OFFICIAL TOURIST BOARD GUIDE

Places to Stay and Visit
South West England

visit**Britain** ™

Contents

Isles of
Scilly

Salisbury Cathedral

VisitBritain

VisitBritain is the organisation created to
market Britain to the rest of the world, and
England to the British.

Formed by the merger of the British Tourist
Authority and the English Tourism Council,
its mission is to build the value of tourism
by creating world-class destination brands
and marketing campaigns.

It will also build partnerships with – and
provide insights to – other organisations
which have a stake in British and English
tourism.

Gold Hill, Shaftesbury

The guide that gives you more

This official VisitBritain guide is packed with information from where to stay, to how to get there and what to see and do. In fact, everything you need to know to enjoy South West England.

Quality accommodation

Choose from a wide range of quality-assessed accommodation to suit all budgets and tastes. This guide contains a comprehensive listing of hotels, bed and breakfast accommodation, self-catering properties, and camping & caravan parks in South West England. Each establishment is a member of an Enjoy England Quality Rose assessment scheme – just look for the Quality Rose, the official marque of Enjoy England quality-assessed accommodation – or The British Graded Holiday Parks Scheme.

Regional information

Every region within South West England has something unique and exciting to offer, whether it's coast or country, adventure or culture, retail therapy or romance you crave. There's something for everyone whatever their age and interests, from families to couples.

At the beginning of each regional section you can find a smattering of suggestions for eating out in the area. Inspirational ideas for memorable days out start on page 171 and, if you turn to the back of the guide, there's a calendar of events. For more possibilities and ideas, log on to **visitsouthwest.co.uk**.

Tourist Information Centres

For local information phone or call into a Tourist Information Centre. Location and contact details can be found starting on page 241. Alternatively, you can text INFO to 62233 to find your nearest Official Partner Tourist Information Centre.

Head South West

Lyme Regis, Dorset

There's much more than meets the eye – 60% of England's heritage coast is in the South West. How's that for starters? But it's much more than just coast...

What's in the South West?

The area is divided into seven regions: Bristol & Bath, Cornwall & the Isles of Scilly, Cotswolds and Forest of Dean, Devon, Dorset – Bournemouth & Poole, Somerset and Wiltshire – Salisbury & Stonehenge. Each has its own distinctive scenery and culture. Find out all you need to know on **visitsouthwest.co.uk**.

Where to start?

If you're looking for accommodation, start right here with this guide. It gives details of a large selection of places to stay – from five-star hotels to B&Bs, from seafront apartments and country cottages to the open air of holiday parks.

What to do?

A beach holiday? Walking or cycling? High adventure? Heritage? Whatever you enjoy doing, you can do it in the South West. Turn the following pages for great ideas. We've split them into themes to help you choose and each has its own website with useful searches so you can find exactly what you're looking for.

Alternatively contact:

South West Tourism
Woodwater Park, Exeter EX2 5WT
(01392) 360050

sheer indulgence

Push the boat out and indulge in a few days aboard a luxury motor yacht, touring the coast at your leisure. Back on land, atmospheric Thornbury Castle, near Bristol, offers bedchambers with four-posters and open fires as well as fine cuisine. Or why not hire a private chef for the evening in an exclusive self-catering property? Spoil yourself even more with a visit to Dart Marina, Dartmouth for total pampering with spa and beauty treatments.

Tailor your own itinerary in a luxury chauffered car from Godolphin Heritage Tours and let your driver/guide take you to tucked-away places and tell you their history.

Treat yourself to succulent seafood, plucked from the Atlantic only hours earlier, or sigh with satisfaction as your taste buds tingle with the taste of Red Devon beef or Greyface Dartmoor lamb. Wine or champagne? Discover the best places to dine by ordering a copy of The Trencherman's Guide to Fine Food on indulgesouthwest.co.uk.

For further information visit

indulgesouthwest.co.uk

close to nature

Taste the tang of salt on your lips as you stride out along the South West Coast Path National Trail, enjoying spectacular views of sun-dappled sea, sweeping sandy bays and hidden coves.

Experience 'up close' the unique and beautiful natural environment, whether by foot, by bike or on horseback. And enjoy the magic of seeing wildlife in its natural habitat.

Hop on a boat across to Brownsea Island and focus your binoculars on peacocks, terns and visiting waders. See marine life close up on an exciting sea-safari from Falmouth or watch falcons fly at Bovey Castle, Newton Abbot. Nightingale Wood in South Marston is also an excellent spot for a stroll and some wildlife spotting.

Satisfyingly weary, head for your holiday home – perhaps a country inn or hotel where wildlife wanders in the grounds, or, to get really close to nature, choose a farm stay with hearty, local produce served at every meal.

For further information visit

naturesouthwest.co.uk

it's adventure!

Paddle fast, ducking and diving, fighting the force of white water at Spirit of Adventure, near Yelverton or scud across the surface of the sea at high speeds as the wind fills your kiteboard at Extreme Academy, Watergate Bay.

Wait for that superwave to bring you to shore on a surfing break at The Adventure Centre at Lusty Glaze in Newquay or brace gentle breezes in sailing boat or canoe on inland waters like Wimbleball Lake, near Dulverton or Croft Farm Leisure and Waterpark, Tewkesbury.

Prefer dry land? Swing through the trees on an aerial assault course at Go Ape! near Ringwood or speed down steep slopes on a mountain bike from Dunkery Beacon, the highest point on Exmoor. Four wheels are faster than two, so instead drive a 4x4 across rough terrain with Land Rover Experience, near Honiton.

For further information visit

itsadventuresouthwest.co.uk

beach and beyond

Join the children and dabble in a salty pool to net that elusive crab; dip your toes in a calm sea or bodyboard on breakers; build a big sandcastle on a beautiful beach. Choose a tiny cove, vast sands or a bustling resort – you can enjoy a beach holiday anywhere, from St Ives and Paignton to Weston-super-Mare and Bournemouth.

But beyond the beaches there's fantastic family fun and entertainment. Hear lions roar at Longleat, come nose to nose with a shark at Newquay's Blue Reef Aquarium, feed 1,000 swans at Abbotsbury Swannery or take a walk on the wild side at At-Bristol.

Find the witch in Wookey Hole Caves, near Wells, hunt for fossils along the Jurassic Coast, puff along on the South Devon Railway from Buckfastleigh to Totnes, or turn upside down on one of the rides at The Flambards Experience in Helston.

For further information visit

familyholidaysouthwest.co.uk

easy preschool

Delight in the sight of your little ones happily pottering on a clean, safe beach. You'll find Blue Flag beaches throughout the South West – from the farthest tip of Cornwall at Sennen Cove to Oddicombe Beach in Torquay and Canford Cliffs Chine in Poole. But if you want more than a beach, there are plenty of other things to keep young children happy.

They'll love bottle-feeding lambs at The Big Sheep, near Bideford, discovering dinosaurs at The Dinosaur Museum, Dorchester and finding Postman Pat at Longleat. The cuddly animals and soft play areas of Dartmouth's Woodland Leisure Park or The Milky Way Adventure Park near Bideford will keep them happy for hours.

And wherever you are you'll find plenty of places to eat that welcome young children and cater especially for them.

For further information visit

easypreschoolsouthwest.co.uk

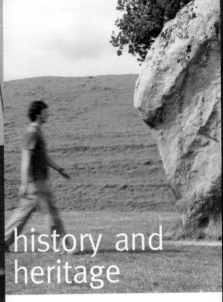

history and heritage

With over 10,000 sites of archaeological importance in the region, and four UNESCO World Heritage Sites (more than any other region outside London), you will never be short of something old to explore.

Cornwall and West Devon Mining Landscape is the latest addition to our list of World Heritage Sites, which include the Jurassic Coastline, Avebury and Stonehenge, and the Georgian city of Bath.

Discover Geevor Tin Mine Heritage Centre in Penzance, Cornwall; explore Portland Castle, one of Henry VIII's great coastal fortresses; find out about photography at Lacock Abbey, or visit the highest fountain in Britain at Stanway House in Cheltenham.

A garden lover? In spring see snowdrops at Painswick Rococo Garden and early daffodils on the Isles of Scilly. Summer brings a riot of roses at Hidcote Manor Garden in the Cotswolds, while Westonbirt Arboretum is the place to be for the reds and golds of autumn.

For further information visit

livingheritagesouthwest.co.uk

relax and recharge

Unwind, chill out, take it easy. There's plenty of opportunity to recharge the batteries. Book a country hotel or a cosy cottage by the sea with some friends and don't make too many plans.

If the mood takes you, head into the countryside for a gentle stroll or amble along the beach. Choose a circular walk like the one through spectacular Lydford Gorge near Okehampton, and enjoy stunning views from the chalk hills of Fontmell and Melbury Downs.

Blow away the cobwebs on a gentle cycle ride around the Cotswolds Area of Outstanding Natural Beauty. Pedal your way through captivating villages and unforgettable landscape, or follow the Family Cycle Trail through the Forest of Dean.

Slow right down on a narrow boat in Wiltshire, drift over the dramatic countryside in a balloon or pamper yourself for the weekend in a boutique hotel with spa treatments.

For further information visit

relaxsouthwest.co.uk

Dartmoor, Devon

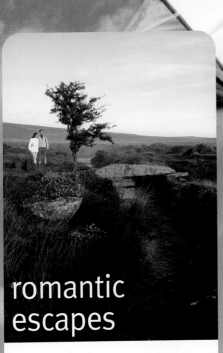

romantic escapes

A wedding anniversary, birthday or a chance to escape for a few days, just the two of you – there's always a reason for a romantic break. Choose a five-star hotel, small country inn or cosy hideaway cottage and start the day with a champagne breakfast.

Make the most of your time together – hire a tandem and pedal The Camel Trail; soar above cities and countryside in a hot-air balloon, floating across ever-changing landscapes; picnic in the heart of a National Park or simply stroll along the beach at sunset.

Alternatively, contact Berrybrook Motors in Exminster and hire that open-top Morgan tourer you've always fancied – pretend it's yours, just for the day. And in the evening, treat yourselves to an intimate dinner at one of the South West's many excellent restaurants.

For further information visit

romancesouthwest.co.uk

tops for teams

So you're in the South West for a conference or team-building exercise. Could be rather dull – but not necessarily! Organisers know that teams 'gel' and work better together if they also 'play' together or take part in team activities, so you could find yourself sailing in style on the luxury, modern skippered yacht The Grand Lady from The Grand Hotel. Or maybe you'll be skimming closer to the waves with a day's surfing instruction at The Adventure Centre at Lusty Glaze on a private Newquay beach.

Back on land you could be revving the engine of a 4x4 and driving over rough terrain at Keypitts Stables and Quads, Ilfracombe.

In complete contrast your day might be spent checking the form and placing your bets at the Cheltenham Races.

For further information visit

swtourism.co.uk

How to use this guide

In this new, fully updated South West guide, you'll find a great choice of hotels, B&B guest accommodation, self-catering properties, and camping & caravan parks in South West England.

Each property has been visited annually by Enjoy England assessors who apply nationally agreed standards so that you can book with confidence knowing your accommodation has been checked and rated for quality.

Detailed accommodation entries include descriptions, prices and facilities. You'll also find special offers and themed breaks to suit your tastes, interests and budget.

Finding accommodation is easy

Regional entries
The guide is divided into seven regional sections and accommodation is listed alphabetically by place name within each region.

Colour maps
Use the colour maps, starting on page 26, to pinpoint the location of all accommodation featured in the regional sections. Then refer to the place index at the back of the guide to find the page number. The index also includes tourism areas such as Dartmoor.

Indexes
A place index at the back makes it easy to find accommodation in a particular area – and if you know the name of the establishment, use the property index.

Ratings and awards at a glance

Reliable, rigorous, easy to use – look out for the following ratings and awards to help you choose with confidence:

Ratings made easy

★ Simple, practical, no frills

★★ Well presented and well run

★★★ Good level of quality and comfort

★★★★ Excellent standard throughout

★★★★★ Exceptional with a degree of luxury

For full details of the Enjoy England Quality Rose assessment schemes, go online at
enjoyengland.com/quality

Star ratings

Establishments are awarded a rating of one to five stars based on a combination of quality of facilities and services provided. Put simply, **the more stars, the higher the quality and the greater the range of facilities and level of service**.

The process to arrive at a star rating is very thorough. Enjoy England professional assessors visit establishments annually and work to strict criteria to rate the available facilities and service.

A quality score is awarded for every aspect of the experience. For hotels and guest accommodation this includes the comfort of the bed, the quality of the breakfast and dinner and, most importantly, the cleanliness. For self-catering properties assessors also consider the layout and design of the accommodation, the ease of use of appliances, the range and quality of the kitchen equipment, and the variety and presentation of visitor information. Camping and caravan parks are awarded a rating following an assessment of the quality, cleanliness, maintenance and condition of the facilities. The warmth of welcome and level of care that each establishment offers are noted, and places that go the extra mile will be awarded high scores for quality.

All the national assessing bodies (VisitBritain, VisitScotland, Visit Wales and the AA*) now operate to a common set of standards for rating hotels, guest accommodation and self-catering properties, giving holidaymakers and travellers a clear guide on exactly what to expect at each level. An explanation of all star ratings can be found on pages 224-225.

*The AA does not assess self-catering properties.

Gold and Silver Awards

These highly-prized Enjoy England awards are only given to hotels and bed and breakfast accommodation offering the highest levels of quality within their star rating (see page 22).

South West Tourism Excellence Awards

Prestigious South West Tourism Excellence Awards showcase the very best in tourism in the area and celebrate people whose contribution to its success is outstanding. A list of winners for the accommodation categories can be found on page 20.

National Accessible Scheme

Establishments with a National Accessible Scheme rating have been thoroughly assessed to set criteria and provide access to facilities and services for guests with visual, hearing or mobility impairment (see page 24).

Welcome Schemes

Enjoy England runs four special Welcome schemes: Cyclists Welcome, Walkers Welcome, Welcome Pets! and Families Welcome. Scheme participants go out of their way to make special provision for guests who enjoy these activities to ensure they have a welcoming, comfortable stay.

Caravan Holiday Home Award Scheme

VisitBritain runs an award scheme for individual holiday caravan homes on highly-graded caravan parks. In addition to complying with standards for Holiday Parks, these exceptional caravans must have a shower or bath, toilet, mains electricity and water heating (at no extra charge) and a fridge (many also have a colour TV).

Classifications explained

The following classifications will help you decide which type of accommodation is right for you, whether you are seeking a non-stop, city-buzz holiday; a quiet weekend away; a home-from-home break or camping fun for all the family.

Hotels

Hotel	A minimum of six bedrooms, but more likely to have over 20.
Small Hotel	A maximum of 20 bedrooms and likely to be more personally run.
Country House Hotel	Set in ample grounds or gardens, in a rural or semi-rural location, with the emphasis on peace and quiet.
Town House Hotel	In a city or town-centre location, high quality with a distinctive and individual style. Maximum of 50 bedrooms, with a high ratio of staff to guests. Possibly no dinner served, but room service available. Might not have a dining room, so breakfast may be served in the bedrooms.
Metro Hotel	A city or town-centre hotel offering full hotel services, but no dinner. Located within easy walking distance of a range of places to eat. Can be of any size.
Budget Hotel	Part of a large branded hotel group, offering limited services. A Budget Hotel is not awarded a star rating.

Bed and Breakfast

Guest Accommodation	Encompassing a wide range of establishments from one-room bed and breakfasts to larger properties, which may offer dinner and hold an alcohol licence.	
Bed and Breakfast	Accommodating no more than six people, the owners of these establishments welcome you into their home as a special guest.	

Guest House	Generally comprising more than three rooms. Dinner is unlikely to be available (if it is, it will need to be booked in advance). May possibly be licensed.
Farmhouse	Bed and breakfast, and sometimes dinner, but always on a farm.
Restaurant with Rooms	A licensed restaurant is the main business but there will be a small number of bedrooms, with all the facilities you would expect, and breakfast the following morning.
Inn	Pubs with rooms, and many with restaurants as well.

Self Catering

Self Catering	Choose from cosy country cottages, smart town-centre apartments, seaside villas, grand country houses for large family gatherings, and even quirky conversions of windmills, railway carriages and lighthouses. Most take bookings by the week, generally from a Friday or Saturday, but short breaks are increasingly offered, particularly outside the main season.

Serviced Apartments	City-centre serviced apartments are an excellent alternative to hotel accommodation, offering hotel services such as daily cleaning, concierge and business centre services, but with a kitchen and lounge area that allow you to eat in and relax when you choose. A telephone and Internet access tend to be standard. Prices are generally based on the property, so they often represent excellent value for money for families and larger groups. Serviced apartments tend to accept bookings for any length of period, and many are operated by agencies whose in-depth knowledge and choice of properties makes searching easier at busy times.
Approved Caravan Holiday Homes	Approved caravan holiday homes are let as individual self-catering units and can be located on farms or holiday parks. All the facilities, including a bathroom and toilet, are contained within the caravan and all main services are provided. There are no star ratings, but all caravans are assessed annually to minimum standards.

Camping and Caravan Parks

Camping Park   These sites only have pitches available for tents.

Touring Park   If you are planning to travel with your own caravan, motor home or tent, then look for a Touring Park.

Holiday Park   If you want to hire a caravan holiday home for a short break or longer holiday, or are looking to buy your own holiday home, a Holiday Park is the right choice. They range from small, rural sites to larger parks with all the added extras, such as a pool.

Many parks will offer a combination of these categories.

Holiday Village   Holiday Villages usually comprise a variety of types of accommodation, with the majority in custom-built rooms, chalets for example. The option to book on a bed and breakfast, or dinner, bed and breakfast basis is normally available. A range of facilities, entertainment and activities are also provided which may, or may not, be included in the tariff.

Holiday Villages must meet a minimum entry requirement for both the provision and quality of facilities and services, including fixtures, fittings, furnishings, decor and any other extra facilities. Progressively higher levels of quality and customer care are provided at each star level.

Forest Holiday Village   A holiday village which is situated in a forest setting with conservation and sustainable tourism being a key feature. It will usually comprise a variety of accommodation, often purpose built; and with a range of entertainment, activities and facilities available on site free of charge or at extra cost.

Quality
visitor attractions

VisitBritain operates a Visitor Attraction Quality Assurance Service.

Participating attractions are visited annually by trained, impartial assessors who look at all aspects of the visit, from initial telephone enquiries to departure, customer service to catering, as well as all facilities and activities.

Only those attractions which have been assessed by Enjoy England and meet the standard receive the quality marque, your sign of a Quality Assured Visitor Attraction.

Look out for the quality marque and visit with confidence.

Accommodation entries explained

Each accommodation entry contains detailed information to help you decide if it is right for you. This has been provided by proprietors and our aim is to ensure that it is as objective and factual as possible.

BATH, Bath and North East Somerset Map ref 5C1   **BED & BREAKFAST**

★★★
BED AND BREAKFAST SILVER AWARD

Bretherton House

17 Easton Road, Bath BA21 3LN **t** (01225) 123222 **f** (01225) 123333
e bretherton@bath.co.uk **w** brethertonhouse.co.uk

B&B per room per night
s £52.00-£65.00
d £80.00-£120.00
Evening meal per person
£20.00-£30.00

open All year except Christmas and New Year
bedrooms 3 double
bathrooms 3 en suite
payment Credit/debit card, euros

Elegant stone house set in beautiful large garden. Peaceful yet near to the city centre. Spacious, comfortable interior with very attractive bedrooms and modern bathrooms. Ideal for exploring this beautiful Georgian city and the West Country. A warm welcome guaranteed.

⊕ M4, jct 18. A46 to Bath. Right at roundabout, A420 towards Bristol. Left at T-junction. Right at traffic lights. Bretherton House is 200yds on right.

♥ Discounts on stays of 4 or more days (excl Saturdays) – see website for details.

Room 🛏 📶 📺 📞 General 🐕 P 🅿 ✴ 🐾 Leisure ♪ ▶ 🏠

Sample enhanced entry

1 Listing under town or village with map reference

2 Enjoy England star rating plus Gold or Silver Award where applicable

3 Category

4 Prices

Hotels – per room for bed and breakfast (B&B) and per person for half board (HB)

Bed and breakfast – per room for bed and breakfast (B&B) and per person for evening meal

Self catering – per unit per week for low and high season

Camping and caravan parks – per pitch per night for touring pitches; per unit per week for caravan holiday homes

5 Establishment name and booking details

6 Indicates when the establishment is open

7 Accommodation details and payment accepted

8 Walkers, cyclists, pets and families welcome

9 Accessible rating where applicable

10 At-a-glance facility symbols

11 Travel directions

12 Special promotions and themed breaks

A key to symbols can be found on the back-cover flap. Keep it open for easy reference.

South West Tourism Awards

South West Tourism Excellence Awards are all about telling the world what a fantastic place the area is to visit, whether it's for a day trip, a weekend break or a fortnight's holiday.

The awards comprise 15 categories including Large and Small Visitor Attraction of the Year, Tourism Website of the Year and Best Tourism Experience and they were presented on 29 October 2007.

All nominees for the accommodation categories had to demonstrate exceptionally high customer care and continual improvement of facilities. Other criteria included a commitment to recycling and the environment, accessibility for disabled customers and the use of local food and drink produce.

Details of winners in the additional categories can be found on **swtourism.co.uk**

**Tourism
Excellence
Awards
2007 - 2008**

Accommodation winners and nominees
South West Tourism Excellence Awards 2007:

Large Hotel of the Year

GOLD **The Hotel & Extreme Academy,** Watergate Bay, *Cornwall*

SILVER **St Michael's Hotel & Spa,** Falmouth, *Cornwall*

SILVER **Bovey Castle Hotel,** Dartmoor, *Devon*

Small Hotel of the Year

GOLD **Combe House Country House Hotel,** Gittisham, *Devon*

SILVER **- Calcot Manor,** Nr Tetbury, *Gloucestershire*

SILVER **- Hotel du Vin,** Bristol

SILVER **- Lucknam Park,** Nr Bath, *Somerset*

Gidleigh Park, Chagford, *Devon*

Bed and Breakfast of the Year

GOLD **The Salty Monk Restaurant with Rooms,** Sidford, *Devon*

SILVER **Lower Barn,** St Ewe, *Cornwall*

Butlers Hotel, Cheltenham, *Gloucestershire*

Camilla House, Penzance, *Cornwall*

Fern Cottage, Pucklechurch, *Gloucestershire*

Self Catering Holiday of the Year

GOLD **Compton Pool Farm,** Compton, *Devon*

SILVER **Tone Dale House,** (let by The Big House Co), Wellington, *Somerset*

Bosinver Farm Cottages, Trewith, St Austell, *Cornwall*

Crylla Valley, *Cornwall*

Caravan Holiday Park of the Year

GOLD **Beverley Park,** Paignton, *Devon*

SILVER **Hidden Valley Park,** Nr Ilfracombe, *Devon*

SILVER **Hendra Holiday Park,** Newquay, *Cornwall*

Woodovis Park, Tavistock, *Devon*

Above, left to right: Lower Barn, St Ewe; Bovey Castle Hotel, Dartmoor; Hendra Holiday Park, Newquay.

Gold and Silver Awards

Gold and Silver Awards are unique to Enjoy England and are given in recognition of exceptional quality in hotel and guest accommodation.

Enjoy England professional assessors make recommendations for Gold and Silver Awards during assessments. They will look at the quality provided in all areas, in particular housekeeping, service and hospitality, bedrooms, bathrooms and food, to see if it meets the highest quality for the star level achieved.

While star ratings are based on a combination of quality, range of facilities and level of service offered, Gold and Silver Awards are based solely on quality. You may therefore find that a two-star Gold Award hotel offering superior levels of quality may be more suited to your needs if, for example, enhanced services such as a concierge or 24-hour room service are not essential for your stay.

Here we list hotels and guest accommodation featured in this guide with a Gold or Silver Award. Use the property index starting on page 250 to find their page numbers.

Exceptional properties excelling in outstanding quality

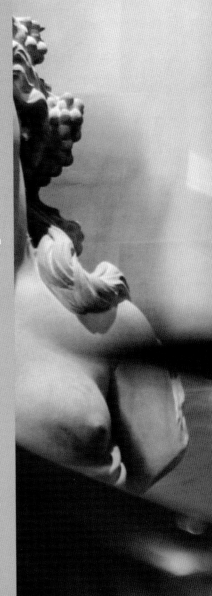

Gold Award Hotels

The Berbury Hotel,
Torquay, *Devon*

Island Hotel,
Isles of Scilly

Hotel Riviera,
Sidmouth, *Devon*

Tides Reach Hotel,
Salcombe, *Devon*

Gold Award Guest Accommodation

Anchorage House,
St Austell, *Cornwall*

Athole Guest House,
Bath, *Somerset*

Brookfield House,
Bovey Tracey, *Devon*

Dolvean House,
Falmouth, *Cornwall*

The Galley 'Fish and Seafood' Restaurant & Spa with Cabins,
Exeter, *Devon*

Heatherly Cottage,
Corsham, *Wiltshire*

The Residence,
Bath, *Somerset*

The Roundham House,
Bridport, *Dorset*

Silver Award Hotels

Aviary Court,
Portreath, *Cornwall*

Corbyn Head Hotel,
Torquay, *Devon*

Garrack Hotel,
St Ives, *Cornwall*

The Grange at Oborne,
Sherborne, *Dorset*

Green Lawns Hotel,
Falmouth, *Cornwall*

The Manor House Hotel,
Studland, *Dorset*

New Inn,
Isles of Scilly

Hotel Penzance,
Penzance, *Cornwall*

Royal Castle Hotel,
Dartmouth, *Devon*

Royal York and Faulkner Hotel and Aspara Spa,
Sidmouth, *Devon*

Wellington Hotel,
Boscastle, *Cornwall*

Silver Award Guest Accommodation

Beaumont House,
Cheltenham, *Gloucestershire*

The Castleton,
Swanage, *Dorset*

Chestnuts House,
Bath, *Somerset*

Corran Farm B&B,
Mevagissey, *Cornwall*

Crofton Lodge,
Marlborough, *Wiltshire*

The Denes Guest House,
Lynton, *Devon*

Dovers House,
Looe, *Cornwall*

Glebe Farm,
Shaftesbury, *Dorset*

Great Sloncombe Farm,
Moretonhampstead, *Devon*

Harefield Cottage,
Bude, *Cornwall*

Honeysuckle Cottage,
Bradford-on-Avon, *Wiltshire*

Lanscombe House,
Torquay, *Devon*

Primrose Cottage,
Launceston, *Cornwall*

The Rokeby Guest House,
Salisbury, *Wiltshire*

Strete Barton House,
Dartmouth, *Devon*

The Wayside B&B,
Bilbrook, *Somerset*

White Cottage,
Athelhampton, *Dorset*

National Accessible Scheme

Finding suitable accommodation is not always easy, especially if you have to seek out rooms with level entry or large print menus. Use the National Accessible Scheme to help you make your choice.

The criteria VisitBritain and national/regional tourism organisations have adopted do not necessarily conform to British Standards or to Building Regulations. They reflect what the organisations understand to be acceptable to meet the practical needs of guests with mobility or sensory impairments and encourage the industry to increase access to all.

Proprietors of accommodation taking part in the National Accessible Scheme have gone out of their way to ensure a comfortable stay for guests with special hearing, visual or mobility needs. These exceptional places are full of extra touches to make everyone's visit trouble-free, from handrails, ramps and step-free entrances (ideal for buggies too) to level-access showers and colour contrast in the bathrooms. Members of the staff or owners may have attended a disability awareness course and will know what assistance will really be appreciated.

Appropriate National Accessible Scheme symbols are included in the guide entries (shown opposite). If you have additional needs or special requirements we strongly recommend that you make sure these can be met by your chosen establishment before you confirm your reservation.

For a wider selection of accessible accommodation, order a copy of the Easy Access Britain guide featuring almost 500 places to stay. Available from Tourism for All for £9.99 (plus P&P).

tourismforall

The National Accessible Scheme forms part of the Tourism for All Campaign that is being promoted by VisitBritain and national/regional tourism organisations. Additional help and guidance on finding suitable holiday accommodation can be obtained from:

Tourism for All
c/o Vitalise, Shap Road Industrial Estate, Kendal LA9 6NZ

information helpline 0845 124 9971
reservations 0845 124 9973
(lines open 9-5 Mon-Fri)
f (01539) 735567
e info@tourismforall.org.uk
w tourismforall.org.uk

Mobility Impairment Symbols

 Typically suitable for a person with sufficient mobility to climb a flight of steps but who would benefit from fixtures and fittings to aid balance.

 Typically suitable for a person with restricted walking ability and for those who may need to use a wheelchair some of the time and can negotiate a maximum of three steps.

 Typically suitable for a person who depends on the use of a wheelchair and transfers unaided to and from the wheelchair in a seated position. This person may be an independent traveller.

 Typically suitable for a person who depends on the use of a wheelchair in a seated position. This person also requires personal/mechanical assistance to aid transfer (eg carer, hoist).

 Access Exceptional is awarded to establishments that meet the requirements of independent wheelchair users or assisted wheelchair users shown above and also fulfil more demanding requirements with reference to the British Standards BS8300:2001.

Visual Impairment Symbols

 Typically provides key additional services and facilities to meet the needs of visually impaired guests.

Typically provides a higher level of additional services and facilities to meet the needs of visually impaired guests.

Hearing Impairment Symbols

 Typically provides key additional services and facilities to meet the needs of guests with hearing impairment.

 Typically provides a higher level of additional services and facilities to meet the needs of guests with hearing impairment.

25

Map 1

Location
Maps

Every place name featured in the regional accommodation sections of this guide has a map reference to help you locate it on the maps which follow. For example, to find Bournemouth, which has 'Map ref 2B3', turn to Map 2 and refer to grid square B3.

All place names appearing in the regional sections are shown in black type on the maps. This enables you to find other places in your chosen area which may have suitable accommodation – the place index (at the back of this guide) gives page numbers.

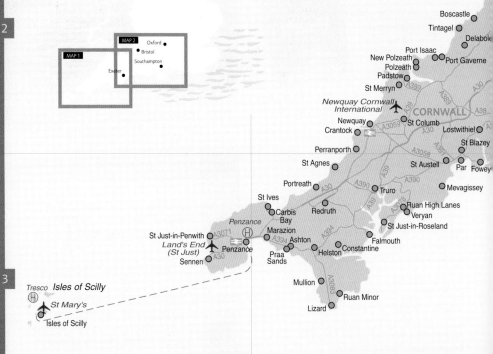

Map 1

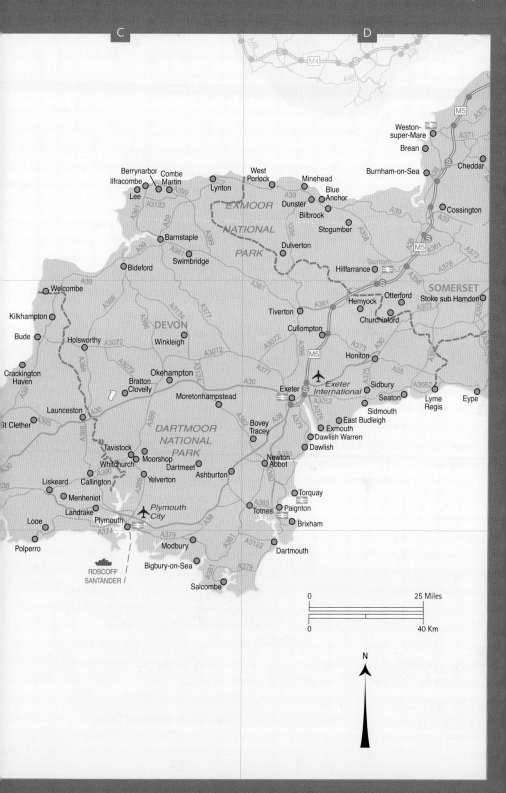

C   D

Weston-super-Mare
Brean
Burnham-on-Sea
Cheddar

Berrynarbor   Combe
Ilfracombe   Martin
Lee
Lynton
West Porlock
Minehead
Blue Anchor
Dunster
Bilbrook
Stogumber
Cossington

A3123
A361
A399

EXMOOR
NATIONAL
PARK

Barnstaple
Swimbridge
Dulverton

Bideford

M5
A39
A361

SOMERSET

Welcombe
Hillfarrance
Taunton
S

Kilkhampton
DEVON
Tiverton
Hemyock
Otterford
Stoke sub Hamdon

Bude
Holsworthy
Winkleigh
Cullompton
Churchinford

A3124
A386
A3072

A361
A373
A30
A35

Crackington Haven
Okehampton
Honiton

Bratton Clovelly
Moretonhampstead
Exeter
Exeter International
Sidbury
Seaton
Lyme Regis
Eype

St Clether
Launceston
Bovey Tracey
Sidmouth
Sidmouth

DARTMOOR
NATIONAL
PARK

East Budleigh
Exmouth
Dawlish Warren
Dawlish

Tavistock
Moorshop
Whitchurch
Dartmeet
Newton Abbot

Liskeard
Callington
Yelverton
Ashburton

Menheniot
Torquay
Paignton
Brixham

Landrake
Totnes
Plymouth
Plymouth City

Looe
Modbury
Dartmouth

Polperro
Bigbury-on-Sea

ROSCOFF
SANTANDER
Salcombe

0   25 Miles

0   40 Km

N

Map 2

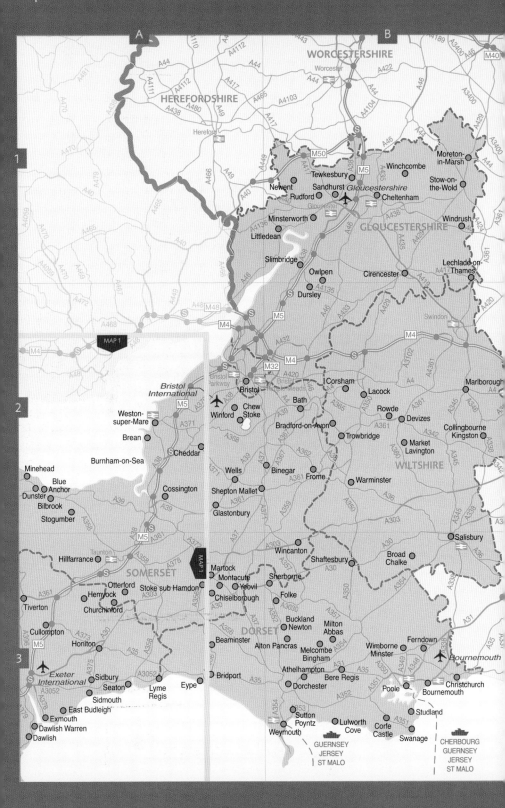

Map 2

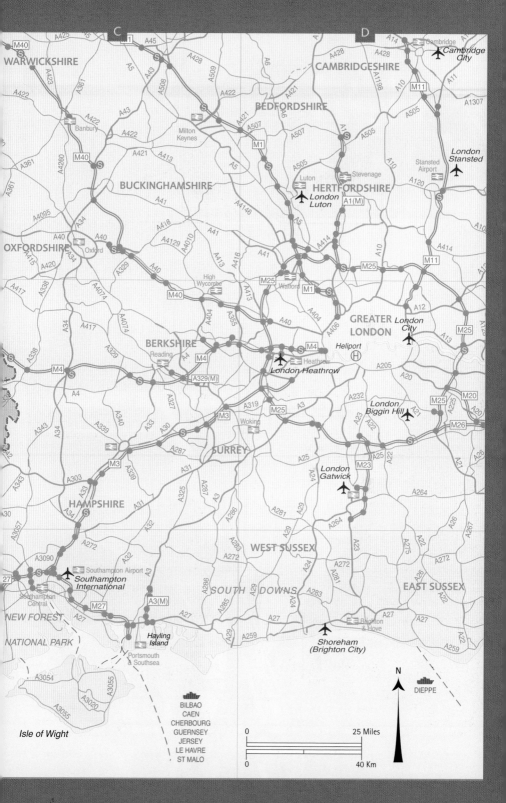

Bath International Music Festival

Thermae Bath Spa

ss Great Britain, Bristol

Explore Bristol & Bath

Two cities. Two different stories. Immerse yourself in Roman times in Bath. In Bristol, experience the energy and excitement of this aspirational centre of culture; the liveliest city in the South West.

Golden terraces

Feel a frisson of excitement as you stroll among Bath's superb Georgian architecture. Take a walking tour and learn about the city's past as the streets unfold before you. Uncover the history of Bath's 2,000-year spa tradition at The Roman Baths. Next? You've some 40 museums, galleries and attractions to choose from – not to mention the shops! Foot weary? Then you're ready for a dip in the natural thermal waters of the Thermae Bath Spa. Emerge relaxed and refreshed, all set for another day.

Dine in style

In between all this busy sightseeing, sink your teeth into a Bath bun at Sally Lunn's, set in one of Bath's oldest houses, or take tea in the elegant surroundings of the Pump Room. This is where Georgian society came to 'take the waters' and it was the place to be seen.

For lunch or dinner, dine in style in Bath's award-winning restaurants. Enjoy gourmet treats and lovely settings at the Michelin-starred Bath Priory Hotel or Lucknam Park Hotel. Or try The Dower House at The Royal Crescent Hotel, The Vellore Restaurant at the MacDonald Bath Spa Hotel and The Olive Tree at the Queensbury Hotel – they all have rosettes.

Innovative Bristol

Bristol has always been a magnet for pioneers and inventors, none more so than Isambard Kingdom Brunel whose presence is keenly felt throughout the city. Call into the old station building, which now houses the intriguing British Empire & Commonwealth Museum, then head down to the docks to explore Brunel's ss Great Britain, one of the world's most exciting and accessible historic ships, with glass sea, real-life cabins, interactive displays and a fascinating museum. The Clifton Suspension Bridge is an amazing engineering feat and a cultural icon not to be missed.

Clifton Suspension Bridge

At-Bristol

Roman Baths, Bath

Balloon Festival, Bristol

Beyond Brunel

Mingle with the crowds and feel the buzz on Bristol's lively waterfront. Stroll along the docks and quays, relax in a stylish bar or cafe or take to the water to see the city from a different perspective on a boat trip. Go into the Watershed to enjoy its programme of art and cinema and venture into the eye of a tornado in At-Bristol. Then turn into the town centre and explore Georgian King Street and quaint Welsh Back with its Tudor-framed buildings.

Move on to the splendid Georgian crescents of elegant Clifton and spend your money in its boutiques, galleries and antique shops before returning to the city centre for dinner and your evening entertainment. Tap your feet to the jazz beat emanating from The Old Duke as you sip your drink at the Llandoger Trow.

Food & drink

Fancy a bite to eat, a relaxing drink or some fresh local produce? Here's a selection of food and drink venues to get you started. For lots more ideas go online at enjoyengland.com/taste.

Restaurants

Bathwick Boatman
European
Forest Road, Bath BA2 6QE
t (01225) 428844
w bathwickboatman.com

Bordeaux Quay
English/European
V-Shed, Canons Way,
Bristol BS1 5UH
t (0117) 906 5550
w bordeaux-quay.co.uk

City Cafe
European
Temple Way, Bristol BS1 6BF
t (0117) 910 2700
w cityinn.com/bristol

Culinaria
European
1 Chandos Road, Redland,
Bristol BS6 6PG
t (0117) 973 7999
w culinariabristol.co.uk

Eastern Eye
Indian
8a Quiet Street, Bath BA1 2JS
t (01225) 422323
w easterneye.com

The Hole in the Wall
English
16 George Street, Bath BA1 2EH
t (01225) 425242
w theholeinthewall.co.uk

Hunstrete House
Fine dining
Pensford, near Bath BS39 4NS
t (01761) 490490
w hunstretehouse.co.uk

Mezzaluna Ristorante
Italian
7a Kingsmead Square,
Bath BA1 2AB
t (01225) 466688
w mezzaluna-bath.co.uk

Oakwood Restaurant
Fine dining
The Park, Wick, near Bath
BS30 5RN
t (0117) 937 1800
w theparkresort.com

POSH at The Rodney Hotel
Anglo/French
4 Rodney Place, Clifton,
Bristol BS8 4HY
t (0117) 973 5422
w cliftonhotels.com

Rajpoot
Indian
Rajpoot House, 4 Argyle Street,
Bath BA2 4BA
t (01225) 466833
w rajpoot.com

San Carlo Restaurant
Italian
44 Corn Street, Bristol BS1 1HQ
t (0117) 922 6586
w sancarlo.co.uk

The Shoots Floating Bar and Restaurant
International
Hotwells Road, Bristol BS8 4RU
t (0117) 925 0597

Zerodegrees
Mediterranean
53 Colston Street, Bristol BS1 5BA
t (0117) 925 2706
w zdrestaurants.com/zerodegrees

Pubs

The Bowl Inn
Church Road, Lower
Almondsbury BS32 4DT
t (01454) 612757
w thebowlinn.co.uk

Ha! Ha! Bar & Canteen
The Tram Shed, Beehive Yard,
Walcot Street, Bath BA1 5BD
t (01225) 421200
w hahaonline.co.uk

Hunters Rest Inn
King Lane, Clutton Hill,
Bristol BS39 5QL
t (01761) 452303
w huntersrest.co.uk

Ring O Bells
Widcombe Parade, Bath BA2 4JT
t (01225) 448870

Tearooms, coffee shops and cafes

Blackstones Kitchen
10a Queen Street,
Bath BA1 1HE
t (01225) 338803
w blackstonefood.co.uk

Farrington's Cafe
Farrington's Farm Shop,
Home Farm, Farrington Gurney,
Bristol BS39 6UB
t (01761) 451698
w farringtons.co.uk

Mud Dock Cycleworks and Cafe
40 The Grove, Bristol BS1 4RB
t (0117) 934 9734
w mud-dock.co.uk

Sally Lunn's
4 North Parade Passage,
Bath BA1 1NX
t (01225) 461634
w sallylunns.co.uk

Searcy's at the Pump Room
Stall Street, Bath BA1 1LZ
t (01225) 444477
w searcys.co.uk

Watershed Cafe Bar
1 Canon's Road, Harbourside,
Bristol BS1 5TX
t (0117) 927 6444
w watershed.co.uk

A special welcome

To help make your selection of accommodation easier there are four special Welcome schemes which accommodation can be assessed to. Owners participating in these schemes go the extra mile to welcome walkers, cyclists, families or pet owners and provide additional facilities and services to make your stay even more comfortable.

Families Welcome

If you are searching for a great family break look out for the Families Welcome sign. The sign indicates that the proprietor offers additional facilities and services catering for a range of ages and family units. For families with young children, the accommodation will have special facilities such as cots and highchairs, storage for push-chairs and somewhere to heat baby food or milk. Where meals are provided, children's choices will be clearly indicated, with healthy options available. They'll also have information on local walks, attractions, activities or events suitable for children, as well as local child-friendly pubs and restaurants. Not all accommodation is able to cater for all ages or combinations of family units, so do check when you book.

Welcome Pets!

Want to travel with your faithful companion? Look out for accommodation displaying the Welcome Pets! sign. Participants in this scheme go out of their way to meet the needs of guests bringing dogs, cats and/or small birds. In addition to providing water and food bowls, torches or nightlights, spare leads and pet washing facilities, they'll buy in food on request, and offer toys, treats and bedding. They'll also have information on pet-friendly attractions, pubs, restaurants and recreation. Of course, not everyone is able to offer suitable facilities for every pet, so do check if there are any restrictions on the type, size and number of animals when you book.

Walkers Welcome

If walking is your passion seek out accommodation participating in the Walkers Welcome scheme. Facilities include a place for drying clothes and boots, maps and books for reference and a first-aid kit. Packed breakfasts and lunch are available on request in hotels and guesthouses, and you have the option to pre-order basic groceries in self-catering accommodation. A wide range of information is provided including public transport, weather, local restaurants and attractions, details of the nearest bank and all night chemists.

Cyclists Welcome

If you like to explore by bike seek out accommodation displaying the Cyclists Welcome symbol. Facilities include a lockable undercover area and a place to dry outdoor clothing and footwear, an evening meal if there are no eating facilities available within one mile, and a packed breakfast or lunch on request. Information is also provided on cycle hire and cycle repair shops, maps and books for reference, weather and details of the nearest bank and all night chemists and more.

For further information go online at enjoyengland.com/quality

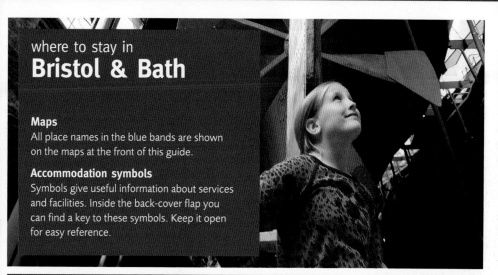

where to stay in
Bristol & Bath

Maps
All place names in the blue bands are shown on the maps at the front of this guide.

Accommodation symbols
Symbols give useful information about services and facilities. Inside the back-cover flap you can find a key to these symbols. Keep it open for easy reference.

BATH, Somerset Map ref 2B2 **HOTEL**

★★★
SMALL HOTEL

B&B per room per night
s £100.00–£125.00
d £135.00–£225.00

Dukes Hotel

Great Pulteney Street, Bath BA2 4DN **t** (01225) 787960 **f** (01225) 787961 **e** info@dukesbath.co.uk
w dukesbath.co.uk

open All year
bedrooms 7 double, 3 twin, 1 family, 6 suites
bathrooms All en suite
payment Credit/debit cards

An ideally located, elegant town house hotel which combines Georgian splendour with comfort and modern conveniences. The rooms are tastefully decorated with period furniture, fine fabrics, prints and portraits to create a stunning overall effect. Superb cuisine served in the Cavendish Restaurant. Stylish bar and secluded patio garden. Room service.

⊕ Exit M4 jct18. Follow signs into Bath. Turn left at traffic lights towards A36, right at the next lights and right into Great Pulteney Street.

♥ Midweek leisure breaks from £125 per night B&B. Two-night weekend breaks to include breakfast and dinner on one night from £370.

Room 🛏 🖼 ☎ 📺 ☕ 🍴   General 🛋 🏛 🔥 ☕ 🍽 🕯 ⊙ 🍷 ✱ 🏐   Leisure ▶ 🚲

BATH, Somerset Map ref 2B2 **GUEST ACCOMMODATION**

★★★★
GUEST ACCOMMODATION

B&B per room per night
s £55.00–£79.00
d £65.00–£110.00

Aquae Sulis

174/176 Newbridge Road, Bath BA1 3LE **t** (01225) 420061 **f** (01225) 446077
e enquiries@aquaesulishotel.co.uk **w** aquaesulishotel.co.uk

Conveniently situated period bed and breakfast 1.5 miles from Bath centre. Lovely en suite rooms with new bathrooms and lots of extras. Sky, Freeview, Wi-Fi. Bar, patio-garden, car park. Easy access to sights.

open All year except Christmas
bedrooms 5 double, 2 twin, 3 single, 3 family
bathrooms 11 en suite, 2 private
payment Credit/debit cards, cash/cheques

Room 🛏 ☎ 📺 ☕ 🍴   General 🛋 🏛 🔥 P 🍴 🍷 🚲 ✱

Key to symbols
Open the back flap for a key to symbols.

BATH, Somerset Map ref 2B2   GUEST ACCOMMODATION

★★★★★
**GUEST ACCOMMODATION
GOLD AWARD**

Athole Guest House

33 Upper Oldfield Park, Bath BA2 3JX **t** (01225) 320000 **f** (01225) 320009
e info@atholehouse.co.uk **w** atholehouse.co.uk

B&B per room per night
s £55.00–£65.00
d £75.00–£88.00

open All year
bedrooms 4 double, 1 family
bathrooms All en suite
payment Credit/debit cards, cash/cheques, euros

Large Victorian home restored to give bright, inviting, quiet bedrooms, sleek furniture, sparkling bathrooms, digital TV, Wi-Fi Internet in all bedrooms, safe. Hospitality is old style. Award-winning breakfasts. Relax in our gardens, or let us help you explore the area. Secure parking behind remote-control gates or in garage. Twelve minutes' walk from centre. Free transfer from/to station.

⊕ M4 jct 18 to Bath. Once in Bath, follow signs for through traffic and Bristol until you see sign for Radstock (Wells Road). Upper Oldfield Park is 1st right.

♥ 3 nights for 2/50% off second night, Nov-Feb. 4 nights for 3/50% off third night, Mar-May and Sep-Oct.

Room 📞 📺 ♿ 🍴 General 🗝 🏢 ♿ P ✂ 🅿 🍴 🦺 ✳ Leisure 🚴

BATH, Somerset Map ref 2B2   GUEST ACCOMMODATION

★★★★★
GUEST ACCOMMODATION

The Carfax

13-15 Great Pulteney Street, Bath BA2 4BS **t** (01225) 462089 **f** (01225) 443257
e reservations@carfaxhotel.co.uk **w** carfaxhotel.co.uk

B&B per room per night
s £69.00–£79.00
d £96.00–£145.00
Evening meal per person
£9.00–£17.00

open All year
bedrooms 13 double, 7 twin, 6 single, 4 family, 1 suite
bathrooms All en suite
payment Credit/debit cards, cash/cheques

A trio of Georgian houses overlooking Henrietta Park with a view to the surrounding hills. A stroll to the Pump Rooms, Roman baths, canal and river. Recently restored and refurbished, well-appointed rooms. Lift to all floors. Car park for 13 cars. Senior Citizens' rates all year.

⊕ From M4 jct 18, A4 to London Road. At city traffic lights over Cleveland Bridge, sharp right at Holburne Museum.

♥ 4 nights for the price of 3, midweek booking Sun to Thu inclusive, quote ETB08.

Room ♿ 📞 📺 ♿ 🍴 General 🗝 🏢 ♿ P ✂ ✕ 🍴 🅿 🔲 Leisure U ♪ 🚴 🚣

BATH, Somerset Map ref 2B2   GUEST ACCOMMODATION

★★★★
**GUEST ACCOMMODATION
SILVER AWARD**

Chestnuts House

16 Henrietta Road, Bath BA2 6LY **t** (01225) 334279 **e** reservations@chestnutshouse.co.uk
w chestnutshouse.co.uk

B&B per room per night
s £65.00–£85.00
d £70.00–£100.00

open All year except Christmas
bedrooms 3 double, 1 twin, 1 family
bathrooms All en suite
payment Credit/debit cards, cash/cheques, euros

Chestnuts House is a high quality B&B set in the heart of the city with an enclosed garden and private off-street parking. The house is built from natural stone and has five excellent en suite guest rooms and one suite, all of which are tastefully decorated and very well appointed.

Room ♿ 📺 ♿ 🍴 General 🗝 🏢 ♿ P ✂ 🍴 🅿 🦺 🔲 ✳ Leisure U

BATH, Somerset Map ref 2B2   **GUEST ACCOMMODATION**

★ ★ ★
FARMHOUSE

B&B per room per night
s Min £50.00
d Min £60.00

Church Farm

Monkton Farleigh, Bradford-on-Avon BA15 2QJ **t** (01225) 858583 **f** 08717 145859
e reservations@churchfarmmonktonfarleigh.co.uk **w** churchfarmmonktonfarleigh.co.uk

Converted farmhouse barn with exceptional
views in peaceful, idyllic setting. Ten minutes
from Bath, ideal base for touring/walking South
West England. Families/dogs welcome.

open All year
bedrooms 2 double, 1 twin
bathrooms All en suite
payment Cash/cheques

Room 📺 💧 ⛶ General 🛏 ▥ 👫 P ⅙ ✿ 🐾 Leisure ⌇ ⌑

BATH, Somerset Map ref 2B2   **GUEST ACCOMMODATION**

★ ★ ★
GUEST HOUSE

B&B per room per night
s £40.00–£50.00
d £65.00–£110.00

Pulteney House

14 Pulteney Road, Bath BA2 4HA **t** (01225) 460991 **f** (01225) 460991 **e** pulteney@tinyworld.co.uk
w pulteneyhotel.co.uk

open All year
bedrooms 7 double, 3 twin, 2 single, 5 family
bathrooms 16 en suite, 1 private
payment Credit/debit cards, cash/cheques

Large, elegant, Victorian house in picturesque,
south-facing gardens with fine views of Bath Abbey.
Large, private car park. Only five to ten minutes'
walk from city centre. An ideal base for exploring
Bath and surrounding areas. All rooms (except one)
en suite with hairdryer, TV, tea/coffee facilities and
radio/alarm clocks.

⊕ *Hotel situated on A36, which runs through Bath. From M4
follow signs to Bath on A46. Then follow signs to A36,
Exeter and Wells.*

❤ *Reduced rates for stays of 3 nights or more – each booking
assessed individually.*

Room 🛋 🖥 📺 💧 ⛶ General 🛏 ▥ 👫 P ⅙ 🔊 ✿ Leisure ☍ ♨

BATH, Somerset Map ref 2B2   **GUEST ACCOMMODATION**

★ ★ ★ ★ ★
**GUEST ACCOMMODATION
GOLD AWARD**

B&B per room per night
s Min £135.00
d Max £300.00
Evening meal per person
£9.50–£40.00

The Residence

Weston Road, Bath BA1 2XZ **t** (01225) 750180 **f** (01225) 750181 **e** info@theresidencebath.com
w theresidencebath.com

open All year
bedrooms 5 double, 1 suite
bathrooms 5 en suite, 1 private
payment Credit/debit cards, cash/cheques, euros

The Residence is unique in Bath, offering just six
rooms. It brings together the exclusivity of a private
club and the service of a modern hotel within a large
Georgian house near the city centre. Our aim is
simple: to be the best home from home you ever
had.

Room 📞 📺 💧 ⛶ General 🛏 7 P 🍽 🍴 ✿ Leisure ☍ ♨

Place index

If you know where you want to stay, the index at the back of the guide will give you
the page number listing accommodation in your chosen town, city or village. Check
out the other useful indexes too.

BATH, Somerset Map ref 2B2 — SELF CATERING

★★★
SELF CATERING

Units **3**
Sleeps **3**
Low season per wk
£440.00–£470.00
High season per wk
£440.00–£470.00

Bath Spa Apartments, Beau Street, Bath

contact Mr Anthony O'Flaherty, 59 Upper Oldfield Park, Bath BA1 3LB
t (01225) 310005 e info@beaustreetapartments.co.uk w bath-selfcatering.co.uk

Three stylish apartments (one double, one single bedroom) in quiet street in town centre. One minute's walk to Spa, Roman Baths and shops. Parking. Tree-lined view. Friday change-over. Wi-Fi. TV/DVD.

open All year
payment Cash/cheques

Unit ▥ TV ▤ ▣ ▧ 🔥 ▥ ⬚ 🍴
General 11 P ⚡ Shop < 0.5 miles Pub < 0.5 miles

BATH, Somerset Map ref 2B2 — SELF CATERING

★★★★
SELF CATERING

Units **7**
Sleeps **2–4**
Low season per wk
£285.00–£645.00
High season per wk
£465.00–£875.00

Church Farm Country Cottages, Bradford-on-Avon

contact Mrs Trish Bowles, Church Farm, Winsley, Bradford-on-Avon BA15 2JH
t (01225) 722246 f (01225) 722246 e stay@churchfarmcottages.com w churchfarmcottages.com

open All year
payment Credit/debit cards, cash/cheques, euros

Tastefully converted single-storey traditional cow byres sleeping two or four persons. Bath four miles. Working farm with sheep, free-range hens and horses. Swim in our luxurious, heated indoor pool (12m x 5m), whatever the weather! Pub/shop 500m. Kennet & Avon Canal nearby for boating, cycling and walking. Regular buses. Welcome cream tea. Green Tourism Business Scheme Silver Award.

⊕ M4 jct 18, take A46 to Bath, then A363 to Bradford-on-Avon. B3108 to Winsley (2 miles). At roundabout, 2nd exit to Bath/Limpley Stoke. Farm 0.75 miles on right.

♥ 4-night midweek break (Mon–Thu) available at same price as 3-night weekend break (Fri–Sun), excl school holidays.

Unit ▥ TV ▥ V ▤ ▣ ▧ 🔥 ▥ ⬚ 🍴 ✿
General ⬚ ▥ ▸ P ⚡ ⬚ S 🐾 Leisure ♨ 🔥 U ♪ ▸ ⚙ 🏊 Shop < 0.5 miles Pub < 0.5 miles

BRISTOL, City of Bristol Map ref 2A2 — HOTEL

★★
SMALL HOTEL

B&B per room per night
s £51.50–£82.50
d £79.00–£99.50

The Bowl Inn and Lilies Restaurant

16 Church Road, Almondsbury, Bristol BS32 4DT t (01454) 612757 f (01454) 619910
e reception@thebowlinn.co.uk w thebowlinn.co.uk

open All year
bedrooms 10 double, 3 twin
bathrooms All en suite
payment Credit/debit cards, cash/cheques

Whether travelling on business or just taking a leisurely break, you will find all the comforts of modern life housed in this historic 12thC village inn. Real ales, fine wines, extensive bar fare and a la carte restaurant. Five minutes junction 16, M5.

⊕ Located 1 mile from M5 jct 16 in lower part of village next to Church of St Mary.

♥ Fri, Sat, Sun inclusive weekend break – single 3 nights £148, double 3 nights £228.

Room ⛲ ☎ TV 📶 🔥 🔥 General ⬚ 4 ▸ P ♟ 🎱 ❶ 𝕀 ✿ 🚐 🐾

It's all quality-assessed accommodation

Our commitment to quality involves wide-ranging accommodation assessment. Rating and awards were correct at the time of going to press but may change following a new assessment. Please check at time of booking.

For key to symbols open the back-cover flap.

BRISTOL, City of Bristol Map ref 2A2 — **GUEST ACCOMMODATION**

★★★★
BED & BREAKFAST

B&B per room per night
s £59.00–£79.00
d £75.00–£98.00
Evening meal per person
£10.00–£22.00

Westfield House

37 Stoke Hill, Sneyd Park, Bristol BS9 1LQ t (0117) 962 6119 f (0117) 911 8434
e admin@westfieldhouse.net w westfieldhouse.net

open All year
bedrooms 1 double, 2 twin
bathrooms All en suite
payment Credit/debit cards, cash/cheques, euros

Westfield House offers the discerning guest, whether on business or on holiday, the opportunity to relax in luxurious, modern accommodation and to savour extremely high quality and beautifully prepared food. Westfield House is run solely by family members therefore you benefit from the family-run environment and personal attention.

⊕ Brochure and clear travel instructions from any direction available on request.

♥ 3 nights accommodation between Thu-Sun incl breakfast and supper for 2: £400.00. Feel free to bring your own wine!

Room ☎ 📺 🛜 🍵 General ☁11 P ✂ ✕ 🍽 🎿 ⚽ ☀ Leisure ∪ ▶ 🏊

BRISTOL, City of Bristol Map ref 2A2 — **SELF CATERING**

★★★★
SELF CATERING

Units   1
Sleeps   2
Low season per wk
£210.00–£280.00
High season per wk
£210.00–£280.00

The Byre, Nr Pilning, Bristol

contact Mrs Penny Withers, The Byre, Laurel Farm, Pilning Street, Bristol BS35 4HN
t (01454) 632315 e david.withers51@btinternet.com

On a working farm, The Byre is a converted cowshed comprising large bed-sitting room, separate kitchen and bathroom, patio and garden. Within easy reach of Bristol, Bath and surrounding areas.

open All year except Christmas and New Year
payment Cash/cheques

Unit 🏠 📺 🖥 📠 🍵 🔲 🔲 🛒 ❄
General P ✂ Ⓢ Leisure ▶ 🏊 Shop 3 miles Pub 0.75 miles

BRISTOL, City of Bristol Map ref 2A2 — **CAMPING & CARAVANNING**

★★★★
TOURING PARK

🚐 (55) £14.30–£27.70
🚙 (55) £14.30–£27.70
55 touring pitches

Baltic Wharf Caravan Club Site

Cumberland Road, Bristol BS1 6XG t (0117) 926 8030 w caravanclub.co.uk

open All year
payment Credit/debit cards, cash/cheques

A waterside site, right in the heart of Bristol's beautifully redeveloped dockland. Linked in the summer by a river ferry to the city centre. For families there is the zoo and Downs Park; a safe place for young children to play in and an ideal picnic spot.

⊕ M5 jct 18, A4, under bridge. Left lane, follow Historic Harbour/SS Great Britain, into Hotwells Road. Right lane at lights, left lane after pedestrian crossing. Over bridge, site on left.

♥ Special member rates mean you can save your membership subscription in less than a week. Visit our website to find out more.

THE CARAVAN CLUB

General P 🚐 🍴 🚿 🚾 🛁 📶 ☀ Leisure ▶

Check the maps

Colour maps at the front pinpoint all the places you will find accommodation entries in the regional sections. Pick your location and then refer to the place index at the back to find the page number.

Eden Project, near St Austell

Minack Theatre, Porthcurno

Polzeath

Explore Cornwall & the Isles of Scilly

Explore hidden coves and harbours of whitewashed cottages. Stride out along mighty cliffs and across brooding moorland. Discover maritime museums and historic houses. Enjoy it all!

Harbours and heritage

Start your Cornish voyage of discovery in the beautiful surroundings of Newquay harbour. Head off to the nearby Blue Reef Aquarium to explore Conwall's hidden treasures in a dazzling undersea safari through the oceans of the world. Visit Polperro for picture-postcard scenes of white cottages against a harbour full of bobbing boats.

Explore Charlestown Shipwreck & Heritage Centre that commemorates achievement and heartbreak in a unique 18th-century setting. Then search out the Eden Project and make your way to the top of the tropical dome, gazing in amazement at the fronds and ferns.

On land and sea

Tack through the waves on a sailing holiday at Falmouth or learn the ropes at the National Maritime Museum Cornwall. Here you can try your hand at steering a boat into the harbour, all in the safety of dry land! Nearby visit some of Cornwall's colourful gardens: stroll along woodland walks beside the river at Trelissick Garden, or wander around Trebah's wild garden where a canopy of rhododendrons grows among glades of 100-year-old tropical tree ferns.

To the south and back

Down on the Lizard Peninsula chill out on countless beaches, check out the tiny coves tucked under giant jagged cliffs and search for caves, stacks and blowholes, or head for the very tip of Britain at Land's End and contemplate the stunning rocky vistas out into the Atlantic. Treat yourself to a performance at the Minack Theatre at Porthcurno where the stage seems to almost hang on the cliff-edge and its setting just adds to the drama.

Tate St Ives

Isles of Scilly

Kitesurfing

Land's End

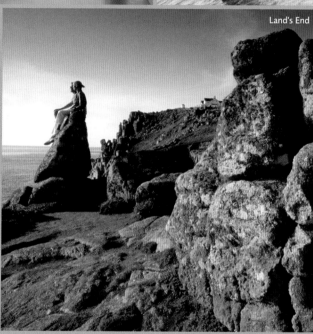

Drive on the open road, racing the clouds as you go, along the rugged north Cornish coast, steeped in folklore and alive with tales of shipwrecks and smugglers. Stop in St Ives and enjoy the works of art in Tate St Ives and the Barbara Hepworth Museum, or pause in Padstow to sample the superb seafood served up in Rick Stein's famous restaurants.

At Tintagel climb the steps up to the ruined castle perched high above the sea and experience the atmosphere of the legends of King Arthur, or bustle about in Boscastle's harbour, peering into the piled-up lobster pots, then taste their earlier contents at lunch or dinner!

Jewels in the ocean

Hop on a helicopter from Penzance and be dazzled by the sparkling jewels of the Atlantic – the Isles of Scilly. Stretch out on silver sands, dip into translucent turquoise waters and relax in the perfect peace and total tranquillity of these islands – only five are inhabited. At the Abbey Garden on Tresco find ferns from New Zealand, acacias from Australia and proteas from South Africa. The waters of the Gulf Stream kiss these shores, keeping them warm and encouraging the growth of subtropical plants. Is this really part of Britain?

Food & drink

Fancy a bite to eat, a relaxing drink or some fresh local produce? Here's a selection of food and drink venues to get you started. For lots more ideas go online at enjoyengland.com/taste.

Restaurants

Barclay House
British
St Martins Road,
East Looe PL13 1LP
t (01503) 262929
w barclayhouse.co.uk

Bay Restaurant
Fine dining
Britons Hill, Penzance TR18 3AE
t (01736) 366890
w bay-penzance.co.uk

Bedruthan Steps Hotel
English
Mawgan Porth, Cornwall TR8 4BU
t (01637) 860555
w bedruthan.com

Castaways
Seafood
Old Admiralty House, Mylor
Harbour, Falmouth TR11 5UF
t (01326) 377710
w eatoutcornwall.com

The Cove Restaurant
Fine dining
Maenporth, Falmouth
TR11 5HN
t (01326) 251136
w thecovemaenporth.co.uk

Fifteen Cornwall
European
On the Beach, Watergate Bay
TR8 4AA
t (01637) 861000
w fifteencornwall.co.uk

Porthminster Cafe
Seafood
Porthminster Beach, St Ives
TR26 2EB
t (01736) 795352
w porthminstercafe.co.uk

The Rising Sun
European
St Mawes, Truro TR2 5DJ
t (01326) 270233
w risingsunstmawes.co.uk

The Sticky Prawn
Seafood
Flushing Quay, Flushing, Falmouth
TR11 5TY
t (01326) 373734
w thestickyprawn.co.uk

Tapenades Restaurant
English
14 Dean Street,
Liskeard PL14 4AA
t (01579) 344844

Trawlers on the Quay
Seafood
East Looe PL13 1AH
t (01503) 263593
w trawlersrestaurant.co.uk

Pubs

5 Degrees West
7 Grove Place, Falmouth
TR11 4AU
t (01326) 311288
w 5degreeswest.net

The Bay View Inn
Marine Drive, Widemouth Bay
EX23 0AW
t (01288) 361273
w bayviewinn.co.uk

The New Inn
Tresco, Isles of Scilly TR24 0QE
t (01720) 422844

The Springer Spaniel
Treburley, Launceston PL15 9NS
t (01579) 370424
w thespringerspaniel.org.uk

Victoria Inn
Perranuthnoe, Penzance
TR20 9NP
t (01736) 710309
w victoriainn-penzance.co.uk

Tearooms, coffee shops and cafes

de Wynns Tea & Coffee House
55 Church Street, Falmouth
TR11 3DS
t (01326) 319259

Muffins
32 Fore Street, Lostwithiel
PL22 0BN
t (01208) 872278
w muffins32.fsnet.co.uk

The Venus Cafe and Beach Shop
Tolcarne Beach Village,
Narrowcliff, Newquay TR7 2QN
t (01637) 876028
w venuscompany.co.uk

Wylde's Cafe
Bossiney Road, Tintagel
PL34 0AH
t (01840) 770007
w wyldestogo.co.uk

Delis

Kings Delicatessen
9 Whitehart Arcade,
Launceston PL15 8AA
t (01566) 774743

Purely Cornish
Buller Street, East Looe
PL13 1AR
t (01503) 262696
w purelycornish.co.uk

Tiffins Deli and Bakery
24 Fore Street, Fowey PL23 1AQ
t (01726) 832322
w tiffinsdeli.co.uk

Farm shops and local produce

St Kew Harvest Farm Shop
St Kew Highway,
Bodmin PL30 3EF
t (01208) 841818

Trevaskis Farm Shop
12 Gwinear Road, Connor
Downs, Hayle TR27 5JQ
t (01209) 713931
w trevaskisfarm.co.uk

enjoy**England** ™

official tourist board guides

Hotels, including country house and town house hotels, metro and budget hotels in England 2008

£10.99

Guest accommodation, B&Bs, guest houses, farmhouses, inns, restaurants with rooms, campus and hostel accommodation in England 2008

£11.99

Self-catering holiday homes, including serviced apartments and approved caravan holiday homes, boat accommodation and holiday cottage agencies in England 2008

£11.99

Touring parks, camping holidays and holiday parks and villages in Britain 2008

£8.99

informative, easy to use and great value for money

Pet-friendly hotels, B&Bs and self-catering accommodation in England 2008

£9.99

Great ideas for places to visit, eat and stay in England

£10.99

Places to stay and visit in South West England

£9.99

Places to stay and visit in Northern England

£9.99

Accessible places to stay in Britain

£9.99

Now available in good bookshops.
For special offers on VisitBritain publications,
please visit **enjoyenglanddirect.com**

where to stay in
Cornwall &
the Isles of Scilly

Maps
All place names in the blue bands are shown
on the maps at the front of this guide.

Accommodation symbols
Symbols give useful information about services
and facilities. Inside the back-cover flap you
can find a key to these symbols. Keep it open
for easy reference.

ASHTON, Cornwall Map ref 1B3 | **SELF CATERING**

★★★
SELF CATERING

Units **9**
Sleeps **1–4**

Low season per wk
£110.00–£240.00
High season per wk
£300.00–£470.00

Chycarne Farm Cottages, Helston
contact Mrs Ross, Chycarne Farm Cottages, Balwest, Ashton TR13 9TE
t (01736) 762473 **f** (01736) 762473 **e** chycarnefarmcottages@hotmail.com
w chycarne-farm-cottages.co.uk

payment Credit/debit cards, cash/cheques

Nestling in the tranquil countryside of Tregonning
Hill, 17thC granite farm buildings converted into
cosy self-contained cottages, set in five acres with
parking. Stunning views over Mounts Bay. Located in
historic World Heritage Site. Many places of interest
within easy reach. Coastal and country walks. Pub/
restaurant one mile. Colour brochure. Closed
February, March and November.

⊕ Take A394 Penzance to Helston road. At Ashton post office
turn left into Higher Lane. Chycarne Farm entrance exactly
1 mile on right-hand side.

♥ 3-and 4-night breaks available in off-peak periods. Call for
details.

Unit TV 🖥 🍴 🖼 📺 ❄
General ♿ ☂ P ✂ ◌ 🐾   Leisure ✈ ↟   Shop 1 mile   Pub 1 mile

Country Code

always follow the Country Code

• Be safe – plan ahead and follow any signs
• Leave gates and property as you find them
• Protect plants and animals, and take your litter home
• Keep dogs under close control
• Consider other people

BOSCASTLE, Cornwall Map ref 1B2 — HOTEL

★★
HOTEL
SILVER AWARD

B&B per room per night
s £40.00–£45.00
d £80.00–£130.00
HB per person per night
£60.00–£85.00

Wellington Hotel

The Harbour, Boscastle PL35 0AQ t (01840) 250202 e info@boscastle-wellington.com
w boscastle-wellington.com

open All year
bedrooms 8 double, 1 twin, 4 single, 2 family
bathrooms All en suite
payment Credit/debit cards, cash/cheques

Listed 16thC coaching inn in the Elizabethan harbour of Boscastle. Fantastic fine-dining restaurant. Traditional pub with Cornish ales, home-cooked food and log fire. Ten acres of private woodland walks and close to coastal path. Ideal location for discovering Cornwall. Recently refurbished after the Boscastle floods.

⊕ From Exeter, A30 to Launceston. At Kennards House junction, A395 to Camelford. At Davidstowe, B3262 to A39. Turn left, then right onto B3266. Follow signs to Boscastle.

♥ Special breaks available throughout the year. 10% discount for 4 or more nights; 15% discount for 7 or more nights.

Room 📞 📺 ♿ 🍴 🛋 General 🛏 🏛 🎿 P ♟ 🍽 📠 ☎ 🛎 ✤ 🍺 Leisure 🎵 🛥 🚶 🏇 🚴 🏊

BOSCASTLE, Cornwall Map ref 1B2 — SELF CATERING

★★★★
SELF CATERING

Units   5
Sleeps   4–6

Low season per wk
£195.00–£280.00
High season per wk
£280.00–£630.00

Cargurra Farm, Boscastle

contact Mrs Gillian Elson, Hennett, St Juliot, Boscastle PL35 0BT
t (01840) 261206 e gillian@cargurra.co.uk w cargurra.co.uk

open All year
payment Credit/debit cards, cash/cheques

Secluded farm setting within the beautiful Valency Valley where Thomas Hardy met his love. Well-appointed, traditional cottage, log fire, central heating. Spacious gardens, barbecue, games room with pool and table tennis. Wi-Fi Internet access, communal computer. Private road, ample parking. Country and coastal walks. Also, cottages converted from Victorian barn.

⊕ Travel directions provided once booking is confirmed.

Unit 🏨 📺 🍴 🛋 🚿 🖥 🍽 🔒 🛋 ✤
General 🛏 🏛 🎿 P 🅿 Leisure ♠ Shop 2 miles Pub 2 miles

BUDE, Cornwall Map ref 1C2 — GUEST ACCOMMODATION

★★★
GUEST ACCOMMODATION

B&B per room per night
d £56.00–£76.00

Beach House

Marine Drive, Widemouth Bay, Bude EX23 0AW t (01288) 361256
e beachhousebookings@tiscali.co.uk w beachhousewidemouth.co.uk

bedrooms 8 double, 1 twin, 2 family
bathrooms All en suite
payment Credit/debit cards, cash/cheques

The Wilkins family welcome you to their unique site, with private access onto Widemouth Beach. All bedrooms are en suite, the majority with sundeck balconies. Sun lounge, new bar lounge, on-site post office, shop, surf shop and hire. Restaurant serving traditional Cornish and seafood menus. Outside dining on decked patios. Open Easter to end of October.

⊕ Enter Bude from A39. Left at mini-roundabout, proceed over Falcon Bridge. After 2.5 miles Beach House is to the right on the foreshore.

♥ Discounts on bookings of 4 days or more.

Room 📺 ♿ General 🛏 🎿 P ♟ ✕ 🍽 ✤ Leisure 🛥

For key to symbols open the back-cover flap.

BUDE, Cornwall Map ref 1C2 — GUEST ACCOMMODATION

★★★★
GUEST HOUSE
SILVER AWARD

Harefield Cottage

Upton, Bude EX23 0LY t (01288) 352350 f (01288) 352712 e sales@coast-countryside.co.uk
w coast-countryside.co.uk

B&B per room per night
s Min £40.00
d Min £54.00
Evening meal per person
Min £20.00

open All year
bedrooms 2 double, 1 twin
bathrooms All en suite
payment Credit/debit cards, cash/cheques

Stone-built cottage with outstanding views. Luxurious and spacious en suite bedrooms, king-size beds and four-poster available. Home cooking our speciality. All diets catered for. Personal attention assured at all times. Only 250yds from the coastal footpath. One mile downhill to the National Cycle network. Hot tub available.

⊕ From A39 follow signs to Bude town centre, turn left at mini-roundabout, over Canal bridge, uphill for 1 mile. Red telephone box on right-hand side, past this there is a left-hand turn to Upton. Harefield Cottage on left.

♥ Special 3-night breaks including DB&B and packed lunch – £130. With walking – £150.

Room 🛏 📺 ⬙ ♙ General ⌘ ▥ ⚲ P ⚡ ✕ ⌨ 🏵 ❀ ⋔ Leisure 🚲 🏖

BUDE, Cornwall Map ref 1C2 — SELF CATERING

★★★★
SELF CATERING

Broomhill Manor Country Estate, Bude

contact Mr A Biggs & Ms L Winstanley, Broomhill Manor Country Estate, Broomhill Manor, Bude EX23 9HA
t (01288) 352940 f (01288) 356526 e info@broomhillmanor.co.uk w broomhillmanor.co.uk

Units **18**
Sleeps **1–6**

Low season per wk
£340.00–£595.00
High season per wk
£785.00–£1,415.00

open All year
payment Credit/debit cards, cash/cheques

Quality cottages in extensive grounds of old manor house. Own riding stables. Indoor swimming pool with jacuzzi, gymnasium, sauna and treatment room. Outdoor pool (seasonal), tennis court. Play areas. Hot tubs. Close to beaches. Easy access to all attractions.

⊕ From the A39 in Stratton turn west up Stamford Hill, then turn left again almost immediately by a white cottage. We are on the right.

♥ Short breaks (Mon-Fri/Fri-Mon) available Oct-Easter.

Unit ▥ 📺 📶 🍳 📼 🔌 📷 ♙ ▢ 🕯 ✿
General ⌘ ▥ ⚲ ⚡ ◎ S ⋔ Leisure 🐟 ⚒ ⚓ ⚲ U ♪ ► 🚲 Shop 1 mile Pub 1 mile

BUDE, Cornwall Map ref 1C2 — SELF CATERING

★★★★
SELF CATERING

Ivyleaf Combe, Bude

contact Mr Cheeseman, Ivyleaf Combe, Ivyleaf Hill, Stratton EX23 9LD
t (01288) 321323 f (01288) 321323 e tony@ivyleafcombe.com w ivyleafcombe.com

Units **10**
Sleeps **4–6**

Low season per wk
£295.00–£335.00
High season per wk
£645.00–£810.00

open All year
payment Cash/cheques

Discover this superbly appointed selection of lodges in a tranquil and beautiful setting. These spacious and contemporary lodges offer the perfect place in which to unwind and relax. All have their own deck/patio, and some have hot tubs. Large, safe play area. Ivyleaf Combe is perfect for that romantic break or the family holiday.

⊕ M5 jct 27, A361 to Barnstaple, left onto A39 towards Bude. Through Kilkhampton. Turn off A39 left towards Ivyleaf golf course. Ivyleaf Combe at bottom of hill on left.

♥ 3- and 4-night stays available. Romantic-break packages in lodges with 4-poster bed and hot tub.

Unit ▥ 📺 🍳 📼 📷 ▢ 🕯 ✿
General ⌘ ▥ ⚲ ⚡ ◎ S ⋔ Leisure U ♪ ► 🚲 Shop 1 mile Pub 1.5 miles

BUDE, Cornwall Map ref 1C2 | **SELF CATERING**

★★★
SELF CATERING

Units **8**
Sleeps **2–6**

Low season per wk
£210.00–£370.00
High season per wk
£340.00–£820.00

Langfield Manor, Bude

contact Suzanne Walker, Langfield Manor, Broadclose, Bude EX23 8DP
t (01288) 352415 **e** langfieldmanor@btconnect.com **w** langfieldmanor.co.uk

open All year
payment Cash/cheques

Langfield Manor is an old Edwardian house that has been converted into eight self-catering apartments, including a heated swimming pool and a full-size snooker table. It is located in a secluded corner of Bude, three minutes' walk from the shops and sandy beaches, and adjacent to Bude Golf Club.

⊕ A39 to Bude past Morrisons, down hill after Esso garage, take 2nd right Killerton Road, 1st left Holnicote Road, 1st right Broadclose, right into manor.

♥ Short breaks. Also the opportunity to book the whole manor house for special occasions or Christmas & New Year.

Unit 🏠 📺 📻 🍳 📷 🍴 🔥 🍷 🔌 🍽 ☕ ❄
General 🐕 🏠 ⚿ P Ⓟ Ⓢ Leisure 🎣 🔍 ∪ ⏊ ♪ 🚴 Shop 3 miles Pub 3 miles

BUDE, Cornwall Map ref 1C2 | **CAMPING & CARAVANNING**

★★★★★
TOURING PARK

🚐 (145) £9.00–£24.00
🚐 (145) £9.00–£24.00
⛺ (145) £9.00–£24.00
145 touring pitches

Budemeadows Park

Budemeadows, Bude EX23 0NA **t** (01288) 361646 **f** 0870 7064825 **e** infootb@budemeadows.com
w budemeadows.com

open All year
payment Credit/debit cards, cash/cheques

Superb centre for surfing, scenery and sightseeing. All usual facilities including heated pool, licensed bar, shop, launderette, playground. Well kept and maintained grounds.

⊕ Signposted on A39, 3 miles south of Bude, 200yds past crossroad to Widemouth Bay.

♥ Discounts for large families and longer stays. Please phone for details.

General 🖥 ♿ P 🔌 ☕ 🍴 🚿 ☉ 📷 🔥 🐕 ☀ Leisure 🎣 📺 🍴 🏊 🔍 ⚲ ∪ ⏊

BUDE, Cornwall Map ref 1C2 | **CAMPING & CARAVANNING**

★★★★
HOLIDAY &
TOURING PARK

🚐 (20) £8.50–£19.50
🚐 (20) £8.50–£19.50
⛺ (20) £8.50–£19.50
🏠 (150) £102.00–£579.00
60 touring pitches

Sandymouth Bay Holiday Park

Sandymouth Bay, Bude EX23 9HW **t** (01288) 352563 **f** (01288) 354822
e reception@sandymouthbay.co.uk **w** sandymouthbay.co.uk

payment Credit/debit cards, cash/cheques

Friendly family park set in 24 acres of meadowland in an area rich with beautiful beaches, bustling coastal resorts and picturesque fishing villages. Inland, the rolling countryside is a fascinating contrast to the rugged coast. Licensed club, indoor pool, sauna, crazy golf, toilets and launderette. Open March to October.

⊕ On M5 from north, exit jct 27. Travel on A361/A39 towards Bude. Just past the village of Kilkhampton, take right-hand turning signposted Sandymouth.

♥ Various promotions for certain times of the year – call us or see website.

General 🔥 🖥 ♿ P 🔌 ☕ 🍴 🔍 ☉ 📷 🔥 🐕 ✕ ☀ Leisure 🎣 📺 🍴 ♪ ⚲ 🔍 ∪ ⏊ 🚴

Key to symbols
Open the back flap for a key to symbols.

CALLINGTON, Cornwall Map ref 1C2 | GUEST ACCOMMODATION

★★★★
GUEST HOUSE

B&B per room per night
s £44.95–£49.95
d £69.90–£79.90
Evening meal per person
£12.95–£15.90

Hampton Manor

Alston, Callington PL17 8LX t (01579) 370494 f (01579) 370494 e hamptonmanor@supanet.com
w hamptonmanor.co.uk

open All year
bedrooms 2 double, 2 twin, 1 family, 1 suite
bathrooms All en suite
payment Cash/cheques

Small Victorian country-house hotel set in 2.5 acres amidst tranquil countryside bordering Devon. High-quality accommodation (wheelchair access), personal service and home-cooked food (diets catered for). Thirty minutes' drive from north and south coasts, historic Plymouth, Dartmoor and Bodmin Moor. The Eden Project and many well-known gardens are also nearby.

⊕ A30 to Launceston, then A388 towards Callington. After 7 miles turn left towards Horsebridge. Straight on at 2 crossroads, then left at sign for Alston/Tutwell.

♥ Romantic DB&B packages, activity weekends for bridge players, walkers, ornithologists etc. Up to 15% discount for groups and long stays.

Room 📶 ♨ 🍷 General 🛏 🍽 🕴 P ⚡ 🍽 ✕ 🍽 🗑 ❄ Leisure ♦ ∪ ♪ ⌐ ⚓

CARBIS BAY, Cornwall Map ref 1B3 | GUEST ACCOMMODATION

★★★★
GUEST ACCOMMODATION

B&B per room per night
d £56.00–£105.00

Beechwood House

St Ives Road, Carbis Bay, St Ives TR26 2SX t (01736) 795170 f (01736) 795170
e beechwood@carbisbay.wanadoo.co.uk

open All year
bedrooms 5 double, 1 twin, 2 family
bathrooms All en suite
payment Credit/debit cards, cash

Five minutes' walk to sandy beach. Looks out over St Ives Bay. All rooms are en suite. Guests' private lounge, garden and parking. We have golf, fishing, St Michael's Mount and trips to the Isles of Scilly all within easy reach. Courtesy lift from local train or bus stations, when available.

⊕ Exit A30 at St Ives, following A3074 signs. Proceed through Lelant to Carbis Bay. You will pass a convenience store. We are about 50yds further on left.

Room 📶 📺 ♨ 🍷 General 🛏 🍽 🕴 P ⚡ 🍽 ❄ Leisure ∪ ♪ ⌐ 🚲 ⚓

CONSTANTINE, Cornwall Map ref 1B3 | SELF CATERING

★★★★
SELF CATERING

Units **1**
Sleeps **2–6**

Low season per wk
£285.00–£345.00
High season per wk
£585.00–£785.00

Green Bank Cottage, Seworgan, Falmouth

contact Mrs Carole Scobie-Allin, Selective Cornish Retreats, Green Valley, Seworgan, Constantine, Falmouth TR11 5QN
t (01326) 340147 & 07767 896359 f (01326) 340147 e caroleselectiveretreats@yahoo.com
w connexions.co.uk/schr

A traditional cottage in a peaceful hamlet, close to the Helford River. Well-equipped with log fire. One double, two twin bedrooms. Private use of spa, sauna and gym. Dogs welcome.

open All year
payment Cash/cheques

Unit 🏠 📺 📻 🍴 🖥 💻 🛁 📻 ♨ 🗑 🍽 🧺 ❄
General 🛏 🍽 🕴 P S 🐕 Leisure ∪ ⌐ ⚓ Shop 2 miles Pub 4 miles

Using map references
Map references refer to the colour maps at the front of this guide.

CRACKINGTON HAVEN, Cornwall Map ref 1C2 — CAMPING & CARAVANNING

★★★
HOLIDAY, TOURING
& CAMPING PARK

⬛ (20)	£10.00–£16.50
⬛ (12)	£10.00–£16.50
⬛ (35)	£10.00–£16.50
⬛ (8)	£160.00–£560.00
43 touring pitches	

Hentervene Caravan & Camping Park

Crackington Haven, Bude EX23 0LF t (01840) 230365 f (01840) 230065
e contact@hentervene.co.uk w hentervene.co.uk

Peaceful park in an Area of Outstanding Natural Beauty. Sandy beaches and coastal path nearby. Spacious, level pitches. Modern caravans to hire/buy. Excellent base for exploring North Cornwall and Devon.

open All year
payment Credit/debit cards, cash/cheques

General ⬛ P ⬛ ⬛ ⬛ ⬛ ⊙ ⬛⬛ ⬛ ⬛ ⬛ ☼ Leisure 📺 ⬛ ⬛ ⊍ ⬛

CRANTOCK, Cornwall Map ref 1B2 — SELF CATERING

★★★–★★★★★
SELF CATERING

Units	**6**
Sleeps	**4–8**
Low season per wk	£220.00–£480.00
High season per wk	£700.00–£1,850.00

Seaspray Holiday Cottages, Crantock

Cornwall Holiday Cottages, PO Box 24, Truro TR1 9AG
t 0845 226 5507 e rentals@cornwall-cottages.biz w cornwall-cottages.biz

open All year
payment Cash/cheques

Comfortable cottages, some with spectacular sea views at West Pentire; others are period properties with conservation listing located in the village; all have gardens; some have log burners; some welcome dogs; all are within easy reach of popular Crantock village and beach. Sleeping from two to eight people, all are equipped to a high standard.

⊕ Take A392 from A30 to Newquay, follow signs to Crantock.

♥ Short breaks Nov-Mar. Christmas and New Year packages.

Unit ⬛ 📺 ⬛ ⬛ ⬛ ⬛ ⬛ ⬛ ⬛ ✻
General ⬛ ⬛ ⬛ P ⬛ ⬛ ⬛ ⬛ Leisure ⬛ Shop 1 mile Pub 1 mile

DELABOLE, Cornwall Map ref 1B2 — SELF CATERING

★
SELF CATERING

Units	**6**
Sleeps	**6**
Low season per wk	£180.00–£280.00
High season per wk	£320.00–£400.00

Delamere Holiday Bungalows, Delabole

contact Mrs Snowden, Delamere Holiday Bungalows, 8 Warren Road, Ickenham UB10 8AA
t (01895) 234144 w delamerebungalows.com

Traditional bungalows in lawned setting. Ideal location, panoramic country views. Sleep four – occasional five/six. Close sandy beaches. Suitable all tastes – spring/summer breaks, family holidays, exploring, surfing. No dogs. Open March to November.

payment Cash/cheques

Unit 📺 ⬛ ⬛
General ⬛ ⬛ P ⬛ Leisure ⊍ ⬛ ⬛ ⬛ Shop < 0.5 miles Pub < 0.5 miles

For key to symbols open the back-cover flap.

FALMOUTH, Cornwall Map ref 1B3   **HOTEL**

★★★
HOTEL
SILVER AWARD

Green Lawns Hotel

Western Terrace, Falmouth TR11 4QJ   t (01326) 312734   f (01326) 211427
e info@greenlawnshotel.com   w greenlawnshotel.com

B&B per room per night
s £55.00–£115.00
d £80.00–£190.00
HB per person per night
£55.00–£140.00

open All year except Christmas
bedrooms 13 double, 12 twin, 6 single, 8 family
bathrooms All en suite
payment Credit/debit cards, cash/cheques

Elegant, chateau-style hotel in prize-winning gardens with views across Falmouth Bay. Distinguished by its ivy exterior, the hotel is between the main beaches and town centre. The Green Lawns offers the perfect holiday setting or business retreat. It is privately owned and renowned for friendly hospitality and professional service.

⊕ A30 onto A39 to Truro. Carry on to Falmouth.

♥ Special terms on DB&B based on 2 people sharing a twin/double for 3/5/7 nights. Spring and autumn breaks.

Room ⌂ ▦ ℂ TV ♨ ℞ ⚘   General ☒ ▥ ♣ P ⛽ ♒ ♨ ◑ ☰ ⌕ ✿ ⊞ ⛾   Leisure ⚷ ⌘ ⚘ ♫ ∪ ⚲ ⌁

FALMOUTH, Cornwall Map ref 1B3   **GUEST ACCOMMODATION**

★★★★★
GUEST ACCOMMODATION
GOLD AWARD

Dolvean House

50 Melvill Road, Falmouth TR11 4DQ   t (01326) 313658   f (01326) 313995
e reservations@dolvean.co.uk   w dolvean.co.uk

B&B per room per night
s £35.00–£45.00
d £70.00–£90.00

open All year except Christmas
bedrooms 6 double, 2 twin, 2 single
bathrooms All en suite
payment Credit/debit cards, cash/cheques

Award-winning Victorian home in an ideal location for exploring Cornwall. Relaxing ambience, good food and romantic bedrooms to make every stay a special occasion.

⊕ Situated on A39 to Pendennis Castle.

♥ Special breaks available in winter, spring and autumn. Check our website for more details.

Room ⌂ TV ♨ ℞   General ☒12 P ⚿ ⛽ ♒ ⚘ ✿

FALMOUTH, Cornwall Map ref 1B3   **SELF CATERING**

★★
SELF CATERING

Units   **1**
Sleeps   **7**

High season per wk
£550.00–£650.00

8 Marine Crescent, Falmouth

contact Mrs Pauline Spong, 42 Westleigh Avenue, Leigh-on-Sea SS9 2LF
t (01702) 712596 & 07989 653639   f (01702) 712596   e rcspong@hotmail.com
w cornwall-online.co.uk/self-catering/falmouth/8mari

Comfortable harbourside house. Ideally located near Maritime Museum, beach, shops and restaurants. Fully equipped. Regret no singles, no pets. Open early July to late September.

payment Cash/cheques

Unit ▥ TV ▣ ▢ ▣ ⬚ ⬚ ⬚ ⬚ ✿
General ☒ P ⑤   Leisure ⚘ ⚱   Shop < 0.5 miles   Pub < 0.5 miles

Place index

If you know where you want to stay, the index at the back of the guide will give you the page number listing accommodation in your chosen town, city or village. Check out the other useful indexes too.

★★★
SELF CATERING

Units **5**
Sleeps **1-6**
Low season per wk
£120.00-£260.00
High season per wk
£315.00-£485.00

Bay View Self Catering, Falmouth

contact Mr & Mrs Walker, Bay View Self Catering, Gyllyngvase Road, Falmouth TR11 4DJ
t (01326) 312429   **e** bay.viewfalmouth@btinternet.com   **w** bayviewselfcatering.co.uk

Ideal holiday location, 100 yds from Gyllyngvase Beach and tropical gardens. Short walk into town, harbour and Events Square.

open All year
payment Cash/cheques

Unit 🏠 📺 🍳 🖥 🛏 ✎ 🍽 ❄
General 🛋 🏛 ⚲ P ⚖ S 🐕   Shop 1 mile   Pub < 0.5 miles

★★★
SELF CATERING

Units **6**
Sleeps **2-5**
Low season per wk
£220.00-£395.00
High season per wk
£415.00-£475.00

Good-Winds Holiday Apartments, Falmouth

contact Mrs Goodwin, Good-Winds Holiday Apartments, 13 Stratton Terracce, Falmouth TR11 2SY
t (01326) 313200   **f** (01326) 313200   **e** goodwinds13@aol.com

open All year
payment Cash/cheques, euros

Modern, two-bedroom apartments with balconies having marvellous views over the harbour, River Pen and the quaint fishing village of Flushing. Under-cover parking for two cars. Walking distance to town. One double bed, two singles and extra single in three units.

⊕ Follow signs into Falmouth. When you see 'Park and Float' signs, left at next roundabout. 1 mile. Right into Symons Hill. Right into Penwerris Lane.

♥ Three-day plus short breaks available out of season.

Unit 🏠 📺 🖥 ⚲ 🖨
General 🛋 🏛 ⚲ P S 🐕   Shop 0.5 miles   Pub 0.75 miles

★★★
HOTEL

B&B per room per night
s £67.00-£220.00
d £90.00-£220.00
HB per person per night
£65.00-£130.00

Fowey Hotel

The Esplanade, Fowey PL23 1HX   **t** (01726) 832551   **f** (01726) 832125
e reception@thefoweyhotel.co.uk   **w** thefoweyhotel.co.uk

open All year
bedrooms 29 double, 6 twin, 1 family, 1 suite
bathrooms All en suite
payment Credit/debit cards, cash/cheques

Majestically positioned on the bank of the Fowey Estuary, the Fowey Hotel, built in 1882, offers friendly service, comfortable rooms and rosette award-winning food. Located only 20 minutes from the Eden Project, the hotel is in the ideal location for exploring many of the gardens and attractions in Cornwall. DB&B rates available on request.

⊕ On entering Fowey, take Daglands Road (on right), continue for 200yds. The Fowey Hotel drive is on the left before the bend in the road.

♥ Special midweek and 3-day Eden breaks available throughout the year.

Room 🖥 ☎ 📺 ☕ 🛜 🎧   General 🛋 🏛 ⚲ P ♨ 🍽 🛗 ● 🖨 🍸 ❄ 🚐 🐕

It's all quality-assessed accommodation

Our commitment to quality involves wide-ranging accommodation assessment. Rating and awards were correct at the time of going to press but may change following a new assessment. Please check at time of booking.

FOWEY, Cornwall Map ref 1B3 | **SELF CATERING**

★★
SELF CATERING

Units **1**
Sleeps **1–4**

Low season per wk
£210.00–£230.00
High season per wk
£270.00–£370.00

Lugger Cottage, Fowey

contact Vicki Medlen, c/o Victoria Inn, Roche, St Austell PL26 8LQ
t 0845 241 1133 **f** (01726) 891233 **e** reservations@smallandfriendly.co.uk **w** smallandfriendly.co.uk

open All year
payment Credit/debit cards, cash/cheques

Polruan is, in many ways, the little twin of Fowey over the river. The Lugger Inn overlooks the water's edge and serves fine food, wine and ales. The cottage has a lounge, kitchen, main bedroom with a double bed, second bedroom with bunk beds, shower room and wc.

⊕ Follow A38 from Plymouth, turn off at Dobwalls and go through East Taphouse. At the brow of the hill, turn left for Polruan; then it's signposted.

Unit ▦ TV ▣ 🗑 🍽 📶 🌐
General ⛱ ▥ ⊀ P ⅍ S Leisure ∪ ♪ ♭ Shop 0.5 miles Pub < 0.5 miles

---

FOWEY, Cornwall Map ref 1B3 | **CAMPING & CARAVANNING**

★★★★
TOURING &
CAMPING PARK

🚐 (65) £12.00–£18.00
🚕 (65) £12.00–£18.00
⛺ (65) £12.00–£18.00
65 touring pitches

Penmarlam Caravan & Camping Park

Bodinnick by Fowey, Fowey PL23 1LZ **t** (01726) 870088 **f** (01726) 870082
e info@penmarlampark.co.uk **w** penmarlampark.co.uk

payment Credit/debit cards, cash/cheques, euros

A quiet, grassy site on the Fowey Estuary, an Area of Outstanding Natural Beauty. Choose from our lawned, sheltered field or enjoy breathtaking views from the upper field. Shop and off-licence, immaculately clean heated amenity block, electric hook-ups and serviced pitches, Wi-Fi Internet access, boat launching and storage adjacent. Open Easter to October.

⊕ A38 in Dobwalls, take A390 (signposted St Austell). In East Taphouse, left onto B3359 (signposted Looe, Polperro). After 5 miles, right (signposted Bodinnick, Fowey via ferry). Site 5 miles.

General ⛽ P ⊙ 🕿 ☕ ⛽ ⟲ ⊙ 🗑 🛁 🐕 🦮 ☼ Leisure ∪ ♪ ♭

HELSTON, Cornwall Map ref 1B3 | **GUEST ACCOMMODATION**

★★★★
GUEST HOUSE

B&B per room per night
s £30.00–£35.00
d £50.00–£55.00

Lyndale Cottage Guest House

4 Greenbank, Meneage Road, Helston TR13 8JA **t** (01326) 561082
e enquiries@lyndalecottage.co.uk **w** lyndalecottage.co.uk

open All year
bedrooms 3 double, 2 twin, 1 single
bathrooms All en suite
payment Credit/debit cards, cash/cheques

Friendly, delightfully cosy Cornish cottage. Providing modern en suite bedrooms, Freeview TVs, CD/DVD players, hospitality trays, lounge with wood-burning stove, garden with patio, private parking. Completely non-smoking. Breakfast is prepared from local produce, free-range eggs, home-made jams and yoghurt. Ideally situated for exploring West Cornwall's gardens, coastline, beaches and seaside towns.

⊕ Please contact us for easy-to-follow directions.

Room ♿ 📞 TV 👝 🍵 General P ⅍ ▥ 🍴 🔌 ✿ Leisure ∪ ♪ ♭ 🚴 🏊

Rest assured

All accommodation in this guide has been rated, or is awaiting assessment, by a professional assessor.

HELSTON, Cornwall Map ref 1B3   **GUEST ACCOMMODATION**

★ ★ ★
GUEST HOUSE

B&B per room per night
s £38.00–£50.00
d £54.00–£58.00

Mandeley Guesthouse

Clodgey Lane, Helston TR13 8PJ   t (01326) 572550   f (01326) 572550   e mandeley@btconnect.com
w mandeley.co.uk

Mandeley is a family-run guesthouse offering accommodation of the highest quality. Centrally located to explore the south-west peninsula. Secure off-road car parking. Bus stop nearby.

open All year except Christmas
bedrooms 1 double, 1 twin, 1 family
bathrooms 2 en suite, 1 private
payment Credit/debit cards, cash/cheques

Room 🖭 📺 🕯 🕮   General ⟿ P 🚭 🛏 🐾 🐕   Leisure ∪ ✔ 🚲 🎣

HELSTON, Cornwall Map ref 1B3   **SELF CATERING**

★ ★ ★
SELF CATERING

Units   **3**
Sleeps   **1–6**
Low season per wk
£150.00–£250.00
High season per wk
£250.00–£425.00

Mudgeon Vean Farm Holiday Cottages, Helston

contact Mr & Mrs Trewhella, Mudgeon Vean Farm Holiday Cottages, St Martin, Helston TR12 6DB
t (01326) 231341   f (01326) 231933   e mudgeonvean@aol.com   w mudgeonvean.co.uk

open All year
payment Cash/cheques

Cosy cottages on small 18thC farm producing apple juice and cider, near Helford River. Equipped to high standard and personally supervised. Night storage heaters and log fires. National Trust walk to the river, outdoor play area for children, games room. Peaceful location in an Area of Outstanding Natural Beauty.

⊕ *A3083 Helston, B3293 Mawgan village. Through Mawgan to St Martins Green. Left at St Martins Green, to next crossroads. Turn left. We are 2nd turning on right down lane.*

Unit 📺 📼 🍳 📠 🖥 🔒 🗄 🖲 🍴 ☼
General ⟿ 🍴 🛏 P Ⓢ 🐕   Leisure ❀ ∪ ✔ 🎣   Shop 1 mile   Pub 2 miles

---

HELSTON, Cornwall Map ref 1B3   **SELF CATERING**

★ ★ ★ ★
SELF CATERING

Units   **1**
Sleeps   **3–9**
Low season per wk
Min £470.00
High season per wk
Max £1,707.00

Tregoose Farmhouse, Helston

contact Mrs Hazel Bergin, Tregoose Farmhouse, Southern Cross, Boundervean Lane, Penponds, Camborne TR14 7QP
t (01209) 714314   e hazel.bergin@dsl.pipex.com   w tregooselet.co.uk

open All year
payment Cash/cheques

A spacious and luxuriously renovated farmhouse in a peaceful, rural setting. Indoor swimming pool. Games room. Sleeps three (plus one cot) or nine (plus two cots). Two ground-floor bedrooms and wetroom. Far-reaching views. Conveniently positioned for exploring south and west Cornwall's coastline, gardens and attractions. Three doubles, one twin and two singles.

⊕ *From A394 (Helston to Penzance), turn right onto B3302. Take 2nd right signposted Gwavas/Lowertown. Left at crossroad. 30yds turn right. Top of hill on left.*

♥ *Ground floor offered at separate tariff off-peak and late availability. Mobility and rehabilitation products available for hire through local supplier.*

Unit 📐 📺 📼 🍳 📠 🖥 🔒 🗄 🖲 🍴 ☼
General ⟿ 🍴 🛏 P 🚭   Leisure 🏊 ❀ ✔ 🎣   Shop 1 mile   Pub 2 miles

---

Quality-assured help

Official Partner Tourist Information Centres offer quality assured help with accommodation as well as suggestions of places to visit and things to do. You'll find contact details at the back of the guide.

HELSTON, Cornwall Map ref 1B3 — CAMPING & CARAVANNING

★★★★
HOLIDAY, TOURING
& CAMPING PARK

🚐 (13) £8.50–£12.50
🚙 (13) £8.50–£12.50
⛺ (13) £8.50–£12.50
🏠 (7) £135.00–£465.00
13 touring pitches

Poldown Camping & Caravan Park

Carleen, Breage, Helston TR13 9NN **t** (01326) 574560 **f** (01326) 574560 **e** info@poldown.co.uk
w poldown.co.uk

Small and pretty countryside site. Peace and quiet guaranteed. Within easy reach of West Cornwall's beaches, walks and attractions. Very good touring facilities. Modern holiday caravans.

payment Cash/cheques, euros

General 🛇 P 🔌 ⟳ 🐾 🎇 ☉ 🗐 🖥 🔥 🪑 ☼ Leisure ⛰ ⤢ ⚓

ISLES OF SCILLY, Isles of Scilly Map ref 1A3 — HOTEL

★★★
HOTEL
GOLD AWARD

HB per person per night
£130.00–£275.00

Island Hotel

Tresco TR24 0PU **t** (01720) 422883 **f** (01720) 423008 **e** islandhotel@tresco.co.uk
w islandhotel.co.uk

bedrooms 6 double, 6 twin, 5 single, 28 family, 3 suites
bathrooms All en suite
payment Credit/debit cards, cash/cheques

'One of Britain's 50 best', says The Independent; 'the ultimate romantic escape', according to Vogue. A gourmet paradise with its own beach and seasonal sailing school, on a private, subtropical island served by direct flights from Penzance. Famous Abbey Gardens, four miles of white beaches – but no crowds; heaven! Open February to October.

⊕ Penzance to Tresco or St Mary's by helicopter or boat. Direct flights to St Mary's from Southampton, Bristol, Exeter, Newquay and Land's End.

♥ Please see our website for all special rates and breaks.

Room 🛏 ☎ 📺 🖐 🍵 ⚭ General 🛋 🎏 🎣 🍷 🍴 🎱 🖥 ⓘ 🍸 ⚮ Leisure ⤢ 🔍 🎾 ⚓ ⛳ 🚴

ISLES OF SCILLY, Isles of Scilly Map ref 1A3 — HOTEL

★★
HOTEL
SILVER AWARD

B&B per room per night
d £140.00–£210.00

New Inn

Tresco TR24 0QE **t** (01720) 422844 **f** (01720) 423200 **e** newinn@tresco.co.uk **w** tresco.co.uk

open All year
bedrooms 16 double
bathrooms All en suite
payment Credit/debit cards, cash/cheques

The only pub on Tresco. A cosy inn with 16 en suite rooms. Eclectic menu served in three dining areas, with great alfresco garden. Great selection of real ales, wines and spirits. The social centre of the private island of Tresco.

⊕ Penzance to Tresco or St Mary's by helicopter or boat. Direct flights from Southampton, Bristol, Exeter, Newquay and Land's End.

♥ Please see our website for all special rates and breaks.

Room 🛏 ☎ 📺 🖐 🍵 ⚭ General 🛋 🎏 🎣 ✂ 🍷 🍴 🎱 🖥 ⚮ Leisure ⤢ 🎾 ⚓ ⛳ 🚴

A holiday on two wheels

For a fabulous freewheeling break, seek out accommodation participating in our Cyclists Welcome scheme. Look out for the symbol and plan your route online at nationalcyclenetwork.org.

ISLES OF SCILLY, Isles of Scilly Map ref 1A3 — SELF CATERING

★★★★
SELF CATERING

Units **1**
Sleeps **4**
Low season per wk
£275.00–£475.00
High season per wk
£525.00–£700.00

The Stable, St Martin's

contact Mrs D Williams, The Stable, Middle Town, St Martin's TR25 0QN
t (01720) 422810 f (01720) 422810 e fiestydee2002@yahoo.co.uk w middletownscilly.co.uk

Converted stable offering very comfortable, well-equipped and beautifully presented accommodation in quiet location. Two bedrooms (one double, one twin).

open All year
payment Cash/cheques

Unit 🛏 📺 📼 🖥 💻 ⚡ 🔥 🍽 🔌 ❄
General 🛏10 🍴 ◎ Shop 0.5 miles Pub < 0.5 miles

KILKHAMPTON, Cornwall Map ref 1C2 — SELF CATERING

★★★
SELF CATERING

Units **1**
Sleeps **4**
Low season per wk
£150.00–£240.00
High season per wk
£295.00–£490.00

Villa Nostra, Kilkhampton, Bude

contact Ms Lea Deely, 32 Fosters Way, Bude EX23 8HF
t 07773 845663 e villanostra@btinternet.com w villanostra.co.uk

Two-bedroom bungalow in grounds of Penstowe Manor. Ideal base for relaxing on the beach, safe swimming and surfing, countryside/coastal walks, and golf. Tamar Lakes nearby.

open All year
payment Cash/cheques, euros

Unit 🛏 📺 📼 🖥 💻 ⚡ 🔥 ❄
General 🛏 P 🍴 ◎ Leisure ⚓ U ♪ ▶ 🚴 Shop 0.5 miles Pub 0.5 miles

LANDRAKE, Cornwall Map ref 1C2 — CAMPING & CARAVANNING

★★★★
TOURING &
CAMPING PARK
🚐(60) £10.80–£18.60
🚍(60) £10.80–£18.60
⛺ (11) £3.50–£18.60
60 touring pitches

Dolbeare Caravan & Camping Park

St Ive Road, Landrake, Saltash PL12 5AF t (01752) 851332 f (01752) 547871
e reception@dolbeare.co.uk w dolbeare.co.uk

open All year
payment Credit/debit cards, cash/cheques

Friendly, well-maintained park which offers you that personal touch. Set amidst rolling countryside from which to explore varied coastal resorts. Enjoy both Cornwall and Devon from Dolbeare. Internet and Wi-Fi available.

General 🅿 🔌 🚿 🚻 📶 🔥 ⊙ 📶 🔋 🐕 🪝 ❄ Leisure ⛰ ♪ ▶

Accessible needs?

If you have special hearing, visual or mobility needs, there's an index of National Accessible Scheme participants featured in this guide.
For more accessible accommodation buy a copy of Easy Access Britain available online at visitbritaindirect.com.

★★★★
BED & BREAKFAST

B&B per room per night
s £25.00–£27.50
d £50.00–£55.00

Oakside

South Petherwin, Launceston PL15 7JL **t** (01566) 86733 **e** janet.crossman@tesco.net

open All year
bedrooms 2 double, 1 twin
bathrooms 2 en suite, 1 private
payment Cash/cheques

Panoramic views of Bodmin Moor from farm bungalow, nestling peacefully amongst delightful surroundings, conveniently situated one minute from A30. Ideal base for touring Devon and Cornwall. Twenty-five minutes from Eden Project. English breakfasts a speciality with home-made bread and preserves. Warm welcome awaits. Cosy, well-equipped rooms. Ideal place to relax.

⊕ *A30 into Cornwall. Three miles west of Launceston, underneath A395, still on A30. Slow down, no slip road. Next left, Oakside 1st bungalow on right.*

Room ♨ 📺 ♿ ☜ General ⌛ ▥ ♯ P ⊱ ◲ ❄ Leisure ▸ 🏛

★★★★★
BED & BREAKFAST
SILVER AWARD

B&B per room per night
s £60.00–£80.00
d £70.00–£120.00
Evening meal per person
£10.00–£14.00

Primrose Cottage

Lawhitton, Launceston PL15 9PE **t** (01566) 773645 **e** enquiry@primrosecottagesuites.co.uk
w primrosecottagesuites.co.uk

open All year
bedrooms 2 double, 1 twin
bathrooms All en suite
payment Credit/debit cards, cash/cheques

Primrose Cottage is set in gardens and woodland leading to the River Tamar. Each luxury suite has its own sitting room, entrance and en suite facilities with beautiful views across the Tamar Valley. Five minutes from the A30 with easy access to both north and south coasts and the moors.

⊕ *Leave Launceston on the A388 Plymouth road. After 1 mile turn left on B3362 signposted Tavistock. Primose Cottage is on the left after 2.5 miles.*

♥ *Discounts on stays of 2 or 3 days. Please see website for details.*

Room ♨ 📺 ♿ ☜ General 12 P ⊱ ✗ ▥ ◲ ❄ Leisure ⌒ 🏛

★★★★
BED & BREAKFAST

B&B per room per night
s Max £39.99
d Min £60.00
Evening meal per person
£15.00–£25.00

Trekenner Court

Pipers Pool, Nr Bodmin Moor, Launceston PL15 8QG **t** (01566) 880118
e trekennercourt@hotmail.co.uk **w** trekennercourt.co.uk

open All year except Christmas
bedrooms 2 double, 1 twin
bathrooms All en suite
payment Cash/cheques, euros

Trekenner Court is in a tranquil setting enjoying glorious views over Bodmin Moor. This 200-year-old barn conversion is set in four acres. Ideal for visiting the gardens and houses of Cornwall and Devon and only 20 minutes from the north coast.

⊕ *Leave the A30 at the A395 to Camelford. Drive through Pipers Pool. After approx 1 mile, on the crest of the incline, turn left.*

♥ *Evening meals available by arrangement. Tickets held for the Eden Project.*

Room ♨ 📺 ♿ ☜ General P ⊱ ▥ ◲ ⚅ ❄ Leisure ∪ ⌒ ▸ 🚲 🏛

★★★★
SELF CATERING

Units **3**
Sleeps **4–6**
Low season per wk
£150.00–£300.00
High season per wk
£250.00–£600.00

Frankaborough Farm Cottages, Lifton

contact Mrs Linda Banbury, Frankaborough Farm Cottages, Lifton PL16 0JS
t (01409) 211308 **f** (01409) 211308 **e** banbury960@aol.com **w** devonfarmcottage.co.uk

Close to Devon/Cornwall border, 260-acre mixed dairy farm offering imaginative barn conversions decorated to a high standard, set in a rural location but easily accessible to the A30.

open All year
payment Cash/cheques, euros

Unit 🔥 📺 🍳 🍽 🖥 🗄 🛋 🗑 🧺 📻 🚪 ✴
General 🛏 🚪 ♿ P 🅿 Ⓢ 🐾   Leisure 🏊 🏞   Shop 4 miles   Pub 4 miles

---

★★★–★★★★★
SELF CATERING

Units **4**
Sleeps **2–4**
Low season per wk
£140.00–£260.00
High season per wk
£260.00–£450.00

Langdon Farm Holiday Cottages, Launceston

contact Mrs Fleur Rawlinson, Langdon Farm Holiday Cottages, Langdon Farm, Launceston PL15 8NW
t (01566) 785389 **e** g.f.rawlinson@btinternet.com **w** langdonholidays.com

One- and two-bedroom, well-equipped cottages, four-poster beds, countryside setting, near pub, ten miles from sea. Easy drive to Eden Project. Short breaks available.

open All year
payment Credit/debit cards, cash/cheques

Unit 🔥 📺 🍳 🍽 🖥 🗄 🛋 🗑 ✴
General 🛏 🚪 ♿ P 🅿 Ⓢ 🐾   Leisure ∪ 🚣 🏇 🚵 🏞   Shop 4 miles   Pub 1 mile

---

★★★
SELF CATERING

Units **2**
Sleeps **2–5**
Low season per wk
£170.00–£300.00
High season per wk
£300.00–£590.00

Lodge Barton, Liskeard

contact Mr & Mrs Hodin, Lodge Barton, Lodge Hill, Liskeard PL14 4JX
t (01579) 344432 **e** lodgebart@aol.com **w** selectideas.co.uk/lodgebarton

Idyllic farm setting with river valley and woods. Sunny character cottages, well equipped and within easy reach of beaches and moors.

open All year
payment Cash/cheques

Unit 🔥 📺 🍳 🖥 🗄 🗑 🛋 🗑 ✴
General 🛏 🚪 ♿ P 🐾   Leisure 🚣 🏇   Shop 2 miles   Pub 1 mile

★★★
SELF CATERING

Units **1**
Sleeps **4**
Low season per wk
Max £350.00
High season per wk
Max £500.00

Trelyn Cottage, Liskeard

contact Ms Angie Fisher, Trelyn Cottage, Trelyn, Keason, St Ive, Liskeard PL14 3NE
t (01579) 383881 **f** (01579) 383881 **e** trelyn@kingfisher-training.freeserve.co.uk
w http://trelyncottage.mysite.wanadoo-members.co.uk

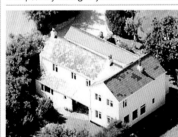

open All year
payment Cash/cheques

One double and one twin bedroom, both en suite. Edge of village location, stunning countryside views. An ideal base for touring Cornwall and West Devon. Within easy reach of local Heritage sites, good walking country, golf courses, National Trust properties, the Eden Project and popular towns such as Looe and Polperro.

⊕ M5/A38 to Plymouth, A388 Saltash-Callington, then A390. Or M5/A30 to Launceston, A388 to Callington, then A390. Or across Dartmoor: A390 from Tavistock.

Unit 🔥 📺 🍳 🖥 🗄 🗑 🛋 📻 ✴
General 🛏 P Ⓢ   Leisure ∪ 🏞   Shop 2.5 miles   Pub 0.75 miles

---

What's in a quality rating?

Information about ratings can be found at the back of this guide.

LIZARD, Cornwall Map ref 1B3 — GUEST ACCOMMODATION

★★★★
INN

B&B per room per night
s £50.00–£60.00
d £70.00–£80.00
Evening meal per person
£7.00–£15.00

The Top House Inn

The Top House, Helston TR12 7NQ t (01326) 290974 w thetophouselizard.co.uk

Britain's most southerly inn, offering eight beautiful en suite bedrooms. After enjoying the breathtaking scenery, relax and let us provide you with excellent home-cooked food. You won't want to leave!

open All year
bedrooms 4 double, 2 twin, 2 family
bathrooms All en suite
payment Credit/debit cards, cash/cheques

Room 🛏 📺 ♿ General 🚭 🏠 ♨ P ⚿ ⛊ ❅ Leisure ∪ ⚲ ⏳

LOOE, Cornwall Map ref 1C2 — HOTEL

★★★
HOTEL

B&B per room per night
s £48.00–£78.00
d £88.00–£140.00
HB per person per night
£50.00–£86.00

Hannafore Point Hotel

Marine Drive, Looe PL13 2DG t (01503) 263273 f (01503) 263272
e stay@hannaforepointhotel.com w hannaforepointhotel.com

open All year
bedrooms 33 double, 4 single
bathrooms All en suite
payment Credit/debit cards, cash/cheques

A warm welcome awaits you. Set in picturesque Cornish village with spectacular, panoramic sea views. Indulge in superb home-cooked food. Varied dining options featuring quality local produce and fresh fish. The terrace is a popular rendezvous for cream teas or cocktails alike. Extensive leisure facilities. Traditional hospitality and excellent service.

⊕ A38 from Plymouth, then A387 to Looe. Cross over stone bridge, turn 1st left (sign 'Hannafore') and uphill until overlooking bay.

♥ Special-event packages. Extensive range of conference and business facilities. Weddings and special occasions. Christmas and New Year celebrations.

Room 🖥 ☎ 📺 ♿ 🍽 General 🚭 🏠 ♨ P ⚑ 🛏 ▥ ● 🗌 ☒ ♨ ❅ 🚐 ⛩ Leisure ☇ ✄ 🏹 ⚡ ∪ ⚲ ⏳ 🚴

LOOE, Cornwall Map ref 1C2 — GUEST ACCOMMODATION

★★★★
GUEST HOUSE

B&B per room per night
s £50.00–£70.00
d £68.00–£82.00

Coombe Farm

Widegates, Looe PL13 1QN t (01503) 240223 e coombe_farm@hotmail.com
w coombefarmhotel.co.uk

open All year except Christmas and New Year
bedrooms 1 double, 1 twin, 1 family
bathrooms All en suite
payment Credit/debit cards, cash/cheques

Coombe Farm country house has 11 acres of lawns, woods and paddock. Guests relax in spacious, en suite cottage rooms. Breakfast is served in your room. Heated outdoor pool, ponies, peacocks, small animals and a dog. Nearby are beautiful beaches, gardens, Eden, Heligan and National Trust properties.

⊕ A38 across Tamar Bridge. Six miles later, at Trerule Foot roundabout, left on A374 to Looe. Follow Looe signs, then Hessenford. Coombe Farm 1 mile after Hessenford on left.

Room 🛏 ☎ 📺 ♿ 🍽 General 🚭 P ⚿ ❅ ⛩ Leisure ☇ ∪ ⚲ ⏳ 🚴 🏞

---

enjoyEngland.com

Big city buzz or peaceful panoramas? Take a fresh look at England and you may be surprised at what's right on your doorstep. Explore the diversity online at enjoyengland.com

★★★★
GUEST HOUSE
SILVER AWARD

Dovers House

St Martins Road, St Martin, Looe PL13 1PB **t** (01503) 265468 **e** twhyte@btconnect.com
w dovershouse.co.uk

B&B per room per night
s £45.00–£60.00
d £55.00–£75.00

open All year except Christmas
bedrooms 2 double, 1 twin, 1 family
bathrooms All en suite
payment Credit/debit cards, cash/cheques

Just a few minutes drive from Looe harbour, Dovers House is an ideal base for exploring or visiting Cornwall's many attractions and scenic views. Looe is an old fishing port with friendly people and good inns and restaurants. Our accommodation offers twin, double and large family rooms, all with en suite. Comfortably designed to make your stay pleasant and relaxing.

⊕ *Dovers House is located on the B3253 road to Looe. 1.7 miles from the harbour.*

❤ *Call, or visit our website for special promotions.*

Room 📺 🐾 ⌖ General ⌖8 P ✂ ⌖ ⌖ ⌖ Leisure ∪ ♪ ⟩ ⌖

Rating Applied For
SELF CATERING

Barclay House Luxury Cottages, Looe

contact Mr Graham Brooks, Barclay House Luxury Cottages, St Martins Road, East Looe, Looe PL13 1LP
t (01503) 262929 **f** (01503) 262632 **e** info@barclayhouse.co.uk **w** barclayhouse.co.uk

Units **8**
Sleeps **2–6**

Low season per wk
£275.00–£775.00
High season per wk
£855.00–£1,375.00

"WE ARRIVED STRESSED - LEFT CHILLED"
McCafferty family, Manchester

open All year
payment Credit/debit cards, cash/cheques

Luxury, award-winning holiday cottages. Breathtaking views over the Looe River valley. Heated pool nestled in a natural sun trap. Five minutes' walk to harbour, town and beach. Superb award-winning restaurant and bar/lounge on site. Come stay at Barclay House, you will be glad you did!

⊕ *From A387 signposted Looe. After 1 mile turn right and follow road for 8 miles. First hotel on left on entering Looe.*

❤ *Special short breaks available – please call for details.*

Unit ⌖ 📺 ⌖ ⌖ ⌖ ⌖ ⌖ ⌖ ⌖ ⌖ ⌖
General ⌖ ⌖ ⌖ ✂ S ⌖ Leisure ⌖ ∪ ♪ ⟩ Shop < 0.5 miles Pub < 0.5 miles

★★★
SELF CATERING

Talehay, Looe

contact Neil & Theresa Dennett, Talehay, Tremaine, Looe PL13 2LT
t (01503) 220252 **e** infobooking@talehay.co.uk **w** talehay.co.uk

Units **5**
Sleeps **2–5**

Low season per wk
£165.00–£450.00
High season per wk
£319.00–£665.00

open All year
payment Credit/debit cards, cash/cheques

Tastefully converted and very comfortable stone holiday cottages set around 17thC non-working farmstead. Set in unspoilt, peaceful countryside with breathtaking coastal walks and beaches nearby. Close to Eden Project, Lost Gardens of Heligan and many National Trust properties. An ideal base for exploring the many varied delights of Cornwall.

⊕ *Over Tamar bridge, A38 for 16 miles. Dobwalls traffic lights, A390 St Austell road (2.5 miles). B3359, left on Looe road. After 6 miles right at crossroads.*

❤ *Short breaks available Oct-Mar (excl Christmas and New Year), minimum 2 nights.*

Unit ⌖ 📺 ⌖ ⌖ ⌖ ⌖ ⌖ ⌖ ⌖
General ⌖ ⌖ ⌖ P ✂ ⌖ Leisure ∪ ♪ ⟩ ⌖ ⌖ Shop 1 mile Pub 1 mile

For key to symbols open the back-cover flap.

LOSTWITHIEL, Cornwall Map ref 1B2   **HOTEL**

★★★
HOTEL

B&B per room per night
s £35.00–£54.00
d £70.00–£108.00
HB per person per night
£49.00–£73.00

Lostwithiel Hotel Golf & Country Club

Lower Polscoe, Lostwithiel PL22 0HQ **t** (01208) 873550 **f** (01208) 873479
e reception@golf-hotel.co.uk **w** golf-hotel.co.uk

open All year
bedrooms 6 double, 16 twin, 2 single, 3 family
bathrooms All en suite
payment Credit/debit cards, cash/cheques

Charming hotel in the heart of Cornwall, overlooking the River Fowey and close to the ancient town of Lostwithiel. A friendly and relaxed atmosphere, coupled with great facilities, make this a very popular destination. Restaurant, bar, gymnasium, indoor heated swimming pool, tennis courts, beautiful 18-hole golf course.

⊕ Off A390 0.5 miles from Lostwithiel.

♥ Cheaper rates if you arrive on a Sun (or Bank Holiday Mon) and stay for 3 or more nights.

Room   General   Leisure

LOSTWITHIEL, Cornwall Map ref 1B2   **SELF CATERING**

★★★–★★★★★
SELF CATERING

Units   **8**
Sleeps   **1–6**

Low season per wk
£210.00–£330.00
High season per wk
£330.00–£895.00

Lanwithan Cottages, Lostwithiel

contact Mr V B Edward-Collins, Lanwithan Cottages, Lanwithan Road, Lostwithiel PL22 0LA
t (01208) 872444 **f** (01208) 872444 **e** info@lanwithancottages.co.uk **w** lanwithancottages.co.uk

open All year
payment Cash/cheques, euros

Charming selection of Georgian estate cottages nestling in the Fowey Valley with two delightful waterside properties. Cottages with leaded-light windows, crackling log fires, four-poster bed and glass-topped well. Parkland, river frontage and boat. Woodland and riverside walks from your garden gate. Come and relax and soak up the Cornish atmosphere.

⊕ Liskeard – Lostwithiel A390, pass National garage on left. 1st left, Great Western units, 1st left again. 300yds sign – follow to house, not farm.

♥ Short breaks out of season. Reduced green fees. Pets accepted in some cottages. Canoe trips available with safety boat.

Unit   General   Leisure   **Shop** 0.5 miles   **Pub** 0.5 miles

---

MARAZION, Cornwall Map ref 1B3   **SELF CATERING**

★★★
SELF CATERING

Units   **13**
Sleeps   **1–5**

Low season per wk
£170.00–£320.00
High season per wk
£410.00–£850.00

Trevarthian Holiday Homes, Marazion

contact Mrs Sally Cattran, Trevarthian Holiday Homes, Trevarthian House, West End TR17 0EG
t (01736) 710100 **f** (01736) 710111 **e** info@trevarthian.co.uk **w** trevarthian.co.uk

open All year
payment Credit/debit cards, cash/cheques

Converted from a Victorian hotel in Mount's Bay location, 50yds from beach. Superb views of St Michael's Mount, Mousehole, Newlyn, Penzance. A selection of the finest self-catering accommodation available. One-minute to five-minute walk to safe sandy beach, playground, pubs, restaurants, galleries, shops, bus routes for Land's End, St Ives, Penzance.

⊕ Enter Marazion and you will find our signs at the bottom of our drive opposite the folly field before you reach the children's playground.

♥ £100 for 2 nights per unit in off-peak time.

Unit   General   Leisure

MENHENIOT, Cornwall Map ref 1C2   **SELF CATERING**

★★★★
SELF CATERING

Units   **6**
Sleeps **1–6**

Low season per wk
£198.00–£305.00
High season per wk
£260.00–£750.00

Hayloft Courtyard Cottages, Liskeard

contact Michele & Stephen Hore, Hayloft Courtyard Cottages, Lower Clicker Road, Menheniot, Liskeard PL14 3PU
t (01503) 240879 **e** courtyardcottage@btconnect.com **w** hayloftcourtyardcottages.com

open All year
payment Credit/debit cards, cash/cheques

A warm welcome and Cornish cream tea await your arrival at our family-run cottages. Lovingly converted from original stone barns and equipped to a high standard with many home-from-home comforts. Recently refurbished bathrooms all with jacuzzi baths. Ideally situated for touring coast, moors and attractions. Children's play area. Restaurant on-site offering popular meal delivery service.

⊕ *Tamar Bridge, A38 for Liskeard. Three miles from 2nd roundabout, up hill on dual carriageway. Sign right for Menheniot. Cross dual carriageway. Hayloft opposite (2nd entrance for cottage).*

♥ *Short breaks – off-peak. Special offers spring/autumn.*

Unit 🛏 📺 🗄 🖥 🔥🛁 💷 🗑 🧺 ✿
General 🛋 🏬 ⚓ P ⓟ Ⓢ ⚙   Leisure ∪ 🎣 ⚑ 🚲   Shop 1 mile   Pub < 0.5 miles

---

MEVAGISSEY, Cornwall Map ref 1B3   **GUEST ACCOMMODATION**

★★★★
**FARMHOUSE
SILVER AWARD**

B&B per room per night
s £31.00–£35.00
d £52.00–£56.00

Corran Farm B&B

St Ewe, Mevagissey, St Austell PL26 6ER **t** (01726) 842159 **e** terryandkathy@corranfarm.fsnet.co.uk
w corranfarm.co.uk

Quality farmhouse B&B on working farm in open countryside with own farm shop. Farm adjoins Heligan Gardens. Choice of delicious breakfast, beautiful walks, beaches, inns. Ideal for exploring Cornwall. Open February to November.

bedrooms 2 double, 1 twin
bathrooms All en suite
payment Cash/cheques

Room 📺 💷 🗑   General 🛋 P 🍴 🧺 🍷 ✿

MEVAGISSEY, Cornwall Map ref 1B3   **CAMPING & CARAVANNING**

★★★★★
**HOLIDAY, TOURING
& CAMPING PARK**
ROSE AWARD

🚐(189) £7.00–£30.00
🚙(189) £7.00–£30.00
⛺(189) £7.00–£30.00
🏠(38) £149.00–£999.00
189 touring pitches

Sea View International

Boswinger, Gorran, St Austell PL26 6LL **t** (01726) 843425 **f** (01726) 843358
e holidays@seaviewinternational.com **w** seaviewinternational.com

payment Credit/debit cards, cash/cheques

Close to Eden Project and New Maritime Museum. AA's best campsite many times. 3.5 miles south west of Mevagissey, parkland setting with panoramic views. Luxury caravans and chalets, mains services, colour television etc. Statics: mid-March to end of October. Touring: May to end of September.

⊕ *From St Austell roundabout take B3273 to Mevagissey. Prior to village turn right and follow signs to Gorran and Gorran Haven and brown tourism signs to park.*

♥ *Please visit the website for special offers.*

General 🔌 📺 🚿 P 🚐 🛒 🚽 🚰 📮 ⊙ 🚮 🛒 🧺 🍷 ☀   Leisure ➰ 🎾 ⚲ 🏊 ∪ 🎣 ⚑ 🚲

Take a break

Look out for special promotions and themed breaks. This could be your chance to indulge an interest, find a new one, or just relax and enjoy exceptional value. Offers (highlighted in colour) are subject to availability.

     For key to symbols open the back-cover flap.

MULLION, Cornwall Map ref 1B3 | **HOTEL**

★★★
HOTEL

B&B per room per night
s £53.00–£84.00
d £106.00–£168.00
HB per person per night
£63.00–£94.00

Polurrian Hotel

Polurrian Road, Mullion, Helston TR12 7EN t (01326) 240421 f (01326) 240083
e relax@polurrianhotel.com w polurrianhotel.com

open All year
bedrooms 14 double, 14 twin, 2 single, 8 family, 1 suite
bathrooms All en suite
payment Credit/debit cards, cash/cheques

Friendly, privately owned hotel set in 12 acres overlooking our sandy beach with stunning views across Mounts Bay. Sun terraces, secluded small walled gardens and leisure club. Two restaurants serve local seasonal produce. Facilities include indoor and outdoor pools, snooker room, beauty room, gym, squash, tennis, games room, climbing frames and creche.

⊕ A3083 from Helston towards The Lizard for about 6m. Then right on B3296 to Mullion. 0.5m past Mullion turn right at brown sign 'Polurrian Hotel'.

♥ Christmas packages. Reduced rates for 7 days and for children sharing with adults. Occasional themed weekends. Free Leisure Club membership.

Room 🛏 🖭 ☎ 📺 🕯 🍵 General 🛆 🏠 🔥 P 🍽 ⌨ 🅿 ◉ 🖭 🍴 ⚙ 🚗 🐾
Leisure 🎿 ☂ 🏊 🎯 🎱 🎣 ∪ 🏌 🚴 🐎

NEW POLZEATH, Cornwall Map ref 1B2 | **SELF CATERING**

★★★
SELF CATERING

Units **1**
Sleeps **6**

Low season per wk
£350.00–£450.00
High season per wk
£620.00–£750.00

Treheather, Wadebridge

contact Dr Elizabeth Mayall, Osmond House, Chestnut Crescent, Exeter EX5 4AA
t (01392) 841219

Spacious, modern bungalow. About 200yds from sandy surfing beach with rock pools. Garden, coastal walks. Open March to November. One double bedroom, one twin with 3ft beds, one twin with 2ft6in beds.

payment Cash/cheques

Unit 🛏 📺 🍴 🖭 🖾 🗄 🍲 ✳
General 🛆 🏠 🔥 P Leisure 🏌 Shop 0.5 miles

NEWQUAY, Cornwall Map ref 1B2 | **GUEST ACCOMMODATION**

★★
GUEST ACCOMMODATION

B&B per room per night
s Min £22.00
d Min £44.00

Chichester Interest Holidays

14 Bay View Terrace, Newquay TR7 2LR t (01637) 874216 e sheila.harper@virgin.net
w http://freespace.virgin.net/sheila.harper

Comfortable, licensed, convenient for shops, beaches and gardens. Showers in most bedrooms, many extras. Walking, mineral collecting, archaeology and Cornish Heritage holidays in spring and autumn. Open March to October.

bedrooms 3 double, 2 twin, 1 single, 1 family
payment Cash/cheques

Room 🕯 General 🛆 2 P 🍽 ⌨ 🅿 🍴 🖭 Leisure 🏖

To your credit

If you book by phone you may be asked for your credit card number. If so, it is advisable to check the proprietor's policy in case you have to cancel your reservation at a later date.

★★★★
SELF CATERING

Units **4**
Sleeps **2–6**

High season per wk
£475.00–£995.00

Cornwall Coast Holidays, Newquay

contact Mrs Deborah Spencer-Smith, Cornwall Coast Holidays
t (020) 8440 7518 & 07910 583050 **e** debbie@cornwallcoastholidays.com
w cornwallcoastholidays.com

open All year
payment Cash/cheques

Cornwall Coast Holidays offer apartments and cottages that are in the perfect location for wonderful beach holidays. The cottages are modern, and the apartments have stunning sea views. Both apartments and cottages have one en suite bathroom and are close to the town centre, golf course and other amenities.

Unit 🏠 📺 ☐ ☐ ☐ ☐ ☐ ☐ ☐ ☐ ☐ ✳
General ☐ ☐ ☐ P ☐

★★★★
SELF CATERING

Units **5**
Sleeps **6**

Low season per wk
£400.00–£700.00
High season per wk
£850.00–£1,530.00

Tolcarne Beach Village, Newquay

contact Mrs Veronica McCann, Narrowcliff, Newquay TR7 2QN
t (01209) 712651 & (01637) 872489 **e** info@tolcarnebeach.co.uk **w** tolcarnebeach.co.uk

open All year
payment Cash/cheques

Wake up, smell the fresh sea air and watch the surf roll in. Beautifully appointed luxury apartments situated right on the crescent-shaped sandy beach.

♥ *Short breaks from £325.00: 4 people including fuel, linen, towels. Surfing breaks including boards, wetsuits from £175.00 per person.*

Unit 🏠 📺 ☐ ☐ ☐ ☐
General ☐ ☐ ☐ ☐ Ⓢ Leisure ☐ ☐ Shop < 0.5 miles Pub < 0.5 miles

★★★★
HOLIDAY, TOURING
& CAMPING PARK
ROSE AWARD

🚐 £10.00–£36.00
🏕 £10.00–£36.00
⛺ £8.00–£36.00
🏠 (18) £210.00–£705.00
200 touring pitches

Porth Beach Tourist Park

Porth, Newquay TR7 3NH **t** (01637) 876531 **f** (01637) 871227 **e** info@porthbeach.co.uk
w porthbeach.co.uk

payment Credit/debit cards, cash/cheques

Situated in a valley with small trout stream, and only 100m from Porth Beach – the perfect family beach. Premium pitches have all facilities including satellite hook-up, as do the 18 static caravans. Bookings only accepted from families or couples (maximum three couples). Open March to November.

⊕ *A30 then A392 Newquay Road. At Quintrell Downs roundabout follow signs for Porth. Turn right at Porth Four Turnings, Park is 0.5 miles on.*

General ☐ P ☐ ☐ ☐ ☐ ☐ ☐ ☐ ☐ ☀ Leisure ☐ ☐ ☐ ☐ ☐

Check it out
Please check prices, quality ratings and other details when you book.

NEWQUAY, Cornwall Map ref 1B2 | **CAMPING & CARAVANNING**

★★★★
HOLIDAY, TOURING
& CAMPING PARK
🚐 £13.00–£17.00
🏕 (19) £200.00–£675.00
98 touring pitches

Riverside Holiday Park

Gwills Lane, Newquay TR8 4PE **t** (01637) 873617 **f** (01637) 877051
e info@riversideholidaypark.co.uk **w** riversideholidaypark.co.uk

Peaceful riverside family park. Two miles to
Newquay. Sheltered, level touring pitches, luxury
lodges and caravans. Covered, heated pool and
bar. Open March to October.

payment Credit/debit cards, cash/cheques

General 🔌 P 🔌 ⌂ 🛉 🍴 ⬚⬚ ⬚⬚ ✕ 🐕   Leisure ⟲ 📺 🍷 🔍 ⚓

NEWQUAY, Cornwall Map ref 1B2 | **CAMPING & CARAVANNING**

★★★★
TOURING &
CAMPING PARK
🚐 (140) £8.50–£14.50
🏕 (140) £8.50–£14.50
Å (140) £8.50–£14.50
140 touring pitches

Treloy Touring Park

Newquay TR8 4JN **t** (01637) 872063 & (01637) 876279 **e** treloy.tp@btconnect.com **w** treloy.co.uk

payment Credit/debit cards, cash/cheques

A family-run park catering exclusively for touring
caravans, tents and motor homes. We aim to offer
fun and enjoyable holidays for families and couples,
in a pleasant, relaxed setting with clean, modern
facilities. Nearby is Treloy Golf Club and driving
range. Coarse fishing available at Porth Reservoir,
one mile away. Open April to September.

⊕ Leave A30 at Highgate Hill, take 3rd exit (Newquay). At
Halloon roundabout take A39 Wadebridge (3rd exit). Then
Trekenning roundabout 1st left, Treloy 4 miles.

♥ Free-night offers early and late season. Conditions apply.

General 🔌 P 🔌 ⌂ 🛉 🍴 ⊙ ⬚⬚ ⬚⬚ ✕ 🐕 🔫 ☼ Leisure ⟲ 📺 🍷 🎵 ⚓ ⚲ ∪ 🚶 ♪

PADSTOW, Cornwall Map ref 1B2 | **GUEST ACCOMMODATION**

★★★★
BED & BREAKFAST

B&B per room per night
s £40.00–£50.00
d £60.00–£80.00

Pendeen House

28 Dennis Road, Padstow PL28 8DE **t** (01841) 532 724 **e** enquire@pendeenhousepadstow.co.uk
w pendeenhousepadstow.co.uk

open All year except Christmas
bedrooms 3 double, 1 single, 1 family
bathrooms All en suite
payment Credit/debit cards, cash/cheques

Pendeen House overlooks Padstow's Camel Estuary
with beautiful views to Rock and Daymer Bay. Newly
refurbished, Pendeen retains its Edwardian
character, complemented by stylish, contemporary
decor. Quality bed and breakfast with attention to
the details that make your stay special. Just three
minutes' walk to Padstow centre with private
parking.

⊕ Take the A389 to Padstow. Follow the road into town, bear
right into Dennis Road, Pendeen is a short distance on the
right.

♥ Winter breaks available; 3 nights for the price of 2, Sun-Thu
inclusive. Please mention this guide when booking.

Room 🛏 📺 ♿ 🍵 General ⚲ 1 🏢 🛉 P ✗ ⬚ 🍴 ✿ Leisure ∪ ⚲

Best foot forward

Walkers feel at home in accommodation participating in our Walkers Welcome scheme.
Look out for the symbol. Consider walking all or part of a long-distance route – go
online at nationaltrail.co.uk.

PADSTOW, Cornwall Map ref 1B2 — SELF CATERING

★★★★
SELF CATERING

Units **1**
Sleeps **6**
Low season per wk
Min £300.00
High season per wk
Max £850.00

Hideaway Cottage, Padstow

contact Mr & Mrs Sutton, 7 Dorchester Way, Elstow, Bedford MK42 9FF
t (01234) 353499 **e** dnl.holidays@ntlworld.com **w** dnlholidays.co.uk

Luxury Cornish cottage offering a high standard of accommodation. Two minutes' walk from picturesque harbour, restaurant and shops. Three en suite bedrooms, plus master bedroom offering views of the Camel estuary.

open All year
payment Cash/cheques

Unit 🏠 📺 🔥 🖥 🍽️ 🛁 🔥 🚽 📻
General 🛏️ ⚰️ Leisure 🚣 🚲

PADSTOW, Cornwall Map ref 1B2 — SELF CATERING

★★★–★★★★★
SELF CATERING

Units **4**
Sleeps **1–8**
Low season per wk
£210.00–£525.00
High season per wk
£540.00–£1,295.00

Yellow Sands Apartments & House, Padstow

contact Mr Dakin, Yellow Sands Apartments & House, Harlyn Bay, Padstow PL28 8SE
t (01841) 520376 **e** martin@yellowsands.fsnet.co.uk **w** yellowsands.net

open All year
payment Cash/cheques

Resident proprietor provides spacious, quality accommodation with stunning sea views! Just 200yds from superb sandy beach and coastal footpath in a designated Area of Outstanding Natural Beauty. Landscaped gardens. Shops and golf one mile. Historic Padstow 2.5 miles. For sightseeing daytrips, all parts of Cornwall within one hour's drive.

⊕ *Exit M5 at jct 31 (Okehampton). Carry on along A30 to Bodmin. Follow signs for Wadebridge, Padstow and Harlyn Bay. We're 200yds up from beach.*

♥ *Special offers available upon request for low season (Nov–May) for couples and long-weekend stays.*

Unit 🏠 📺 📻 🔥 🖥 🍽️ 🛁 🔥 🚽 📻 ✳️
General 🛏️ 🏠 🚶 P ✂️ 🐕 Leisure ∪ 🚣 🚲 Shop 1 mile Pub < 0.5 miles

PADSTOW, Cornwall Map ref 1B2 — CAMPING & CARAVANNING

★★★
TOURING &
CAMPING PARK

🚐 (180) £10.00–£17.50
🚐 (180) £10.00–£17.50
▲ (180) £10.00–£17.50
180 touring pitches

Padstow Touring Park

Padstow PL28 8LE **t** (01841) 532061 **e** mail@padstowtouringpark.co.uk **w** padstowtouringpark.co.uk

Located one mile from Padstow with footpath access; panoramic views; quiet family park; open all year; sandy beaches two miles; some en suite pitches; easy access from main road.

open All year
payment Credit/debit cards, cash/cheques

General 🖥 🔌 P 🔥 🚰 🚿 🚐 📻 ☺ 🔥 🛏️ 🐕 🐾 ☀️ Leisure ⛰️ ∪ 🚣 🚲

PAR, Cornwall Map ref 1B3 — GUEST ACCOMMODATION

★★★★
INN

B&B per room per night
s £35.00–£40.00
d £60.00–£65.00
Evening meal per person
£8.50–£15.00

The Royal Inn

66 Eastcliffe Road, Par PL24 2AJ **t** (01726) 815601 **f** (01726) 816415 **e** info@royal-inn.co.uk
w royal-inn.co.uk

Completely refurbished in 2003, The Royal offers excellent en suite accommodation at an affordable price. Four miles from Eden, close to bus and rail links, licensed bar and restaurant on site.

open All year except Christmas and New Year
bedrooms 4 double, 9 twin, 1 family, 3 suites
bathrooms All en suite
payment Credit/debit cards, cash/cheques

Room 🛏️ 🔥 ☎ 📺 ♨️ 📻 General 🛏️ 🏠 🚶 P ✂️ 🍽️ 🛋️ ♨️ ✳️ Leisure 🚣 🏴

Confirm your booking

It's always advisable to confirm your booking in writing.

For key to symbols open the back-cover flap.

PENZANCE, Cornwall Map ref 1A3   HOTEL

★★★
HOTEL

B&B per room per night
s £54.50–£69.50
d £109.00–£139.00
HB per person per night
£69.50–£89.50

Beachfield Hotel

Promenade, Penzance TR18 4NW t (01736) 362067 f (01736) 331100 e office@beachfield.co.uk
w beachfield.co.uk

open All year except Christmas and New Year
bedrooms 6 double, 4 twin, 6 single, 2 family
bathrooms All en suite
payment Credit/debit cards, cash/cheques, euros

An elegant modernised Victorian hotel on the promenade with a warm and friendly atmosphere, offering panoramic views of St Michael's Mount and Mount's Bay. Central to the shops and waterside of Penzance, the fishing port of Newlyn is close by. The Beachfield makes an ideal base from which to explore the delights of Penwith.

⊕ *A30 to Penzance. Follow signs to seafront. We are located on the only roundabout.*

Room ... General ... Leisure ...

PENZANCE, Cornwall Map ref 1A3   HOTEL

★★★
HOTEL
SILVER AWARD

B&B per room per night
s £75.00–£80.00
d £110.00–£170.00
HB per person per night
£80.00–£105.00

Hotel Penzance

Britons Hill, Penzance TR18 3AE t (01736) 363117 f (01736) 350970
e enquiries@hotelpenzance.com w hotelpenzance.com

open All year
bedrooms 12 double, 9 twin, 3 single
bathrooms All en suite
payment Credit/debit cards, cash/cheques

Be assured of consistently high levels of comfort and friendly service at this Cornwall Tourism Awards Hotel of the Year 2006 and also Restaurant of the Year 2006 for The Bay. Traditional or contemporary-style rooms with sea views across Penzance Harbour and towards St Michael's Mount.

⊕ *Enter Penzance on A30. Dual carriageway past heliport. At roundabout keep left. Third turn right onto Brittons Hill. Hotel 70m on right.*

♥ *Oct-Apr: dinner in The Bay restaurant included in room rate.*

Room ... General ... Leisure ...

PENZANCE, Cornwall Map ref 1A3   HOTEL

★★★
HOTEL

B&B per room per night
s £68.00–£85.00
d £136.00–£170.00
HB per person per night
£78.00–£96.00

Queens Hotel

The Promenade, Penzance TR18 4HG t (01736) 362371 e enquiries@queens-hotel.com
w queens-hotel.com

open All year
bedrooms 18 double, 24 twin, 19 single, 9 family
bathrooms All en suite
payment Credit/debit cards, cash/cheques

Discover Britain's Hotel of The Year 2000/2. Elegant Victorian hotel on the seafront promenade of Penzance with majestic views across Mount's Bay and St Michael's Mount. We are ideally situated for Tate St Ives, Land's End and the Eden Project. Our award-winning dining room offers local fresh fish and produce.

⊕ *From A30 head towards Penzance, then follow signs to promenade.*

♥ *We offer special seasonal breaks and yoga weekends. Please call our reception for further details.*

Room ... General ... Leisure ...

★★★
BED & BREAKFAST

B&B per room per night
s £52.00
d £60.00

Harbour Heights Bed and Breakfast

Boase Street, Newlyn, Penzance TR18 5JE **t** (01736) 350976 **e** anneofnewlyn@aol.com
w harbour-heights.co.uk

open All year except Christmas and New Year
bedrooms 2 double, 1 twin
payment Credit/debit cards, cash/cheques

In an old and quaint 17thC cobbled street and situated only 25 metres from Newlyn Harbour, the property enjoys views over Mount's Bay and down the Lizard Peninsula. Visit the areas many beautiful coves and beaches. Locally sourced produce and extensive breakfast menu. Comfortable rooms and warm welcome.

⊕ *A30 through Cornwall to Penzance. Follow promenade to Newlyn. At crossroads turn left signposted Mousehole. After sharp left bend, take 2nd right – Boase street, (25m from harbour).*

♥ *Book 3 nights in a row – get 4th free!*

Room 📺 👜 🍴   General ⏱12 P ⚡ ✕ 🎮 🛏 🔥▫   Leisure ⌇ 🚲 🎣

★★★
FARMHOUSE

B&B per room per night
s Min £27.00
d Min £54.00
Evening meal per person
Min £12.00

Menwidden Farm

Ludgvan, Penzance TR20 8BN **t** (01736) 740415 **e** cora@menwidden.freeserve.co.uk

bedrooms 4 double, 1 twin
bathrooms 3 en suite
payment Cash/cheques

Quiet farmhouse set in countryside with views towards St Michael's Mount. Centrally situated in West Cornwall. Land's End, St Ives, Lizard Peninsula and Penzance Heliport all within easy reach. Good home-cooking. Open March to October.

⊕ *Turn towards Ludgvan at Crowlas crossroads. 3rd turning right signposted Vellanoweth. Last farm on left, 1 mile up this road.*

Room 👜   General P ⚡ ✕ 🛏 ✿ 🐾   Leisure ∪ ⌇

★★★
GUEST HOUSE

B&B per room per night
s £29.00–£38.00
d £50.00–£56.00

Penrose Guest House

8 Penrose Terrace, Penzance TR18 2HQ **t** (01736) 362782 **e** enquiries@penrosegsthse.co.uk
w penrosegsthse.co.uk

open All year except Christmas
bedrooms 1 double, 1 twin, 1 family
bathrooms 2 en suite, 1 private
payment Credit/debit cards, cash/cheques

Marc and Anne offer a warm welcome to their small, friendly, family-run guesthouse. We offer quality en suite accommodation and good food. Situated close to the bus and train stations, town centre, heliport and harbour. The perfect base for exploring the beauty of West Cornwall.

⊕ *Follow signs for town centre. Turn right just before train station building, into Penrose Terrace. We are 30m up on the right.*

♥ *3 nights for the price of 2 Nov-Feb. Discounts for stays of 7 nights or more.*

Room 📺 👜 🍴   General 5 ⚡ 🎮 🔥 ✿   Leisure ∪ ⌇ 🏌 🚲

        For key to symbols open the back-cover flap.

PENZANCE, Cornwall Map ref 1A3   SELF CATERING

Rospannel Farm, Penzance

★★★
SELF CATERING

Units   **2**
Sleeps   **3–8**
Low season per wk
£200.00–£300.00
High season per wk
£350.00–£450.00

contact Mr Hocking, Rospannel Farm, Crows-An-Wra, Penzance TR19 6HS
t (01736) 810262   **e** gbernardh@btinternet.com   **w** rospannel.com

Old-fashioned, very quiet and peaceful farm. Own pool and hide for bird-watchers. Moth light for insect enthusiasts. Badgers, foxes and lots of wildlife.

open All year
payment Cash/cheques

Unit 🛏 📺 📠 🚪 🌀 🔲 📶 ✳
General ♨ P 🐾

PERRANPORTH, Cornwall Map ref 1B2   GUEST ACCOMMODATION

Tides Reach

★★★★
GUEST HOUSE

B&B per room per night
s £33.00–£35.00
d £33.00–£38.00
Evening meal per person
£10.50–£15.00

Ponsmere Road, Perranporth TR6 0BW   **t** (01872) 572188   **f** (01872) 572188
e jandf.boyle@virgin.net   **w** tidesreachhotel.com

Charming, older style, family-run hotel close to shops and one minute from the beach. Dinner, bed and breakfast, and licensed bar. Private garden.

open All year except Christmas and New Year
bedrooms 5 double, 2 twin, 2 single, 1 family
bathrooms 9 en suite, 1 private
payment Credit/debit cards, cash/cheques, euros

Room 🛏 📺 🍵 🌀   General ♨5 P 🔥 ⚓ 🎱 🛏 📶 ✳   Leisure ∪ 🚣 🏇 🏊

PERRANPORTH, Cornwall Map ref 1B2   SELF CATERING

Penhale Villa, Perranporth

★★★★
SELF CATERING

Units   **1**
Sleeps   **1–10**
Low season per wk
£750.00–£1,000.00
High season per wk
£1,200.00–£1,950.00

contact Mrs Lauretta Wright
t 07971 590131   **e** lauretta@btconnect.com   **w** cornwall-breaks.co.uk

open All year
payment Cash/cheques, euros

Luxury five-bedroom, three-bathroom seaside villa. Super garden with summerhouse, hot tub, games/ party/gym room, Wendy House. Two minutes to super beach. Sleeps eight adults, two children. Jacuzzi baths, deluge showers. Furnished and equipped to the highest standard. Great for family get-togethers. Plenty of parking.

⊕ Property is at the end of a no-through-road (off Cliff Road) – offering peace and quiet but very close to the beach and all amenities.

♥ Out-of-season discounts for midweek, weekend breaks and for 4 persons or less. Early booking discounts available. Out of season discounts.

Unit 🛏 📺 📠 📶 📇 📷 📺 🍵 🚪 🌀 🔲 📶 ✳
General ♨ 🍴 🅿 🔥 ◯ Ⓢ 🐾   Leisure ● ∪ 🚣 🏇 🚲 🏊   Shop < 0.5 miles   Pub < 0.5 miles

---

Don't forget www.

Web addresses throughout this guide are shown without the prefix www. Please include www. in the address line of your browser. If a web address does not follow this style it is shown in full.

POLPERRO, Cornwall Map ref 1C3 — GUEST ACCOMMODATION

★ ★ ★
INN

B&B per room per night
s £40.00–£45.00
d £60.00–£70.00
Evening meal per person
£6.00–£16.00

Crumplehorn Inn and Mill

Crumplehorn, Polperro, Looe PL13 2RJ t (01503) 272348 f (01503) 273148
e host@crumplehorn-inn.co.uk w crumplehorn-inn.co.uk

open All year
bedrooms 6 double, 3 twin, 2 family, 8 suites
bathrooms All en suite
payment Credit/debit cards, cash/cheques

14thC character Cornish inn and mill in quaint, historic fishing village. B&B and self-catering available. En suite, non-smoking rooms with TV, telephone, clock radio and tea and coffee. Local ales and scrumpy. Varied bar menu with daily specials featuring locally caught fish. Pets welcome. Car parking on site.

⊕ Full directions (via car, train and taxi) available on our website.

❤ Winter-break scheme in operation.

Room 🛏 📞 📺 ♿ 🍵   General ➤ ♨ 🔥 P ♟ 🛏 🗑 ❄ 🐕   Leisure ∪ ♪

POLZEATH, Cornwall Map ref 1B2 — SELF CATERING

★ ★
SELF CATERING

Units   8
Sleeps   1–8
Low season per wk
£350.00–£500.00
High season per wk
£500.00–£700.00

Oystercatcher Bar, Wadebridge

contact Vicki Medlen, Central Reservations, 63 Trevarthian Road, St Austell PL25 4BY
t 0845 241 1133 f (01726) 67970 e reservations@smallandfriendly.co.uk w smallandfriendly.co.uk

open All year
payment Credit/debit cards, cash/cheques

The Oystercatcher Bar and beautifully refurbished apartments are situated overlooking Polzeath beach, North Cornwall. All apartments have a kitchen, bathroom and one or two bedrooms depending on the size. Many of them have amazing sea views, and are only five minutes' walk to the beach.

⊕ Take the A30 or A38 to Bodmin, then take the A39 to Wadebridge and Polzeath is then signposted.

Unit 🛏 📺 ▪ 🗄 🖥 ❄
General ➤ ♨ 🔥 P ✂ ⃝ 🆂 🐕   Leisure ∪ ♪ ⌖ 🚲   Shop < 0.5 miles   Pub < 0.5 miles

POLZEATH, Cornwall Map ref 1B2 — SELF CATERING

★ ★ ★
SELF CATERING

Units   1
Sleeps   2–8
Low season per wk
Min £250.00
High season per wk
Max £825.00

Trehenlie, Polzeath, Wadebridge

contact Mrs Julie Angwin, Sunrise, Lower Boscarne, Nanstallon, Bodmin PL30 5LG
t (01208) 75243 f (01208) 75243 e sangwin@tiscali.co.uk

Spacious, detached bungalow, excellently furnished and equipped. Central heating. Minutes from local amenities and wonderful surfing. Beach perfect for children. Glorious coastal walks, golf, tennis, riding. Quiet location.

open All year
payment Cash/cheques

Unit 🛏 📺 📼 🗄 🖥 ▪ 🗄 🗄 🗄 🖥 ❄
General ➤ ♨ 🔥 P ⃝ 🆂 🐕   Leisure ⌖ 🚲   Shop < 0.5 miles   Pub < 0.5 miles

Using map references

The map references refer to the colour maps at the front of this guide. The first figure is the map number, the letter and figure that follow indicate the grid reference on the map.

For key to symbols open the back-cover flap.

PORT GAVERNE, Cornwall Map ref 1B2 — SELF CATERING

★★★–★★★★★
SELF CATERING

Units **10**
Sleeps **2–8**

Low season per wk
£357.00–£553.00
High season per wk
£595.00–£1,218.00

Green Door Cottages, Port Isaac

contact Mrs Ross, Green Door Cottages, Port Isaac PL29 3SQ
t (01208) 880293 f (01208) 880151 e enquiries@greendoorcottages.co.uk
w greendoorcottages.co.uk

open All year
payment Credit/debit cards, cash/cheques

A delightful collection of restored 18thC Cornish buildings built around a sunny enclosed courtyard and two lovely apartments with stunning sea views. Picturesque, tranquil cove ideal for children. Half a mile from Port Isaac, on the South West Coast Path. Polzeath beach and Camel Trail nearby. Traditional pub opposite. Dogs welcome.

⊕ From A30 right onto A395 at Kennards House. Right at T-junction with A39. After 1 mile right onto B3314, signposted Boscastle. Two miles after Delabole, right to Port Gaverne.

♥ 3-night weekend or 4-night midweek short breaks available Jan-May, Sep-Dec.

Unit 🖳 📺 ⛽ 🍳 🗄 🐕 ❄
General 🛏 🚶 P ◎ S ♞ Leisure ∪ ♪ ♭ ⚲ Shop 0.5 miles Pub < 0.5 miles

PORT ISAAC, Cornwall Map ref 1B2 — GUEST ACCOMMODATION

★★★★
INN

B&B per room per night
s £75.00–£110.00
d £95.00–£140.00
Evening meal per person
£12.00–£30.00

The Slipway

Harbour Front, Port Isaac PL29 3RH t (01208) 880264 f (01208) 880408
e slipway@portisaachotel.com w portisaachotel.com

open All year except Christmas
bedrooms 7 double, 1 twin, 2 suites
bathrooms All en suite
payment Credit/debit cards, cash/cheques, euros

The Slipway Hotel is a small, friendly, family-run hotel of great character. Bedrooms are stylishly furnished and many overlook the harbour. Guests can combine their stay with the delights of one of the area's finest seafood restaurants. Menus are highly imaginative, concentrating on the use of the best, locally sourced fresh fish, meat and produce.

⊕ In Port Isaac pass Co-op on right. 100m, turn left down Back Hill and follow road to harbour (narrow streets) where you will find The Slipway.

♥ Special out-of-season breaks available – DB&B and 3 nights' B&B for the price of 2.

Room ☎ 📺 ♿ 🍳 General 🛏 🚶 🅿 ⚒ ♥ ✗ 🍴 🐾 ❄ Leisure ∪ ♪ ♭

PORTREATH, Cornwall Map ref 1B3 — HOTEL

★★
COUNTRY HOUSE HOTEL
SILVER AWARD

B&B per room per night
s £50.00
d £78.00–£82.00
HB per person per night
£57.00–£59.00

Aviary Court

Marys Well, Redruth TR16 4QZ t (01209) 842256 f (01209) 843744 e info@aviarycourthotel.co.uk
w aviarycourthotel.co.uk

open All year
bedrooms 4 double, 1 twin, 1 family
bathrooms All en suite
payment Credit/debit cards, cash/cheques

Charming country house in two acres of secluded, well-kept gardens with tennis court. Family run, personal service, good food. Superior en suite bedrooms with TV, telephone, tea/coffee, fresh fruit. Ideal touring location (coast five minutes). St Ives, Tate, Heligan and Eden Project all within easy reach. Half-board prices are based on two people sharing.

⊕ Follow Portreath and Illogan signs from A30 at Pool.

Room ☎ 📺 ♿ 🍳 General 🛏 3 🅿 ♥ 🐾 ❄ Leisure 🎾 ♭

PORTREATH, Cornwall Map ref 1B3 **SELF CATERING**

★★★★★
SELF CATERING

Units **3**
Sleeps **1–6**
Low season per wk
£220.00–£300.00
High season per wk
£300.00–£750.00

Higher Laity Farm, Redruth

contact Mrs Lynne Drew, Higher Laity Farm, Portreath Road, Redruth TR16 4HY
t (01209) 842317 **f** (01209) 842317 **e** info@higherlaityfarm.co.uk **w** higherlaityfarm.co.uk

open All year
payment Credit/debit cards, cash/cheques

Come and relax in our tastefully converted luxury barns. En suite bedrooms, central heating, linen provided, gas cooker, fridge/freezer, microwave, dishwasher, washer/dryer, hi-fi, video, DVD. Close to beaches and the breathtaking North Cornish coast. Ideal for walking, relaxing and exploring Cornwall. A friendly welcome is guaranteed. One cottage wheelchair accessible.

⊕ *From M5 take A30 to Redruth/Porthtowan slip road towards Redruth. For full travel directions please contact us directly.*

♥ *Short breaks available Oct-Mar, also discounted rates for couples, out of season.*

Unit 🏠 📺 📠 🗄 📠 🖥 🛏 ⏻ 🔥 💡 🔌
General 🏃 🏠 👤 P 🍴 S   Leisure ∪ 🚣 ► 🚴   Shop 1 mile   Pub 0.5 miles

---

PORTREATH, Cornwall Map ref 1B3   **CAMPING & CARAVANNING**

★★★★
HOLIDAY, TOURING
& CAMPING PARK

🚐 (18)   £10.00–£14.00
🚍 (3)   £10.00–£14.00
▲ (18)   £10.00–£14.00
🏕 (20) £140.00–£575.00

Tehidy Holiday Park

Harris Mill, Illogan, Redruth TR16 4JQ **t** (01209) 216489 **e** holiday@tehidy.co.uk **w** tehidy.co.uk

payment Credit/debit cards, cash/cheques

Tehidy Holiday Park has been developed to a high standard and includes a range of clean and modern facilities to ensure you have a comfortable and enjoyable stay. Children's play area. Shop/off licence, payphone, games room. Toilet block with laundrette. Open from March to November.

⊕ *Off A30 at Redruth, right to Porthtowan. After 275m left onto B3300 (Portreath). Straight over at crossroads. Past Cornish Arms. Site 500m on left.*

General 🛒 P 🔌 🚻 ☎ 🔥 ⊙ 🗑 📦 🛒   Leisure 📺 ♦ ⚠ ∪ 🚣 🚴

PRAA SANDS, Cornwall Map ref 1B3   **SELF CATERING**

★★★
SELF CATERING

Units **5**
Sleeps **2–8**
Low season per wk
£330.00–£465.00
High season per wk
£745.00–£1,195.00

Sea Meads Holiday Homes, Penzance

contact Ms Pierpoint, Best Leisure, Old House Farm, Slough SL3 6HU
t (01753) 664336 **f** (01753) 663740 **e** enquiries@bestleisure.co.uk **w** bestleisure.co.uk

open All year
payment Cash/cheques

Well-equipped detached houses, each with private garden, situated in superb sub-tropical position on a private estate. Spacious lounge with large patio windows. Balcony to the first floor from which to enjoy the view of the glorious mile-long Praa Sands beach, only five minutes' walk away.

⊕ *From Helston take A394 to Penzance, halfway at Ashton Village turn left at Hendra Lane, follow road to the sea.*

Unit 🏠 📺 🗄 📠 🖥 🛏 ⏻ 🔥 💡 🔌
General 🏃 🏠 👤 P 🍴 S 🐾   Leisure ♦ ∪ 🚣 ►   Shop 0.5 miles   Pub 0.5 miles

---

Travel update
Get the latest travel information – just dial RAC on 1740 from your mobile phone.

For key to symbols open the back-cover flap.

REDRUTH, Cornwall Map ref 1B3 — **GUEST ACCOMMODATION**

★★★★
GUEST HOUSE

B&B per room per night
s Min £38.00
d Min £56.00
Evening meal per person
£12.50–£15.00

Goonearl Cottage

Wheal Rose, Scorrier, Redruth TR16 5DF **t** (01209) 891571 **f** (01209) 891916
e goonearl@onetel.com **w** goonearlcottage.com

open All year
bedrooms 4 double, 1 twin, 1 family, 1 suite
bathrooms 5 en suite, 2 private
payment Credit/debit cards, cash/cheques, euros

Family-run guesthouse; beaches close by; easy access to the whole of Cornwall; superb English breakfast.

⊕ Leave the A30 at the Scorrier/A3047 sign. Turn right at The Plume of Feathers, first left into Wheal Rose.

Room 🛏 📺 ♨ ⚲ General ♿ ⊞ 🅿 🍽 ✕ 📺 🕮 ✿ Leisure ∪ ⌨ ⌂ 🚲 🏊

REDRUTH, Cornwall Map ref 1B3 — **SELF CATERING**

★★★
SELF CATERING

Units **1**
Sleeps **2–6**
Low season per wk
£225.00–£300.00
High season per wk
£300.00–£525.00

The Barn at Little Trefula, Redruth

contact Mr & Mrs Higgins, The Barn at Little Trefula, Little Trefula Farm, Trefula TR16 5ET
t (01209) 820572 **e** barn@trefula.com **w** trefula.com

The Barn at Little Trefula, in Cornwall's historical mining country yet surrounded by fields, is an architect-designed recent conversion offering panoramic views and the perfect base for a peaceful and comfortable family holiday.

open All year
payment Cash/cheques, euros

Unit 📺 ⊡ 🖥 🖵 ♨ 🗑 🖳 ✿
General ♿ ⊞ 🅿 ⚟ Ⓢ 🛍 Leisure ∪ 🚲 Shop 0.5 miles Pub < 0.5 miles

---

RUAN HIGH LANES, Cornwall Map ref 1B3 — **GUEST ACCOMMODATION**

★★★
FARMHOUSE

B&B per room per night
s £26.00–£38.00
d £52.00–£56.00

Trenona Farm Holidays

Ruan High Lanes, Truro TR2 5JS **t** (01872) 501339 **f** (01872) 501253
e info@trenonafarmholidays.co.uk **w** trenonafarmholidays.co.uk

bedrooms 1 double, 3 family
bathrooms 3 en suite, 1 private
payment Credit/debit cards, cash/cheques

Enjoy a warm welcome in our Victorian farmhouse on a working farm on the beautiful Roseland Peninsula. Our guest bedrooms have en suite or private bathrooms, and we welcome children and pets. Public footpaths lead to Veryan and the south coast (three miles). Open between March and November.

⊕ A390 to Truro. At Hewaswater take B3287 to Tregony then A3078 to St Mawes at Tregony Bridge. After 2 miles, pass Esso garage. 2nd farm on left-hand side.

♥ Discounts for stays of 4 or more nights for children and for family rooms.

Room 📺 ♨ ⚲ General ♿ ⊞ 🅿 ⚟ 🕮 ✿ 🛍 Leisure ∪

Town, country or coast

The entertainment, shopping and innovative attractions of the big cities, the magnificent vistas of the countryside or the relaxing and refreshing coast – this guide will help you find what you're looking for.

RUAN MINOR, Cornwall Map ref 1B3 — CAMPING & CARAVANNING

★★★★
HOLIDAY, TOURING
& CAMPING PARK

🚐 (15) £11.00–£17.00
🚐 (15) £11.00–£17.00
Å (20) £10.00–£14.00
🏕 (14) £99.00–£417.00
35 touring pitches

Silver Sands Holiday Park

Gwendreath, Nr Kennack Sands, Ruan Minor, Helston TR12 7LZ t (01326) 290631 f (01326) 290631
e enquiries@silversandsholidaypark.co.uk w silversandsholidaypark.co.uk

payment Credit/debit cards, cash/cheques

A quiet family-run park set in nine acres of landscaped grounds, offering peace and tranquillity. The large, well-spaced touring emplacements are individually marked and bounded by trees and shrubs. A short, enchanting woodland walk through the Lizard nature reserve brings you to award-winning sandy beaches. David Bellamy Gold award. Open Easter to September.

✦ A3083 from Helston past RNAS Culdrose, left onto B3293 (St Keverne). Right turn after passing Goonhilly satellite station. Left after 1.5 miles to Gwendreath.

General 🚐 P 🔌 🖒 🍴 🚐 📻 ☉ 🎫 🛒 🚲 🛩 ☼ Leisure ⚗ ∪ ♪

ST AGNES, Cornwall Map ref 1B3 — GUEST ACCOMMODATION

★★
GUEST HOUSE

B&B per room per night
s £22.50–£42.50
d £35.00–£55.00
Evening meal per person
Min £15.00

Penkerris

Penwinnick Road, St Agnes TR5 0PA t (01872) 552262 f (01872) 552262 e info@penkerris.co.uk
w penkerris.co.uk

open All year
bedrooms 3 double, 1 twin, 3 family
bathrooms 3 en suite
payment Credit/debit cards, cash/cheques, euros

Penkerris is a creeper-clad Edwardian residence with a lawned garden and parking. A 'home from home' offering real food, comfortable bedrooms with all facilities (three en suite) and cosy lounge (log fires in winter). Licensed. Dramatic cliff walks and three really beautiful beaches one kilometre away. Excellent surfing, riding and gliding nearby.

✦ Easy to find on B3277 road from Chiverton roundabout on A30, just by the village sign.

Room 📺 💧 General 🛋 🎱 ♿ P ⦿ ✕ 🍴 🅿 🦮 💺 ☼ 🛩 Leisure ∪ ♪ 🚴 🏄

ST AGNES, Cornwall Map ref 1B3 — SELF CATERING

★★★★★
SELF CATERING

Units   1
Sleeps   1–5
Low season per wk
£295.00–£395.00
High season per wk
£450.00–£875.00

The Owl House, St Agnes

contact Ms Hicks, The Owl House, Chy Ser Rosow, Barkla Shop, St Agnes TR5 0XN
t (01872) 553644 e enquiries@the-owl-house.co.uk w the-owl-house.co.uk

open All year
payment Credit/debit cards, cash/cheques

Spacious detached cottage enjoying the seclusion of woodland with meandering stream. Superbly equipped and with its own private patio, The Owl House is a luxurious base from which to explore Cornwall, with many walks from the doorstep. The lovely village of St Agnes is less than one mile away. Brochure available.

✦ See website for map.

♥ Short breaks available in low season from £225.

Unit 🍳 📺 🕮 📼 📀 🖥 📶 🍴 🗄 🔢 🍽 ⌨ ❀
General 🛋 🎱 ♿ P ✂ Ⓢ Leisure ∪ ♪ Shop 1 mile Pub 0.5 miles

Take a break

Look out for special promotions and themed breaks highlighted in colour.
(Offers subject to availability.)

For key to symbols open the back-cover flap.

ST AGNES, Cornwall Map ref 1B3 — CAMPING & CARAVANNING

★★★★
TOURING PARK

(70)	£14.00–£19.00
(70)	£14.00–£19.00
(70)	£14.00–£19.00

70 touring pitches

Beacon Cottage Farm Touring Park

Beacon Drive, St Agnes TR5 0NU t (01872) 552347 e beaconcottagefarm@lineone.net
w beaconcottagefarmholidays.co.uk

Peaceful, secluded park on a working farm in an
Area of Outstanding Natural Beauty. Pitches in six
small, landscaped paddocks. Beautiful sea views,
lovely walks, ten minutes' walk to sandy beach.
Open April to October.

payment Credit/debit cards, cash/cheques

General 🔌🖥️🚗P🔌🚽🔐🚿🛎️🔋🍳🎿🚻🕯️🔆 Leisure ⚠️ ∪ 🏊 🚴 🏕️

ST AUSTELL, Cornwall Map ref 1B3 — HOTEL

★★★
HOTEL

B&B per room per night
s £60.00–£70.00
d £120.00–£190.00
HB per person per night
£80.00–£115.00

Cliff Head Hotel

Sea Road, Carlyon Bay, St Austell PL25 3RB t (01726) 812345 f (01726) 815511
e info@cliffheadhotel.com w cliffheadhotel.com

open All year
bedrooms 19 double, 17 twin, 14 single, 8 family
bathrooms All en suite
payment Credit/debit cards, cash/cheques

South-facing hotel, close to the beach with fine sea
views and cliff walks, and standing in its own
grounds. Situated in the centre of the Cornish
Riviera, it is ideally positioned for exploring Cornwall
and visiting the Eden Project.

⊕ A390 south to just before St Austell, Carlyon Bay signed on
left. Go under bridge, turn left at mini-roundabout. Sea
Road is next right.

♥ Please check website or telephone hotel for seasonal
specials.

Room 🛗🖥️📺📶☕ General 🛏️🍴P🍽️🔋🅿️🍷✿🚗 Leisure 🎾 🏐 ⛳ 🏊

ST AUSTELL, Cornwall Map ref 1B3 — GUEST ACCOMMODATION

★★★★★
GUEST ACCOMMODATION
GOLD AWARD

B&B per room per night
s £85.00–£125.00
d £110.00–£150.00
Evening meal per person
£29.00–£35.00

Anchorage House

Nettles Corner, Boscundle, St Austell PL25 3RH t (01726) 814071 e info@anchoragehouse.co.uk
w anchoragehouse.co.uk

bedrooms 1 double, 2 suites
bathrooms All en suite
payment Credit/debit cards, cash/cheques

A luxury, national-award-winning, Georgian-style
lodge with indoor swimming complex located in the
centre of Cornwall and only five minutes from the
Eden Project and Carlyon Bay beach. Open March to
December.

⊕ 2 miles east of St Austell off the A390. Across from the St.
Austell Garden Centre, turn left and then immediately left
again into the drive leading to the courtyard.

Room 📺📶☕ General 🛏️16 P🍷✗🔋🅿️☕✿ Leisure 🎾 🏐 🅿️ 🏊

It's all in the detail

Please remember that all information in this guide has been supplied by the
proprietors well in advance of publication. Since changes do sometimes occur it's a
good idea to check details at the time of booking.

ST AUSTELL, Cornwall Map ref 1B3 — SELF CATERING

★★★★
SELF CATERING

Units	2
Sleeps	3

Low season per wk
Min £245.00
High season per wk
Max £510.00

Lanjeth Farm Holiday Cottages, St Austell

contact Mrs Anita Webber, Lanjeth Farm, Lanjeth, St Austell PL26 7TN
t (01726) 68438 **e** anita@cornwall-holidays.uk.com **w** cornwall-holidays.uk.com

open All year
payment Cash/cheques

Gardens and art interests. Two peaceful, quality, fully-equipped cottages overlooking plantsman's garden on smallholding. Double and single bedroom in each (no under 12s). Cornish etchings and pine furniture throughout. Eden, Heligan and coast nearby. Secluded, yet easy access to whole of Cornwall.

⊕ From St Austell take A3058 Newquay road. Lanjeth is after Trewoon. Left at old school. Bottom of hill turn right. Farm at end of lane.

♥ Short breaks available during low season (min 3 nights).

Unit 🍳 TV 🛖 💻 🕯️ 🔌 🎱 🧺 🗲
General 12 **P** ✂️ Leisure 🗲 Shop 1 mile Pub 1 mile

ST BLAZEY, Cornwall Map ref 1B2 — SELF CATERING

★★★★
SELF CATERING

Units	5
Sleeps	2

Low season per wk
Min £230.00
High season per wk
Max £420.00

Woodmill Farm Holiday Cottages, Par

contact Mrs Michelle Hume, Woodmill Farm Holiday Cottages, Prideaux Road, St Blazey, Par PL24 2SR
t (01726) 810171 **e** enquiries@woodmill-farm.co.uk **w** woodmill-farm.co.uk

open All year
payment Credit/debit cards, cash/cheques

A 17thC former flour mill set in seven acres on the edge of the picturesque Prideaux Wood. Eden one mile, Lost Gardens of Heligan six miles. Glorious beaches, historic ports, excellent local restaurants all within easy reach. Ideally situated to explore Cornwall. A perfect retreat at any time of year.

⊕ A38 to Liskeard, then A390 to St. Blazey. At St. Blazey, after level crossing take first right signposted to Eden Project, then first right.

♥ Off season weekends and short breaks.

Unit 🍳 TV 🛖 💻 🕯️ 🔌 🎱 🧺 🗲
General ♿ **P** ✂️ ◎ Leisure ∪ 🗲 🚲 🛶 Shop < 0.5 miles Pub < 0.5 miles

ST CLETHER, Cornwall Map ref 1C2 — SELF CATERING

★★★★
SELF CATERING

Units	2
Sleeps	4–6

Low season per wk
£280.00–£350.00
High season per wk
£350.00–£950.00

Forget-me-not Farm Holidays, Launceston

contact Mr & Mrs James & Sheila Kempthorne, Forget-me-not Farm Holidays, Trefranck, St Clether PL15 8QN
t (01566) 86284 **f** (01566) 86284 **e** holidays@trefranck.co.uk **w** forget-me-not-farm-holidays.co.uk

open All year
payment Cash/cheques

Superb location between Bodmin Moor and spectacular North Cornwall Heritage Coast on our 300-year-old family working farm. The cottage and barn are superbly equipped and spacious, yet warm and cosy with real log fire, romantic four-poster bed and secluded garden. Ideal base for outdoor activities. A welcome retreat all year round.

⊕ From M5 turning off to A30, onto A395, travel through Pipers Pool. Pass Moorview Garage. 1st left at Coldnorthcott. One mile to crossroads; cottage on left.

♥ Long weekends or short breaks welcome – out of school holidays at short notice.

Unit 🍳 TV 🛖 💻 🕯️ 🔌 🎱 🧺 🗲
General ♿ 🛏️ 🚼 **P** ✂️ ◎ Ⓢ Leisure ∪ 🗲 🚲 🛶 Shop 5 miles Pub 3 miles

ST COLUMB, Cornwall Map ref 1B2 | **SELF CATERING**

★★★
SELF CATERING

Units **1**
Sleeps **4**

Low season per wk
£250.00–£350.00
High season per wk
£450.00–£600.00

The Chalet, Nr Tregonetha, St Columb

contact Mr & Mrs David & Diana Chambers, Dennis Farm, St Columb TR9 6DY
t (01637) 881200 e info@dennisfarm.co.uk w dennisfarm.co.uk

Peaceful, secure, disabled-friendly, comfortable, warm chalet set on 75 accessible, historic and rural acres. Easy drives to Eden, Newquay and Padstow. Ideal for seaside, country or heritage holidays.

open All year
payment Cash/cheques

Unit 🏠 TV 📺 💻 🍽 🛏 🧺 🍳 💡 ❄
General 🐕 P ♿ 🅾 S Leisure ✎ ⛱ Shop 3 miles Pub 3 miles

ST IVES, Cornwall Map ref 1B3 | **HOTEL**

★★★
HOTEL
SILVER AWARD

B&B per room per night
s £65.00–£135.00
d £130.00–£210.00
HB per person per night
£84.00–£115.00

Garrack Hotel

Burthallan Lane, St Ives TR26 3AA t (01736) 796199 f (01736) 798955 e etc@garrack.com
w garrack.com

open All year except Christmas
bedrooms 11 double, 5 twin, 2 single
bathrooms All en suite
payment Credit/debit cards, cash/cheques

Small, family-run hotel and restaurant. Secluded position, set in two acres of gardens with 30 miles of coastal views. Overlooking Porthmeor beach and the Tate Gallery St Ives. Facilities include indoor pool, sauna, four-poster bed, sea-view rooms and car park. Award-winning restaurant with an emphasis on local seafood.

⊕ Exit A30 for A3074, past garden centre, left at 1st roundabout, left at 2nd. Follow signs for St Ives B3311 and brown signs for Tate Gallery.

❤ Special winter rates available.

Room 🛁 🚪 ☎ TV 🛏 🍳 🔌 General 🐕 🏠 ♿ P 🍽 🎱 🕺 ⚙ ● I ❄ 🐾 Leisure 🎣 🏊 🎿 ⛳ 🚴

ST IVES, Cornwall Map ref 1B3 | **SELF CATERING**

★★★
SELF CATERING

Units **1**
Sleeps **1–4**

Low season per wk
Min £200.00
High season per wk
Max £650.00

9 Ayr Lane, St Ives

contact Ms Sue Kibby, 115 Earlsfield Road, London SW18 3DD
t (020) 8870 3228 e sue.kibby@btinternet.com w btinternet.com/~stives.cottage

open All year
payment Cash/cheques

Cosy, modernised, ancient, granite, three-storey cottage overlooking town and harbour. Central location. Self-guided walking pack available. Also local history books and maps. Easily accessible by car, train or coach. Perfect all year round. Linen and electricity included.

⊕ From Carbis Bay, right at Porthminster Hotel down Tregunna Hill into Tregunna Place. Then towards harbour, at market building towards Hepworth Museum into Ayr Lane.

❤ Low-season discounts for short breaks of 4 days or less.

Unit TV 📺 💻 🍳 🔌 🧺 💡 ❄
General 🐕 🏠 ♿ ♿ S Leisure ⛱ Shop < 0.5 miles Pub < 0.5 miles

Check it out

Information on accommodation listed in this guide has been supplied by proprietors.
As changes may occur you should remember to check all relevant details at the time of booking.

ST IVES, Cornwall Map ref 1B3 — SELF CATERING

★★★★
SELF CATERING

Units **1**
Sleeps **14**
Low season per wk
£595.00–£895.00
High season per wk
£995.00–£2,495.00

Accommodation Orla-Mo, St Ives

Pednolver Terrace, St Ives, Cornwall TR26 2EL
t 0845 644 2833 e info@surfives.co.uk w surfives.co.uk

Luxuriously refurbished captain's house, centrally located, with breathtaking views. Three king-size, two twin beds, three en suites, bathroom, designer kitchen, parking. Wi-Fi Internet access (2Mb), phone, PlayStation 2 plus games. Short breaks available.

open All year
payment Cash/cheques, euros

Unit 🔥 📺 ⬛ 🍽 🛏 ▣ 🍴 📶 📞 🔒 🧺 ❄
General 🚭 ⛺ 🚶 P ✂ S   Leisure ∪ ⚓ ⛵ 🚴 🛶   Shop < 0.5 miles   Pub < 0.5 miles

ST IVES, Cornwall Map ref 1B3 — SELF CATERING

★★★
SELF CATERING

Units **7**
Sleeps **1–7**
Low season per wk
£185.00–£300.00
High season per wk
£490.00–£675.00

Chy Mor and Premier Apartments, St Ives

contact Michael Gill, Chy Mor and Premier Apartments, Beach House, The Wharf, St Ives TR26 1QA
t (01736) 798798 f (01736) 796831 e enquiry@stivesharbour.com w stivesharbour.com

Situated on St Ives harbour front with uninterrupted views of the harbour and bay. Visit our website, www.stivesharbour.com.

open All year
payment Credit/debit cards, cash/cheques

Unit 🔥 📺 ⬛ 🍽 🍴 📶 🛏
General 🚭 🏠 S   Leisure ⚓   Shop < 0.5 miles   Pub < 0.5 miles

ST IVES, Cornwall Map ref 1B3 — SELF CATERING

★★★
SELF CATERING

Units **1**
Sleeps **1–8**
Low season per wk
£330.00–£520.00
High season per wk
£540.00–£730.00

Lifeboat Inn, St Ives

contact Vicki Medlen, Central reservations, 63 Trevarthian Road, St Austell PL25 4BY
t 0845 241 1133 f (01726) 67970 e reservations@smallandfriendly.co.uk w smallandfriendly.co.uk

open All year
payment Credit/debit cards, cash/cheques

The Lifeboat Inn has a superb self-catering flat with glorious views across St Ives. The flat sleeps a maximum of eight people and has two double bedrooms, one bunk-bed room and a sofa bed in the lounge. The pub and restaurant serve fine food, wine and ales.

⊕ *Follow the A30 to Hayle, and then take the St Ives road. Follow signs to the harbour, and it's near the lifeboat station.*

Unit 🔥 📺 ⬛ 🍽 🍴 📶 🛏 📞 🔒
General 🚭 🚶 P ✂ S   Leisure ∪ ⚓ ⛵ 🚴 🛶   Shop 0.5 miles   Pub < 0.5 miles

ST IVES, Cornwall Map ref 1B3 — SELF CATERING

★★★★
SELF CATERING

Units **8**
Sleeps **4–6**
Low season per wk
£295.00–£425.00
High season per wk
£475.00–£765.00

Rotorua Apartments, Carbis Bay

contact Mrs Linda Roach, Rotorua Apartments, Trencrom Lane, Carbis Bay, St Ives TR26 2TD
t (01736) 795419 f (01736) 795419 e rotorua@btconnect.com w stivesapartments.com

Holiday apartments situated in quiet, wooded lane, with heated outdoor pool and gardens. All apartments are furnished and equipped to a high standard, including dishwasher, microwave, fridge/freezer and electric cooker.

open All year
payment Credit/debit cards, cash/cheques

Unit 🔥 📺 ⬛ 🍽 🛏 ▣ 🍴 📶 🔒 ❄
General 🚭 🏠 🚶 P ✂ ▢   Leisure ≈ ∪ ⚓ 🚴   Shop 0.5 miles   Pub 1 mile

Stay focused

Don't forget your camera. Take home shots of the greatest scenery, super seascapes and family fun.

ST IVES, Cornwall Map ref 1B3 | **SELF CATERING**

★★
SELF CATERING

Units **1**
Sleeps **7–9**

Low season per wk
£325.00–£485.00
High season per wk
£530.00–£715.00

The Studio, St Ives

contact Carol Holland, Little Parc Owles, Pannier Lane, Carbis Bay, St Ives TR26 2RQ
t (01736) 793015

Well-equipped five-bedroom cottage in the picturesque old fishermen's and artists' quarter of St Ives. This converted sail loft also has a spacious living room, kitchen, bath/wc and shower/wc.

open All year
payment Cash/cheques

Unit 🖩 📺 🍳 🗄 🔌 📻 🧺
General 🛏 🐕 Shop < 0.5 miles   Pub < 0.5 miles

ST IVES, Cornwall Map ref 1B3 | **SELF CATERING**

★★★
SELF CATERING

Units **3**
Sleeps **2–5**

Low season per wk
Min £215.00
High season per wk
Max £935.00

Tregowan, St Ives

contact Carole Mincham, Tregowan, Porthmeor Hill, St Ives TR26 1JU
t (01736) 798421   **e** info@tregowanstives.co.uk   **w** tregowanstives.co.uk

Stunning apartments, newly refurbished. Balcony overlooking Porthmeor beach. Apt 1: double bedroom. Apt 2: two double bedrooms. Apt 3: two double bedrooms, one single bedroom.

open All year
payment Cash/cheques

Unit 🖩 📺 🗄 💻 🍳 🔌 🧺 ❄
General 🛏 P ⚡ 💿 S

ST IVES, Cornwall Map ref 1B3 | **CAMPING & CARAVANNING**

★★★★
TOURING &
CAMPING PARK

🚐 (168) £11.50–£21.00
🚙 (168) £11.50–£21.00
⛺ (235) £11.50–£21.00
234 touring pitches

Little Trevarrack Holiday Park

Laity Lane, Carbis Bay, St Ives TR26 3HW   **t** (01736) 797580   **e** info@littletrevarrack.co.uk
w littletrevarrack.co.uk

payment Credit/debit cards, cash/cheques

Little Trevarrack Holiday Park is ideally located for exploring the beautiful West Cornwall peninsula. Our range of superb facilities includes a heated outdoor swimming pool with sun terrace (Whitsun to mid-September). Approximately one mile from the stunning Carbis Bay beach and the coastal footpath into St Ives. Open April to September.

⊕ *From A30 take A3074 to St Ives. Signposted left opposite turning for Carbis Bay beach. Straight across at next crossroads. Approx 200m on right.*

♥ *Please telephone reception for details.*

General 🖩 P 🔌 🐕 🍴 📶 💻 🛏 🐾 ☼   Leisure ⚡ 🎣 ⛰ ∪ ♪ ↑

ST JUST-IN-PENWITH, Cornwall Map ref 1A3 | **GUEST ACCOMMODATION**

★★★
GUEST ACCOMMODATION

B&B per room per night
s £35.00–£45.00
d £60.00–£75.00
Evening meal per person
£7.50–£15.00

The Commercial

Market Square, St Just, Penzance TR19 7HE   **t** (01736) 788455   **f** (01736) 788131
e enquiries@commercial-hotel.co.uk   **w** commercial-hotel.co.uk

A former coaching inn, well-known locally for its great food and friendly atmosphere. Ideal for exploring nearby World Heritage sites and Land's End coastline. Free Wi-Fi broadband connection available.

open All year
bedrooms 5 double, 1 twin, 4 family
bathrooms 7 en suite, 3 private
payment Credit/debit cards, cash/cheques

Room 📺 💷 🍳   General 🛏 11 🅿 P 🍴 📶 🛏 📻 💻 ☼ 🐾   Leisure ⚡ ∪ ♪ ↑ 🚲 🏊

To your credit
If you book by credit card, it's advisable to check the proprietor's cancellation policy in case you have to change your plans.

ST JUST-IN-PENWITH, Cornwall Map ref 1A3 | CAMPING & CARAVANNING

★★★★
HOLIDAY, TOURING
& CAMPING PARK

(10)   £10.00–£12.50
(7)   £10.00–£12.50
A (14)   £8.00–£10.00
(15) £190.00–£450.00
17 touring pitches

Roselands Caravan Park

Dowran, St Just, Penzance TR19 7RS t (01736) 788571 e info@roselands.co.uk w roselands.co.uk

payment Credit/debit cards, cash/cheques

Roselands is a quiet, secluded, family-run park ideal for coastal and moorland walks. Close to beaches and attractions including golf course. Luxury six-berth caravans. Level touring pitches. Bar, evening meals, in our new conservatory. Open 1 January to 31 October.

⊕ *From the A30 Penzance bypass, turn right for St Just on the A3071. Half a mile before reaching St Just, turn left at the caravan sign.*

♥ *Over 55s, 10% off one week's holiday before 14 Jul or after 8 Sep, excl Easter.*

General P ▣ ♻ ♞ ℞ ☉ ▣▣ ⚍ ✕ ☂ ⛺ ☼ Leisure ⚑ ♣ ⌂ ♫ ▶ ⚲

ST JUST IN ROSELAND, Cornwall Map ref 1B3 | GUEST ACCOMMODATION

★★★★
BED & BREAKFAST

B&B per room per night
d £75.00–£85.00

Roundhouse Barns

Truro TR2 5JJ t (01872) 580038 f (01872) 580067 e info@roundhousebarns.co.uk
w roundhousebarns.co.uk

open All year except Christmas and New Year
bedrooms 2 double
bathrooms All en suite
payment Cash/cheques

Beautifully converted 17thC barn set in peaceful surroundings on the Roseland. Instant access to walks by the Fal river. St Just in Roseland church with its subtropical gardens and the picturesque harbour of St Mawes are both nearby. Delightful, comfortable rooms with luxury bedding. Locally sourced breakfasts.

⊕ *A3078 to St Just in Roseland. Right turn, B3289, signposted King Henry Ferry. After 1.5 miles take left turn, signposted Messack. Follow signs to Roundhouse Barns.*

Room ♻ 📺 ♦ ♑ General ➰16 P ⊁ ⚍ ⚭ ✻ Leisure ♫ ▶ 🏠

ST MERRYN, Cornwall Map ref 1B2 | SELF CATERING

★★★★
SELF CATERING

Units   **2**
Sleeps   **6**

Low season per wk
£250.00–£445.00
High season per wk
£475.00–£590.00

141 & 147 Jasmine Way, Padstow

contact Mr & Mrs Griffin, 141 & 147 Jasmine Way, Alverstoke, 9 Shaymoor Lane, Bristol BS35 4JR
t (01454) 632624 e robert.griffin@tiscali.co.uk

Luxurious detached three bedroom, six-plus berth bungalow. Enclosed rear garden, patio and conservatory. Bedding supplied. Dishwasher, washing machine, power shower etc. Ample parking. Near Padstow and many beautiful beaches.

open All year
payment Cash/cheques

Unit ⚏ 📺 ▣ ▨ ▣ ⚍ 🗑 🗑 ⚏ ✻
General ➰ ▥ ⚏ P ⊁ Ⓢ Leisure ⚲ ∪ ♫ ▶ ⚲ Shop < 0.5 miles Pub 1 mile

Check the maps

Colour maps at the front pinpoint all the places you will find accommodation entries in the regional sections. Pick your location and then refer to the place index at the back to find the page number.

SENNEN, Cornwall Map ref 1A3 | SELF CATERING

★★★
SELF CATERING

Units **1**
Sleeps **5**
Low season per wk
£400.00–£425.00
High season per wk
£450.00–£480.00

Little Trevallack, Sennen, Penzance

contact Mrs Nicholas, Trevallack, Mayon, Sennen TR19 7AD
t (01736) 871451 f (01736) 871451 e suenicholas@hotmail.com

Fully equipped bungalow with superb coastal views. Half mile to beach. One family bedroom with en suite bathroom plus one double bedroom. No pets. Private parking.

open All year
payment Cash/cheques

Unit ▥ TV 🖥 🖥 🖥 🖥 ✿
General ♨ ⊨ P ⅋ Shop < 0.5 miles Pub 0.5 miles

SENNEN, Cornwall Map ref 1A3 | SELF CATERING

★★★★
SELF CATERING

Units **1**
Sleeps **2–10**
Low season per wk
Min £310.00
High season per wk
Max £1,135.00

Trevear Farm, Penzance

contact Mrs Thomas, Trevear Farm, Sennen, Penzance TR19 7BH
t (01736) 871205 f (01736) 871205 e trevear.farm@farming.co.uk w trevearfarm.co.uk

open All year
payment Cash/cheques

Large farmhouse, completely refurbished; very clean and well equipped; central heating and woodburner. Five minutes' drive to beautiful Sennen Cove. Ample parking, enclosed garden. Great for walking, beaches, cycling and culture. Activity or relaxation – the choice is yours!

⊕ From Penzance, take A30 towards Land's End. Private drive is on the left, just outside Sennen.

♥ Weekend breaks and discount for under-occupancy (excl school and Bank Holidays).

Unit ▥ TV 🖥 🖥 🖥 🖥 🖥 ✿
General ♨ ⊨ ♣ P S Leisure ∪ ♪ ▸ ⚲ Shop 1.5 miles Pub 1.5 miles

---

TINTAGEL, Cornwall Map ref 1B2 | HOTEL

★★
HOTEL

B&B per room per night
s £40.00–£60.00
d £65.00–£120.00
HB per person per night
£55.00–£80.00

The Wootons Country House Hotel

Fore Street, Atlantic Road, Tintagel PL34 0DD t (01840) 770170 f (023) 9273 2759
e wootons@tiscali.co.uk w wootons.co.uk

open All year
bedrooms 5 double, 3 twin, 2 family, 1 suite
bathrooms All en suite
payment Credit/debit cards, cash/cheques, euros

A converted Victorian country house modernised in 1993 with a restaurant, bar, lounge and full en suite accommodation, situated within walking distance of the world-renowned Tintagel Castle, the legendary birthplace of King Arthur. The coastal path and Castle Cove are also within easy reach. Private parking is provided.

⊕ A30 to A395, follow signs to Camelford/Tintagel. In Tintagel turn left at mini-roundabout. Hotel is situated 400m on left by castle access.

Room 🖥 ☎ TV ♨ ♨ General ♨ ▤ 🍴 ● ✿ Leisure ● ∪ ♪ ⚲

Place index

If you know where you want to stay, the index at the back of the guide will give you the page number listing accommodation in your chosen town, city or village. Check out the other useful indexes too.

TINTAGEL, Cornwall Map ref 1B2 — GUEST ACCOMMODATION

The Mill House

★★★
INN

B&B per room per night
s £50.00–£90.00
d £90.00–£120.00
Evening meal per person
£12.00–£30.00

Trebarwith Strand, Tintagel PL34 0HD t (01840) 770200 f (01840) 770647
e management@themillhouseinn.co.uk w themillhouseinn.co.uk

An 18thC mill, now a stylish hotel with traditional bar and restaurant, using local fish and produce, half a mile from beach.

open All year except Christmas
bedrooms 7 double, 1 twin, 1 single
bathrooms All en suite
payment Credit/debit cards, cash/cheques, euros

Room 📞 📺 👜 🖥 General 🛏 🏄 P 🍴 ♨ ✕ 🎱 🎿 ❀ ♞ Leisure ∪ ♪ ♪ 🚲

TINTAGEL, Cornwall Map ref 1B2 — CAMPING & CARAVANNING

Trewethett Farm Caravan Club Site

★★★★★
TOURING &
CAMPING PARK

🚐 (142) £13.60–£25.60
🚏 (142) £13.60–£25.60
142 touring pitches

Trethevy, Tintagel PL34 0BQ t (01840) 770222 w caravanclub.co.uk

payment Credit/debit cards, cash/cheques

Cliff-top site with breathtaking views. Walk to Boscastle, with its pretty harbour and quayside, or Tintagel to see its dramatic castle. Non-members welcome. Open March to November.

⊕ From A30 onto A395 signposted Camelford. Right onto A39 signposted Bude. Left just before transmitter. Right onto B3266 signposted Boscastle. Left onto B3263. Site entrance is on the right in about 2 miles.

♥ Special member rates mean you can save your membership subscription in less than a week. Visit our website to find out more.

THE CARAVAN CLUB

General P 🔌 🕑 🚐 🅿 ☉ 🗑 🛒 ❅ Leisure ♪ ♪

TRURO, Cornwall Map ref 1B3 — SELF CATERING

Trelowthas, Malpas, Nr Truro

★★★★
SELF CATERING

Units   1
Sleeps   1–6

Low season per wk
Min £250.00
High season per wk
Max £750.00

contact Mr Chris Churm, 16 Morleys Close, Lowdham, Nottingham NG14 7HN
t (0115) 966 5611 f (0115) 966 5611 w 4starcornwall.co.uk

Quality, luxurious accommodation ideal for couples and families. Set in the picturesque riverside village of Malpas, two miles from Truro. Magnificent views and walks, very peaceful, excellent facilities. Mahogany four-poster bed.

open All year
payment Cash/cheques, euros

Unit 🪟 📺 🖥 ▣ 🍴 🗄 ♨ 🗑 🍽 🗄 ❅
General 🛏 P 🍴 Leisure ♪ ♪ Shop < 0.5 miles Pub < 0.5 miles

Discover Britain's heritage

Discover the history and beauty of over 250 of Britain's best-known historic houses, castles, gardens and small manor houses. You can purchase Britain's Historic Houses and Gardens – Guide and Map from good bookshops and online at visitbritaindirect.com.

TRURO, Cornwall Map ref 1B3 | SELF CATERING

★★★★★
SELF CATERING

Units **46**
Sleeps **1–7**

Low season per wk
£480.00–£850.00
High season per wk
£740.00–£1,545.00

The Valley Cottages, Carnon Downs, Truro

The Valley, Bissoe Road, Carnon Downs, Truro TR3 6LQ
t (01872) 862194 f (01872) 864343 e info@the-valley.co.uk w the-valley.co.uk

open All year
payment Credit/debit cards, cash/cheques, euros

A secluded hamlet of contemporary holiday cottages in the centre of Cornwall's beauty and life. Relax in architect-designed luxury with an ambience of contemporary living. Explore spectacular countryside, with indoor, outdoor and spa pools, gym, squash/tennis courts and the stylish Café Azur serving exquisite cuisine on your doorstep … Cornwall's chic country retreat.

⊕ A30 from Exeter to A39/A3076 (Truro). Bypass Truro to A39 (Falmouth). The Valley is signposted from A39 Falmouth road at Carnon Downs roundabout, about 3 miles outside Truro.

♥ Call for short-break special offers and out-of-season discounts at Cornwall's chic country retreat.

Unit 🛏 📺 📼 🖥 🔲 🍳 🔥 🍽 🔲 📶 ✼
General 👶 🎱 🚶 P 🅂 🐾   Leisure 🎣 🏊 ♨ 🏊 ♪ ⛳ 🚲   Shop 0.5 miles Pub 0.5 miles

---

TRURO, Cornwall Map ref 1B3 | CAMPING & CARAVANNING

★★★★
TOURING PARK

🚐 (40) £10.00–£13.00
🚙 (5) £10.00–£13.00
⛺ (15) £10.00–£13.00
60 touring pitches

Summer Valley Touring Park

Shortlanesend, Truro TR4 9DW t (01872) 277878 e res@summervalley.co.uk w summervalley.co.uk

Situated in a sheltered valley surrounded by woods and farmland, we have been awarded for our peaceful, rural environment. We have the ideal site for visiting the gardens in spring. Open April to October.

payment Credit/debit cards, cash/cheques

General 🏕 P 🔌 🚻 🚿 🚰 🐾 ☉ 📶 🔲 ⚓ 🐕 ✼   Leisure 🎯 ♪

VERYAN, Cornwall Map ref 1B3 | SELF CATERING

★★★★
SELF CATERING

Units **2**
Sleeps **6**

Low season per wk
£240.00–£470.00
High season per wk
£470.00–£760.00

Trenona Farm Holidays, Veryan

contact Mrs Pamela Carbis, Trenona Farm, Ruan High Lanes, Truro TR2 5JS
t (01872) 501339 f (01872) 501253 e pam@trenonafarmholidays.co.uk
w trenonafarmholidays.co.uk

open All year
payment Credit/debit cards, cash/cheques

The former farmhouse, and old stone workshop, have been tastefully converted to provide quality accommodation with modern furnishings and appliances for relaxing holidays on a mixed working farm on the beautiful Roseland Peninsula. Private gardens and patios. Many public gardens and attractions nearby. Children/pets welcome. Disabled access.

⊕ A30 past Bodmin, A391 to St Austell, A390 towards Truro. Just beyond Probus take A3078 to St Mawes. After 8 miles pass Esso garage, Trenona Farm 2nd on left.

♥ Short breaks available Oct-Mar.

Unit 🛏 📺 📼 🖥 🔲 🍳 🔥 🔲 ✼
General 👶 🎱 🚶 P 🐾 🐕   Leisure ⛳   Shop 1 mile Pub 2 miles

It's all quality-assessed accommodation

Our commitment to quality involves wide-ranging accommodation assessment. Rating and awards were correct at the time of going to press but may change following a new assessment. Please check at time of booking.

Gloucester Cathedral

Forest of Dean Sculpture Trail

Symonds Yat

Explore Cotswolds & Forest of Dean

Step into Beatrix Potter's world or take the waters in an elegant spa town. Hunt for antiques in mellow-stone villages or walk across gentle hillsides. Go back to the Iron Age or watch peregrines fly. Which do you do first?

Cathedral city

You may be surprised to discover that the cathedral city of Gloucester is actually an inland port. Spend some time down at the docks where Victorian warehouses have become intriguing museums and there's plenty going on. See the brilliantly coloured boats, part of The National Waterways Museum, and take a cruise along the Gloucester & Sharpness Canal. In the city centre, enter the majestic beauty of the cathedral or step into Beatrix Potter's favourite story at The House of The Tailor of Gloucester.

Take the waters

Keep your credit card handy for the elegant stores of Cheltenham Spa and when shopping is done, enjoy the gleaming buildings, tree-lined avenues and decorative ironwork. Sample the spa waters, just as they did in Regency times, in the Pittville Pump Room. A music-lover? Discover the life and works of Gustav Holst in his Birthplace Museum.

Green and gold

Escape into the romantic rolling hills of the Cotswolds, scattered with small towns and villages built of distinctive honey-coloured limestone. Follow the Romantic Road, two easy-to-find routes that will take you through towns, villages and lovely landscapes, tracing the tales of artists and writers. Criss-cross the little bridges over the River Windrush in Bourton-on-the-Water; poke around the antique shops of Stow-on-the-Wold; bustle about in the open-air street market at Moreton-in-Marsh and appreciate the beautifully preserved buildings in Chipping Campden and Tetbury. Get the camera out for idyllic country scenes in the villages of Upper and Lower Slaughter.

Clearwell Caves

Cotswolds cottages, Bibury

Historic Gloucester Docks

Cheltenham Racecourse

Beyond the hills

From the highest points of the Cotswolds you get spectacular views of the Severn Vale, so go west to find out what's there. Take time out in Tewkesbury, a photogenic town of black-and-white timbered buildings, and amble around the abbey admiring its great Norman arches. Then beyond Gloucester make for the mysteries of The Royal Forest of Dean, the 'Queen of Forests'. Get an insight into its fascinating industrial heritage and history at the Cinderbury Iron Age Farm or clamber into Clearwell Caves to see how iron ore has been 'won' here over 4,000 years, from the Bronze Age to the present.

Walk in woodland glades or follow the Family Cycle Trail on two wheels. Drive through the Wye Valley, an Area of Outstanding Natural Beauty, and stop to see peregrines at Symonds Yat where RSPB volunteers make sure you get excellent views as the birds hunt, and feed their young. For a bit more action, dodge and dive on white waters or paddle a canoe gently along the River Wye.

Food & drink

Fancy a bite to eat, a relaxing drink or some fresh local produce? Here's a selection of food and drink venues to get you started. For lots more ideas go online at enjoyengland.com/taste.

Restaurants

Allium
European
1 London Street, Market Place, Fairford GL7 4AH
t (01285) 712200
w allium.uk.net

Barnsley House
Italian
Barnsley, Circencester GL7 5EE
t (01285) 740000
w barnsleyhouse.com

Bibury Court Hotel
Fine dining
Bibury, Cirencester GL7 5NT
t (01285) 740337
w biburycourt.com

Le Champignon Sauvage
Fine dining
24-26 Suffolk Rd,
Cheltenham GL50 2AQ
t (01242) 573449
w lechampignonsauvage.co.uk

The Overton
English
88 St Georges Road,
Cheltenham GL50 3EA
t (01242) 523371
w theoverton.com

The Pepper Pot
English
Lower Wick, Dursley
GL11 6DD
t (01453) 810259

The Pudding Club at Three Ways House Hotel
English
Chapel Lane, Mickleton,
Chipping Camden GL55 6SB
t (01386) 438429
w puddingclub.com

Sophie's Restaurant
French
The Priory, 20 High Street,
Minchinhampton GL6 9BN
t (01453) 885188
w le-midi.co.uk

Pubs

The Bell at Sapperton
Sapperton, Cirencester GL7 6LE
t (01285) 760298
w foodatthebell.co.uk

The Horse and Groom Village Inn
Upper Oddington,
Moreton-in-Marsh GL56 0XH
t (01451) 830584
w horseandgroom.uk.com

The Kings Arms
The Street, Didmarton GL9 1DT
t (01454) 238245
w kingsarmsdidmarton.co.uk

The Ormond at Tetbury
23 Long Street, Tetbury GL8 8AA
t (01666) 505690
w theormondattetbury.co.uk

The Priory Inn
London Road, Tetbury GL8 8JJ
t (01666) 502251
w theprioryinn.co.uk

The Tunnel House Inn
Tarlton Road, Coates,
Cirencester GL7 6PW
t (01285) 770280
w tunnelhouse.com

Tearooms, coffee shops and cafes

Atrium Bar and Restaurant
Tortworth Court Four Pillars
Hotel, Tortworth,
Wotton-under-Edge GL12 8HH
t (01454) 263000
w four-pillars.co.uk

Cotswold Farm Fayre
Denfurlong Farm, Chedworth,
Cheltenham GL54 4NQ
t (01285) 720265
w cotswoldfarmfayre.com

The Kitchen
7 High Street, Minchinhampton,
Stroud GL6 9BN
t (01453) 882655

Thatchers Tea Rooms
101 Montpellier Street,
Cheltenham GL50 1RS
t (01242) 584150
w thatcherscheltenham.co.uk

Delis

Relish
36 Long Street,
Wotton-under-Edge GL12 7BT
t (01453) 844477

Farm shops and local produce

The Butts Farm Shop
South Cerney,
Cirencester GL7 5QE
t (01285) 862224
w buttsfarmshop.com

The Cotswold Cheese Company
5 High Street, Moreton-in-Marsh
GL56 0AH
t (01608) 652862
w cotswoldcheesecompany.co.uk

Cotswold Farm Fayre
Denfurlong Farm, Chedworth,
Cheltenham GL54 4NQ
t (01258) 720265
w cotswoldfarmfayre.com

Old Farm
Dorn, Moreton-in-Marsh
GL56 9NS
t (01608) 650394
w oldfarmdorn.co.uk

Puddleditch Farm Shop
Berkeley Heath, Berkeley
GL13 9EU
t (01453) 810816
w puddleditchfarm.co.uk

Shepherd's Farm Shop
Hazelfield Garden World,
Ledbury Road, Newent GL18 1DL
t (01531) 828590
w shepherdsfarmshop.co.uk

Never has a rose meant so much

Everyone has a trusted friend, someone who tells it straight. Well, that's what the Enjoy England Quality Rose does: reassures you before you check into your holiday accommodation that it will be just what you want, because it's been checked out by independent assessors. Which means you can book with confidence and get on with the real business of having a fantastic break.

enjoy**England**.com

★ ★ ★

BED & BREAKFAST

The **Quality Rose** is the mark of England's *official*, nationwide quality assessment scheme and covers just about every place you might want to stay, using a clear star rating system: from caravan parks to stylish boutique hotels, farmhouse B&Bs to country house retreats, self-catering cottages by the sea to comfy narrowboats perfect for getting away from it all. Think of the Quality Rose as your personal guarantee that your expectations will be met.

Our ratings made easy

★	Simple, practical, no frills
★★	Well presented and well run
★★★	Good level of quality and comfort
★★★★	Excellent standard throughout
★★★★★	Exceptional with a degree of luxury

Look no further. Just look out for the Quality Rose. Find out more at enjoy**England**.com/quality

where to stay in
Cotswolds & Forest of Dean

Maps
All place names in the blue bands are shown on the maps at the front of this guide.

Accommodation symbols
Symbols give useful information about services and facilities. Inside the back-cover flap you can find a key to these symbols. Keep it open for easy reference.

CHELTENHAM, Gloucestershire Map ref 2B1　　　　　　　　　　　　　　　　　　　　**HOTEL**

★★★
SMALL HOTEL

B&B per room per night
s £65.00–£85.00
d £98.00–£125.00

Charlton Kings Hotel

London Road, Charlton Kings, Cheltenham GL52 6UU **t** (01242) 231061 **f** (01242) 241900
e enquiries@charltonkingshotel.co.uk **w** charltonkingshotel.co.uk

open All year
bedrooms 8 double, 2 twin, 2 single, 1 family
bathrooms All en suite
payment Credit/debit cards, cash/cheques

Surrounded by the Cotswold Hills, on the outskirts of Cheltenham. Quality, comfort and friendliness are hallmarks of this privately owned hotel. All rooms have satellite TV. Wi-Fi Internet available. Very comfortable standard rooms. Superior rooms are larger, with many upgraded facilities. Excellent restaurant open seven days a week. Ample parking.

⊕ *On entering Cheltenham from Oxford (A40), hotel is 1st building on the left.*

♥ *2-night weekend break special DB&B from £60pppn sharing a double room. 3- and 5-night breaks also available.*

Room 👥 ☎ 📺 🚭 🍵 🕭, General 🛋 🎱 🅿 ⚡ 🍷 🎳 🍴 📺 ❄ 🐾

The great outdoors

Discover Britain's green heart with this easy-to-use guide. Featuring a selection of the most stunning gardens in the country, The Gardens Explorer is complete with a handy fold-out map and illustrated guide. You can purchase the Explorer series from good bookshops and online at visitbritaindirect.com.

CHELTENHAM, Gloucestershire Map ref 2B1   **GUEST ACCOMMODATION**

★★★★★
GUEST ACCOMMODATION
SILVER AWARD

Beaumont House

56 Shurdington Road, Cheltenham GL53 0JE   **t** (01242) 223311   **f** (01242) 520044
e reservations@bhhotel.co.uk   **w** bhhotel.co.uk

B&B per room per night
s £62.00–£178.00
d £89.00–£193.00
Evening meal per person
£12.00–£30.00

open All year
bedrooms 9 double, 3 twin, 2 single, 1 family,
1 suite
bathrooms All en suite
payment Credit/debit cards, cash/cheques

Owner-managed, set in a lovely garden with ample parking, Beaumont House offers luxury at affordable rates. The stunning, modern en suite rooms with satellite TV/Sky Sports, free broadband, hairdryer and room safe, ensure a comfortable stay in style. Delicious breakfasts and friendly service. Relax and enjoy our warm hospitality.

✪ Situated at the Cheltenham end of the A46 Shurdington Road, which is the extension of the A46 Bath Road, just south of Cheltenham town centre.

♥ Champagne, flowers and chocolates can all be arranged in your room for that special day.

Room 📞 📺 🖥 🕾   General 🕾 10 P 🗲 🏮 🛏 👭 🎇   Leisure 🚴 🏊

CHELTENHAM, Gloucestershire Map ref 2B1   **GUEST ACCOMMODATION**

★★★
GUEST ACCOMMODATION

B&B per room per night
s £35.00–£45.00
d £55.00–£65.00

Cheltenham Guest House

145 Hewlett Road, Cheltenham GL52 6TS   **t** (01242) 521726   **f** 0871 661 4405
e info@cheltenhamguesthouse.biz   **w** cheltenhamguesthouse.biz

Stylish, yet economical, bed and breakfast accommodation; walking distance to town centre. Designer-themed rooms, eg Greek, African, old Scandinavian. Generous breakfasts in grand breakfast room. Free Internet access and car park.

open All year
bedrooms 3 double, 2 twin, 3 single, 1 family
bathrooms 7 en suite, 2 private
payment Credit/debit cards, cash/cheques, euros

Room 📺 🖥   General 🕾 🏵 🏮 P 🗲 👭 🎇   Leisure 🏌

CHELTENHAM, Gloucestershire Map ref 2B1   **SELF CATERING**

★★★
SELF CATERING

Units   **3**
Sleeps   **2–4**

Low season per wk
£145.00–£305.00
High season per wk
£180.00–£355.00

Balcarras Farm Holiday Cottages, Cheltenham

contact Mr & Mrs David & Judith Ballinger, Balcarras Farm, London Road, Charlton Kings,
Cheltenham GL52 6UT
t (01242) 584837   **e** cottage@balcarras-farm.co.uk   **w** balcarras-farm.co.uk

Built in 1992, around three sides of paved courtyard at rear of owners' former farmhouse, these brick-built, single-storey cottages incorporate materials from original stables and cider mill. Footpaths directly onto Cotswold Way.

open All year
payment Credit/debit cards, cash/cheques

Unit 🏠 📺 📺 🖥 🌣
General 🕾 🏵 🏮 P 🗲 🔘 Ⓢ 🦮   Leisure U   Shop < 0.5 miles   Pub < 0.5 miles

---

Check the maps

Colour maps at the front pinpoint all the cities, towns and villages where you will find accommodation entries in the regional sections. Pick your location and then refer to the place index at the back to find the page number.

       For key to symbols open the back-cover flap.

CIRENCESTER, Gloucestershire Map ref 2B1 — **GUEST ACCOMMODATION**

★★★★
GUEST ACCOMMODATION

B&B per room per night
s Min £45.00
d Min £60.00
Evening meal per person
Min £15.00

Riverside House

Watermoor Road, Cirencester GL7 1LF **t** (01285) 647642 **f** (01285) 647615
e riversidehouse@mitsubishi-cars.co.uk **w** riversidehouse.org.uk

open All year
bedrooms 13 double, 11 twin
bathrooms All en suite
payment Credit/debit cards, cash/cheques

Located 15 minutes' walk from the centre of the historic market town of Cirencester with easy access to and from M4/M5 and the Cotswolds. Riverside House is fully licensed and provides superb bed and breakfast for private and corporate guests. Built in the grounds of Mitsubishi UK headquarters.

⊕ Located just off A419 opposite the Tesco superstore. Take the turning at roundabout (Kwik-Fit) for Watermoor and turn left after ATS exhausts.

♥ Special group discounts are available at weekends. Ideal for clubs and societies.

Room ☎ 📺 ♿ 🍽 General ☂ P ✂ 🍷 ✗ 🍳 ✿

DURSLEY, Gloucestershire Map ref 2B2 — **SELF CATERING**

★★★
SELF CATERING

Units   **1**
Sleeps   **1–4**
Low season per wk
£186.00–£231.00
High season per wk
£231.00–£267.00

Two Springbank, Dursley

contact Mrs Freda Jones, 32 Everlands, Cam, Dursley GL11 5NL
t (01453) 543047 **e** lhandfaj32lg@surefish.co.uk

Victorian, mid-terraced cottage in a pleasant, rural location near to a 14thC village church with open fields to rear and within easy reach of the Cotswold Way.

open All year
payment Cash/cheques

Unit 🛏 📺 🍳 🔲 📻 🍽 🧺 📞 ⚙ 🔥 ✿
General ☂ 🍳 ♿ P ✂ S   Leisure ∪ ♪ ► 🚲 🚣   Shop 0.75 miles   Pub 0.75 miles

LECHLADE-ON-THAMES, Gloucestershire Map ref 2B1 — **GUEST ACCOMMODATION**

★★★
INN

B&B per room per night
s £40.00–£60.00
d £45.00–£70.00
Evening meal per person
£10.00–£25.00

New Inn Hotel

Market Square, Lechlade-on-Thames GL7 3AB **t** (01367) 252296 **f** (01367) 252315
e info@newinnhotel.co.uk **w** newinnhotel.co.uk

The New Inn Hotel is where a 250-year tradition of hospitality blends with 21st century comfort and Cotswold charm. On the banks of River Thames in the centre of Lechlade.

open All year except Christmas
bedrooms 10 double, 12 twin, 4 single, 2 family
bathrooms All en suite
payment Credit/debit cards, cash/cheques, euros

Room 🛏 📺 ☎ ♿ 🍽 General P 🍷 🍳 🅿 🔥 ✿ Leisure ⚲ ∪ ♪ ► 🚲

Get on the road

Take yourself on a journey through England's historic towns and villages, past stunning coastlines and beautiful countryside with VisitBritain's series of inspirational touring guides. You can purchase the guides from good bookshops and online at visitbritaindirect.com.

LITTLEDEAN, Gloucestershire Map ref 2B1   SELF CATERING

★★★
SELF CATERING

Units **1**
Sleeps **3**

Low season per wk
£160.00–£260.00
High season per wk
£260.00–£360.00

Brambles, Littledean, Cinderford

contact Mrs Norman, Brambles, Sutton Baynham Farm, Sutton Road, Cinderford GL14 2TU
t (01594) 827311 f (01594) 827345 e lynda@searanckes.com

open All year
payment Cash/cheques, euros

We welcome you to our 30-acre farm in wooded
Soudley Valley. Brambles provides tranquillity next
to our farmhouse. Foray into the woods or picnic in
our fields. Stone steps lead to accommodation with
wooden balcony and view over valley. Sleeps two
adults and two children. One mile to Dean Heritage
Centre.

⊕ *From A48 Elton Corner take A4151 to Littledean. In village,
turn left for Soudley, then take lane on right-hand side after
0.7 miles.*

Unit ▦ TV ⊞ ⊙ ▣ 🗄 🍴 🖫 🖵 ✿
General 🔥 ▥ ⚑ P ⊙ S 🐾 Leisure ∪ ↗ ⅃ 🚲 ⛵ Shop 1 mile Pub 1 mile

MINSTERWORTH, Gloucestershire Map ref 2B1   GUEST ACCOMMODATION

★★★
GUEST ACCOMMODATION

B&B per room per night
s Min £30.00
d Min £60.00

Severn Bank

Minsterworth, Gloucester GL2 8JH t (01452) 750146 f (01452) 750357 e info@severnbank.com
w severn-bank.com

open All year except Christmas and New Year
bedrooms 2 double/twin, 1 family
bathrooms All en suite
payment Cash/cheques

A fine country house set in large gardens with lovely
river walk. All en suite rooms are spacious with
beautiful river views, as is the breakfast room in
which we serve a healthy buffet breakfast including
fruits, yoghurts, cereals and breads. There are good
pubs nearby for evening meals.

⊕ *Travel west from Gloucester on A40. Turn left onto A48
towards Chepstow; continue for 2.3 miles. Just past church
lane turn left into Severn Bank.*

Room TV 🖢 General 🔥10 P ⚡ 🖪 ✿ Leisure ⛵

MORETON-IN-MARSH, Gloucestershire Map ref 2B1   GUEST ACCOMMODATION

★★★★
GUEST HOUSE

B&B per room per night
s £40.00
d £55.00–£60.00

Treetops

London Road, Moreton-in-Marsh GL56 0HE t (01608) 651036 f (01608) 651036
e treetops1@talk21.com w treetopscotswolds.co.uk

Family guesthouse on the A44, set in 0.5 acres of
secluded gardens. Five minutes' walk from the
village centre.

open All year except Christmas
bedrooms 4 double, 2 twin
bathrooms All en suite
payment Credit/debit cards, cash/cheques

Room 🖢 TV 🖢 🍴 General 🔥 ▥ ⚑ P ⚡ 🖪 ✿ Leisure ⅃

Our quality rating schemes

For a detailed explanation of the quality and facilities represented
by the stars, please refer to the information pages at the back of
this guide.

MORETON-IN-MARSH, Gloucestershire Map ref 2B1   **CAMPING & CARAVANNING**

★★★★★
TOURING PARK

(182) £14.30–£27.70
(182) £14.30–£27.70
182 touring pitches

Moreton-in-Marsh Caravan Club Site

Bourton Road, Moreton-in-Marsh GL56 0BT   **t** (01608) 650519   **w** caravanclub.co.uk

open All year
payment Credit/debit cards, cash/cheques

An attractive, well-wooded site within easy walking distance of the market town of Moreton-in-Marsh. On-site facilities include crazy golf, volleyball and boules. Large dog-walking area.

⊕ From Moreton-in-Marsh on A44 the site entrance is on the right 250yds past the end of the speed limit sign.

♥ Special member rates mean you can save your membership subscription in less than a week. Visit our website to find out more.

THE
CARAVAN CLUB

General 🖪 P ⚙ 🚻 🍴 🖵 📷 ☉ 🚮📷 🐕 🛒 ☼   Leisure ⛺ 🛶

NEWENT, Gloucestershire Map ref 2B1   **SELF CATERING**

★★★
SELF CATERING

Units   **1**
Sleeps   **1–4**

Low season per wk
Min £310.00
High season per wk
Max £580.00

The George Hotel, Newent

contact Mr Rhodri Yeandle, The George Hotel, Church Street, Newent GL18 1PU
t (01531) 820203   **f** (01531) 822392   **e** enquiries@georgehotel.uk.com   **w** georgehotel.uk.com

A unique two-bedroom mews apartment converted from coaching stables, within the courtyard of a 17thC coaching inn. Located in the heart of Newent.

open All year
payment Credit/debit cards, cash/cheques, euros

Unit 🛏 📺 🖵 🍳 📻 🖵 🧺 🗑 🔌 🗄 📞 ⌨ // ❄
General 🦮 🍴 🏊 P 🅿 🆂   Leisure ∪ 🛶 🏍 🚲 🛥

OWLPEN, Gloucestershire Map ref 2B1   **SELF CATERING**

★★★–★★★★★
SELF CATERING

Units   **9**
Sleeps   **2–8**

Low season per wk
£295.00–£855.00
High season per wk
£395.00–£1,495.00

Owlpen Manor, Uley

contact Mrs Jayne Simmons, Estate Office, Owlpen Manor, Owlpen, Uley, Nr Dursley GL11 5BZ
t (01453) 860261   **f** (01453) 860819   **e** sales@owlpen.com   **w** owlpen.com

open All year
payment Credit/debit cards, cash/cheques

Romantic Cotswold hamlet, manor house and church in a hidden beech wood valley. Nine self-catering period and historic cottages spread around the 215-acre estate. Antiques, log fires and four-posters in some. 15thC restaurant. Midweek and weekend breaks available all year round. 'The most beautiful place in England' – Fodor's Guide 2000.

⊕ B4066 to Uley. In Uley, follow signs to Owlpen at the Green, by the Old Crown public house.

♥ Excellent value four-night midweek breaks available all year round (excl Xmas and New Year). Also three-night weekend breaks available.

Unit 🛏 📺 🖵 🖵 🍳 🖵 🧺 🗑 🔌 🗄 ❄
General 🦮 🍴 🏊 P 🆂 🐕   Leisure ∪ 🛶 🏍 🚲   Shop 1 mile   Pub 1 mile

It's all quality-assessed accommodation

Our commitment to quality involves wide-ranging accommodation assessment. Rating and awards were correct at the time of going to press but may change following a new assessment. Please check at time of booking.

RUDFORD, Gloucestershire Map ref 2B1 — **GUEST ACCOMMODATION**

★★★★
GUEST ACCOMMODATION

B&B per room per night
s Min £35.00
d Min £55.00
Evening meal per person
Min £10.00

The Dark Barn Cottages

Barbers Bridge, Rudford, Gloucester GL2 8DX **t** (01452) 790412 **f** (01452) 790145
e info@barbersbridge.co.uk **w** barbersbridge.co.uk

open All year except Christmas and New Year
bedrooms 15 double, 1 twin, 1 family
bathrooms All en suite
payment Credit/debit cards, cash/cheques

Four-hundred-year-old, Grade II Listed buildings with adjacent cottages. In a rural setting, equidistant from Gloucester and Newent. Swimming pool and fitness centre, clay-pigeon shooting every other weekend.

⊕ *From M50 jct 2, south on B4215 towards Gloucester, approx 6 miles.*

Room General Leisure

SANDHURST, Gloucestershire Map ref 2B1 — **SELF CATERING**

★★★★
SELF CATERING

Units 3
Sleeps 2–6
Low season per wk
Min £250.00
High season per wk
Max £550.00

Great Coverden, Sandhurst, Gloucester

contact Mrs Deb Warren, Bengrove Farm, Base Lane, Sandhurst GL2 9NU
t (01452) 730231 **f** (01452) 730895 **e** Debs@bengrovefarm.fsnet.co.uk **w** greatcoverden.com

Located on a farm, these converted barns with oak beams offer a high standard of spacious, well-equipped accommodation. Large gardens with fantastic views, close to many places of interest.

open All year
payment Cash/cheques, euros

Unit
General Leisure Shop 3 miles Pub 3 miles

SLIMBRIDGE, Gloucestershire Map ref 2B1 — **GUEST ACCOMMODATION**

★★★
INN

B&B per room per night
s £50.00–£55.00
d £60.00–£70.00
Evening meal per person
£5.00–£15.00

Tudor Arms

Shepherds Patch, Slimbridge, Gloucester GL2 7BP **t** (01453) 890306 **f** (01453) 890103
e ritatudorarms@aol.com

Free house offering real ales, home-cooked food and modern, purpose-built, en suite accommodation. Close to Slimbridge Wildfowl and Wetland Centre. Families and dogs welcome.

open All year
bedrooms 2 double, 5 twin, 5 family
bathrooms All en suite
payment Credit/debit cards, cash/cheques

Room General Leisure

STOW-ON-THE-WOLD, Gloucestershire Map ref 2B1 — **GUEST ACCOMMODATION**

★★★★
INN

B&B per room per night
s Min £85.00
d £85.00–£110.00
Evening meal per person
£8.95–£35.00

Westcote Inn

Nether Westcote, Chipping Norton OX7 6SD **t** (01993) 830888 **f** (01993) 831657
e info@westcoteinn.co.uk **w** westcoteinn.co.uk

open All year
bedrooms 3 double, 1 family
bathrooms All en suite
payment Credit/debit cards, cash/cheques

Traditional Cotswold inn situated in glorious countryside with views as far as the eye can see, complete with all modern facilities. Westcote serves traditional British food from our fine dining restaurant, or if you are looking for something simpler the Tack Room menu serves fabulous pub grub in front of open fireplaces. Situated between Burford and Stow-on-the-Wold, and three miles from Kingham Station with direct trains from Paddington.

Room General Leisure

For key to symbols open the back-cover flap.

TEWKESBURY, Gloucestershire Map ref 2B1 — **CAMPING & CARAVANNING**

★★★★
TOURING &
CAMPING PARK

(154) £12.10–£24.90
(154) £12.10–£24.90
154 touring pitches

Tewkesbury Abbey Caravan Club Site

Gander Lane, Tewkesbury GL20 5PG **t** (01684) 294035 **w** caravanclub.co.uk

payment Credit/debit cards, cash/cheques

Impressive location next to Tewkesbury Abbey. Only a short walk into the old town of Tewkesbury where there is much to explore. Open March to November.

⊕ From M5 leave by exit 9 onto A438. In about 3 miles in town centre, at cross-junction turn right. After 200yds turn left into Gander Lane. From M50 leave by exit 1 on A38. For details on other routes visit caravanclub.co.uk.

♥ Special member rates mean you can save your membership subscription in less than a week. Visit our website to find out more.

General ⊞ P ⊕ ⊕ ⊕ ⊕ ⊕ ⊙ ⊞ ⊞ ☼   Leisure ⤵ ↾

WINCHCOMBE, Gloucestershire Map ref 2B1 — **SELF CATERING**

★★★★
SELF CATERING

Units   1
Sleeps   2–6

Low season per wk
£250.00–£285.00
High season per wk
£385.00–£475.00

Muir Cottage, Winchcombe, Cheltenham

contact Mark Grassick, Postlip Estate Co, Postlip Stables, Winchcombe, Cheltenham GL54 5AQ
t (01242) 603124 **e** enquiries@thecotswoldretreat.co.uk **w** thecotswoldretreat.co.uk

Attractive, high-quality, Arts and Crafts-inspired, Cotswold-stone cottage converted from 18thC barn. Quietly located on historic country estate adjacent to Cotswold Way. Log fire, satellite TV. The ideal hideaway.

open All year
payment Cash/cheques, euros

Unit ⊞ ⊞ ⊞ ⊞ ⊞ ⊞ ⊞ ⊞ ⊞ ⊞ // ☼
General ⊞ ⊞ ⊞ P ⑤ ↾   Leisure ↾ ⚬ ⚲   Shop 1.5 miles   Pub 1.5 miles

---

WINDRUSH, Gloucestershire Map ref 2B1 — **SELF CATERING**

★★★★
SELF CATERING

Units   1
Sleeps   4

Low season per wk
Max £395.00
High season per wk
Max £495.00

Keeper's Cottage, Windrush

contact Mrs Collette Carmichael, 34 Upper High Street, Thame OX9 2DN
t (01844) 215417 & 07730 456789 **f** (01844) 214407 **e** enquiries@gamekeeperscottage.co.uk
w gamekeeperscottage.co.uk

open All year
payment Cash/cheques

Set in peaceful rolling countryside in an Area of Outstanding Natural Beauty, Keeper's Cottage is a Grade II Listed Cotswold stone cottage dating back to the 19th century. The cottage forms part of the National Trust Sherborne Estate and enjoys stunning views across open meadow and woodland from all windows.

⊕ Turning for Windrush is off main A40 approximately 6 miles after Burford in Cheltenham direction. Directions sent with booking confirmation.

♥ Short breaks available for 3 or 4 nights. Please telephone to check availability.

Unit ⊞ ⊞ ⊞ ⊞ ⊞ ⊞ ⊞ ⊞ ⊞ ⊞ ☼
General ⊞ ⊞ ⊞ ⚥ ⑤   Leisure ∪   Shop 1 mile   Pub 0.5 miles

Quality-assured help

Official Partner Tourist Information Centres offer quality assured help with accommodation as well as suggestions of places to visit and things to do. You'll find contact details at the back of the guide.

Surfers in Torquay, Devon

On the beach at Woolacombe

Lynton cliffs

Explore Devon

Watch white sails scudding about on sun-dappled seas. Take bracing walks along rusty-red cliff tops. Surf on breakers and swim from safe sandy beaches. Hunt for fossils and spot wildlife. Enjoy peace and quiet or activity and excitement. It's up to you.

Southern charms

Begin your exploration with time spent in Exeter. Walk along the historic quayside, a buzzing area of stylish shops, cafes and restaurants; shop in the city's many stores or visit the cool, airy cathedral. Then take a trip way back in time down on Devon's Jurassic Coast. Hunt for fossils as you explore 185 million years' of the earth's history at this World Heritage Site. Wander along cliffs of rusty-red sandstone or potter about on beautiful beaches along the south coast.

Enjoy lazy days in quiet seaside towns such as Sidmouth or Exmouth or choose the lively buzz and activity of Torquay, with top entertainment and superb shopping as well as the sea and the sand. Adopt a penguin or a puffin on a visit to Living Coasts, an amazing world-class aquatic centre, and at nearby Greenaway, where Dame Agatha Christie wrote many of her novels, stroll around the woodland garden with lovely views over the River Dart. Buy freshly caught fish on the harbourside at Brixham or find family fun at Paignton.

Safe sailing

Alternatively set sail from Devon's southern tip and tack through sheltered waters around Dartmouth, Kingsbridge and Salcombe. Beginners can learn the ropes on a sailing course while experienced sailors can hoist their spinnakers and set out to sea from safe havens. If you prefer to keep your feet on dry land, meander through narrow streets, searching for maritime memorabilia or amble around harbours, watching boats beavering in and out. Travel inland to Totnes on a hunt for antiques and a perfect pub lunch.

Start Point Lighthouse, near Kingsbridge, Devon

Bayards Cove

Quaywest Waterpark, Paignton

Kite flying on Dartmoor

Moody moorland

Dartmoor beckons now – a National Park. Explore it on foot or by bike and you'll be rewarded with views of ancient stone clapper bridges, sparkling clear rivers, heather-clad hills and the characteristic craggy outcrops of rock. Discover strange standing stones, burrows and hill forts – proof of prehistoric settlements – or examine the evidence of one-time mining activity for lead, copper and tin. There are woodland walks and wildlife to observe and towns like Chagford and Tavistock for rest and recuperation. Beyond the moors, enjoy the heady scents at Rosemoor, the Royal Horticultural Society's glorious garden at Great Torrington.

Beaches and breakers

See a different side to Devon over on the north coast. Gone are the red cliffs, replaced instead with broad beaches and bigger breakers. Take a board and ride the surf at Croyde and Woolacombe or bring a bucket and spade and build a castle on the soft sands at Ilfracombe. While here, pop into 11 The Quay, Damien Hirst's restaurant, for a spot of local produce.

In complete contrast walk down the incredibly steep cobbled street of Clovelly, lined with pretty cottages, to the harbour below. If you don't fancy the walk back up, there's transport to help you out! Avoid more steep hills by stepping into the cliff railway at Lynmouth down at sea level and clank to the top at Lynton where the views are stunning.

Food & drink

Fancy a bite to eat, a relaxing drink or some fresh local produce? Here's a selection of food and drink venues to get you started. For lots more ideas go online at enjoyengland.com/taste.

Restaurants

Café Paradiso @ Hotel Barcelona
European
Alias Hotel Barcelona, Magdalen Street, Exeter EX2 4HY
t (01392) 281000
w aliashotels.com

Combe House Hotel & Restaurant
Fine dining
Gittisham, Honiton EX14 3AD
t (01404) 540400
w thishotel.com

English House Restaurant & Rooms
English
Teignmouth Road, Maidencombe, Torquay TQ1 4SY
t (01803) 328760
w english-house.co.uk

The Horn of Plenty
Fine dining
Gulworthy, Tavistock PL19 8JD
t (01822) 832528
w thehornofplenty.co.uk

La Petite Maison
English
35 Fore Street, Topsham, Exeter EX3 0HR
t (01392) 873660
w lapetitemaison.co.uk

Michael Caines at ABode Exeter
Fine dining
Cathedral Yard, Exeter EX1 1HD
t (01392) 223638
w michaelcaines.com

Ode
European
21 Fore Street, Shaldon TQ14 0DE
t (01626) 873977
w odetruefood.co.uk

Orchid Restaurant
European
Corbyn Head Hotel, Torbay Road, Torquay TQ2 6RH
t (01803) 296366
w orchidrestaurant.net

Restaurant 42
European
Fore Street, Salcombe TQ8 8JG
t (01548) 843408
w restaurant42.co.uk

Pubs

The Diggers Rest Inn
Woodbury Salterton, Exeter EX5 1PQ
t (01395) 232375
w diggersrest.co.uk

The Grove Inn
Kings Nympton EX37 9ST
t (01769) 580406
w thegroveinn.co.uk

The Jack in the Green Inn
Rockbeare, near Exeter EX5 2EE
t (01404) 822240
w jackinthegreen.uk.com

The Merry Harriers
Forches Corner, Clayhidon EX15 3TR
t (01823) 421270
w merryharriers.co.uk

Victoria Inn
Fore Street, Salcombe TQ8 8BU
t (01548) 842604
w victoriainnsalcombe.co.uk

The White Hart Bar & Dining Room
Dartington Hall, Dartington, Totnes TQ9 6EL
t (01803) 847111
w dartingtonhall.com

Tearooms, coffee shops and cafes

Food Dreckly – Cattle Market Café
Whitchurch Road, Tavistock PL19 9BB
t (01822) 832897
w fooddreckly.com

Fremington Quay Cafe
Bickington, near Barnstaple EX31 2NH
t (01271) 378783
w fremingtonquaycafe.co.uk

Georgian Tea Room
Broadway House, 35 High Street, Topsham, Exeter EX3 0ED
t (01392) 873465
w broadwayhouse.com

The Venus Cafe – Blackpool Sands
Melverley, Ravensbourne Lane, Stoke Fleming, Dartmouth TQ6 0QR
t (01803) 712648
w venuscompany.co.uk

The Venus Cafe
The Warren, Bigbury-on-Sea, near Modbury TQ7 4AZ
t (01548) 810141
w venuscompany.co.uk

Farm shops and local produce

Darts Farm
Topsham, Exeter EX3 0QH
t (01392) 878200
w dartsfarm.co.uk

D J Haggett Butchers Ltd
2 Newcourt Road, Silverton, Exeter EX5 4HA
t (01392) 860226
w djhaggett.co.uk

Lifton Strawberry Fields Farm Shop
Lifton PL16 0DE
t (01566) 784605
w liftonstrawberryfields.co.uk

Pipers Farm
27 Magdalen Road, Exeter EX2 4TA
t (01392) 274504
w pipersfarm.com

Stokeley Farm Shop
Stokeley Barton, Stokenham, Kingsbridge TQ7 2SE
t (01548) 581010
w stokeley.co.uk

where to stay in
Devon

Maps
All place names in the blue bands are shown on the maps at the front of this guide.

Accommodation symbols
Symbols give useful information about services and facilities. Inside the back-cover flap you can find a key to these symbols. Keep it open for easy reference.

ASHBURTON, Devon Map ref 1C2 | SELF CATERING

★★★★
SELF CATERING

Units **2**
Sleeps **2-4**
Low season per wk
Min £210.00
High season per wk
Max £430.00

Wren & Robin Cottages, Newton Abbot

contact Mrs Margaret Phipps, Wren & Robin Cottages, New Cott Farm, Ashburton TQ13 7PD
t (01364) 631421 **f** (01364) 631421 **e** enquiries@newcott-farm.co.uk **w** newcott-farm.co.uk

Enjoy Dartmoor National Park with tors, moors and tiny villages. Stress free, plenty of fresh air. Wren/Robin Cottages are peacefully situated and beautifully furnished. Prices all-inclusive.

open All year
payment Credit/debit cards, cash/cheques

Unit ▦ TV ▯ ▭ ☐ ▯ ◌ ▯ ▯ ✿
General ☌3 P ✄ S Leisure ∪ ♪ Shop 4 miles Pub 1 mile

BARNSTAPLE, Devon Map ref 1C1 | GUEST ACCOMMODATION

★★★★
GUEST ACCOMMODATION

B&B per room per night
s Min £50.00
d Min £90.00
Evening meal per person
Min £24.50

Westcott Barton

Middle Marwood, Barnstaple EX31 4EF **t** (01271) 812842 **e** westcott_barton@yahoo.co.uk
w westcottbarton.co.uk

open All year
bedrooms 5 double, 2 twin
bathrooms 5 en suite
payment Cash/cheques

Historic country estate with fine example of a Saxon farmstead; ornamental gardens, streams, ponds and acres of ancient woodland. Perfect for artists, photographers, birdwatchers and naturalists. Beautiful en suite bedrooms in beamed stone cottages and our longhouse. Locally and organically sourced home-cooked breakfasts. Evening meals available on request.

⊕ *Please contact us or see our website for directions.*

Room ♿ TV ✒ ☖ General ☌10 P ♥ ✗ ▦ ☖ ✿ Leisure ∪ ♪ ▱ ▱

Place index

If you know where you want to stay, the index at the back of the guide will give you the page number listing accommodation in your chosen town, city or village. Check out the other useful indexes too.

For key to symbols open the back-cover flap.

BERRYNARBOR, Devon Map ref 1C1 | SELF CATERING

★★★
SELF CATERING

Units **4**
Sleeps **2–7**

Low season per wk
£95.00–£301.00
High season per wk
£320.00–£894.00

Smythen Farm Coastal Holiday Cottages, Ilfracombe

contact Mr & Ms Thompson & Elstone, Smythen Farm Coastal Holiday Cottages, Symthen, Sterridge Valley, Berrynarbor, Ilfracombe EX34 9TB
t (01271) 882875 f (01271) 882875 e jayne@smythenfarmholidaycottages.co.uk
w smythenfarmholidaycottages.co.uk

payment Cash/cheques

Near golden sands with sea and coastal views. Heated, covered swimming pool in a suntrap enclosure, gardens and games room with pool table, table tennis, football machine. Tree-house on two levels. Free pony rides, ball pond and bouncy castle, 14-acre recreation field and dog walk. For colour brochure phone Jayne. Open March to January.

⊕ A361 to Barnstaple then A39 for 1 mile towards Lynton. Left onto B3230, through Muddiford and Milltown. Right by garage onto A3123, next left to Sterridge Valley.

Unit 🏠 📺 📱 🔲 🔄 🔳 🍴 🔥 🧺 🔌 ✳
General 🛏 🖼 🏃 P 🖸 🆂 🐕 Leisure 🎣 🏹 ● ∪ ♪ 🚲 🏊 Shop 1.5 miles Pub 1.5 miles

BIDEFORD, Devon Map ref 1C1 | SELF CATERING

★★★
SELF CATERING

Units **1**
Sleeps **2**

Low season per wk
£150.00–£200.00
High season per wk
£200.00–£275.00

Coachmans Cottage, Monkleigh, Bideford

contact Mr & Mrs Tom & Sue Downie, Cream Tea Cottages, Staddon House, Monkleigh, Bideford EX39 5JR
t (01805) 623670 f (01805) 624549 e tom.downie@ukonline.co.uk w creamteacottages.co.uk

Charming character cottage set in traditional courtyard surroundings. Our price includes all linen, logs for the wood-burner and a cream tea to help you settle in after your journey.

open All year
payment Credit/debit cards, cash/cheques

Unit 📺 📱 🔲 🔥 🧺 🔌 🔌 🔳 🔌 ✳
General 🛏 🖼 🏃 P 🖸 🆂 🐕 Leisure 🚲 🏊 Shop < 0.5 miles Pub < 0.5 miles

BIGBURY-ON-SEA, Devon Map ref 1C3 | SELF CATERING

★★★★★
SELF CATERING

Units **1**
Sleeps **1–4**

Low season per wk
£450.00–£1,024.00
High season per wk
£1,148.00–£1,580.00

Apartment 5, Burgh Island Causeway, Bigbury-on-Sea

Helpful Holidays, Mill Street, Chagford, Newton Abbot TQ13 8AW
t (01647) 433593 f (01647) 433694 e help@helpfulholidays.com w helpfulholidays.com

open All year
payment Credit/debit cards, cash/cheques

Luxury, modern, ground-floor apartment set into cliff with panoramic southerly views from large patio. Facilities include pool, gym, sauna, cafe/bar, grassy cliff-top grounds and direct access to beautiful large sandy beach and coastal path. Popular for surfing and near golf course and village shop/post office. View www.burghislandcauseway.com

⊕ From A38 at Ivybridge, take the 'B' road to Modbury then the A379 towards Kingsbridge. Very soon leave on B3392 for Bigbury-on-Sea.

♥ Bargain weekend and short-stay breaks available in autumn and winter months.

Unit 🏠 📺 📱 🔲 🔄 📷 🔲 🔥 🧺 🔌 🔌 🔳 🔌 ✳
General 🛏 🖼 🏃 P 🆂 🐕 Leisure 🎣 ♪ 🏃 Shop < 0.5 miles Pub < 0.5 miles

It's all quality-assessed accommodation

Our commitment to quality involves wide-ranging accommodation assessment. Rating and awards were correct at the time of going to press but may change following a new assessment. Please check at time of booking.

BOVEY TRACEY, Devon Map ref 1D2 — GUEST ACCOMMODATION

★★★★★
**BED & BREAKFAST
GOLD AWARD**

Brookfield House

Challabrook Lane, Bovey Tracey TQ13 9DF t (01626) 836181 e enquiries@brookfield-house.com
w brookfield-house.com

B&B per room per night
s £47.00–£53.00
d £64.00–£76.00

bedrooms 2 double, 1 twin
bathrooms 2 en suite, 1 private
payment Credit/debit cards, cash/cheques

Spacious, early-Edwardian residence situated on the edge of Bovey Tracey and Dartmoor and set in two acres with panoramic moor views. Secluded tranquillity yet within easy walking distance of town. Individually decorated bedrooms, all with comfortable seating areas. Gourmet breakfasts, including home-made breads and preserves. Open February to November.

⊕ From A38 take A382 towards Bovey Tracey. At 1st roundabout, left into Pottery Road. At T-junction, right into Brimley Road, then left into Challabrook Lane. We are on the right.

♥ Special rates on application for stays of 4 or more nights.

Room TV 🌢 🍵 General 🕭12 P⚡✳ Leisure ∪ ♩ ♭ 🏊

BRATTON CLOVELLY, Devon Map ref 1C2 — CAMPING & CARAVANNING

★★★★
**HOLIDAY, TOURING
& CAMPING PARK**

South Breazle Holidays

Okehampton EX20 4JS t (01837) 871752 e louise@southbreazleholidays.co.uk
w southbreazleholidays.co.uk

🚐(5)   £11.50–£18.00
🚐(20)   £11.50–£18.00
▲ (20)   £11.50–£18.00
25 touring pitches

payment Credit/debit cards, cash/cheques

This peaceful family-owned site with 25 super-sized pitches is set within a 100-acre organic farm, close to Dartmoor and two miles from Roadford Lake. Well-appointed shower block with power showers, on-site shop. Wi-Fi. An ideal place to unwind, and explore the local area. Open 1 March to 31 October.

⊕ Exit A30 at Stowford Cross. Follow signs for Roadford Lake. After 1 mile turn right, then 2nd left (staggered crossroads). 1st farm lane on right.

♥ Get 10% discount when you book 15 nights or more in low or mid-season.

General 🏕P🔌 ♀🖵🌧⊙🔲🔌☼ Leisure ⚠ ♩

BRIXHAM, Devon Map ref 1D2 — HOTEL

★★★
HOTEL

The Berry Head Hotel

Berry Head, Brixham TQ5 9AJ t (01803) 853225 f (01803) 882084 e stay@berryheadhotel.com
w berryheadhotel.com

B&B per room per night
s £48.00–£78.00
d £96.00–£168.00
HB per person per night
£58.00–£94.00

open All year
bedrooms 12 double, 10 twin, 3 single, 7 family
bathrooms All en suite
payment Credit/debit cards, cash/cheques, euros

Steeped in history, nestling on water's edge in acres of outstanding natural beauty. Traditional hospitality, excellent, friendly and personal service with attention to detail. Comfortable accommodation, thoughtfully equipped. Imaginative menus, varied dining options, featuring quality local produce and fresh fish. Lounge, bars and terrace, equally popular with locals and residents.

⊕ Enter Brixham, continue to harbour and around up King Street for 1 mile to Berry Head.

♥ Special-event packages. Extensive range of conference and business facilities. Weddings and special occasions. Christmas and New Year celebrations.

Room 🛏 ☎ TV 🌢 🍵 🔥 General 🕭🚿♿P🍽🕒🅜⊙🔲☕✳🚪🐕 Leisure 🎣♫∪♩♭🚲🏊

For key to symbols open the back-cover flap.

BRIXHAM, Devon Map ref 1D2   SELF CATERING

★★★
SELF CATERING

Units   **7**
Sleeps   **1–4**
Low season per wk
£120.00–£210.00
High season per wk
£250.00–£480.00

Brixham Harbourside Holiday Flats, Brixham

contact Mrs Helgard Stone, 13 Cambridge Road, Brixham TQ5 8JW
t (01803) 851919   **e** david.f.stone@btinternet.com   **w** brixham-harbourside-holiday-flats.com

open All year
payment Cash/cheques

Four one-bedroom, and three two-bedroom, self-contained flats. Clean, well-furnished and comfortable. Sea and harbour views of fishing boats, yachts and pleasure craft. Hot water, central heating, electricity, all bed linen, towels and parking are inclusive. We do our best to make your stay a pleasant one.

⊕ *Last property on the left of Brixham harbour.*

♥ *Short breaks available Nov-Feb.*

Unit 🛏️ 📺 📻 ⚙️ 🔥 🍴 🧺
General 🌳 🏠 ♿ 🐾   Leisure ✦   Shop < 0.5 miles   Pub < 0.5 miles

BRIXHAM, Devon Map ref 1D2   SELF CATERING

★★★
SELF CATERING

Units   **2**
Sleeps   **1–4**
Low season per wk
Min £225.00
High season per wk
Max £515.00

Galmpton Touring Park Cottages, Brixham

contact Mrs Pam Collins, Galmpton Touring Park Cottages, Greenway Road, Brixham TQ5 0EP
t (01803) 842066   **e** galmptontouringpark@hotmail.com   **w** gtpcottages.co.uk

Two comfortable cottages in beautiful countryside on edge of village near Brixham. A quiet base from which to explore South Devon. Beaches and attractions nearby – lovely walks from your doorstep.

open All year
payment Credit/debit cards, cash/cheques

Unit 📺 🍴 📻 ⚙️ ✳️
General 🌳 🏠 ♿ P ♿ 📻 Ⓢ   Leisure ✦   Shop 0.5 miles   Pub 0.5 miles

BRIXHAM, Devon Map ref 1D2   CAMPING & CARAVANNING

★★★★★
TOURING &
CAMPING PARK

🚐 (239) £14.30–£32.00
🚙 (239) £14.30–£32.00
239 touring pitches

Hillhead Holiday Park Caravan Club Site

Hillhead, Brixham TQ5 0HH   **t** (01803) 853204   **w** caravanclub.co.uk

payment Credit/debit cards, cash/cheques

In a great location, with many pitches affording stunning sea views. Swimming pool, evening entertainment, bar, restaurant and much more! Open March to January 2009.

⊕ *Right off A380 (Newton Abbot). Three miles onto ring road (Brixham). Seven miles turn right, A3022. In 0.75 miles, right onto A379. Two miles keep left onto B3025. Site entrance on left.*

♥ *Special member rates mean you can save your membership subscription in less than a week. Visit our website to find out more.*

CARAVAN CLUB

General P 🔌 🚻 🍴 🚐 📶 ☺ 📷 📦 🛁 ✗ 🐾 ☼   Leisure ⚡ 📺 🍴 🎵 ❀ 🎱 U

A breath of fresh air

Love the great outdoors? Britain's Camping, Caravan & Holiday Parks 2008 is packed with information on quality sites in some spectacular locations. You can purchase the guide from good bookshops and online at visitbritaindirect.com.

COMBE MARTIN, Devon Map ref 1C1 — SELF CATERING

★★★★
SELF CATERING

Units **5**
Sleeps **2–9**
Low season per wk
£310.00–£660.00
High season per wk
£530.00–£2,200.00

Coulscott House, Combe Martin, Ilfracombe

contact Dr Sue Jay, Coulscott House, Nutcombe Hill, Combe Martin, Ilfracombe EX34 0PQ
t (01271) 883339 **e** stay@coulscott.co.uk **w** coulscott.co.uk

open All year
payment Cash/cheques

Just five properties set in private valley with streams, meadows, woods. Sleeping two to nine. Indoor heated pool. Close to Exmoor, coastal footpaths, massive surfing beaches, hidden coves, pubs, restaurants. Immaculate, well behaved dogs welcome in selected cottages. Hot tub. Wood-burning stoves. History, nature, beauty, fun, activity, relaxation.

⊕ *One mile out of Combe Martin. Fringes of Exmoor. Nutcombe Hill. Close to sea. 45 minutes from M5 Tiverton.*

♥ *Short breaks out of season. Three nights minimum. Last-minute bargains – phone to enquire.*

Unit 🔲 📺 🔲 🔲 🔳 🔳 🔳 🔳 🔳 🔳 🔳 ✻
General 🛏 🏠 ♿ P 🔥 🔲 Ⓢ 🐾 Leisure 🏊 ∪ ♪ 🏌 🚴 ⛵ Shop 1 mile Pub 1 mile

CULLOMPTON, Devon Map ref 1D2 — GUEST ACCOMMODATION

★★★★
FARMHOUSE

B&B per room per night
s £28.00–£30.00
d £56.00–£60.00

Langford Court North

Langford, Cullompton EX15 1SQ **t** (01884) 277234 **f** (01884) 277234 **e** tchattey@yahoo.co.uk

Beautiful thatched medieval farmhouse with large tastefully furnished rooms. Good home cooking also excellent country pubs nearby. Central for touring and walking in Devon.

open All year except Christmas and New Year
bedrooms 1 double, 1 family
bathrooms 1 en suite, 1 private
payment Cash/cheques

Room 🛏 📺 ♿ 🔳 General 🛏 P 🔥 🔳 ✻ Leisure ♪ 🏌

DARTMEET, Devon Map ref 1C2 — SELF CATERING

★★★
SELF CATERING

Units **1**
Sleeps **2**
Low season per wk
£230.00–£290.00
High season per wk
£315.00–£440.00

Coachman's Cottage, Dartmeet

contact Mrs Toni Evans, Hunter's Lodge, Dartmeet, Princetown PL20 6SG
t (01364) 631173 **e** huntlodge@pobox.com **w** dartmeet.com

open All year
payment Credit/debit cards, cash/cheques, euros

Granite cottage at the meeting of the East and West Darts in the heart of Dartmoor National Park. Fully equipped kitchen/dining room. Large, comfortable lounge and spacious double/twin bedroom. Breathtaking view of the Dart Valley and surrounding tors from bedroom and patio. Immediate access to riverbank, woodland and open moorland.

⊕ *From Pear Tree exit at Ashburton, B3357 towards Two Bridges for 7 miles. Hunter's Lodge is 1st building on right after bridge in Dartmeet.*

♥ *Short breaks available in low season.*

Unit 🔲 📺 🔲 🔳 🔳 🔳 ✻
General 🛏 ♿ P 🔥 🔲 Ⓢ 🐾 Leisure ∪ ♪ 🚴 ⛵ Shop 4 miles Pub 1 mile

DARTMOOR

See under Ashburton, Bovey Tracey, Dartmeet, Moretonhampstead, Okehampton, Tavistock, Yelverton

Quality-assured help

Official Partner Tourist Information Centres offer quality assured help with accommodation as well as suggestions of places to visit and things to do. You'll find contact details at the back of the guide.

For key to symbols open the back-cover flap.

DARTMOUTH, Devon Map ref 1D3 — HOTEL

★★★
HOTEL
SILVER AWARD

Royal Castle Hotel

11 The Quay, Dartmouth TQ6 9PS **t** (01803) 833033 **f** (01803) 835445 **e** enquiry@royalcastle.co.uk
w royalcastle.co.uk

B&B per room per night
s £90.00–£105.00
d £130.00–£219.00

Historic 17thC quayside coaching inn set in the heart of Dartmouth. Two busy bars, a restaurant overlooking the river and 25 luxurious bedrooms.

open All year
bedrooms 14 double, 6 twin, 2 single, 3 family
bathrooms All en suite
payment Credit/debit cards, cash/cheques

Room 📺 ℡ 📺 ♨ ♨   General ℡ ⊞ ♯ ♣ P 🍴 ⊞ 🄼 ◑ ⚏ ☕ ♞   Leisure ∪ ↾ 🚲

DARTMOUTH, Devon Map ref 1D3 — HOTEL

★★★
HOTEL

Stoke Lodge Hotel

Cinders Lane, Stoke Fleming, Dartmouth TQ6 0RA **t** (01803) 770523 **f** (01803) 770851
e mail@stokelodge.co.uk **w** stokelodge.co.uk

B&B per room per night
s £63.00–£70.00
d £91.00–£120.00
HB per person per night
£63.50–£89.00

open All year
bedrooms 9 double, 9 twin, 2 single, 5 family
bathrooms All en suite
payment Credit/debit cards, cash/cheques

Family-run, country-house hotel set in three acres of attractive gardens with sea and village views. En suite bedrooms, indoor and outdoor swimming pools, sauna, jacuzzi, tennis court and full-size snooker table. Reduced green fees at Dartmouth Golf Club. Excellent food and fine wines. Open all year. Ample parking.

⊕ *From Dartmouth take the A379 to Stoke Fleming for about a mile. In the centre of the village turn right into Cinders Lane.*

♥ *Bargain breaks and special offers – please phone for details.*

Room 🛏 📺 ℡ 📺 ♨ ♨   General ℡ ⊞ ♯ ♣ P 🍴 ⊞ 🄼 🍴 ♯ ♞   Leisure ⚓ ⚓ ⚓ ● ⚬ ∪ ↾ ↾ 🏊

DARTMOUTH, Devon Map ref 1D3 — GUEST ACCOMMODATION

★★★★
BED & BREAKFAST

Lower Collaton Farm

Blackawton, Dartmouth TQ9 7DW **t** (01803) 712260 **e** mussen@lower-collaton-farm.co.uk
w lower-collaton-farm.co.uk

B&B per room per night
s £35.00–£45.00
d £60.00–£70.00

open All year except Christmas and New Year
bedrooms 2 double, 1 twin
bathrooms All en suite
payment Credit/debit cards, cash/cheques

Three delightful en suite bedrooms in traditional, comfortable, Devonshire farmhouse overlooking peaceful valley with views over rolling countryside. Six miles from Dartmouth and beaches. Friendly pedigree Shetland sheep, hens and ducks. Price includes delicious breakfast with finest local produce. Two self-catering cottages for four and two also available.

⊕ *Totnes A381 signed Dartmouth. Halwell A3207 signed Dartmouth. After 1 mile turn right, signed 'Collaton, no through traffic.' Farm is 350yds on left behind wooden gate.*

Room 🛏 📺 ♨ ♨   General ℡ ⊞ ♯ P ♨ ⊞ 🄼 ♯   Leisure 🏊

CYCLISTS WELCOME   WELCOME CYCLISTS

A holiday on two wheels

For a fabulous freewheeling break, seek out accommodation participating in our Cyclists Welcome scheme. Look out for the symbol and plan your route online at nationalcyclenetwork.org.

DARTMOUTH, Devon Map ref 1D3 — GUEST ACCOMMODATION

★ ★ ★ ★
**GUEST HOUSE
SILVER AWARD**

B&B per room per night
s £55.00–£75.00
d £65.00–£85.00

Strete Barton House

Totnes Road, Strete, Dartmouth TQ6 0RN t (01803) 770364 f (01803) 771182
e info@stretebarton.co.uk w stretebarton.co.uk

open All year
bedrooms 3 double, 2 twin, 1 family
bathrooms 4 en suite, 2 private
payment Credit/debit cards, cash/cheques

16thC manor house with stunning sea views. Exquisitely furnished bedrooms with either en suite or private facilities. All rooms have TV/DVD, Wi-Fi Internet, hairdryer, radio-alarm and extensive beverage tray. Full English or continental breakfast using local produce. Use of residents' lounge. Close to two beautiful beaches.

⊕ *A381 from Totnes to Kingsbridge. At Halwell, turn left (A3122) to Dartmouth. After Dartmouth Golf Club turn right to Strete. Strete Barton is near the church.*

Room 🖥 📺 👜 ♨ General ⟳3 P ⤬ 🎱 🍴 🐾 ✿ 🐕 Leisure ⤳ ⏻ 🏖

DARTMOUTH, Devon Map ref 1D3 — GUEST ACCOMMODATION

★ ★ ★ ★
BED & BREAKFAST

B&B per room per night
s £60.00–£65.00
d £60.00–£90.00

Valley House

46 Victoria Road, Dartmouth TQ6 9DZ t (01803) 834045 e enquiries@valleyhousedartmouth.com
w valleyhousedartmouth.com

open All year except Christmas
bedrooms 2 double, 1 twin
bathrooms All en suite
payment Cash/cheques

Receive a warm welcome to Dartmouth from Angela and Martin Cairns-Sharp. Central location, five minutes' walk to River Dart and town centre. Off-road (on-site) parking – a particular advantage in Dartmouth. Well-equipped rooms, lovely breakfasts served in dining room. Britain in Bloom prize winner 2005 and 2006.

⊕ *From the end of the M5 at Exeter take A38 (signposted to Plymouth). Leave A38 at Buckfastleigh and follow A384 left to Dartmouth (via Totnes).*

♥ *Discounts for stays of 4 days or more.*

Room 📺 👜 ♨ General ⟳12 P ⤬ Leisure U ⤳ ⏻ 🏖

DARTMOUTH, Devon Map ref 1D3 — SELF CATERING

★ ★ ★
SELF CATERING

Units **4**
Sleeps **2–6**

Low season per wk
£255.00–£385.00
High season per wk
£395.00–£685.00

The Old Bakehouse, Dartmouth

contact Mrs Sylvia Ridalls, The Old Bakehouse, 7 Broadstone, Dartmouth TQ6 9NR
t (01803) 834585 f (01803) 834585 e gparker@pioneerps.co.uk w oldbakehousedartmouth.co.uk

Three character cottages, with beams and old stone fireplaces. In a conservation area, two minutes from historic town centre and river. Free parking. Beach 15 minutes' drive. Dogs free. Non-smoking.

open All year
payment Credit/debit cards, cash/cheques

Unit 🏠 📺 🍳 📺. 📻 🍽
General ⟳ 🎱 🍴 ⤬ S 🐕 Leisure ⤳ Shop < 0.5 miles Pub < 0.5 miles

enjoy**England**.com

Big city buzz or peaceful panoramas? Take a fresh look at England and you may be surprised at what's right on your doorstep. Explore the diversity online at enjoyengland.com

For key to symbols open the back-cover flap.

★★★★
SELF CATERING

Units　　**5**
Sleeps　**4–6**
Low season per wk
£295.00–£335.00
High season per wk
£705.00–£765.00

Cofton Country Cottage Holidays, Dawlish

contact Mrs Valerie Jeffery, Cofton Country Cottage Holidays, Cofton, Starcross, Exeter EX6 8RP
t (01626) 890111　**f** (01626) 891572　**e** info@coftonholidays.co.uk　**w** coftonholidays.co.uk

open All year
payment Credit/debit cards, cash/cheques

On the edge of privately owned Cofton Country
Holiday Park, converted 100-year-old farm buildings
overlooked by ancient Cofton church. Coarse-fishing
lakes. Woodland walks. Within a short drive of the
Exe Estuary and Dawlish Warren. All amenities of the
park available during season, including swimming
pool and pub.

⊕ From M5 jct 30 take A379 for Dawlish; 3 miles Exeter side
of Dawlish.

♥ Short breaks early and late season. 3- or 4-night breaks at
most times. Free coarse fishing Nov-Mar.

Unit ▦ ⊡ ⬚ ⊟ ▣ ▤ ⬚ ⬚ ◫ ✿
General ⬚ ⊞ ⚲ P ⅄ ◫ ⓢ　Leisure ⬚ ⤴　Shop < 0.5 miles　Pub < 0.5 miles

★★★★★
SELF CATERING

Units　　**1**
Sleeps　**4**
Low season per wk
£450.00–£550.00
High season per wk
£650.00–£850.00

Great Cliff Luxury Apartment, Dawlish

contact Mr Roger Smith, 7 Lavington View, Bridgnorth WV15 6BJ
t (01746) 769301　**f** (01746) 769302　**e** rsmith@greatcliff.co.uk　**w** greatcliff.co.uk

Great Cliff is an attractive two-bedroom luxury
self-catering apartment located on the seafront,
Dawlish, with spectacular views.

open All year
payment Cash/cheques

Unit ▦ ⊡ ⊟ ▣ ▤ ⬚ ⬚ ⬚ ◫
General ⬚ P ⅄ ⓢ　Leisure ⤴　Shop < 0.5 miles　Pub < 0.5 miles

★★★★
HOLIDAY, TOURING
& CAMPING PARK
ROSE AWARD

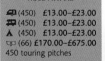
(450)　£13.00–£23.00
(450)　£13.00–£23.00
(450)　£13.00–£23.00
(66)　£170.00–£675.00
450 touring pitches

Cofton Country Holidays

Cofton, Starcross, Exeter EX6 8RP　**t** (01626) 890111　**f** (01626) 891572　**e** info@coftonholidays.co.uk
w coftonholidays.co.uk

payment Credit/debit cards, cash/cheques

A glorious corner of Devon. Family-run holiday park
in 30 acres of delightful parkland. Some of the finest
pitches in South Devon. Heated outdoor swimming
pools. Fun-packed visitor attractions to suit all. David
Bellamy Gold Conservation Award. Two minutes
from Blue Flag beach. Open April to October.

⊕ A379 Exeter to Dawlish road, 3 miles Exeter side of
Dawlish.

♥ £2 off standard pitch per night, low and mid season. Senior
Citizens save an extra £1 each per night (advance
bookings, minimum 3 nights' stay).

General ▣ ▣ P ⬚ ⬚ ⬚ ⬚ ⊙ ⬚ ⬚ ⬚ ✕ ☼　Leisure ⬚ ▮ ⬚ ⬚ ⤴

Take a break

Look out for special promotions and themed breaks. This could be your chance to
indulge an interest, find a new one, or just relax and enjoy exceptional value. Offers
(highlighted in colour) are subject to availability.

DAWLISH, Devon Map ref 1D2 — **CAMPING & CARAVANNING**

Great value family holidays on the glorious South Devon Coast

Your holiday may not be for ever...

Super 4 pool heated water leisure complex

Cruisers Club - Stylish Bar and Show Lounge

Childrens entertainment programme

Close to sandy award-winning beach at Dawlish Warren

Ideal base for exploring the coast and countryside

Holiday Home Ownership www.welcomeholidayhomes.co.uk

...but the memories will be!!!

Tel: 01626 862070

Self-catering, caravans, bungalows and luxury Spanish-style holiday homes

Welcome Family Holiday Park • Dawlish Warren • Sunny South Devon • EX7 0PH - Request a free colour brochure
www.welcomefamily.co.uk • Email: fun@welcomefamily.co.uk

DAWLISH WARREN, Devon Map ref 1D2 — **SELF CATERING**

★★★★
SELF CATERING

Units **5**
Sleeps **4–6**
Low season per wk
£295.00–£349.00
High season per wk
£705.00–£799.00

Eastdon House, Dawlish Warren

contact Mrs Valerie Jeffery, Cofton Country Holidays, Cofton, Starcross, Exeter EX6 8RP
t (01626) 890111 **f** (01626) 891572 **e** info@coftonholidays.co.uk **w** coftonholidays.co.uk

open All year
payment Credit/debit cards, cash/cheques

Magnificent 18thC house converted into luxury apartments. Woodside Cottages – estate workers' cottage conversions. Exe Estuary views, surrounded by fields and 50 acres of unspoilt woodlands. Quiet and restful holidays in a perfect setting. Amenities at Cofton during season.

⊕ From M5 jct 30, take A379 towards Dawlish. Location is 3 miles from the Exeter side of Dawlish.

♥ Short breaks early and late season. 3- or 4-night breaks at most times. Free coarse fishing Nov-Mar.

Unit ▦ ⊡ ⊡ ⊟ ⊡ ⊟ ⊡ ⊡ ⊡ ✿
General ⚞ ▥ ⚲ P ⚡ S Leisure ♪ Shop 0.5 miles Pub 1 mile

Check the maps

Colour maps at the front pinpoint all the cities, towns and villages where you will find accommodation entries in the regional sections. Pick your location and then refer to the place index at the back to find the page number.

For key to symbols open the back-cover flap.

EAST BUDLEIGH, Devon Map ref 1D2   **SELF CATERING**

★★★★
SELF CATERING

Units **1**
Sleeps **6−8**

Low season per wk
£330.00−£435.00
High season per wk
£535.00−£875.00

Brook Cottage, Budleigh Salterton

contact Mrs Jo Simons, Foxcote, Noverton Lane, Prestbury, Cheltenham GL52 5BB
t (01242) 574031   e josimons@tesco.net   w brookcottagebudleigh.co.uk

open All year
payment Cash/cheques

Spacious thatched cottage. Two showers and bathroom. Beaches, walking, golf, karting, bird-watching, riding nearby – but the cottage is so comfortable it's a pleasure to be indoors. Two living rooms with TVs, one for the adults, and a snug, with sofa bed, for the children! Visit our website for more photos.

⊕ From A376 take B3179 signed for Woodbury and Budleigh Salterton; proceed through Woodbury and Yettington; right after Bicton gates and again on entering East Budleigh.

♥ Reduced-rate winter breaks for 3-night stays with or without linen (excl Christmas and New Year).

Unit ▥ 📺 ▯▯▯▯▯▯▯▯▯▯▯
General ♿ ▥ ☂ P ⚡ ▥ 🐕   Leisure ∪ ♪ ► 🚿   Shop 2 miles   Pub < 0.5 miles

---

EXETER, Devon Map ref 1D2   **GUEST ACCOMMODATION**

★★★★★
RESTAURANT WITH ROOMS
GOLD AWARD

B&B per room per night
s £87.50−£100.00
d £125.00−£300.00

The Galley 'Fish and Seafood' Restaurant & Spa with Cabins

41 Fore Street, Topsham, Exeter EX3 0HU   t (01392) 876078   e fish@galleyrestaurant.co.uk
w galleyrestaurant.co.uk

open All year except Christmas and New Year
bedrooms 2 double, 1 twin, 1 suite
bathrooms 4 private
payment Credit/debit cards, cash/cheques

What dreams are made of: our accommodation weaves a different kind of magic in Topsham. Discover our nautical cabins, available with panoramic river views. Master Chef of Britain: Paul Da-Costa-Greaves who also happens to be a spiritual healer and alternative therapist. Jacuzzi/spa/hot tub by prior arrangement.

⊕ M5 jct 30, follow signs to Topsham. The Galley Restaurant with Cabins is near the quay.

Room ☎ 📺 ♿ 🍴   General ♿ 12 P ⚡ ▥ ▯ X ▥ ▥ ▯ ✿   Leisure ↻ ∪ ►

EXETER, Devon Map ref 1D2   **GUEST ACCOMMODATION**

★★
INN

B&B per room per night
s £40.00−£50.00
d £65.00−£80.00
Evening meal per person
£10.00−£20.00

Thorverton Arms

Thorverton, Exeter EX5 5NS   t (01392) 860205   e info@thethorvertonarms.co.uk
w thethorvertonarms.co.uk

open All year
bedrooms 3 double, 1 twin, 1 single, 1 family
bathrooms All en suite
payment Credit/debit cards, cash/cheques

Traditional English country inn set in the heart of the beautiful village of Thorverton. Situated in the Exe Valley, yet only seven miles from Exeter. Comfortable en suite rooms, bar, award-winning restaurant, large south facing garden and car park. Ideal touring base for Exmoor, Dartmoor and the Devon coasts.

⊕ Just off the A396, seven miles north of Exeter. 11 miles from jct 27 of the M5. Eight miles from Exeter Airport.

♥ DB&B – £50 per person (min 2 people).

Room 📺 ♿ 🍴   General ♿ ☂ P ⚡ ▥ X ▥ ▥ ✿ 🐕   Leisure ∪ ♪ 🚿

★★★★
SELF CATERING

Units   **7**
Sleeps   **6–7**

Low season per wk
£280.00–£480.00
High season per wk
£400.00–£875.00

Bussells Farm Cottages, Exeter

contact Andy and Lucy Hines, Bussells Farm, Huxham, Nr Stoke Canon, Exeter EX5 4EN
t (01392) 841238   **f** (01392) 841345   **e** bussellsfarm@aol.com   **w** bussellsfarm.co.uk

open All year
payment Credit/debit cards, cash/cheques

Lovely barn-conversion cottages, heated outdoor swimming pool from May to September, adventure playground, well-equipped games room and excellent coarse fishing in the private lakes. We offer a wonderful base from which to explore the beautiful Exe Valley, Dartmoor, the South Devon beaches and the ancient city of Exeter.

⊕ *At Stoke Canon, take road next to church signposted Huxham and Poltimore; just after Barton Cross Hotel (0.5 miles) turn left. Bussells Farm is 0.5 miles on left.*

♥ *3-night stays available. Low season discounts for 1 or 2 people. Pets welcome.*

Unit ▥ 📺 ▣ 🗄 📶 🍳 🔌 ❄
General 🛏 🏵 ⚷ P ✂ ⊙ S 🐾   Leisure ≈ 🎣 U ⚓ 🚲 🏞   Shop 1 mile   Pub 1 mile

---

★★★★
SELF CATERING

Units   **1**
Sleeps   **6**

Low season per wk
£380.00–£500.00
High season per wk
£500.00–£825.00

Chandler Cottage, Starcross, Exeter

contact Mrs Jewel Goss, Mountbatton, 2 Royal Way, Starcross, Exeter EX6 8EQ
t (01626) 891390 & 07984 005174   **e** regenthouse@eclipse.co.uk
w cottageguide.co.uk/chandlercottage

Luxury self-catering holiday cottage. Two bathrooms, third toilet with washbasin. Utility room with washing machine and dryer. Free parking. Bring your food and clothing only. Come and relax.

open All year
payment Credit/debit cards, cash/cheques, euros

Unit ▥ 📺 🔲 🗄 ▣ 🗄 📶 🍳 🔌 🔌 ❄
General 🛏 🏵 ⚷ P ✂ ⊙ S   Leisure U ⚓ ⚓ 🚲 🏞   Shop < 0.5 miles   Pub < 0.5 miles

---

★★★★★
SELF CATERING

Units   **1**
Sleeps   **4**

Low season per wk
£200.00–£380.00
High season per wk
£410.00–£520.00

Coach House Farm, Exeter

contact Mr & Miss John & Polly Bale, Coach House Farm, Exeter EX5 3JH
t (01392) 461254   **f** (01392) 460931   **e** selfcatering@mpprops.co.uk

open All year
payment Credit/debit cards, cash/cheques, euros

Surrounded by the National Trust Killerton estate, the converted stables of our Victorian coach house provide comfortable ground-floor accommodation (no steps) with private entrance and garden overlooking sheep meadows. Working arable and sheep farm. Spectacular East Devon coastline, Exmoor, Dartmoor and Exeter are easily reached. Good access from M5/A30.

⊕ *Information on the location will be given on confirmation of the booking.*

Unit ▥ 📺 🔲 🗄 ▣ 🗄 📶 🍳 🔌 🔌 ❄
General 🛏 🏵 ⚷ P ✂ 🐾   Shop 1 mile   Pub 1 mile

EXMOOR

See under Combe Martin, Lynton

To your credit

If you book by phone you may be asked for your credit card number. If so, it is advisable to check the proprietor's policy in case you have to cancel your reservation at a later date.

EXMOUTH, Devon Map ref 1D2   **SELF CATERING**

★★★★
SELF CATERING

Units **2**
Sleeps **1–5**
Low season per wk
Min £250.00
High season per wk
Max £570.00

2 & 4 Channel View, Exmouth

contact Mr & Mrs Cliff & Sandra Lenn, C & S Lenn, Channel View, Esplanade, Exmouth EX8 2AZ
t (01395) 222555 e holiday@channelview.eu w channelview.eu

Comfortable, spacious, seafront apartments offering stunning sea, coastal and Exe estuary views and overlooking Exmouth's glorious sandy beach and Beach Gardens. Easy walking distance of Exmouth town centre.

open All year
payment Cash/cheques

Unit ▥ TV 🍳 🖸 🖃 🔥 🖭 ▫ ▱ ❄
General ざ P ⊁   Shop < 0.5 miles   Pub < 0.5 miles

HEMYOCK, Devon Map ref 1D2   **GUEST ACCOMMODATION**

★★★★
FARMHOUSE

B&B per room per night
d £60.00

Pounds Farm

Hemyock EX15 3QS   t (01823) 680802   e shillingscottage@yahoo.co.uk   w poundsfarm.co.uk

open All year
bedrooms 1 double
bathrooms En suite
payment Cash/cheques

Stone farmhouse set in large gardens. Relax beside the outdoor heated pool or next to a log fire. Gorgeous bedroom, en suite with walk-in shower. Extensive views over the Culm Valley Area of Outstanding Natural Beauty. Delicious farmhouse breakfasts with free-range eggs and home-made marmalade. Half a mile to village pub. Within easy reach of M5/A303.

⊕ *M5 jct 26, A38 to Cullompton (signpost Hemyock on left). Follow through village. After sharp right bend 1st left before ornate pump. 0.5 miles on right.*

♥ *Discounts on stays of 2 or more days. Telephone or see website for details.*

Room TV 🍳 🖳   General ざ P ⊁ 🍴 ℳ ❄   Leisure ⳺ U 🚴 🛥

HOLSWORTHY, Devon Map ref 1C2   **SELF CATERING**

★★★★
SELF CATERING

Units **1**
Sleeps **4**
Low season per wk
£400.00–£500.00
High season per wk
£500.00–£575.00

The Barn at Southcombe Farm, Holsworthy

contact Mrs Eileen Clark, Southcombe Farm, Staddon Road, Holsworthy EX22 6NH
t (01409) 253761 e relax@southcombe.net w southcombe.net

open All year
payment Cash/cheques

The Barn is the perfect, peaceful country retreat. Full of character and quality furnishings, it is very comfortable and cosy. For winter breaks the log-burner and underfloor heating will keep you toasty. The two bedrooms can be configured as either twin or double, for couples, friends or families.

⊕ *Proceed south from Holsworthy on the A388. At Whimble turn left into Staddon Road. Southcombe is 0.5 miles on the left.*

♥ *Long weekends available off-season.*

Unit ▥ TV 🖃 🖭 🖳 🖸 ▫ ▱ 🖵 ❄
General ざ 🍴 ♿ P ⊁ [S]   Leisure U ⳻ ⯈ 🚴 🛥   Shop 1 mile   Pub 1 mile

---

WALKERS WELCOME
WELCOME WALKERS

Best foot forward

Walkers feel at home in accommodation participating in our Walkers Welcome scheme. Look out for the symbol. Consider walking all or part of a long-distance route – go online at nationaltrail.co.uk.

★★★★
SELF CATERING

Units **3**
Sleeps **2–5**

Low season per wk
£235.00–£424.00
High season per wk
£601.00–£815.00

Odle Farm, Upottery, Honiton

contact Karen Marshallsay, Odle Farm
t (01404) 861105 **e** info@odlefarm.co.uk **w** odlefarm.co.uk

open All year
payment Credit/debit cards, cash/cheques

A pretty courtyard of cottages in the Blackdown Hills Area of Outstanding Natural Beauty. Our family-run complex offers peace and tranquillity with stunning views. All cottages have log burners in the beamed lounges, fully equipped kitchens and four-poster beds in the main bedroom. Relax under the stars in our hydrotherapy spa.

❤ *Short breaks available. Discount for couples in larger properties outside peak weeks.*

Unit ▥ TV 🔲 🔲 🔲 🔲 🔲 🔲 🔲 🔲
General 🔲 🔲 🔲 🔲 ⑤ 🔲 Leisure 🔲 🔲 🔲 🔲 Shop 3 miles Pub 2 miles

★★★★★
HOLIDAY PARK
🚐 (27) £175.00–£700.00

Beachside Holiday Park

33 Beach Road, Hele, Ilfracombe EX34 9QZ **t** (01271) 863006 **f** (01271) 867296
e enquiries@beachsidepark.co.uk **w** beachsidepark.co.uk

open All year
payment Credit/debit cards, cash/cheques

At Beachside, sea views and the beach are right outside your door; you don't have to get in the car and drive. Peaceful, relaxing, tranquil, unspoilt, quiet, great for all ages and families alike – these are words often used to describe a holiday at Beachside. Open all year round.

⊕ *Just off the A399 between Ilfracombe and Combe Martin.*
❤ *Short breaks out of high season. For specials see our website.*

General 🔲 P 🔲 🔲 🔲 🔲 ☼ Leisure 🔲 🔲 🔲

★★★★
HOLIDAY, TOURING
& CAMPING PARK
ROSE AWARD

🚐 (8) £11.00–£22.00
🏕 (50) £11.00–£27.00
🚐 (20) £180.00–£710.00

Hele Valley Holiday Park

Hele Bay, Ilfracombe EX34 9RD **t** (01271) 862460 **f** (01271) 867926 **e** holidays@helevalley.co.uk
w helevalley.co.uk

open All year
payment Credit/debit cards, cash/cheques

A family-run haven set in a charming peaceful valley within walking distance of Hele Bay beach and Ilfracombe town. An ideal location for touring the beautiful rugged North Devon coastline. Luxury accommodation with private spas. Hele Valley has everything you need for a perfectly peaceful holiday.

⊕ *From Ilfracombe High Street travel east towards Combe Martin. Swimming baths on your left then follow brown tourist signs for Hele Valley.*

General 🔲 🔲 P 🔲 🔲 🔲 🔲 🔲 🔲 🔲 🔲 🔲 🔲 ☼ Leisure 🔲 🔲 🔲 🔲

Key to symbols
Open the back flap for a key to symbols.

LEE, Devon Map ref 1C1 | **SELF CATERING**

★★★–★★★★★
SELF CATERING

Units **8**
Sleeps **2–8**

Low season per wk
£200.00–£495.00
High season per wk
£450.00–£990.00

Lower Campscott Farm, Ilfracombe

contact Mrs Margaret Cowell, Lower Campscott Farm, Lee, Ilfracombe EX34 8LS
t (01271) 863479 **f** (01271) 867639 **e** holidays@lowercampscott.co.uk **w** lowercampscott.co.uk

open All year
payment Credit/debit cards, cash/cheques

Charming, tastefully furnished character cottages converted from our farm buildings. Everything supplied to make your stay special. Also holiday homes and lodges. Peaceful farm setting with views across the Bristol Channel. Lee and Woolacombe beaches are easily accessible.

⊕ Information on the location will be sent when the booking is confirmed.

♥ Short breaks available out of school holidays. Residential craft and hobby courses second and third weeks of the month.

Unit 🔥 📺 📶 🍴 📻 🔌 🍽 🏺 ✳
General 🛏 🏛 🔥 P 🍴 ◻ Ⓢ Leisure 🔍 ♒ ∪ ♣ 🚲 Shop 1.5 miles Pub 1.5 miles

---

LYNTON, Devon Map ref 1C1 | **GUEST ACCOMMODATION**

★★★★
GUEST HOUSE
SILVER AWARD

B&B per room per night
d £46.00–£56.00
Evening meal per person
£12.00–£15.00

The Denes Guest House

15 Longmead, Lynton EX35 6DQ **t** (01598) 753573 **e** j.e.mcgowan@btinternet.com **w** thedenes.com

open All year except Christmas
bedrooms 3 double, 2 family
bathrooms 4 en suite, 1 private
payment Credit/debit cards, cash/cheques

Peacefully located close to Valley of Rocks, but a short walk to the heart of the village, The Denes is an ideal base to explore Exmoor, whether walking, cycling or driving. Our bedrooms are spacious, all with en suite or private facilities. Freshly cooked breakfasts and evening meals appeal to discerning appetites.

⊕ M5 jct 23 signposted Bridgwater. M5 jct 25 onto A358 signposted Minehead. M5 jct 27 onto A361 signposted Tiverton. In Lynton follow signs to Valley of Rocks.

♥ Beaujolais Nouveau weekend. New Year specials. Gift vouchers. 3-night DB&B.

Room 📺 ♿ 🍴 General 🛏 🏛 🔥 P 🍴 ♥ ✕ 🍽 🏛 ✳ Leisure ♒

LYNTON, Devon Map ref 1C1 | **SELF CATERING**

★★★★
SELF CATERING

Units **1**
Sleeps **1–2**

Low season per wk
Min £255.00
High season per wk
Max £595.00

Royal Castle Lodge, Lynton

contact Mr M Wolverson, Primespot Character Cottages, c/o Stag Cottage, Holdstone Down, Combe Martin EX34 0PF
t (01271) 882449

open All year
payment Cash/cheques, euros

Something special! High-quality, 16thC, detached, thatched stone cottage with rustic balcony, stable door, real fire, garden. Idyllic coastal setting in England's 'Little Switzerland'. Exmoor National Park, wooded outlook with harbour, pubs, restaurants, shops within walking distance. Spectacular walks. Spotless, warm and cosy. Off-season short breaks. Perfect honeymoon/anniversaries.

⊕ Follow A39 via Minehead for Lynton and Lynmouth. Telephone from anywhere in Lynton/Lynmouth and we will come and meet you.

♥ De-stressing breaks Nov-Mar.

Unit 🔥 📺 📻 🏺 🔌 🍽 🍴 ✳
General 🛏 P Ⓢ 🔥 Leisure ∪ ♣ Shop < 0.5 miles Pub < 0.5 miles

MODBURY, Devon Map ref 1C3   **SELF CATERING**

★★★★
SELF CATERING

Units   **4**
Sleeps   **2–6**
Low season per wk
£240.00–£305.00
High season per wk
£460.00–£640.00

Oldaport Farm Cottages, Modbury, Ivybridge

contact Miss C M Evans, Oldaport Farm Cottages, Modbury, Nr Ivybridge PL21 0TG
t (01548) 830842   **f** (01548) 830998   **e** cathy@oldaport.com   **w** oldaport.com

open All year
payment Cash/cheques

Four comfortable fully equipped cottages converted from redundant stone barns. Peaceful setting in beautiful South Hams valley on historic 70-acre working sheep farm and miniature Shetland Pony stud. There is an abundance of wildlife and many fascinating walks, the South West Coast Path is nearby. Dartmoor eight miles.

⊕ *A28 south of Exeter – exit at Ugborough, onto A3121 towards Ermington, onto A379 towards Modbury – turn right signpost Orcheton, then continue to Oldaport.*

♥ *Short breaks available 21 Sep-1 May.*

Unit 📺 📶 🖥 💻 🍳 🧺 ♿
General 🛏 🏊 ⚓ ◎ Ⓢ 🐕   Shop 2.5 miles   Pub 2 miles

MODBURY, Devon Map ref 1C3   **CAMPING & CARAVANNING**

★★★★
TOURING PARK

🚐 (112) £12.10–£24.90
🚏 (112) £12.10–£24.90
112 touring pitches

Broad Park Caravan Club Site

Higher East Leigh, Modbury, Ivybridge PL21 0SH   **t** (01548) 830714   **w** caravanclub.co.uk

payment Credit/debit cards, cash/cheques

Situated between moor and sea, this makes a splendid base from which to explore South Devon. Head for Dartmoor, or seek out the small villages of the South Hams. Open March to November.

⊕ *From B3207, site on left.*

♥ *Midweek discount: pitch fee for standard pitches for stays on any Tue, Wed or Thu night outside peak season dates will be reduced by 50%.*

THE
CARAVAN
CLUB

General P 🚐 🗑 🚐 🐾 🍳 🐕 🚶

MOORSHOP, Devon Map ref 1C2   **SELF CATERING**

★★★
SELF CATERING

Units   **2**
Sleeps   **1–4**
Low season per wk
£150.00–£250.00
High season per wk
£220.00–£400.00

Higher Longford, Tavistock

Higher Longford, Tavistock PL19 9LQ
t (01822) 613360   **f** (01822) 618722   **e** stay@higherlongford.co.uk   **w** higherlongford.co.uk

Excellently presented, comfortable, stone-built cottages with all the comforts from home, set within the Dartmoor National Park. Ideal for touring Devon and Cornwall. Children/pets welcome.

open All year
payment Credit/debit cards, cash/cheques

Unit 📺 📶 🖥 💻 🍳 🧺 ♿
General 🛏 🏊 ⚓ P 🚶 ◎ Ⓢ 🐕   Leisure ⚓ ∪ 🎣 🚲   Shop < 0.5 miles   Pub 1 mile

---

MOORSHOP, Devon Map ref 1C2   **CAMPING & CARAVANNING**

★★★★
TOURING &
CAMPING PARK

🚐 (80) £6.00–£12.00
🚏 (10) £6.00–£12.00
▲ (40) £5.00–£12.00
🏕 (4) £150.00–£480.00
100 touring pitches

Higher Longford Caravan & Camping Park

Moorshop, Tavistock PL19 9LQ   **t** (01822) 613360   **f** (01822) 618722   **e** stay@higherlongford.co.uk
w higherlongford.co.uk

Beautiful, quiet family-run park with scenic views of Dartmoor. Spacious pitches, electric hook-ups, grass, hardstanding and multiserviced pitches available all year. Modern, clean and warm facilities. Dogs welcome. Ideal for Devon, Cornwall and Dartmoor.

open All year
payment Credit/debit cards, cash/cheques

General 🚐 🗑 P 🚐 🗑 🍳 🐾 ◎ 🍴 🐕 🚶 ☼   Leisure 📺 ⚓ 🏔 ∪ 🎣 🚲

     For key to symbols open the back-cover flap.

MORETONHAMPSTEAD, Devon Map ref 1C2 — GUEST ACCOMMODATION

★★★★
FARMHOUSE
SILVER AWARD

Great Sloncombe Farm
Moretonhampstead, Newton Abbot TQ13 8QF t (01647) 440595 f (01647) 440595
e hmerchant@sloncombe.freeserve.co.uk w greatsloncombefarm.co.uk

B&B per room per night
s £30.00–£35.00
d £60.00–£70.00

13thC farmhouse in a magical Dartmoor valley. Meadows, woodland, wild flowers and animals. Farmhouse breakfast with freshly baked bread. Everything provided for an enjoyable break.

open All year
bedrooms 2 double, 1 twin
bathrooms All en suite
payment Cash/cheques

Room 🛏 📺 ♿ 🍴   General ☞8 ⚡ ♨ ✿ 🐾   Leisure ∪ ♪ ► 🚴 ⛵

NEWTON ABBOT, Devon Map ref 1D2 — CAMPING & CARAVANNING

★★★★★
TOURING &
CAMPING PARK

Dornafield
Two Mile Oak, Newton Abbot TQ12 6DD t (01803) 812732 f (01803) 812032
e enquiries@dornafield.com w dornafield.com

🚐(135) £12.50–£19.80
🚗 £12.50–£19.80
⛺ £13.50–£20.80

payment Credit/debit cards, cash/cheques

Beautiful 14thC farmhouse located in 30 acres of glorious South Devon countryside. So quiet and peaceful, yet so convenient for Torbay and Dartmoor. Superb facilities to suit the discerning caravanner, including many hardstanding, all-service pitches. Shop, games room, adventure play area, tennis and golf. Our brochure is only a phone call away.

⊕ Take A381 Newton Abbot to Totnes road. In 2.5 miles at Two Mile Oak Inn turn right. In 0.5 miles 1st turn to left. Site 200yds on right.

♥ Early- and late-season bookings. Book for 7 days and only pay for 5. Details on request.

THE CARAVAN CLUB

General 🅿 P 🔌 🚰 🍴 🍳 🛒 ⊙ 🚻 🐾 ♨ ☼   Leisure 📺 ⚡ ⛰ 🎣 ►

OKEHAMPTON, Devon Map ref 1C2 — SELF CATERING

★★★★
SELF CATERING

Units 4
Sleeps 4–6

Low season per wk
£195.00–£370.00
High season per wk
£370.00–£670.00

Beer Farm, Okehampton
contact Bob & Sue Annear, Beer Farm, Okehampton EX20 1SG
t (01837) 840265 f (01837) 840245 e info@beerfarm.co.uk w beerfarm.co.uk

open All year
payment Cash/cheques

Enjoy a peaceful holiday on our small farm situated on the northern edge of Dartmoor in mid-Devon. Comfortable and well-equipped two- and three-bedroomed cottages with DVDs and CD players. One offers accessibility for the less mobile. Games room, some covered parking. Dogs/horses by arrangement. Good walking, cycling and touring base.

⊕ A30 towards Okehampton. Leave at Sticklepath, Belstone junction. Take old A30 towards Sticklepath. Left at Tongue End crossroads. Right to Taw Green. After 800yds, Beer Farm on left.

♥ 5% discount on second (lower price) cottage if booked together. Short breaks often available (minimum 3 nights).

Unit 🛏 📺 🍴 🖥 📻 🍳 🧺 🔌 ⚡   General ☞ 🍴 ♨ P Ⓢ 🐾   Leisure ⚡ ∪ ♪ 🚴 ⛵ Shop 1 mile Pub 1.5 miles

Using map references
The map references refer to the colour maps at the front of this guide. The first figure is the map number, the letter and figure that follow indicate the grid reference on the map.

PAIGNTON, Devon Map ref 1D2 — SELF CATERING

★★
SELF CATERING

Units **8**
Sleeps **2-6**
Low season per wk
£121.00-£204.00
High season per wk
£258.00-£465.00

Tregarth, Paignton

contact Mr & Mrs Haskins, Tregarth, 8 Adelphi Road, Paignton TQ4 6AW
t (01803) 558458 **e** tregarthpaignton@aol.com **w** tregarthpaignton.co.uk

These delightful holiday flats are located on the English Riviera, close to the sea and Paignton railway station. Modern, fully equipped rooms and on-site parking. An ideal base to explore the Devon coast.

open All year
payment Cash/cheques

Unit 🛏 📺 🖥 🖳
General ⏰ 🏛 ♠ P ⓘ 🏇 Shop < 0.5 miles Pub 0.5 miles

PLYMOUTH, Devon Map ref 1C2 — GUEST ACCOMMODATION

★★★★
GUEST ACCOMMODATION

B&B per room per night
s £30.00-£40.00
d £44.00-£54.00

Athenaeum Lodge

4 Athenaeum Street, The Hoe, Plymouth PL1 2RQ **t** (01752) 665005 & (01752) 670090
f (01752) 665005 **e** us@athenaeumlodge.com **w** athenaeumlodge.com

open All year except Christmas and New Year
bedrooms 3 double, 2 twin, 1 single, 3 family
bathrooms 7 en suite
payment Credit/debit cards, cash/cheques

Elegant, Grade II Listed guesthouse, ideally situated on The Hoe. Centrally located for the Barbican, Theatre Royal, Plymouth Pavilions, ferry port and the National Marine Aquarium. The city centre and university are a few minutes' walk. Divers' and sailors' paradise. Excellent, central location for touring Devon and Cornwall. Wi-Fi Internet and free use of computer if required.

⊕ Follow signs for the city centre, Barbican and Hoe. Pass the Barbican on your left and continue along Notte Street to the Walrus Pub. Turn left.

Room 🛏 📺 🖥 🍵 General ⏰5 P ⚡ 🍴 ♿ Leisure ⚓ 🎱

PLYMOUTH, Devon Map ref 1C2 — GUEST ACCOMMODATION

★★★★
GUEST ACCOMMODATION

B&B per room per night
s £35.00-£45.00
d £55.00-£70.00

Berkeleys of St James

4 St James Place East, Plymouth PL1 3AS **t** (01752) 221654 **f** (01752) 221654
e enquiry@onthehoe.co.uk **w** onthehoe.co.uk

Non-smoking Victorian town house ideally situated for seafront, Barbican, theatre, ferry port and city centre. Flexible accommodation between double/twin/triple. Excellent breakfast serving free-range, organic produce where possible.

open All year except Christmas and New Year
bedrooms 2 double, 1 twin, 1 single, 1 family
bathrooms 4 en suite, 1 private
payment Credit/debit cards, cash/cheques

Room 🛏 📺 🖥 🍵 General ⏰ 🏛 P ⚡ 🍴 Leisure 🎱

PLYMOUTH, Devon Map ref 1C2 — GUEST ACCOMMODATION

★★★★
GUEST HOUSE

B&B per room per night
s £30.00-£40.00
d £45.00-£55.00

Brittany Guest House

28 Athenaeum Street, The Hoe, Plymouth PL1 2RQ **t** (01752) 262247
e enquiries@brittanyguesthouse.com **w** brittanyguesthouse.co.uk

Non-smoking, all rooms en suite, some 5ft beds, crisp white linen. Private car park, close to shops, bars, pavilions, seafront. Credit and debit cards taken. Run by resident proprietors.

open All year except Christmas and New Year
bedrooms 4 double, 2 twin, 2 single, 2 family
bathrooms All en suite
payment Credit/debit cards, cash/cheques, euros

Room 🛏 📺 🖥 🍵 General ⏰3 P ⚡ 🍴

Check it out
Please check prices, quality ratings and other details when you book.

PLYMOUTH, Devon Map ref 1C2 | **GUEST ACCOMMODATION**

★★★
FARMHOUSE

B&B per room per night
s £22.00–£26.00
d £42.00–£46.00
Evening meal per person
Min £12.00

Gabber Farm

Gabber Lane, Down Thomas, Plymouth PL9 0AW **t** (01752) 862269 **f** (01752) 862269
e gabberfarm@tiscali.co.uk

A courteous welcome at this farm, near coast and Mount Batten Centre. Lovely walks. Special weekly rates, especially for Senior Citizens and children. Directions provided.

open All year
bedrooms 1 double, 1 twin, 1 single, 2 family
bathrooms 3 en suite
payment Credit/debit cards, cash/cheques

Room 📺 ♿ General 🍳🏠🔥P✗🏚🅿♿ Leisure 🚲

PLYMOUTH, Devon Map ref 1C2 | **CAMPING & CARAVANNING**

★★★★
**HOLIDAY &
TOURING PARK**

🚐(60) £8.60–£18.00
🚙(60) £8.60–£18.00
60 touring pitches

Plymouth Sound Caravan Club Site

Bovisand Lane, Down Thomas, Plymouth PL9 0AE **t** (01752) 862325 **w** caravanclub.co.uk

payment Credit/debit cards, cash/cheques

Within easy reach of the historic port. Superb views over the Sound. Close to the South West Coast Path and lovely beaches. Open March to October.

⊕ *Turn right at village signposted Down Thomas into Bovisand Lane. Site on right.*

♥ *Special member rates mean you can save your membership subscription in less than a week. Visit our website to find out more.*

General P 🔌 💧 🅦 🐾 🛁 Leisure ▶

SALCOMBE, Devon Map ref 1C3 | **HOTEL**

★★★
**HOTEL
GOLD AWARD**

HB per person per night
£65.00–£160.00

Tides Reach Hotel

Cliff Road, Salcombe TQ8 8LJ **t** (01548) 843466 **f** (01548) 843954 **e** enquire@tidesreach.com
w tidesreach.com

bedrooms 14 double, 14 twin, 2 single, 3 family, 2 suites
bathrooms All en suite
payment Credit/debit cards, cash/cheques

Elegant and well-appointed hotel in an unrivalled position of outstanding natural beauty on edge of a secluded tree-fringed sandy cove. Well-equipped indoor pool and leisure complex with tropical atmosphere. Award-winning cuisine and friendly, caring staff. All this combines to produce an ideal location for a short break or holiday. Closed December to January.

⊕ *Leave A38 at Buckfastleigh to Totnes, then take A381 to Salcombe, then follow signs to South Sands.*

♥ *Winter, Spring and Autumn Bargain Breaks.*

Room 📞📺♿🍷🏋 General 🍳8 P❗🏚🅿●🖥♿🐾 Leisure 🎾🏊✗🎱∪🎣▶

Town, country or coast

The entertainment, shopping and innovative attractions of the big cities, the magnificent vistas of the countryside or the relaxing and refreshing coast – this guide will help you find what you're looking for.

SEATON, Devon Map ref 1D2 — SELF CATERING

West Ridge Bungalow, Seaton

★★★
SELF CATERING

Units **1**
Sleeps **1–4**

Low season per wk
£225.00–£325.00
High season per wk
£385.00–£525.00

contact Mrs Hildegard Fox, West Ridge Bungalow, Harepath Hill, Seaton EX12 2TA
t (01297) 22398 **f** (01297) 22398 **e** foxfamily@westridge.fsbusiness.co.uk
w cottageguide.co.uk/westridge

payment Cash/cheques

Comfortably furnished bungalow on elevated ground in 1.5 acres of gardens. Beautiful, panoramic views of Axe Estuary and sea. Close by are Beer and Branscombe. Lyme Regis seven miles, Sidmouth ten miles. Excellent centre for touring, walking, sailing, fishing, golf. Full gas central heating, double glazing throughout. Open March to October.

⊕ *From M5 jct 25 (Taunton exit) take A358 southwards for 25 miles. At A3052 turn right. West Ridge is 400m to the west of Colyford.*

♥ *10% reduction for 2 persons only, throughout booking period.*

Unit 🛏 📺 🚪 🍽 💻 🛗 🔌 🥄 ☼
General 🧺 ♨ ⛺ P 🚭 🐕 Leisure ▸ 🏞 Shop 0.5 miles Pub 1 mile

SIDBURY, Devon Map ref 1D2 — CAMPING & CARAVANNING

Putts Corner Caravan Club Site

★★★★★
TOURING PARK
🚐(113) £12.10–£24.90
🚐(113) £12.10–£24.90
113 touring pitches

Sidbury, Sidmouth EX10 0QQ **t** (01404) 42875 **w** caravanclub.co.uk

payment Credit/debit cards, cash/cheques

A quiet site in pretty surroundings, with a private path to the local pub. Bluebells create a sea of blue in spring, followed by foxgloves. Open March to November.

⊕ *From M5 jct 25, A375 signposted Sidmouth. Turn right at Hare and Hounds onto B3174. In about 0.25 miles turn right into site entrance.*

♥ *Special member rates mean you can save your membership subscription in less than a week. Visit our website to find out more.*

THE
CARAVAN
CLUB

General 🖥 P 🔥 🍳 🍴 🖥 🔌 ☉ 🚽 🐕 ☼ Leisure 🎱 ▸

SIDMOUTH, Devon Map ref 1D2 — HOTEL

Hotel Riviera

★★★★
HOTEL
GOLD AWARD

B&B per room per night
s £94.00–£148.00
d £188.00–£274.00
HB per person per night
£109.00–£175.00

The Esplanade, Sidmouth EX10 8AY **t** (01395) 515201 **f** (01395) 577775
e enquiries@hotelriviera.co.uk **w** hotelriviera.co.uk

open All year
bedrooms 11 double, 7 twin, 6 single, 2 suites
bathrooms All en suite
payment Credit/debit cards, cash/cheques

The hotel has a long tradition of hospitality and is perfect for unforgettable holidays, long weekends, unwinding breaks and all the spirit of the glorious festive season... you will be treated to the kind of friendly, personal attention that can only be found in a private hotel of this quality.

⊕ *M5 jct 30 then follow A3052.*

♥ *Luxury 3-day breaks and carefree weekend breaks at certain times of year. Christmas and New Year programme also available.*

Room 📞 📺 ♿ 🍵 🛋 General 🧺 ♨ ⛺ P 🍷 🍽 🛗 ● 🚪 ✝ ☼ 🐕 Leisure 🎵 🏊 ♪ ▸ 🚴 🏞

What's in a quality rating?
Information about ratings can be found at the back of this guide.

For key to symbols open the back-cover flap.

★★
HOTEL
SILVER AWARD

Royal York and Faulkner Hotel and Aspara Spa

The Esplanade, Sidmouth EX10 8AZ **t** 0800 220714 & (01395) 513043 **f** (01395) 577472
e stay@royalyorkhotel.co.uk **w** royalyorkhotel.co.uk

B&B per room per night
s £42.00–£70.00
d £84.00–£140.00
HB per person per night
£52.00–£92.00

bedrooms 9 double, 29 twin, 22 single, 8 family, 2 suites
bathrooms All en suite
payment Credit/debit cards, cash/cheques

Magnificent Regency hotel enjoying an unrivalled position on Sidmouth's esplanade, overlooking the sea and adjacent to the picturesque town centre. Owned and personally run by the Hook family, the hotel has a long-standing reputation for hospitality and service, is beautifully appointed, offers all amenities and boasts a superb new spa. Closed January.

⊕ M5, jct 30: follow A3052 to Sidmouth. A303: follow A30 to Sidmouth.

♥ Special offers available throughout the year. Freephone 0800 220714 for details.

Room 🛗 📺 🕭 General 🛏 ♿ P 🍽 🎱 🎬 🖥 ⊹ 🚲 🐾 Leisure 🏊 ♨ 🎵 🎯 ♿ 🎣

★★★
GUEST HOUSE

Ryton Guest House

52-54 Winslade Road, Sidmouth EX10 9EX **t** (01395) 513981 **f** (01395) 519210
e info@ryton-guest-house.co.uk **w** ryton-guest-house.co.uk

B&B per room per night
s £25.00–£35.00
d £50.00–£70.00

Ryton is a friendly, established guesthouse, offering spacious, comfortable en suite rooms, private parking and hospitality second to none. River walks and coastal path close by.

open All year except Christmas and New Year
bedrooms 3 double, 1 twin, 3 single, 2 family
bathrooms 6 en suite, 3 private
payment Cash/cheques

Room 📺 🕭 General 🛏 5 P 🎬 🖥 ⊹ 🐾 Leisure ♿ 🎯 ♿ 🏌

★★★★
SELF CATERING

Flat 4 Western Court, Sidmouth

contact Mr G M Corr, Glendevon, Cotmaton Road, Sidmouth EX10 8QX
t (01395) 512216 **f** (01395) 512216 **e** sidmouthholidayflats@yahoo.co.uk
w sidmouth-selfcatering.co.uk

Units   **1**
Sleeps   **2**
Low season per wk
£260.00–£335.00
High season per wk
£395.00–£425.00

A one-bedroom apartment sleeping two in the centre of Sidmouth in a quiet complex. It is close to the seafront and town centre. Modernised. Lift, garage, parking space, balcony.

open All year
payment Cash/cheques, euros

Unit 🛏 📺 🍴 🖥 🔲 🍳 🖥 🗑 ⊹
General P 🎬   Shop < 0.5 miles   Pub < 0.5 miles

Take a break

Look out for special promotions and themed breaks. It's a golden opportunity to indulge an interest, find a new one, or just relax and enjoy exceptional value. Offers and promotions are highlighted in colour (and are subject to availability).

SIDMOUTH, Devon Map ref 1D2   **SELF CATERING**

★★★★
SELF CATERING

Units   **8**
Sleeps   **4**

Low season per wk
£194.00–£329.00
High season per wk
£345.00–£648.00

Leigh Cottages, Sidmouth

contact Mr & Mrs Terry & Alison Clarke, Leigh Cottages, The Leighs, Weston, Sidmouth EX10 0PH
t (01395) 516065   **f** (01395) 512563   **e** alison@leigh-cottages.co.uk
w streets-ahead.com/leighcottages

open All year
payment Credit/debit cards, cash/cheques

Bungalows and cottages in delightful gardens and countryside. 150yds from a National Trust valley leading to the World Heritage Coastline and Weston Mouth beach. Lovely coastal path and cliff-top walks and level walks around nearby donkey sanctuary fields. Ideal base for exploring the coastal towns and villages in the area.

⊕ *M5 jct 30, join A3052. At Sidford straight on then right at top of hill, signposted Weston. Follow signs to hamlet, 1st property on right.*

Unit 🏠 📺 ▣ ▭ 🍳 🖳 ✿   General 🐕 🏳 🚶 P ✄ ◎ 🎄   Leisure ∪ ♪ ▸ 🚲   Shop 1.5 miles   Pub 1.5 miles

---

SWIMBRIDGE, Devon Map ref 1C1   **SELF CATERING**

★★★★
SELF CATERING

Units   **4**
Sleeps   **2–9**

Low season per wk
£190.00–£443.00
High season per wk
£355.00–£959.00

Lower Hearson Farm, Barnstaple

contact Mr & Mrs G Pelling, Swimbridge, Barnstaple EX32 0QH
t (01271) 830702   **e** info@hearsoncottagesdevon.co.uk   **w** hearsoncottagesdevon.co.uk

open All year
payment Cash/cheques

Former dairy farm set in 13 acres of gardens, field and woodland. Tucked away in the heart of the North Devon countryside, it's perfect for a relaxing holiday. Our holiday cottages, games facilities and pool are surrounded by two acres of gardens, making this a safe place for children.

Unit 🏠 📺 ▣ ▭ ▤ 🖨 ◎ 🖳 ✿   General 🐕 🏳 🚶 P ✄ S 🎄   Leisure ⚡ ♣ ♪ ▸   Shop 2 miles   Pub 1.5 miles

---

TAVISTOCK, Devon Map ref 1C2   **SELF CATERING**

★★★★
SELF CATERING

Units   **1**
Sleeps   **1–4**

Low season per wk
£250.00–£350.00
High season per wk
£350.00–£450.00

Edgemoor Cottage, Middlemoor, Tavistock

contact Mrs Mary Susan Fox, Edgemoor, Middlemoor, Tavistock PL19 9DY
t (01822) 612259   **f** (01822) 617625   **e** Foxes@dartmoorcottages.info   **w** edgemoorcottage.co.uk

open All year
payment Credit/debit cards, cash/cheques, euros

Attractive country cottage in peaceful hamlet. Two en suite bedrooms (one twin, one double, both with TV), kitchen/dining room, upstairs living room leading into a sun lounge/diner with patio overlooking fields. Perfect base to explore Dartmoor, Devon and Cornwall. North and south coasts are within an hour's drive.

⊕ *At Tavistock follow road signs to Whitchurch. At Whitchurch post office turn up the hill. Turn right at the cattle grid to Middlemoor.*

♥ *£25 discount to holidaymakers booking a second week with us. £25 discount to holidaymakers booking a subsequent holiday with us.*

Unit 🏠 📺 ▣ ▭ 🖨 🖳 ✿   General 🐕 🏳 🚶 P   Leisure ∪ ♪ ▸ 🚲   Shop < 0.5 miles   Pub < 0.5 miles

---

     For key to symbols open the back-cover flap.

TAVISTOCK, Devon Map ref 1C2 | **SELF CATERING**

★★★
SELF CATERING

Units **1**
Sleeps **2**

Low season per wk
£150.00
High season per wk
£150.00

Higher Chaddlehanger Farm, Tavistock

contact Mrs Ruth Cole, The Annexe, Higher Chaddlehanger Farm, Tavistock PL19 0LG
t (01822) 810268 **f** (01822) 810268

Holiday flatlet in farmhouse on beef and sheep farm, close to Moors. Own entrance, private garden.

open All year
payment Cash/cheques

Unit 🔲 📺 🔲 🔲 🔲 🔲 ❄
General 🛏 🏠 ♿ 🐾

TAVISTOCK, Devon Map ref 1C2 | **CAMPING & CARAVANNING**

★★★★
HOLIDAY, TOURING
& CAMPING PARK
ROSE AWARD

🚐(40)   £9.50–£14.50
🚙(40)   £9.50–£14.50
⛺(40)   £9.50–£14.50
🏠(12) £195.00–£445.00
120 touring pitches

Harford Bridge Holiday Park

Peter Tavy, Tavistock PL19 9LS **t** (01822) 810349 **f** (01822) 810028 **e** enquiry@harfordbridge.co.uk
w harfordbridge.co.uk

open All year
payment Credit/debit cards, cash/cheques

Beautiful, level, sheltered park set in Dartmoor with delightful views of Cox Tor. The River Tavy forms a boundary, offering riverside and other spacious, level camping pitches. Luxury, self-catering caravan holiday homes. Ideal for exploring Devon and Cornwall, walking the moor or just relaxing on this beautiful park.

⊕ *M5 onto A30 to Sourton Cross; take left turn onto A386 Tavistock Road; 2 miles north of Tavistock, take the Peter Tavy turning; entrance 200yds on left.*

♥ *Holiday let: £15 off 2-week booking. £10 Senior Citizen discount.*

General 🔌 🐕 P 🔲 🔲 🔲 🔲 🔲 🔲 🔲 🔲 🐾 ⚲ ☼   Leisure 📺 🔍 🎢 ⚲ 🛶 🚴 🏊

TIVERTON, Devon Map ref 1D2 | **SELF CATERING**

★★★★
SELF CATERING

Units **4**
Sleeps **1–4**

Low season per wk
£270.00–£480.00
High season per wk
£410.00–£780.00

Tiverton Castle, Tiverton

contact Mrs Alison Gordon, Tiverton Castle, Park Hill, Tiverton EX16 6RP
t (01884) 253200 & (01884) 255200 **f** (01884) 254200 **e** tiverton.castle@ukf.net
w tivertoncastle.com

Extremely comfortable and well-equipped apartments inside historic castle in centre of Tiverton. All modern comforts in medieval surroundings. Beautiful garden. Wonderful touring centre for the best that Devon offers.

open All year
payment Cash/cheques

Unit 🔲 📺 🔲 🔲 🔲 🔲 🔲 🔲 🔲 ❄
General 🛏 🏠 ♿ P 🍴   Leisure 🛶 🚴 🏊   Shop < 0.5 miles   Pub < 0.5 miles

---

TORQUAY, Devon Map ref 1D2 | **HOTEL**

★★
HOTEL
GOLD AWARD

B&B per room per night
s £53.00–£82.00
d £66.00–£118.00
HB per person per night
£67.00–£78.00

The Berburry Hotel

64 Bampfylde Road, Torquay TQ2 5AY **t** (01803) 297494 **f** (01803) 215902
e bsellick@berburry.co.uk **w** berburry.co.uk

Relive the memory of a West Country experience at The Berburry. Remember fresh produce, the expertise of our chef-proprietor, traditional hospitality, en suite bedrooms and meticulous attention to detail. Open March to November.

bedrooms 5 double, 4 twin
bathrooms All en suite
payment Credit/debit cards, cash/cheques

Room 🛏 📺 ♿ 🔲 🔲   General P 🍴 ♿ 🍷 🔲 🔲 ❄

Look at the maps

Colour maps at the front pinpoint the location of all accommodation found in the regional sections.

TORQUAY, Devon Map ref 1D2 | HOTEL

★★★
HOTEL
SILVER AWARD

Corbyn Head Hotel

Torbay Road, Torquay TQ2 6RH t (01803) 213611 f (01803) 296152 e info@corbynhead.com
w corbynhead.com

B&B per room per night
s £45.00–£150.00
d Min £70.00
HB per person per night
£35.00–£160.00

open All year
bedrooms 29 double, 10 twin, 3 single, 3 family
bathrooms All en suite
payment Credit/debit cards, cash/cheques, euros

The Corbyn Head Hotel is one of Torquay's leading hotels with its seafront location. Many of the bedrooms boast sea views and have private balconies. With two award-winning restaurants to choose from, and with its outstanding service, you can expect an enjoyable stay.

♥ Please enquire about special promotions. Stay 7 nights for the price of 6.

Room ♿ ☎ 📺 ♨ 🍵 ✎   General 🖨 🖳 ⚿ P ☕ 🍴 ♨ ● 🖵 ✕ ✿ 🚗 🐾   Leisure ↺ 🏊 🎿 ♬ ∪ 🏌 🚴

TORQUAY, Devon Map ref 1D2 | HOTEL

★★
HOTEL

Red House Hotel

Rousdown Road, Torquay TQ2 6PB t (01803) 607811 f (01803) 200592
e stay@redhouse-hotel.co.uk w redhouse-hotel.co.uk

B&B per room per night
s £38.00–£48.00
d £56.00–£76.00
HB per person per night
£35.00–£53.00

Small, friendly hotel offering indoor/outdoor pools, spa, sauna, gym and beauty salon. Adjoining self-catering or serviced apartments. Convenient for seafront and other amenities.

open All year
bedrooms 5 double, 2 twin, 3 family
bathrooms 10 en suite
payment Credit/debit cards, cash/cheques

Room ☎ 📺 ♨ 🍵 ✎   General 🖨 🖳 ⚿ P ☕ 🍴 ♨ 🖵 🖵 ✿ 🐾   Leisure ↺ ↻ 🏊 🎿 ⚗

TORQUAY, Devon Map ref 1D2 | GUEST ACCOMMODATION

★★★
GUEST HOUSE

Brocklehurst

Rathmore Road, Torquay TQ2 6NZ t (01803) 390883 e enquiries@brocklehursthotel.co.uk
w brocklehursthotel.co.uk

B&B per room per night
d £50.00–£60.00

open All year except Christmas and New Year
bedrooms 1 double, 3 twin, 1 family
bathrooms All en suite
payment Credit/debit cards, cash/cheques

A small, family-run guesthouse with a friendly atmosphere. We are set on the level, in a quiet area of Torquay, but within easy walking distance of Torquay station, the Riviera Conference Centre, the main seafront and local shops. We are conveniently placed for buses to local attractions.

⊕ Approaching Torquay from the north (A380/3022). Turn right at the second traffic lights after Torre Station into Walnut Road. Rathmore Road is first right turn.

Room ♿ 📺 ♨ 🍵   General 🖨 P ✂ 🖳 🖵 ✎ ✿

Our quality rating schemes

For a detailed explanation of the quality and facilities represented by the stars, please refer to the information pages at the back of this guide.

For key to symbols open the back-cover flap.

★ ★ ★ ★ ★
GUEST ACCOMMODATION

B&B per room per night
s £55.00–£88.00
d £70.00–£136.00

Haldon Priors

Meadfoot Sea Road, Torquay TQ1 2LQ t (01803) 213365 f (01803) 215577
e travelstyle.ltd@talk21.com w haldonpriors.co.uk

bedrooms 4 double, 1 twin, 1 family
bathrooms All en suite
payment Credit/debit cards, cash/cheques

Haldon Priors is a beautiful Victorian villa adjacent to Meadfoot Bay, set in exquisite subtropical gardens with heated outdoor pool and sauna. All rooms have everything needed to make your stay memorable, with complimentary refreshments on arrival and all the beauty of Devon on the doorstep. Open Easter to end of September. No smoking in hotel.

⊕ *Pass Torquay Harbour on your right. Turn left at the clock tower, right at the 1st lights, to Meadfoot Road. On the left just before the beach.*

Room 📺 ♨ ❑ General ❑ ≣ ♟ P ✕ ♨ ✳ Leisure ⚓ ◑ ♪ ⚐ ⌂

★ ★ ★ ★
GUEST ACCOMMODATION
SILVER AWARD

B&B per room per night
s £50.00
d £60.00–£100.00

Lanscombe House

Cockington Village, Torquay TQ2 6XA t (01803) 606938 f (01803) 607656
e enquiries@lanscombehouse.co.uk w lanscombehouse.co.uk

bedrooms 6 double, 1 twin, 1 family
bathrooms All en suite
payment Credit/debit cards, cash/cheques, euros

Relax and unwind, this country-house B&B is tucked away in the picturesque thatched village of Cockington, surrounded by Cockington Country Park – a peaceful haven just a short stroll to the sea. The luxury accommodation is fully refurbished, and includes a four-poster room. Open Easter to October.

⊕ *Follow signs for Torbay and head for seafront. Turn right to Paignton. At Livermead turn right (Cockington). As you enter village we are on left.*

Room 🛏 🖥 📺 ♨ ❑ General ≣ ♟ P ✂ ⛌ 🍴 ♨ ✳ Leisure ♪ ⌂

★ ★ ★
SELF CATERING

Units **24**
Sleeps **1–6**

Low season per wk
£200.00–£420.00
High season per wk
£330.00–£715.00

Maxton Lodge Holiday Apartments, Torquay

contact Mark Shephard and Alex Brook, Maxton Lodge Holiday Apartments, Rousdown Road, Torquay TQ2 6PB
t (01803) 607811 f (01803) 605357 e stay@redhouse-hotel.co.uk w redhouse-hotel.co.uk

Well-appointed, self-contained apartments providing superior accommodation. Close to shops and seafront and an ideal base for touring. Indoor/outdoor pools, spa, sauna, gymnasium. Beauty salon, solarium, games room, licensed bar, restaurant.

open All year
payment Credit/debit cards, cash/cheques

Unit 🛏 📺 🖥 ❑ 🍴 🗎 🍽 📻 ∥ ✳
General ❑ ≣ ♟ P ◉ Ⓢ ♞ Leisure ⚓ ⚓ ◑ U Shop < 0.5 miles Pub < 0.5 miles

It's all in the detail

Please remember that all information in this guide has been supplied by the proprietors well in advance of publication. Since changes do sometimes occur it's a good idea to check details at the time of booking.

TORQUAY, Devon Map ref 1D2 — SELF CATERING

★★★★★
SELF CATERING

Units **1**
Sleeps **2–10**
Low season per wk
£500.00–£800.00
High season per wk
£1,100.00–£1,950.00

St Christophers Holiday Home, Torquay
contact Mr David Perry, Wildewood, Meadfoot Road, Torquay TQ1 2JP
t (01803) 297471 **e** cperry@lineone.net **w** torquayholiday.com

Luxury, detached holiday home within walking distance of three beaches, town and harbour. Warm and cosy in winter with central heating and woodburner. Patio and parking.

open All year
payment Cash/cheques

Unit 🌐 📺 🍳 📷 💻 ⊟ ⊟ ♦ 🎞 🔲 🏮 ✳
General 👶 🛏 🅿 ⚡ Ⓢ Leisure ∪ ♪ Shop < 0.5 miles Pub < 0.5 miles

TOTNES, Devon Map ref 1D2 — HOTEL

★★★
HOTEL

B&B per room per night
s £85.00–£115.00
d £109.00–£140.00

Royal Seven Stars Hotel
The Plains, Totnes TQ9 5DD **t** (01803) 862125 **f** (01803) 867925 **e** enquiry@royalsevenstars.co.uk
w royalsevenstars.co.uk

An ancient coaching inn at the heart of Totnes. Its stylish decor provides a unique blend of tradition with a contemporary twist.

open All year
bedrooms 14 double, 2 twin, 1 single, 1 family
bathrooms All en suite
payment Credit/debit cards, cash/cheques

Room 🖥 ☎ 📺 🛁 ♦ 🍳 ⚅ General 👶 🏮 🛏 🅿 ♟ 🎱 🍺 🍴 ● ⊟ 🍷 ✳ 🐕 Leisure ⚲

TOTNES, Devon Map ref 1D2 — CAMPING & CARAVANNING

★★★★
TOURING &
CAMPING PARK

🚐 £8.00–£15.00
🚏 £8.00–£15.00
⛺ £8.00–£15.00
35 touring pitches

Broadleigh Farm Park
Coombe House Lane, Aish, Stoke Gabriel, Totnes TQ9 6PU **t** (01803) 782309 **f** (01803) 782422
e enquiries@broadleighfarm.co.uk **w** gotorbay.com/accommodation

Situated in beautiful South Hams village of Stoke Gabriel close to the River Dart and Torbay's wonderful, safe beaches. Many local walks. Bus stop at end of lane. Dartmoor within easy reach by car. Open March to end of October.

payment Cash/cheques

General 🅿 🔌 🚻 🔥 🔆 ⊙ 🔲 🐕 ♿ ☼ Leisure ♪ ⚲ 🚴

WELCOMBE, Devon Map ref 1C2 — SELF CATERING

★★★–★★★★★
SELF CATERING

Units **5**
Sleeps **2–8**
Low season per wk
£205.00–£404.00
High season per wk
£562.00–£1,154.00

Mead Barn Cottages, Welcombe, Bideford
contact Mr & Mrs Rob & Lisa Ireton, Mead Barn Cottages, Welcombe, Bideford EX39 6HQ
t (01288) 331721 **e** holidays@meadbarns.com **w** meadbarns.com

open All year
payment Cash/cheques

Five comfortable, well-equipped stone barns, two/four bedrooms sleeping four/eight people. Located on coast in North Devon Area of Outstanding Natural Beauty, 0.5 miles from unique local cove, beach, rock pools, surfing, walking. Providing good additional facilities: trampoline, swings, barbecue area etc. Three miles from A39 and Cornwall/Devon border, we offer easy access for touring.

⊕ *Turn off A39 at Welcombe Cross (Devon/Cornwall border) signposted Welcombe. Follow lane for 3 miles. Gate 150yds after Mead Corner on right.*

♥ *Short breaks and discounts offered for couples, and two-week bookings, off-peak. Special Romantic Retreat with flowers, chocolates, wine and four-poster.*

Unit 🌐 📺 🍳 📷 💻 ⊟ ⊟ ♦ 🎞 🔲 🏮 ✳
General 👶 🛏 🅿 Ⓞ Ⓢ 🐕 Leisure 🔍 ⚲ ∪ ♪ ⚲ Shop 2.5 miles Pub 0.5 miles

Rest assured
All accommodation in this guide has been rated, or is awaiting assessment, by a professional assessor.

For key to symbols open the back-cover flap.

★★★★
SELF CATERING

Units **1**
Sleeps **1–8**

Low season per wk
£600.00–£700.00
High season per wk
£700.00–£800.00

Challonsleigh, Whitchurch, Tavistock

contact Mary Susan Fox, Edgemoor, Middlemoor, Tavistock PL19 9DY
t (01822) 612259   **e** vicky@dartmoorcottages.info   **w** challonsleigh.co.uk

open All year
payment Credit/debit cards, cash/cheques

Spacious, detached family house surrounded by gardens; spectacular views overlooking fields adjacent to extensive moorland. Two double and two twin bedrooms. Within an hour of South and North Devon and Cornish beaches, the Eden Project, the aquarium, gardens and places of historic interest. Wonderful walking, riding and cycling over Dartmoor.

⊕ A30, then A386 to Tavistock. Take Whitchurch road to the post office/shop crossroads. Turn left past pub and church. Last house on right before cattlegrid.

Unit ▦ TV 🖵 💻 ⊟ 🍳 🔥 🗄 🔲 📺 ❈
General ⌂ 🛏 🚭 P   Leisure ∪ ♪ ⚑ 🚲 ⌂   Shop < 0.5 miles   Pub < 0.5 miles

---

★★★★
GUEST ACCOMMODATION

B&B per room per night
s £35.00
d £60.00

The Old Parsonage

Court Walk, Winkleigh EX19 8JA   **t** (01837) 83772   **f** (01837) 680074   **e** tony@lymingtonarms.co.uk

open All year
bedrooms 4 double
bathrooms All en suite
payment Cash/cheques

Typical Devon thatched and cob-walled house. Park-like gardens have many magnificent trees, rhododendrons and azaleas. Comfortable, en suite bedrooms with lots of old-world charm. Garden gate leads to village square. Five minutes away at Wembworthy we recommend the Lymington Arms for its excellent restaurant and blackboard menus.

⊕ From M5 jct 27, follow signs to Tiverton (A361). Follow signs to Witheridge, Eggesford, Wembworthy, Winkleigh.

Room ⌂ TV 🐾   General ⌂5 P ✕ ❈ 🐾

★★★★
GUEST ACCOMMODATION

B&B per room per night
s £37.50–£42.50
d £65.00–£70.00

Overcombe House

Old Station Road, Yelverton PL20 7RA   **t** (01822) 853501   **f** (01822) 853602
e enquiries@overcombehotel.co.uk   **w** overcombehotel.co.uk

open All year except Christmas
bedrooms 4 double, 3 twin, 1 single
bathrooms All en suite
payment Credit/debit cards, cash/cheques

Offering a warm, friendly welcome in relaxed, comfortable surroundings with a substantial breakfast using local and home-made produce. Enjoying beautiful views over the village and Dartmoor. Conveniently located for exploring the varied attractions of both Devon and Cornwall, in particular Dartmoor National Park and the adjacent Tamar Valley.

⊕ Situated between Plymouth and Tavistock. Located on the edge of the village of Horrabridge and just over a mile north-west of Yelverton heading towards Tavistock.

Room ⌂ TV 🐾 🍵   General ⌂5 P ⚡ 🍽 🍴 ❈   Leisure ∪ ♪ ⚑ 🚲 ⌂

If you have access needs...

Look for the National Accessible Scheme symbols if you have special hearing, visual or mobility needs.

Corfe Castle

Oceanarium, Bournemouth

Jurassic Coast, Dorset

Explore Dorset

Hunt for fossils at a World Heritage Site. Walk, cycle and ride in contrasting countryside. Stretch out on Blue Flag beaches. Opt for the bustle and entertainment of big Bournemouth or chill out in peaceful Poole. The choice is yours.

Big, big Bournemouth

It's a seaside resort, first-class shopping centre and lively, buzzing, bustling town all rolled into one. Delve into department stores and individual boutiques, lingering over the lingerie and stocking up on shoes, or stroll through sweet-scented pine trees and flower-filled gardens to a different world beyond. The prom, the pier, the sandy beach and the gentle waves – everything you need for a break beside the sea. Take a look under the surface in the Oceanarium, feast on fine fish and chips or dine in the town centre on cuisines from around the world. As dusk falls and the lights come on, Bournemouth transforms into a heady nightspot, so swap shorts and sandals for designer denims and head for the clubs, pubs and bars.

Peaceful Poole

Take life at a gentler pace in picture-perfect Poole. Go down to the quayside and drift drowsily past little stores stocked with maritime paintings and distinctive Poole Pottery. Sip your drink outside a pub or cafe and watch the action as boats ply their way in and out of the massive natural harbour, or hop on a ferry yourself and spend a day walking among the wildlife of Brownsea Island. Uncover tales of smugglers and ghosts on the Cockle Trail around the Quay and Old Town then delve deeper into the town's history in the redeveloped Poole Museum. Poole's beaches have held coveted Blue Flags for 20 years so relax and soak up the sun at Sandbanks and Canford Cliffs, relaxed in the knowledge that you're in safe hands.

Hardy's Cottage, Higher Brockhampton

Abbotsbury Swannery

Sandbanks Peninsula, Poole

Shaftesbury

Jurassic Coast

This is fossil hunting country! Look for ammonites, belemnites and even bones from ichthyosaurs which are frequently uncovered on this stretch of coast, made up entirely of rocks formed during the Jurassic period, some 185 million years ago! The beaches around Charmouth and Lyme Regis are the best places to hunt for fossils and the Charmouth Heritage Coast Centre, together with The Philpot Museum and Dinosaurland in Lyme Regis, give advice and run regular guided fossil-collecting walks. If you prefer basking on beaches to poking among pebbles, then head for traditional resorts like Lyme Regis, Weymouth and Swanage where you can do all the things you like to do beside the seaside. Parade along the promenade, doze in a deckchair or join in the family fun and entertainment.

Walk, cycle or ride

Inland, explore mile upon mile of open countryside and green rolling hills by foot, by bike, on horseback or by car. Wander in woodlands carpeted with bluebells; look out for rabbits and hares, foxes and deer. To uncover Dorset's wildlife why not join a badger watch, or take a llama for a walk? Visit Lyme Regis Marine Aquarium or Abbotsbury Swannery, Dorset's world-famous sanctuary, home to hundreds of free-flying swans. Ride a steam train from Swanage to Corfe and clamber among the ruins of one of England's most evocative castles. A Thomas Hardy fan? The pages of his novels will come alive as you travel around in Dorset. Admire the pretty garden at his home in Higher Bockhampton or see a reconstruction of his study in the Dorset County Museum in Dorchester.

Food & drink

Fancy a bite to eat, a relaxing drink or some fresh local produce? Here's a selection of food and drink venues to get you started. For lots more ideas go online at enjoyengland.com/taste.

Restaurants

The Broad Street Restaurant
English
57-58 Broad Street,
Lyme Regis DT7 3QF
t (01297) 445792

Chideock House Hotel
English
Main Street, Chideock,
Bridport DT6 6JN
t (01297) 489242
w chideockhousehotel.com

Hensleigh Hotel
English
Lower Sea Lane,
Charmouth DT6 6LW
t (01297) 560830
w hensleighhotel.co.uk

Les Bouviers Restaurant & Hotel
European
Arrowsmith Road, Canford
Magna, Wimborne BH21 3BD
t (01202) 889555
w lesbouviers.co.uk

The Manor Hotel
English
Beach Road, West Bexington,
Dorchester DT2 9DF
t (01308) 897616
w themanorhotel.com

The Mansion House Hotel & Restaurant
English
Thames Street, Poole BH15 1JN
t (01202) 685666
w themansionhouse.co.uk

Riverside Restaurant
Seafood
West Bay, Bridport DT6 4EZ
t (01308) 422011
w thefishrestaurant-westbay.co.uk

Splinters
European
12 Church Street,
Christchurch BH23 1BW
t (01202) 483454
w splinters.uk.com

The White House Hotel
English
2 Hillside, The Street,
Charmouth DT6 6PJ
t (01297) 560411
w whitehousehotel.com

Yalbury Cottage Hotel and Restaurant
European
Lower Bockhampton,
Dorchester DT2 8PZ
t (01305) 262382
w yalburycottage.com

Pubs

The European Inn
Piddletrenthide, Dorchester
DT2 7QT
t (01300) 348308
w european-inn.co.uk

The Fiddleford Inn
Fiddleford, Sturminster Newton
DT10 2BX
t (01258) 472489
w fiddlefordinn.co.uk

The Langton Arms
Tarrant Monkton, near Blandford
DT11 8RX
t (01258) 830225
w thelangtonarms.co.uk

The Shave Cross Inn
Marshwood Vale, Bridport
DT6 6HW
t (01869) 868358

Tearooms, coffee shops and cafes

Downhouse Farm Garden Cafe
Higher Eype, Bridport DT6 6AH
t (01308) 421232

The Green Yard Cafe
4-6 Barrack Street, Bridport
DT6 3LY
t (01308) 459466

The Lookout Cafe
Durlston Castle, Durlston Country
Park, Lighthouse Road, Swanage
BH19 2JL
t (01929) 424443
w durlston.co.uk

Delis

Forbidden Fruits
43 South Street, Bridport
DT6 3NY
t (01308) 422794

Turnbulls Delicatessen & Cafe
9 High Street, Shaftesbury
SP7 8HZ
t (01747) 858575
w turnbulls-deli.co.uk

Wyndhams Delicatessen
Victor Jackson Avenue,
Poundbury, Dorchester DT1 3GY
t (01305) 259359
w wyndhamsfood.com

Farm shops and local produce

The Green House
Gold Hill Organic Farm, Child
Okeford, Blandford DT11 8HB
t (01258) 863716
w thegreenhouse.biz

Town Mill Bakery
Unit 2 Riverside Studios, Coombe
Street, Lyme Regis
DT7 3PY
t (01297) 444035
w townmillbakery.com

Village Store
Brewers Quay, Hope Square,
Weymouth DT4 8TR
t (01305) 777622
w brewers-quay.co.uk

Washingpool Farm Shop
North Allington, Bridport DT6 5HP
t (01308) 459549
w washingpool.co.uk

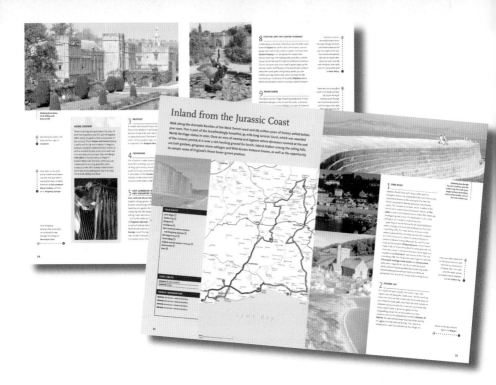

Take a tour of England

VisitBritain presents a series of **three** inspirational touring guides to the regions of England: South and South West, Northern England and Central England.

Each guide takes you on a fascinating journey through stunning countryside and coastlines, picturesque villages and lively market towns, historic houses and gardens.

- Easy-to-use maps
- Clear directions to follow the route
- Lively descriptions of all the places for you to discover
- Stunning photographs bring each area to life

Touring Central England – £14.99
Touring Northern England – £14.99
Touring South and South West England – £14.99
plus postage and handling

where to stay in
Dorset

Maps
All place names in the blue bands are shown on the maps at the front of this guide.

Accommodation symbols
Symbols give useful information about services and facilities. Inside the back-cover flap you can find a key to these symbols. Keep it open for easy reference.

ALTON PANCRAS, Dorset Map ref 2B3 | **SELF CATERING**

★★★★–★★★★★
SELF CATERING

Units   **4**
Sleeps   **4–10**
Low season per wk
£330.00–£550.00
High season per wk
£500.00–£1,100.00

Bookham Court, Dorchester

contact Mr & Mrs Andrew Foot, Whiteways, Bookham, Alton Pancras, Dorchester DT2 7RP
t (01300) 345511   **f** (01300) 345511   **e** andy.foot1@btinternet.com   **w** bookhamcourt.co.uk

Luxurious and tranquil cottages with disabled access. Games room, wildlife hide, private fishing, glorious walks in Hardy Country. 20 miles from sea. Sleeps two to ten people.

open All year
payment Cash/cheques

Unit 🛏 📺 🍴 ▯ ▭ ▯ ▯ 🍷 ⬚ ◻ ✿
General ♨ 🏠 🖈 P Ⓢ ✠   Leisure ♣ ∪ ✦   Shop 1 mile   Pub 1 mile

---

ATHELHAMPTON, Dorset Map ref 2B3 | **GUEST ACCOMMODATION**

★★★★
BED & BREAKFAST
SILVER AWARD

B&B per room per night
s £45.00–£55.00
d £70.00–£120.00

White Cottage

Dorchester DT2 7LG   **t** (01305) 848622   **e** markjamespiper@aol.com
w freewebs.com/whitecottagebandb

open All year except Christmas
bedrooms 1 double, 1 twin, 1 family
bathrooms 2 en suite, 1 private
payment Cash/cheques

A beautiful 300-year-old cottage, recently refurbished. Double room looks over river and hills, whereas the twin room looks over field and woodland. The new family suite has a large lounge and can sleep up to four. Each room has dressing gowns, fresh fruit and flowers and a mini-fridge. Athelhampton House 200yds.

⊕ White Cottage is situated in the hamlet of Athelhampton, between the villages of Puddletown and Tolpuddle, just off the A35, 6 miles from Dorchester.

♥ 3 nights or more: single £35-£40, double £50-£60. Children under 3: free, children under 12: £15 sharing room.

Room 🛏 ♿ 🍷   General ♨ 🏠 🖈 P ⚡ ✕ 🖭 ✿   Leisure ✦ 🏛

Key to symbols
Open the back flap for a key to symbols.

BEAMINSTER, Dorset Map ref 2A3 — **SELF CATERING**

★★★★
SELF CATERING

Units **1**
Sleeps **2–3**
Low season per wk
Min £175.00
High season per wk
Max £400.00

Stable Cottage, Beaminster

contact Mrs Diana Clarke, Stable Cottage, Meerhay Manor, Beaminster DT8 3SB
t (01308) 862305 **f** (01308) 863972 **e** meerhay@aol.com **w** meerhay.co.uk

Ground-floor conversion of old barn in grounds of old manor. Wheelchair accessible. Idyllic setting in 40 acres of farmland. Plantsman's garden, tennis court, stabling. Seven miles coast.

open All year
payment Cash/cheques

Unit
General Leisure Shop 1 mile Pub 1 mile

BERE REGIS, Dorset Map ref 2B3 — **CAMPING & CARAVANNING**

★★★
TOURING & CAMPING PARK

(71)	£11.00–£16.50
(71)	£11.00–£16.50
(71)	£11.00–£16.50

71 touring pitches

Rowlands Wait Touring Park

Rye Hill, Bere Regis, Wareham BH20 7LP **t** (01929) 472727 **f** (01929) 472275
e enquiries@rowlandswait.co.uk **w** rowlandswait.co.uk

payment Credit/debit cards, cash/cheques

Set in an Area of Outstanding Natural Beauty. Modern amenity block with family/disabled facilities. Centrally situated for many attractions and places of interest. Direct access to heathland, ideal for walkers, cyclists, couples, families and nature lovers. Open March to October, winter by arrangement.

⊕ *At Bere Regis follow signs to Wool/Bovington. Rowlands Wait is 0.75 miles (1.2km) from the village, top of the hill on the right.*

General Leisure

BOURNEMOUTH, Dorset Map ref 2B3 — **GUEST ACCOMMODATION**

★★★★
GUEST ACCOMMODATION

B&B per room per night
s £35.00–£42.00
d £60.00–£78.00

The Blue Palms

26 Tregonwell Road, Bournemouth BH2 5NS **t** (01202) 554968 **f** (01202) 294197
e bluepalmshotel@btopenworld.com **w** bluepalmshotel.com

Attractive town-centre hotel with own car park and garden. Good standard of accommodation, service and food. Short walk from beaches, shops, Bournemouth International Centre etc.

open All year except Christmas
bedrooms 5 double, 2 twin, 1 single, 2 family
bathrooms All en suite
payment Credit/debit cards, cash

Room General

Using map references

Map references refer to the colour maps at the front of this guide.

BOURNEMOUTH, Dorset Map ref 2B3 | GUEST ACCOMMODATION

★★★
GUEST ACCOMMODATION

B&B per room per night
s £22.00–£30.00
d £50.00–£60.00

Denewood

1 Percy Road, Bournemouth BH5 1JE t (01202) 394493 f (01202) 391155 e info@denewood.co.uk
w denewood.co.uk

Friendly family hotel ideally situated to take advantage of the famous Bournemouth beaches. On-site parking, varied breakfasts served, health and beauty centre.

open All year except Christmas and New Year
bedrooms 4 double, 2 twin, 2 single, 3 family
bathrooms All en suite
payment Credit/debit cards, cash/cheques

Room 📺 ♿ General ⌂ 🏠 ♿ P ♨ 🐾 🐕 Leisure ♨ 🚲 🏊

BOURNEMOUTH, Dorset Map ref 2B3 | GUEST ACCOMMODATION

★★★
GUEST ACCOMMODATION

B&B per room per night
s £35.00–£65.00
d £50.00–£76.00
Evening meal per person
£10.00

The Kings Langley

1 West Cliff Road, Bournemouth BH2 5ES t (01202) 557349 f (01202) 789739
e john@kingslangleyhotel.com w kingslangleyhotel.com

open All year
bedrooms 10 double, 6 twin, 4 family
bathrooms All en suite
payment Credit/debit cards, cash/cheques

Warm, friendly, family-run hotel providing excellent accommodation and traditional home-cooked food. Located just a few minutes' walk from beach, shops and entertainment. Free parking for all our guests, central heating, tea-making facilities, Sky TV and hairdrying facilities in all bedrooms.

Room 🛏 📺 ♿ 🍴 General ⌂ 🏠 ♿ P ♨ ✕ 🍽 🐾 🐕 Leisure 🏊

BOURNEMOUTH, Dorset Map ref 2B3 | GUEST ACCOMMODATION

★★★★
GUEST ACCOMMODATION

B&B per room per night
s £25.00–£31.70
d £46.00–£49.00

Wenrose

23 Drummond Road, Boscombe, Bournemouth BH1 4DP t (01202) 396451 & 07778 800804
f (01202) 396451 e wenrose@bigfoot.com w bournemouthbedandbreakfast.co.uk

open All year except Christmas and New Year
bedrooms 2 double, 1 twin, 1 single
bathrooms 2 en suite
payment Credit/debit cards, cash/cheques, euros

Tranquil guesthouse with garden. Close to shops, sea and public transport. Rooms include desks, tea trays, TVs and wireless broadband. Ideal for business people. Parking. Patio, garden, cooked or continental breakfast, special diets catered for. Non-smoking. No children or pets.

⊕ M27 to Ringwood, left onto A338 (A35) to Bournemouth, over flyover, first (St Pauls) roundabout turn left (1st exit) – straight over next roundabout (Asda on left). Left at (St Swithins) roundabout. 5th turning on left.

♥ 10% discount for staying 7 consecutive nights or more. £6 per person extra for one-night stay.

Room 📺 ♿ 🍴 General P ✂ 🍽 🐾 ✿ Leisure ▶ 🚲 🏊

Place index

If you know where you want to stay, the index at the back of the guide will give you the page number listing accommodation in your chosen town, city or village. Check out the other useful indexes too.

BRIDPORT, Dorset Map ref 2A3 — GUEST ACCOMMODATION

★★★★★
**GUEST ACCOMMODATION
GOLD AWARD**

The Roundham House

Roundham Gardens, West Bay Road, Bridport DT6 4BD **t** (01308) 422753
e cyprencom@compuserve.com **w** roundhamhouse.co.uk

B&B per room per night
s £44.00–£57.00
d £76.00–£98.00

bedrooms 4 double, 2 twin, 1 single, 1 family
bathrooms 7 en suite, 1 private
payment Credit/debit cards, cash/cheques, euros

An Edwardian country house set in an acre of gardens on elevated ground overlooking the rolling West Dorset hills, the majestic World Heritage Coastline and the sea. Many awards for quality. Spacious, en suite bedrooms with glorious views. Ten minutes' walk to the sea. Open March to November. Licensed bar.

⊕ *From centre of Bridport, take road south to West Bay. Hotel is 0.25 miles on the left-hand side.*

Room 📞 📺 🕯 🍷   General 👜7 P ⅍ ☎ 🛏 ✳ 🐾   Leisure ►

BRIDPORT, Dorset Map ref 2A3 — SELF CATERING

★★★★
SELF CATERING

Units **10**
Sleeps **2–6**

Low season per wk
£283.00–£467.00
High season per wk
£483.00–£835.00

Rudge Farm, Bridport

contact Mr Michael Hamer, Rudge Farm, Chilcombe, Bridport DT6 4NF
t (01308) 482630 **e** enquiries@rudgefarm.co.uk **w** rudgefarm.co.uk

open All year
payment Credit/debit cards, cash/cheques

Rudge Farm provides a beautiful countryside location for a stress-free holiday, a short distance away from the World Heritage Coastline. The old farm buildings have been converted into comfortable and cosy cottages, ranging from one to three bedrooms. There are a number of leisure facilities on the farm, including a tennis court and games barn.

⊕ *From Dorchester, take the A35 towards Bridport for 10 miles, turning left 2 miles before Bridport. Follow road for 1 mile. Rudge Farm is on your left.*

♥ *Short breaks available all year.*

Unit 🏠 📺 📋 ▣ 🖥 🍴 🎁 ✳
General 👜 🍴 ♿ P ⅍ 🚭 Ⓞ Ⓢ   Leisure ♦ ⚲ ∪ ♪ ►   Shop 2 miles   Pub 1 mile

BRIDPORT, Dorset Map ref 2A3 — CAMPING & CARAVANNING

★★★★
**HOLIDAY, TOURING
& CAMPING PARK**

🚐 (350) £11.00–£31.00
🚍 (50) £11.00–£31.00
⛺ (100) £11.00–£31.00
🏚 (60) £160.00–£740.00
500 touring pitches

Freshwater Beach Holiday Park

Burton Bradstock, Bridport DT6 4PT **t** (01308) 897317 **f** (01308) 897336
e office@freshwaterbeach.co.uk **w** freshwaterbeach.co.uk

payment Credit/debit cards, cash/cheques

Family park with a large touring and camping field. Own private beach on Dorset's spectacular World Heritage Coastline. Surrounded by countryside and within easy reach of Dorset's features and attractions. Free nightly family entertainment and children's activities. Horse and pony rides, donkey derby, beach fishing, cliff and seaside walks. Open mid-March to mid-November.

⊕ *From Bridport take B3157, situated 2 miles on the right.*

♥ *Pitch prices include up to 6 people and club membership.*

General 🏪 P 🅿 🍴 ☎ 🆚 ⟲ ⊙ 📧 🖥 🍴 ✗ 🐾 ☼   Leisure ⚡ 📺 ♟ 🎵 ♦ ⚲ ∪ ♪ ►

Check it out
Please check prices, quality ratings and other details when you book.

BUCKLAND NEWTON, Dorset Map ref 2B3 — SELF CATERING

★★★★
SELF CATERING

Units **3**
Sleeps **4**

Low season per wk
£225.00–£345.00
High season per wk
£375.00–£500.00

Domineys Cottages, Buckland Newton, Nr Dorchester

contact Mrs Jeanette Gueterbock, Domineys Cottages, Domineys Yard, Buckland Newton, Dorchester DT2 7BS
t (01300) 345295 **f** (01300) 345596 **e** cottages@domineys.com **w** domineys.com

open All year
payment Cash/cheques

Delightful, Victorian, two-bedroomed cottages, comfortably furnished and equipped and maintained to highest standards. Surrounded by beautiful gardens with patios. Heated summer swimming pool. Peaceful location on village edge in heart of Hardy's Dorset. Well situated for touring Wessex, walking and country pursuits. Regret no pets. Children 5+ and babies welcome.

⊕ A352 Dorchester. Left on B3146, follow signs for Buckland Newton. In village take no-through road on left just past pub and telephone box.

Unit 🏠 📺 🖥 💻 🔲 📼 ♨
General 🛏5 🍴 ☕ P   Leisure 🎣 ♨ ⚓   Shop 1 mile   Pub < 0.5 miles

CHRISTCHURCH, Dorset Map ref 2B3 — GUEST ACCOMMODATION

★★★
BED & BREAKFAST

B&B per room per night
s £30.00–£35.00
d £60.00–£80.00
Evening meal per person
£7.00–£10.00

Golfers Reach

88 Lymington Road, Highcliffe, Christchurch BH23 4JU **t** (01425) 272903 **e** caoy@amserve.com

open All year
bedrooms 2 double, 1 twin, 1 single, 1 family
bathrooms All en suite
payment Credit/debit cards, cash/cheques

Golfers Reach offers non-smoking accommodation. All rooms are en suite with colour TV and tea-/coffee-making facilities. Close to local amenities and Highcliffe Castle.

Room 🛏 📺 ☕ 🍴   General 🏠 ☕ ✂ ✕ 🛏 🔌 ♨ 🐾

CORFE CASTLE, Dorset Map ref 2B3 — GUEST ACCOMMODATION

★★★★
BED & BREAKFAST

B&B per room per night
s Min £45.00
d £65.00

Westaway

88 West Street, Corfe Castle, Wareham BH20 5HE **t** (01929) 480188 **e** ray_hendes@btinternet.com
w westaway-corfecastle.co.uk

open All year except Christmas and New Year
bedrooms 2 double, 1 twin
bathrooms 2 en suite, 1 private
payment Cash/cheques

Luxury accommodation comprising two double en suites and twin with private bathroom, situated in the beautiful village of Corfe Castle, with wonderful views of the Purbeck Hills. First-class Aga breakfast, lovely rear garden, including large wildlife pond. Plenty of local walks including Jurassic Coast – a World Heritage site.

⊕ A351 from Wareham to Corfe Castle. Turn right into village square, bear left into West Street. Westaway is 0.25 miles on right.

♥ All year: book 7 nights and only pay for 6.

Room 📺 ☕ 🍴   General 🛏8 P ✂ 🛏 ♨   Leisure ♨ ⚓ ▶ 🚲 🏠

DORCHESTER, Dorset Map ref 2B3 | **SELF CATERING**

★★★
SELF CATERING

Units 1
Sleeps 4
High season per wk
£301.00–£669.00

Wolfeton Lodge, Dorchester

contact Mrs Thimbleby, Wolfeton House, Wolfeton, Dorchester DT2 9QN
t (01305) 263500 **f** (01305) 265090 **e** kthimbleby@wolfeton.freeserve.co.uk

Idyllic lodge beside River Frome, in water meadows below historic Wolfeton House. A c1820 core with large conservatory for sitting and dining. Own garden. Sleeps four plus child. Open May to end of October.

payment Cash/cheques

Unit 〰 ⊡ ▣ 🍴🗄🗄🍽❀
General ⏳8 P 🐾 Leisure ⮐ ▶ Shop 1 mile Pub 1.5 miles

DORCHESTER, Dorset Map ref 2B3 | **CAMPING & CARAVANNING**

★★
TOURING &
CAMPING PARK

🚐(50) £7.00–£12.00
🚎(50) £7.00–£12.00
▲ (50) £7.00–£12.00
50 touring pitches

Giants Head Caravan & Camping Park

Old Sherborne Road, Dorchester DT2 7TR **t** (01300) 341242 **e** holidays@giantshead.co.uk
w giantshead.co.uk

Two miles north-east of Cerne Abbas, three miles south of Middlemarsh, eight miles from Dorchester.

payment Cash/cheques

General ⛽🗂🏕P🔌🚰🚻🅵☉🗄 🎣 🏕. Leisure ⮐ ▶

EYPE, Dorset Map ref 1D2 | **HOTEL**

★★
COUNTRY HOUSE HOTEL

B&B per room per night
s £55.00–£70.00
d £85.00–£103.00
HB per person per night
£55.00–£80.00

Eype's Mouth Country Hotel

Eype, Bridport DT6 6AL **t** (01308) 423300 **f** (01308) 420033 **e** info@eypesmouthhotel.co.uk
w eypesmouthhotel.co.uk

open All year
bedrooms 12 double, 3 twin, 2 single, 1 family
bathrooms All en suite
payment Credit/debit cards, cash/cheques, euros

Set in the picturesque small village of Eype, the hotel nestles amidst the downland and cliff tops that form the Heritage Coastline. Stunning sea views in a peaceful setting are matched by excellent hospitality. Good food and drink, served in the comfortable surroundings of this family-run hotel, make the perfect venue for a relaxing break.

⊕ A35, Bridport bypass, take turning to Eype, also signed to service area, then 3rd right to beach. Hotel 0.5 miles down lane.

♥ Special DB&B 3-night breaks available throughout the year.

Room ⊡ 📞 ⊡ 🚿 🍵 General ⏳ ⛪ ☂ P 🍷 🎱 🍴 ❀ 🐾 Leisure ⮐ ▶

Suit yourself

The symbols at the end of each entry mean you can enjoy virtually made-to-measure accommodation with the services and facilities most important to you. A key to the symbols can be found inside the back-cover flap. Keep this open for easy reference.

For key to symbols open the back-cover flap.

FERNDOWN, Dorset Map ref 2B3 `SELF CATERING`

★★★
SELF CATERING

Units **1**
Sleeps **1–8**

Low season per wk
£380.00–£600.00
High season per wk
£675.00–£1,080.00

Birchcroft, Ferndown

contact Miss Leanne Hemingway, Dorset Cottage Holidays, 11 Tyneham Close, Sandford, Wareham BH20 7BE
t (01929) 553443 **f** (01929) 552714 **e** enq@dhcottages.co.uk **w** dhcottages.co.uk

open All year
payment Credit/debit cards, cash/cheques

A nature lover's secret hideaway, Birchcroft is surrounded by rhododendron bushes in over an acre of land. With accessible accommodation, it's large enough for two families. Terrace enjoys breathtaking local views. Deer, foxes, rabbits, and birds are often seen. Only five miles from Bournemouth beaches. Great for walkers and golfers.

⊕ *A338 towards Bournemouth. Take B3073, passing airport and through Parley Cross. Pass Coppins Nursery. Entrance to the lane is immediately after Knowle House on right.*

♥ *Weekend breaks available during low seasons. Special activity weekends for golfers, etc. Fully-catered group bookings.*

Unit 🖳 📺 🖸 🖃 🖾 🛢🛢 🖲 🖳 🗍 ✿
General 🕭 P ⊱ Ⓢ Leisure ∪ ♪ ▶ Shop 0.5 miles Pub 0.5 miles

FOLKE, Dorset Map ref 2B3 `SELF CATERING`

★★★★
SELF CATERING

Units **4**
Sleeps **4–8**

Low season per wk
£330.00–£550.00
High season per wk
£500.00–£1,200.00

Folke Manor Farm Cottages, Folke, Sherborne

contact Mr & Mrs John & Carol Perrett, Folke Manor Farm, Folke, Sherborne DT9 5HP
t (01963) 210731 & 07929 139472 **e** folkemanorfarm@aol.com **w** folkemanorholidays.co.uk

Folke Manor Farm Cottages are spacious barn conversions in a quiet part of the Blackmore Vale close to Sherborne. Ideal place for walking and to relax in our beautiful gardens.

open All year
payment Cash/cheques

Unit 🖳 📺 🖸 🖃 🖾 🛢🛢 🖲 🖳 🗍 ✿
General 🕭 🛏 🏃 P ⊱ Ⓢ 🐕 Leisure ♪ ▶ 🚣 Shop 0.5 miles Pub 0.5 miles

LULWORTH COVE, Dorset Map ref 2B3 `HOTEL`

★★
HOTEL

B&B per room per night
s £42.50–£60.00
d £66.00–£95.00
HB per person per night
£49.00–£69.00

Cromwell House Hotel

Lulworth Cove, West Lulworth, Wareham BH20 5RJ **t** (01929) 400253 **f** (01929) 400566
e cromwell@lulworthcove.co.uk **w** lulworthcove.co.uk

open All year except Christmas and New Year
bedrooms 7 double, 7 twin, 2 single, 3 family
bathrooms All en suite
payment Credit/debit cards, cash/cheques

Lulworth Cove 200yds, all en suite rooms, spectacular sea views, direct access Jurassic Coast, excellent walking and country pursuits. Good home cooking – local fish, including Lulworth Cove lobsters, a speciality. Bar and extensive wine list, beautiful gardens and sea-facing terrace, home-made cream teas, all-day refreshments, swimming pool (May to October). Groups welcome.

⊕ *M3, M27, A31 to Bere Regis, B3071 to West Lulworth. Hotel situated on slip road, on left, 200yds beyond end of West Lulworth village heading for Lulworth Cove.*

♥ *Art and photography courses – apply for details. 3-day special breaks available.*

Room 🖐 🛏 📞 📺 📶 🛎 🖐 General 🕭 🛏 🏃 P 🍽 🎱 ⊱ 🖂 ☎ ✿ 🐕 Leisure 🎣 ∪ ▶ 🚣

Confirm your booking
It's always advisable to confirm your booking in writing.

LYME REGIS, Dorset Map ref 1D2   GUEST ACCOMMODATION

★★★★
GUEST ACCOMMODATION

B&B per room per night
d £50.00–£70.00

St Andrews House

Uplyme Road, Lyme Regis DT7 3LP   **t** (01297) 445495

Quality accommodation in large house. Sea and country views. Parking, swimming pool and gardens. Friendly atmosphere and extensive breakfast menu.

open All year
bedrooms 3 double
bathrooms All en suite
payment Cash/cheques

Room TV ⓦ 🍵   General 🛏 P 🏠 ✿   Leisure 🐾

LYME REGIS, Dorset Map ref 1D2   SELF CATERING

★★★★
SELF CATERING

Units   **2**
Sleeps   **2–4**

Low season per wk
£295.00–£420.00
High season per wk
£465.00–£595.00

Sea Tree House, Lyme Regis

contact Mr David Parker, Sea Tree House, 18 Broad Street, Lyme Regis DT7 3QE
t (01297) 442244   **f** (01297) 442244   **e** seatree.house@ukonline.co.uk
w lymeregis.com/seatreehouse

open All year
payment Cash/cheques

Romantic, elegant apartments overlooking the sea, three minutes from the beach. Spacious living room with dining area overlooking the sea. Central position giving easy access to restaurants, pubs and walks in Area of Outstanding Natural Beauty. Wi-Fi Internet. Warm, friendly welcome from owners.

⊕ *Approach Lyme Regis from either A35 or A3052. Sea Tree House is on Broad Street, the main street, just before you reach the sea.*

♥ *Short breaks available in the low season.*

Unit 🛏 TV 🍴🔲▦🖥▪ 🍽🍵 🍵🔆🖥 🖥✿
General 🛏 🏠 P 🅿 ⓢ 🐾   Leisure U ♣ ⚑   Shop 0.5 miles   Pub 0.5 miles

---

LYME REGIS, Dorset Map ref 1D2   SELF CATERING

★★★★
SELF CATERING

Units   **1**
Sleeps   **5**

Low season per wk
£350.00–£390.00
High season per wk
£450.00–£875.00

Sheepwash Green, Fishpond Bottom, Bridport

contact Mrs Ambra Edwards, Guppys Lodge, Fishpond, Bridport DT6 6NN
t (01297) 678598   **e** ambra@sheepwashgreen.co.uk   **w** sheepwashgreen.co.uk

open All year
payment Cash/cheques

Imagine a secret valley untouched by time, with glorious views over rolling hills to Dorset's Jurassic Coast. Hidden in this Area of Outstanding Natural Beauty, stands Sheepwash Green, a cosy cob cottage with beams, log fires and large sunny garden. No traffic. No noise. No light pollution. Just perfect peace, with outstanding walking from the door. World Heritage coast and beach: four miles.

⊕ *Fishpond Bottom is reached from the B3165 at Marshwood, or the A35 at Morcombelake. Please telephone the owner for directions.*

♥ *Midweek breaks: 4 nights for the price of 3. Bluebell breaks; Christmas escapes – see website for details.*

Unit 🛏 TV 🔲▦ 🖥▪ 🍽🍵 🍵🔆🖥 🖥✿
General 🛏 🏠 🛎 P ✂ ⓢ 🐾   Leisure ♣ ⚑ 🏠   Shop 4 miles   Pub 2 miles

---

It's all quality-assessed accommodation

Our commitment to quality involves wide-ranging accommodation assessment. Rating and awards were correct at the time of going to press but may change following a new assessment. Please check at time of booking.

MELCOMBE BINGHAM, Dorset Map ref 2B3   **SELF CATERING**

★★★★
SELF CATERING

Units   **1**
Sleeps   **1–7**

Low season per wk
£400.00–£575.00
High season per wk
£625.00–£800.00

Greygles, Melcombe Bingham, Dorchester

contact Mr Paul Sommerfeld, 22 Tiverton Road, London NW10 3HL
t (020) 8969 4830   **f** (020) 8960 0069   **e** enquiry@greygles.co.uk   **w** greygles.co.uk

open All year
payment Cash/cheques, euros

Rural peace in spacious, well-equipped stone cottage with delightful views. Hardy Country, on edge of friendly village with well-known pub. Four bedrooms, one on ground floor. Log fire. Wendy house in garden. In an Area of Outstanding Natural Beauty, just off Wessex Ridgeway walkers' path. Coast, abbeys, castles, gardens, many attractions within 30 minutes' drive.

⊕ From Winterbourne Whitechurch on A354 Blandford/ Dorchester road, follow sign to Milton Abbas, then through Milton, Hilton and Ansty to Melcombe Bingham.

♥ Short breaks available outside summer peak, Christmas and Easter. Min 3-night stay. Linen, towels and heating included.

Unit 🏠 📺 🖥 💻 🍴 🔲 📷 🛋 🔌 🍳 🔲 🖁 📠 ❄
General ♨ 🛏 ⚓ P ✎ ◎ 🐾   Leisure 🎣   **Shop** 0.5 miles   **Pub** 0.5 miles

---

MILTON ABBAS, Dorset Map ref 2B3   **SELF CATERING**

★★★★
SELF CATERING

Units   **1**
Sleeps   **2–6**

Low season per wk
£245.00–£305.00
High season per wk
£345.00–£595.00

Primrose Cottage, Blandford Forum

contact Mrs Therese Clemson, 22 Kerrfield, Winchester SO22 5EX
t (01962) 865786   **f** (01962) 865786   **e** therese.clemson@btinternet.com
w miltonabbas-primrosecottage.co.uk

open All year
payment Cash/cheques

Grade II Listed, 18thC, thatched cob cottage set on the street in the unique village of Milton Abbas, created by Lord Milton. Centre of Hardy Country. Ideal for walkers and romantics.

⊕ From A354 follow signs to Milton Abbas.

Unit 🏠 📺 🖥 💻 🍴 🔲 📷 🛋 🔌 🍳 🔲 🖁 ❄
General ♨ 🛏 ⚓ P ⑤ 🐾   Leisure ∪ ♪ ▶

POOLE, Dorset Map ref 2B3   **SELF CATERING**

★★★★★
SELF CATERING

Units   **10**
Sleeps   **2–8**

Low season per wk
£495.00–£650.00
High season per wk
£690.00–£1,150.00

The Dorset Resort, Hyde, Wareham

contact Miss Jackie Langworthy, The Dorset Resort, Hyde, Wareham BH20 7NT
t (01929) 472244   **f** (01929) 471294   **e** resort@dorsetresort.com   **w** dorsetresort.com

open All year
payment Credit/debit cards, cash/cheques

The Scandinavian-style log homes at the Dorset Resort are both beautiful and luxurious. Superbly well crafted, they are set in tranquil woodland in the heart of Dorset's stunning countryside. Each has its own sauna, log-burning stove and balcony. We are minutes from Blue Flag beaches, Jurassic Coast etc.

⊕ See website for details.

♥ Special offers will appear from time to time on our website.

Unit 🏠 📺 🖥 💻 🍴 🔲 📷 🛋 🔌 🍳 🔲 🖁 📠 // ❄
General ♨ 🛏 ⚓ P ✎ ◎ ⑤   Leisure ◉ ♪ ▶ 🚲 🎣   **Shop** 3 miles   **Pub** 3 miles

---

POOLE, Dorset Map ref 2B3 — SELF CATERING

Fripps Cottage, Wimborne

★★★
SELF CATERING

Units **1**
Sleeps **4**

Low season per wk
£250.00–£440.00
High season per wk
£440.00–£655.00

contact Mrs Helen Edbrooke, Stoneleigh House, 2 Rowlands Hill, Wimborne BH21 1AN
t (01202) 884908 **f** 0870 471 2861 **e** helen@stoneleighhouse.com
w stoneleighhouse.com/frippscottage

Two-bedroom detached bungalow set in five acres in beautiful country location, close to town and coast. Large, enclosed, well-maintained garden. All mod cons, and fully equipped for a very comfortable stay.

open All year
payment Cash/cheques

Unit 🏠 📺 ⊟ 🅿 ▦ 🛏 🗲 🗑 🗄 🍳 ❄
General 🛋 ▥ ⚘ P ⚡ ♨ Leisure ∪ ▶ 🏖 Shop 1.5 miles Pub 1 mile

SHAFTESBURY, Dorset Map ref 2B3 — GUEST ACCOMMODATION

Glebe Farm

★★★★★
BED & BREAKFAST
SILVER AWARD

B&B per room per night
s £35.00–£40.00
d £70.00–£80.00
Evening meal per person
£15.00–£20.00

High Street, Ashmore, Salisbury SP5 5AE **t** (01747) 811974 **f** (01747) 811104
e tmillard@glebe.f9.co.uk

open All year except Christmas and New Year
bedrooms 1 double, 1 twin
bathrooms All en suite
payment Cash/cheques

Beautiful, unique, contemporary farmhouse in Dorset's highest village, set in a tranquil location away from traffic noise. Enjoy an evening meal with your bottle of wine and literally soak up the views then retire to bed with open doors and drift off to sleep listening to our resident owls!

Room 🛏 📺 ♨ ♨ General 14 P ✕ Leisure ▶

SHERBORNE, Dorset Map ref 2B3 — HOTEL

The Grange at Oborne

★★★
HOTEL
SILVER AWARD

B&B per room per night
s £90.00–£100.00
d £105.00–£150.00
HB per person per night
£79.50–£112.00

Oborne, Sherborne DT9 4LA **t** (01935) 813463 **f** (01935) 817464 **e** reception@thegrange.co.uk
w thegrangeatoborne.co.uk

Situated just one mile from Sherborne, The Grange is a splendid mellow-stone country-house hotel in a peaceful location.

open All year
bedrooms 15 double, 3 twin
bathrooms All en suite
payment Credit/debit cards, cash/cheques

Room 🛏 🛋 ☎ 📺 ♨ ♨ 🔥 General 🛋 ▥ ⚘ P ⚡ 🍴 🛎 ❄ 🚐 Leisure ▶

SHERBORNE, Dorset Map ref 2B3 — GUEST ACCOMMODATION

The Pheasants B&B

★★★★
BED & BREAKFAST

B&B per room per night
s £50.00–£57.00
d £65.00–£82.00

24 Greenhill, Sherborne DT9 4EW **t** (01935) 815252 **f** (01935) 812938 **e** info@thepheasants.com
w thepheasants.com

A 300-year-old town house in the heart of historic Sherborne, a short walk from the abbey and castles. Elegant guests' lounge. Fine wines by the glass. All rooms en suite.

open All year except Christmas and New Year
bedrooms 1 double, 1 twin, 1 family
bathrooms All en suite
payment Cash/cheques

Room 📺 ♨ ♨ General 🛋 🗲 ▮ 🛎 ❄ Leisure ▶ 🏖

Travel update

Get the latest travel information – just dial RAC on 1740 from your mobile phone.

For key to symbols open the back-cover flap.

SHERBORNE, Dorset Map ref 2B3 | SELF CATERING

★★★
SELF CATERING

Units **1**
Sleeps **4**

Low season per wk
£220.00–£270.00
High season per wk
£320.00–£360.00

Blackberry Cottage, Sherborne

contact Mr John Michael Farr, 17 Marsh Lane, Yeovil BA21 3BX
t (01935) 423148 **f** (01935) 706874

An ideal base for discovering the delights of
Dorset. This 19thC stone cottage is close to the
centre of the historic town of Sherborne.

open All year
payment Cash/cheques

Unit 🏠 📺 ⛶ 🍳 ▭ ⚒ 🗄 🗑 💄❄
General 🐕 P ✂

STUDLAND, Dorset Map ref 2B3 | HOTEL

★★
HOTEL
SILVER AWARD

HB per person per night
£98.00–£134.00

The Manor House Hotel

Manor Road, Studland BH19 3AU **t** (01929) 450288 **f** (01929) 452255
e themanorhousehotel@lineone.net **w** themanorhousehotel.com

open All year
bedrooms 8 double, 4 twin, 5 family, 4 suites
bathrooms All en suite
payment Credit/debit cards, cash/cheques

Romantic 18thC manor house in 20 acres of
secluded grounds overlooking the sea. Residential
and restaurant licence. All rooms en suite with
central heating, TV, telephone, radio, hairdryer, tea/
coffee-making facilities. Four-poster beds. Menus
feature fresh local seafood. Oak-panelled bar and
dining room with conservatory. Two hard tennis
courts. Riding and golf nearby.

♥ *Good discounts on stays of 3 nights or more. Christmas 3-
day package and New Year 2-day package available.*

Room 🛏 🖥 ☎ 📺 🍳 🕯 General 🐕5 P ♨ 🎱 ♫ ❄ 🐾 Leisure ♦ ∪ ⚑

SUTTON POYNTZ, Dorset Map ref 2B3 | SELF CATERING

★★★★
SELF CATERING

Units **1**
Sleeps **1–4**

Low season per wk
£310.00–£540.00
High season per wk
£540.00–£720.00

Ebenezer Cottage, Weymouth

contact Mrs Cathy Varley
t 07778 524199 **e** info@ebenezercottage.co.uk **w** ebenezercottage.co.uk

open All year
payment Cash/cheques

Three-bedroom terraced cottage on picturesque
millstream lane. Sutton Poyntz lies in a horseshoe of
hills, along which runs the South West Coast Path.
Rolling downs and secret valleys provide access to
beautiful scenery. At the heart of the World Heritage
Site, there are spectacular views towards the Jurassic
Coast.

⊕ *A354 Dorchester to Weymouth. 2nd left signposted
Broadmayne/Preston. At small crossroads, right. 1st left
signposted Sutton Poyntz. Silver Street is 1 mile on left.*

♥ *Short breaks available Oct-Mar.*

Unit 🏠 📺 ⛶ ▭ 🍳 🗄 🍴 ⚒ 🗄 🗑 💄❄
General 🐕 🏛 ♨ ✂ Ⓢ Leisure ∪ 🚲 Shop 1 mile Pub 0.5 miles

Check it out

Information on accommodation listed in this guide has been supplied by proprietors.
As changes may occur you should remember to check all relevant details at the time
of booking.

SWANAGE, Dorset Map ref 2B3 — **HOTEL**

★★★
HOTEL

B&B per room per night
s £61.00–£82.00
d £61.00–£176.00
HB per person per night
£74.00–£90.00

The Pines Hotel

Burlington Road, Swanage BH19 1LT **t** (01929) 425211 **f** (01929) 422075
e reservations@pineshotel.co.uk **w** pineshotel.co.uk

open All year
bedrooms 17 double, 8 twin, 2 single, 8 family,
8 suites
bathrooms All en suite
payment Credit/debit cards, cash/cheques

Family-run hotel in the Purbeck countryside at the quiet end of Swanage Bay. Own access to the beach and walks encompassing marvellous coastal views. The Pines prides itself on the friendliness of its staff, the comfort of its sea-facing lounges and its reputation for cuisine served in our recently refurbished restaurant.

⊕ *A351 into Swanage. Left at seafront. 2nd right at the end of Burlington Road.*

♥ *Details of bargain breaks/autumn and winter specials/ Christmas and New Year available on request.*

Room 🛁 📞 📺 ♨ ⛄ General ♨ 🍳 ♿ P ♨ 🕎 🕅 ❍ 🗄 ♨ ♯ 🕇 Leisure ♫ ∪ ♪ ↑ 🚲 🏊

SWANAGE, Dorset Map ref 2B3 — **GUEST ACCOMMODATION**

★★★★
GUEST ACCOMMODATION
SILVER AWARD

B&B per room per night
s £30.00–£50.00
d £60.00–£100.00

The Castleton

1 Highcliffe Road, Swanage BH19 1LW **t** (01929) 423972 **e** stay@castletonhotel-swanage.co.uk
w castletonhotel-swanage.co.uk

open All year except Christmas
bedrooms 5 double, 2 twin, 1 single, 2 family
bathrooms All en suite
payment Cash/cheques

You are invited to our family-run B&B situated 100m from the beach. All rooms are en suite, and furnished to ensure that you have a relaxing and comfortable stay. Be it for one week or two, or one night or two, you will be made just as welcome. Please see virtual tour on our website.

⊕ *From town centre follow signs to Studland. We are 100m from where the road veers away from the beach, on the right.*

Room 🛁 📺 ♨ ⛄ General ♨6 P ♨ 🕎 🕅 ♯ Leisure ♪ ↑ 🚲 🏊

SWANAGE, Dorset Map ref 2B3 — **CAMPING & CARAVANNING**

★★★★★
TOURING PARK
🚐(53) £13.60–£25.60
🚍(53) £13.60–£25.60
53 touring pitches

Haycraft Caravan Club Site

Haycrafts Lane, Swanage BH19 3EB **t** (01929) 480572 **w** caravanclub.co.uk

payment Credit/debit cards, cash/cheques

Peaceful site located five miles from Swanage, with its safe, sandy beach. Spectacular cliff-top walks, Corfe Castle, Lulworth Cove and Durdle Door within easy reach. There are numerous public footpaths and coastal walks nearby. Open March to November.

⊕ *Midway between Corfe Castle and Swanage. Take A351 from Wareham to Swanage, at Harmans Cross turn right into Haycrafts Lane, site 0.5 miles on the left.*

♥ *Special member rates mean you can save your membership subscription in less than a week. Visit our website to find out more.*

THE
CARAVAN
CLUB

General P 🚐 🕃 🍴 🚐 🈺 ☉ 🏕🗄 🕇 ☼ Leisure ♪ ↑

For key to symbols open the back-cover flap.

WEYMOUTH, Dorset Map ref 2B3 | GUEST ACCOMMODATION

★★★★
BED & BREAKFAST

B&B per room per night
s £54.00–£60.00
d £75.00–£85.00

Old Harbour View

12 Trinity Road, Weymouth DT4 8TJ **t** (01305) 774633 & 07974 422241 **f** (01305) 750828
e pv_1st_ind@yahoo.co.uk

Idyllic Georgian harbourside town house, offering two charming double bedrooms. Restaurants, pubs, sandy beach and ferries to the Channel Islands on its doorstep.

open All year except Christmas and New Year
bedrooms 1 double, 1 twin
bathrooms All en suite
payment Credit/debit cards, cash/cheques

Room 📺 ✆ General P ✂ 🍽 🅿 ⚅ 🖥 Leisure ✦ ▸ 🚲 🏊

WEYMOUTH, Dorset Map ref 2B3 | CAMPING & CARAVANNING

★★★★
TOURING PARK
🚐 (120) £11.20–£22.40
🚏 (120) £11.20–£22.40
120 touring pitches

Crossways Caravan Club Site

Crossways, Dorchester DT2 8BE **t** (01305) 852032 **w** caravanclub.co.uk

payment Credit/debit cards, cash/cheques

Set in 35 acres of woodland. Dorchester is nearby, also Weymouth's award-winning, sandy beach. Visit Lawrence of Arabia's house at Cloud's Hill. If you want to leave the car behind for the day, the railway station is just five minutes' walk from the site. Open March to October.

⊕ North from A35 or south from A352, join B3390. Site on right within 1 mile. Entrance to site by forecourt of filling station.

♥ Midweek discount: pitch fee for standard pitches for stays on any Tue, Wed or Thu night outside peak season dates will be reduced by 50%.

THE
**CARAVAN
CLUB**

General 🖼 P 🔌 🕭 ☎ 🚐 🛎 ⊙ 🛍 🖥 🍴 ☼ Leisure 🏔

WIMBORNE MINSTER, Dorset Map ref 2B3 | GUEST ACCOMMODATION

★★
INN

B&B per room per night
s £35.00–£45.00
d £50.00–£70.00

The Albion

High Street, Wimborne Minster BH21 1HR **t** (01202) 882492 **f** (01202) 639333
e albioninn-wimborne@tiscali.co.uk **w** albioninn-wimborne.co.uk

The oldest-surviving coaching house in Wimborne, situated just off the town square opposite the minster. All rooms with modern facilities. Large bathroom with WC, shower and bath.

open All year except Christmas
bedrooms 1 double, 1 twin, 1 family
payment Credit/debit cards, cash/cheques, euros

Room 📺 ✆ 🍷 General 🪑 🍴 ✗ ❄ Leisure ✦ ▸

Glastonbury Tor

Wookey Pier, Cheddar Gorge

Tarr Steps, Exmoor National Park

Explore Somerset

Wander around quaint villages and elegant country houses. See a classic cathedral and captivating caves. Discover mysterious moorland and tales of myth and legend. Choose quiet coastal harbours or fun-filled family resorts.

Contrasting coast

Enter the Castle of Doom or just rotate gently on the Big Wheel in The Grand Pier amusement park at Weston-super-Mare. Or take a bucket and spade to the sandy beach, enjoy a donkey ride and all the traditional pleasures of a family seaside resort, both here and at Burnham-on-Sea. You'll find more safe sands at Minehead before the coast becomes jagged as it reaches Exmoor. Stride out on the South West Coast Path here, or take a journey of pure nostalgia on the West Somerset Railway.

Hills and moors

Exmoor may be one of England's smallest national parks, but it packs a lot in. Follow footpaths and bridleways through high, wild moorland, steeply wooded combes, ancient oak forests and rolling farmland. Take your mountain bike and speed down cycle paths that radiate from Dunkery Beacon, Exmoor's highest point, or take life at a slower pace on horseback – it's a popular place for pony-trekking. While Exmoor is Lorna Doone Country, the Quantock Hills belong to poet Samuel Taylor Coleridge. Follow his footsteps into the landscape that inspired him and walk along all, or part of the 36-mile Coleridge Way.

Mystery and legend

Spend your well-earned pounds on bargain-priced designer outfits at Clarks Village in Street before tracking down tales of mystery and legend at Glastonbury. The Tor, standing like a beacon rising out of the Somerset flats, is said to be the home of Gwyn ap Nudd, the Lord of the Underworld and King of the Fairies – a place where the fairy folk live – and it's also reputed to be the birthplace of King Arthur.

South West Coast Path

Cheddar Caves and Gorge

Somerset Cider

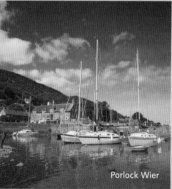

Porlock Wier

In the grounds of ruined Glastonbury Abbey is a cutting from the Glastonbury thorn that is said to have originated from the staff of Joseph of Arimathea. The hawthorn still astonishes by flowering at Christmas as well as in May. Uncover yet more mysteries at Wookey Hole Caves – ask about the witch!

Cathedrals and caves

Take time to wander around the city of Wells dominated by its magnificent cathedral, begun in the 12th century. And while you are here, tuck into afternoon tea on the Garden Terrace at nearby Bishop's Palace which dates back to the early 13th century.

On your travels in the county, visit a Somerset cider producer to see how the local tipple is made and search out the original home of the famous cheese at Cheddar Caves & Gorge. It's now a major attraction where you can go deep underground in Gough's Cave, explore its cathedral-like caverns carved out over a million years, and meet 9,000-year-old Cheddar Man, Britain's oldest complete skeleton. Or stay on the surface and climb the 274 steps of Jacob's Ladder from the Gorge to the top of the Mendip Hills. The views are worth the effort!

Food & drink

Fancy a bite to eat, a relaxing drink or some fresh local produce? Here's a selection of food and drink venues to get you started. For lots more ideas go online at enjoyengland.com/taste.

Restaurants

Andrews on the Weir
Fine dining
Porlock Weir, Minehead
TA24 8PB
t (01643) 863300
w andrewsontheweir.co.uk

Blostin's Restaurant
Bistro
29-33 Waterloo Road,
Shepton Mallet BA4 5HH
t (01749) 343648
w blostins.co.uk

Brazz
Bistro
Castle Bow, Taunton TA1 1NF
t (01823) 252000
w the-castle-hotel.com

Clavelshay Barn Restaurant
English
Lower Clavelshay Farm, North
Petherton, Bridgwater TA6 6PJ
t (01278) 662629
w clavelshaybarn.co.uk

The Full Moon at Rudge
English
near Frome BA11 2QF
t (01373) 830936
w thefullmoon.co.uk

The George & Pilgrim Hotel
English
1 High Street, Glastonbury
BA6 9DP
t (01458) 831146

Kempsters Restaurant
English
Lower Street, West Chinnock,
Crewkerne TA18 7PT
t (01935) 881768

Little Barwick House
English
Barwick, Yeovil BA22 9TD
t (01935) 423902
w littlebarwickhouse.co.uk

Mulberrys Bistro
Bistro
9 Union Street, Yeovil BA20 1PQ
t (01935) 434188
w mulberrysbistro.co.uk

New Farm Restaurant
Fine dining
Over Stratton, South Petherton
TA13 5LQ
t (01460) 240584
w newfarmrestaurant.co.uk

Sharpham Park
Fine dining
Charlton House, Charlton Road,
Shepton Mallet BA4 4PR
t (01749) 342008
w charltonhouse.com

Thomas's Restaurant at Bellplot House Hotel
English
High Street, Chard TA20 1QB
t (01460) 62600
w bellplothouse.co.uk

Truffles Restaurant
English
95 High Street, Bruton
BA10 0AR
t (01749) 812255
w trufflesbruton.co.uk

The Willow Tree Restaurant
British
3 Tower Lane, Taunton TA1 4AR
t (01823) 352835
w willowtreerestaurant.co.uk

Pubs

The Globe
Fore Street, Milverton,
Taunton TA4 1JX
t (01823) 400534
w theglobemilverton.co.uk

The Haymaker Inn
Wadeford, Chard TA20 3AP
t (01460) 64161
w thehaymakerinn.com

The Helyar Arms
Moor Lane, East Coker,
Yeovil BA22 9JR
t (01935) 862332
w helyar-arms.co.uk

The Montague Inn
Shepton Montague,
Wincanton BA9 8JW
t (01749) 813213

The Pilgrims
Lovington, Castle Cary BA7 7PT
t (01963) 240600
w thepilgrimsatlovington.co.uk

The Queen's Arms
Corton Denham DT9 4LR
t (01963) 220317
w thequeensarms.com

Tearooms, coffee shops and cafes

Bank House Café
Bank House, The Square,
Axbridge BS26 2AP
t (01934) 733004
w bankhousecafe.co.uk

East Lambrook Manor Gardens
South Petherton TA13 5HH
t (01460) 240328
w eastlambrook.co.uk

Farm shops and local produce

Barleymow's Farm Shop
Snowdon Hill Farm, Chard
TA20 3PS
t (01460) 62130
w barleymowsfarmshop.com

Jon Thorner's
Bridge Farm Shop, Pylle,
Shepton Mallet BA4 6TA
t (01749) 830138
w jonthorners.co.uk

Pitney Farm Shop
Glebe Farm, Woodsbirdshill Lane,
Pitney, Langport TA10 9AP
t (01458) 253002
w pitneyfarmshop.co.uk

Roots: Fabulous West Country Food
7a Bath Place, Taunton TA1 4ER
t (01823) 337233
w tauntonroots.co.uk

Rumwell Farm Shop
Wellington Road, Rumwell,
near Taunton TA4 1EJ
t (01823) 461599
w rumwellfarmshop.com

Quality
visitor attractions

VisitBritain operates a Visitor Attraction Quality Assurance Service.

Participating attractions are visited annually by trained, impartial assessors who look at all aspects of the visit, from initial telephone enquiries to departure, customer service to catering, as well as all facilities and activities.

Only those attractions which have been assessed by Enjoy England and meet the standard receive the quality marque, your sign of a Quality Assured Visitor Attraction.

Look out for the quality marque and visit with confidence.

where to stay in
Somerset

Maps
All place names in the blue bands are shown on the maps at the front of this guide.

Accommodation symbols
Symbols give useful information about services and facilities. Inside the back-cover flap you can find a key to these symbols. Keep it open for easy reference.

BILBROOK, Somerset Map ref 1D1 **GUEST ACCOMMODATION**

★★★★
GUEST ACCOMMODATION
SILVER AWARD

B&B per room per night
s £37.00–£39.00
d £54.00–£58.00

The Wayside B&B
Bilbrook, Minehead TA24 6HE **t** (01984) 641669 **e** thewayside@tiscali.co.uk **w** thewayside.co.uk

Modern, country accommodation focusing on the highest levels of quality and service. Superb location with easy access to great walking and the coast. Open 1 March to 31 October.

bedrooms 2 double
bathrooms 1 en suite, 1 private
payment Cash/cheques

Room 📺 ♨ ❧ General ☎12 P ⊁ ﷺ ✿ Leisure ∪ ⊁ 🚲 ⛵

BINEGAR, Somerset Map ref 2B2 **SELF CATERING**

★★★★
SELF CATERING

Units **1**
Sleeps **5**

Low season per wk
£360.00–£425.00
High season per wk
£475.00–£590.00

Spindle Cottage, Binegar Green, Nr Bath
contact Mrs Angela Bunting, Spindle Cottage, Binegar Green, Binegar, Near Bath BA3 4UE
t (01749) 840497 **e** angela@spindlecottagelets.co.uk **w** spindlecottagelets.co.uk

open All year
payment Cash/cheques

Fairy-tale 17thC cottage, high on Mendip Hills. Garden has summerhouse, gazebo, conservatory. Cottage is a place of charm and delight. Lovely sitting room with low ceiling and oak beams. Wood-burning stove. Three bedrooms: one double, one twin, one single. Wells, Glastonbury, Bath, Cheddar, Wookey Hole within easy reach.

⊕ 15 miles south of Bath on A367. One mile from A37 at Gurney Slade. Five miles north of Wells on B3139.

♥ Short breaks available Oct-Mar, 3-night stay.

Unit ﷺ 📺 ⌨ 💻 🗄🖥 ⊟🍴 🖨 ⌨🍳 ✿
General ☎ 🛏 ﹩ P ⊁ ⊙ Ⓢ Shop 1 mile Pub 0.5 miles

Place index
If you know where you want to stay, the index at the back of the guide will give you the page number listing accommodation in your chosen town, city or village. Check out the other useful indexes too.

BLUE ANCHOR, Somerset Map ref 1D1 — SELF CATERING

★★★★
SELF CATERING

Units **3**
Sleeps **2–5**

Low season per wk
£265.00–£335.00
High season per wk
£335.00–£545.00

Huntingball Lodge, Blue Anchor

contact Mr & Mrs Brian & Kim Hall, Huntingball Lodge, Blue Anchor, Minehead TA24 6JP
t (01984) 640076 **f** (01984) 640076 **w** huntingball-lodge.co.uk

open All year
payment Cash/cheques

Elegant, quiet country house with spectacular views over the Somerset coastline and Exmoor countryside. Luxurious and spacious self-catering apartments furnished and equipped to a very high standard, each with own private patio or roof terrace. Pub/restaurant, tea rooms and convenience store within easy walking distance. Guaranteed warm welcome from the resident owners.

⊕ *From Taunton, A358 then A39 to Minehead. At Carhampton, right (signed Blue Anchor). Go along seafront, 1st right to Chapel Cleeve. We are 1st on left.*

♥ *Short breaks available Nov-Mar (excl Christmas and New Year).*

Unit 📺 ▢ ▨ 🖥 🗄 🍴 🍲 📁 ❄
General P ⚲ ▢ S 🐾 Shop < 0.5 miles Pub < 0.5 miles

BREAN, Somerset Map ref 1D1 — GUEST ACCOMMODATION

★★★★
GUEST ACCOMMODATION

B&B per room per night
s £30.00–£37.50
d £50.00–£60.00

Yew Tree House

Hurn Lane, Berrow, Nr Brean, Burnham-on-Sea TA8 2QT **t** (01278) 751382
e yewtree@yewtree-house.co.uk **w** yewtree-house.co.uk

open All year except Christmas
bedrooms 2 double, 2 twin, 1 family, 1 suite
bathrooms All en suite
payment Credit/debit cards, cash/cheques

We warmly welcome visitors to our charming old house with its spacious rooms, modern facilities, on-site parking and gardens. We are easy to reach from the motorway and in the perfect location for a break. The house is close to the beach and ideally located for Somerset's many attractions.

⊕ *M5 jct 22. B3140 to Burnham and Berrow. Berrow follow signs to Brean. 0.5miles after church turn right, we are 300yds on left.*

♥ *Reduced rates for longer stays and singles out of season (see website for details).*

Room ⬚ 📺 ☕ 🍲 General ⬚ 🏛 🏠 P ⚲ 🎠 🛌 🔥 ❄ Leisure ∪ ⚓ ▶ 🚣

BURNHAM-ON-SEA, Somerset Map ref 1D1 — HOTEL

★★
HOTEL

B&B per room per night
s £48.00–£58.00
d £68.00–£84.00
HB per person per night
£40.00–£70.00

Laburnum House Lodge Hotel

Sloway Lane, West Huntspill, Highbridge TA9 3RJ **t** (01278) 781830 **f** (01278) 781612
e laburnumhh@aol.com **w** laburnumhh.co.uk

Country house on edge of nature reserve and the River Huntspill. Ideal for fishing and West Country sightseeing. Quiet and peaceful location surrounded by open countryside, where you have the most beautiful sunset over the sea.

open All year
bedrooms 25 double, 25 twin, 3 single, 10 family, 2 suites
bathrooms All en suite
payment Credit/debit cards, cash/cheques, euros

Room ⬚ 🛏 ☎ 📺 ☕ 🍲 🔥 General ⬚ 🏛 🏠 P 🍴 🛌 ● ☕ ☀ 🔥🚌 🐾 Leisure 🎣 🏊 ⛳ 🎯 🔍 ∪ ⚓ ▶ 🚴

It's all quality-assessed accommodation

Our commitment to quality involves wide-ranging accommodation assessment. Rating and awards were correct at the time of going to press but may change following a new assessment. Please check at time of booking.

For key to symbols open the back-cover flap.

BURNHAM-ON-SEA, Somerset Map ref 1D1 | SELF CATERING

★★★-★★★★
SELF CATERING

Units **4**
Sleeps **2-9**

Low season per wk
£100.00-£175.00
High season per wk
£295.00-£595.00

Prospect Farm, Highbridge

contact Mrs Gillian Wall, Prospect Farm Holidays, Strowlands, East Brent, Highbridge TA9 4JH
t (01278) 760507

open All year
payment Cash/cheques

17thC, tastefully restored country cottages set amidst flower gardens and surrounded by the natural West Country beauty of the Somerset Levels, near the legendary Brent Knoll, with remains of Iron Age and Roman settlements. Two miles junction 22 M5, three miles Burnham-on-Sea. Variety of small farm animals and pets. Children welcome.

⊕ M5 jct 22, take A38 for Weston-super-Mare/Bristol, then A370 for Weston-super-Mare. At war memorial, 1st right, then 1st left, then immediately right into Strowlands. Farm 300yds on right.

♥ Special tariffs quoted for midweek and weekend breaks in low season.

Unit 🖳 📺 🖭 🖦 🛢🗄 🍳🍽️ 🍲 ⁄ ✻
General 🛏️ 🏬 🅿️ 🅾️ 🆂 🐾 Leisure ♨ ∪ ⌁ ⸚ 🚲 🚣 Shop < 0.5 miles Pub < 0.5 miles

CHEDDAR, Somerset Map ref 1D1 | GUEST ACCOMMODATION

★★
BED & BREAKFAST

B&B per room per night
s £25.00-£30.00
d £50.00-£60.00

Waterside

Cheddar Road, Axbridge BS26 2DP t (01934) 743182 e gillianaldridge@hotmail.com
w watersidecheddar.co.uk

A warm and friendly welcome awaits you. Surrounded by the Mendip hills, ideal for discovering Glastonbury, Wells, Bream, Weston, Wookey Hole, or Cheddar Gorge and show caves. Children and dogs welcome.

open All year
bedrooms 1 double, 1 twin, 1 family
bathrooms All en suite
payment Cash/cheques, euros

Room 🛏️ 📺 🍵 General 🛏️ 🏬 🅿️ ✂ 🍽️ ✻ 🐾 Leisure ∪ 🚣

CHEDDAR, Somerset Map ref 1D1 | SELF CATERING

★★★
SELF CATERING

Units **4**
Sleeps **1-4**

Low season per wk
£160.00-£180.00
High season per wk
£180.00-£200.00

Sungate Holiday Apartments, Cheddar

contact Mrs M M Fieldhouse, Pyrenmount, Parsons Way, Winscombe BS25 1BU
t (01934) 842273 & (01934) 742264 e sunholapartment@btinternet.com
w sungateholidayapartments.co.uk

Delightful apartments in listed Georgian house. Well furnished and equipped. Level rear entrance. In the centre of Cheddar village close to gorge and caves. Well-behaved children and pets welcome.

open All year
payment Cash/cheques, euros

Unit 🖳 📺 🖭 🖦 🍲 🍳 ✻
General 🛏️ 🏬 🅿️ ✂ 🅾️ 🆂 🐾 Leisure 🚲 Shop < 0.5 miles Pub < 0.5 miles

Our quality rating schemes

For a detailed explanation of the quality and facilities represented by the stars, please refer to the information pages at the back of this guide.

CHEDDAR, Somerset Map ref 1D1 — CAMPING & CARAVANNING

★★★★
HOLIDAY, TOURING
& CAMPING PARK
ROSE AWARD

🚐(100) £13.00–£25.00
🚏(20) £11.00–£19.00
▲ (80) £13.00–£24.00
🚐(37) £180.00–£600.00
200 touring pitches

Broadway House Holiday Touring Caravan and Camping Park

Axbridge Road, Cheddar BS27 3DB t (01934) 742610 f (01934) 744950
e info@broadwayhouse.uk.com w broadwayhouse.uk.com

payment Credit/debit cards, cash/cheques, euros

Nestling at the foot of the Mendip Hills, this family-run park is only one mile, and the closest of its kind, to England's Grand Canyon: Cheddar Gorge. We have every facility your family could ever want: shop, bar, launderette, swimming pool, BMX track, skateboard park, nature trails, archery, caving and canoeing. Open March to November.

⊕ *M5 jct 22. Eight miles. Midway between Cheddar and Axbridge on A371.*

General ⊞P🔌🚿🛢🍴⊙🅿🛒✕🐾♨☀ Leisure ⚓🖳🍽🧺Ѧ☽♪❀

CHEW STOKE, Somerset Map ref 2A2 — GUEST ACCOMMODATION

★★★
GUEST ACCOMMODATION

B&B per room per night
s £30.00–£35.00
d Min £56.00

Orchard House

Bristol Road, Chew Stoke, Bristol BS40 8UB t (01275) 333143 f (01275) 333754
e orchardhse@ukgateway.net w orchardhouse-chewstoke.co.uk

Comfortable accommodation in a carefully modernised Georgian house and coach house annexe. Good eating in local pubs. Convenient access to Bristol and Bath.

open All year
bedrooms 1 double, 2 twin, 1 single, 1 family
bathrooms 4 en suite, 1 private
payment Credit/debit cards, cash/cheques

Room ♿🖳♨ General 🏠🖵Ѧ P🍴🧺◙☼ Leisure ♪🏡

CHISELBOROUGH, Somerset Map ref 2A3 — SELF CATERING

★★★★
SELF CATERING

Units   1
Sleeps   4

Low season per wk
£250.00–£310.00
High season per wk
£310.00–£450.00

One Fair Place, Chiselborough, Stoke-sub-Hamdon

contact Mrs Adrienne Wright, 39 The Avenue, Crowthorne RG45 6PB
t (01344) 772461 f (01344) 778389 e aawright@btopenworld.com w somersetcottageholidays.co.uk

open All year
payment Credit/debit cards, cash/cheques

Golden hamstone cottage in quiet, picturesque village. Wonderful walks from doorstep in lovely countryside. Many National Trust properties and well-known gardens nearby. Ideal touring area. Two bedrooms and bathroom, including shower. Freshly equipped kitchen overlooks pretty cottage garden. Very comfortable sitting room with log-burning stove. Private parking. Linen provided. Brochure.

⊕ *From A303 take A356 Crewkerne Road to Chiselborough. Go through village and take Odcombe road. Take 2nd turning on left and cottage is straight ahead.*

♥ *Short breaks available Oct–Mar, min 2 nights. £60pn. Longer breaks negotiable.*

Unit ⬛ 🖳🅿◙🎛🍴💷◙🝙❀
General 🏠🖵Ѧ P🍴 S Leisure 🏡 Shop 1.5 miles Pub < 0.5 miles

Quality-assured help

Official Partner Tourist Information Centres offer quality assured help with accommodation as well as suggestions of places to visit and things to do. You'll find contact details at the back of the guide.

CHURCHINFORD, Somerset Map ref 1D2 — SELF CATERING

★★★★
SELF CATERING

Units **1**
Sleeps **6**

Low season per wk
£100.00–£250.00
High season per wk
£250.00–£510.00

South Cleeve Bungalow, Taunton

contact Mrs V D Manning, Churchinford, Taunton TA3 7PR
t (01823) 601378 & 07811 362740   **e** enquiries@timbertopbungalows.co.uk
w timbertopbungalows.co.uk

open All year
payment Cash/cheques

Discover all that Somerset and Devon have to offer, and relax in a well-maintained bungalow, ideally located within easy reach of visitor attractions. Watch the wildlife that comes to the large garden whilst enjoying the comfort of the fully equipped bungalow. Two double bedrooms (one en suite) and one twin bedroom.

⊕ From Churchinford, take Red Lane Road out of village. Up to crossroads, turn left. Take first right. Second bungalow on left.

Unit 🛏 📺 📻 🖥 💻 📼 🍴 🔥 🕯 🔔 🛋 ♨
General 🛗 🏛 ♿ P ✂ S 🐾   Leisure 🏊   Shop 1 mile   Pub 1 mile

COSSINGTON, Somerset Map ref 1D1 — SELF CATERING

★★★★★
SELF CATERING

Units **1**
Sleeps **8–13**

Low season per wk
£1,415.00–£2,055.00
High season per wk
£2,195.00–£3,325.00

Cossington Park, Cossington, Bridgwater

contact Ms Lesley Pinnell, Middle Road, Cossington, Bridgwater TA7 8LH
t (01278) 429852 & 07977 040579   **e** info@cossingtonpark.com   **w** cossingtonpark.com

open All year
payment Credit/debit cards, cash/cheques

Cossington Park is a superb period home with extensive, superbly-maintained gardens in one of England's finest tourist locations; owned for 300 years by the same family whose pictures, antiques and 5,000 books are there for your enjoyment; loved by all ages for family reunions, dinners and celebrations.

⊕ In a tranquil Somerset village only 3 miles from the M5 jct 23 – easy to reach from the Midlands, South East and London/Bristol airports.

♥ For special occasions/celebrations, we offer a choice of two superb cordon bleu cooks and wonderful aromatherapy and beauty treatments.

Unit 🛏 📺 📻 🖥 💻 📼 🍴 🔥 🕯 🔔 🛋 ♨
General 🛗 🏛 ♿ P O S 🐾   Leisure ♦ ∪ ♪   Shop 1 mile   Pub 0.5 miles

DULVERTON, Somerset Map ref 1D1 — GUEST ACCOMMODATION

★★★★★
BED & BREAKFAST

B&B per room per night
s £50.00–£70.00
d £60.00–£85.00

Hawkwell Farm House

Dulverton, Somerset TA22 9RU   **t** (01398) 341708   **f** (01398) 341708
e jan@hawkwellfarmhouse.co.uk   **w** hawkwellfarmhouse.co.uk

open All year
bedrooms 1 double, 1 twin, 1 family
bathrooms All en suite
payment Credit/debit cards, cash/cheques

South-facing, 16thC traditional Devonshire longhouse, on the edge of Exmoor National Park, full of charm and character, dating back to the Domesday era. Secluded, yet easily accessible, standing in 14 acres of mature gardens, paddocks, and woodland. Inglenook fireplaces, exposed beams, four-poster beds, providing luxurious, spacious en suite accommodation. Heated swimming pool. Warm welcome and hearty breakfasts.

⊕ Easily accessible from jct 27 of M5. Just a few minutes from Dulverton.

♥ Discounts on stays of 4 or more days (excl Saturdays) – see website for details.

Room 🖥 📺 ♿ 🍵   General 🛗 12 P ✂ 🍴 🍽 ❋ 🐾   Leisure 🎣 ∪ ♪ 🏊

DULVERTON, Somerset Map ref 1D1 — **SELF CATERING**

SELF CATERING

Units **3**
Sleeps **4–20**

Low season per wk
£305.00–£1,550.00
High season per wk
£575.00–£2,700.00

Deer's Leap Country Cottages, Yeo Mill, Nr Dulverton

contact Mrs Heather Fuidge, Deer's Leap Country Cottages, West Anstey EX36 3NZ
t (01398) 341407 **f** (01398) 341407 **e** deersleapcottages@lineone.net **w** deersleap.com

open All year
payment Credit/debit cards, cash/cheques

Deer's Leap is the perfect place to get together with friends or family for a special occasion or just to spend some quality time together. The main house sleeps up to 20 and with a games room, sauna, hot tub and gym, there's something here for everyone.

⊕ *Detailed directions on application.*

Unit ⫿⫿⫿, ⊤⊽ ⊏⊽⊟ ⊞⊡ ⊟⊡ ⊡ ⊡ ✿
General ♨ ⟗ ♯ P ⊱ ○ ⑤ ⊁ Leisure ● ⊹ ∪ ✈ ⊰ **Shop** 0.75 miles **Pub** 2.5 miles

---

DULVERTON, Somerset Map ref 1D1 — **CAMPING & CARAVANNING**

★ ★ ★ ★
TOURING PARK

⛺(64) £12.10–£24.90
⛺(64) £12.10–£24.90
64 touring pitches

Exmoor House Caravan Club Site

Dulverton TA22 9HL **t** (01398) 323268 **w** caravanclub.co.uk

payment Credit/debit cards, cash/cheques

Very quiet and secluded, in the heart of Lorna Doone country. Shops and pubs within walking distance, Exmoor is on the doorstep. Leave your car behind and explore this walker's paradise. Open March to January 2009.

⊕ *From M5 jct 27, B3222 to Dulverton, left over river bridge, 200yds on. Note: 2 narrow hump bridges on B3222, approach carefully.*

♥ *Special member rates mean you can save your membership subscription in less than a week. Visit our website to find out more.*

THE
CARAVAN
CLUB

General P ⟗ ⊖ ♞ ⊞⑤ ⊙ ⊏⊟ ⊁

DULVERTON, Somerset Map ref 1D1 — **CAMPING & CARAVANNING**

★ ★ ★ ★ ★
TOURING PARK

⛺(80) £14.30–£27.70
⛺(80) £14.30–£27.70
80 touring pitches

Lakeside Caravan Club Site

Higher Grants, Exebridge, Dulverton TA22 9BE **t** (01398) 324068 **w** caravanclub.co.uk

payment Credit/debit cards, cash/cheques

Recently redeveloped, Lakeside has splendid new facilities and all pitches (now level) boast superb views of surrounding hills and the Exe Valley. Within easy reach of the National Park and Lorna Doone country. Open March to November.

⊕ *From A396 site on left within 2.5 miles.*

♥ *Special member rates mean you can save your membership subscription in less than a week. Visit our website to find out more.*

THE
CARAVAN
CLUB

General P ⟗ ⊖ ⊞⑤ ⊏⊟ ⊁ Leisure ✈

CYCLISTS
WELCOME
WELCOME
CYCLISTS

A holiday on two wheels

For a fabulous freewheeling break, seek out accommodation participating in our Cyclists Welcome scheme. Look out for the symbol and plan your route online at nationalcyclenetwork.org.

For key to symbols open the back-cover flap.

DUNSTER, Somerset Map ref 1D1 | **HOTEL**

★★★
SMALL HOTEL

B&B per room per night
s £50.00–£70.00
d £80.00–£120.00
HB per person per night
£60.00–£90.00

Yarn Market Hotel (Exmoor)

25 High Street, Dunster, Minehead TA24 6SF t (01643) 821425 f (01643) 821475
e yarnmarket.hotel@virgin.net w yarnmarkethotel.co.uk

open All year
bedrooms 10 double, 2 twin, 1 single, 2 family
bathrooms All en suite
payment Credit/debit cards, cash/cheques

Within Exmoor National Park, our hotel is ideal for walking, riding and fishing. Family-run with a friendly, relaxed atmosphere. All rooms en suite with colour TV. Four-poster and superior rooms available. Totally non-smoking. Home-cooked dishes to cater for all tastes. Group bookings welcomed. Conference facilities. Special Christmas and New Year breaks.

⊕ *From M5 jct 25 follow signs for Exmoor/Minehead A358/ A39. Dunster signed approx 0.5 miles from A39 on left. Hotel in centre of village beside Yarn Market.*

♥ *Discounted rates for longer stays and midweek bookings. Ring for newsletter with information on special events. Group bookings welcome.*

Room 🛏 ☎ 📺 🚶 🍴 🗝 General 🛎 🏧 🕯 🍽 🛗 🚾 🍷 🚗 🐕 Leisure ♨ 🏊 🎣 🚴 🚣

EXMOOR

See under Bilbrook, Dulverton, Dunster, Minehead

FROME, Somerset Map ref 2B2 | **SELF CATERING**

★★★★
SELF CATERING

Units   1
Sleeps   2
Low season per wk
£310.00–£430.00
High season per wk
£350.00–£510.00

Lazy Dog Cottage, Frome

contact Mrs Sophie Elkins, 8 Park Lane, Heywood BA13 4NB
t (01373) 855275 f (01373) 855277 e sophie@lazydogcottage.co.uk w lazydogcottage.co.uk

A lovely, stone, weaver's cottage in a car-free conservation area in the attractive market town of Frome. Find breakfast, champagne, fresh flowers, chocolates and much more.

open All year
payment Credit/debit cards, cash/cheques

Unit 🛗 📺 🗄 🍴 🕯 General 🗝 Ⓢ Leisure ♨ 🎣

GLASTONBURY, Somerset Map ref 2A2 | **GUEST ACCOMMODATION**

★★★
INN

B&B per room per night
s £35.00–£55.00
d £69.00–£79.00

Who'd A Thought It Inn

17 Northload Street, Glastonbury BA6 9JJ t (01458) 834460 e enquiries@whodathoughtit.co.uk
w whodathoughtit.co.uk

Town-centre located traditional inn; five en suite bedrooms; extensive menus with imaginative flair; restaurant-quality food at pub prices. Excellent real ales. Please phone to reserve rooms.

open All year
bedrooms 3 double, 2 twin
bathrooms All en suite
payment Credit/debit cards, cash/cheques

Room 📺 🚶 🍴 General 🛎 🏧 P 🍷 ⚬ 🐕

Don't forget www.

Web addresses throughout this guide are shown without the prefix www. Please include www. in the address line of your browser. If a web address does not follow this style it is shown in full.

GLASTONBURY, Somerset Map ref 2A2   SELF CATERING

★ ★ ★
SELF CATERING

MapleLeaf Middlewick Holiday Cottages, Wick, Glastonbury

Units **8**
Sleeps **2–6**

contact Ms Amanda Ions, Middlewick Holiday Cottages, Wick Lane, Glastonbury BA6 8JW
t (01458) 832351 **e** middlewick@btconnect.com **w** middlewickholidaycottages.co.uk

Low season per wk
£220.00–£525.00
High season per wk
£420.00–£770.00

open All year
payment Credit/debit cards, cash/cheques

The cottages within this Grade II Listed farmstead have been restored to provide comfortable, well-equipped accommodation. Walk to Glastonbury Tor from the back door, explore the region, relax in the heated indoor swimming pool, try out the steam room or have a massage in our treatment room. Wi-Fi Internet access.

✤ *Wick Lane runs between A361 and A39. From A39 we are 1 mile on your right. From A361 1.5 miles on your left.*

♥ *Online booking for last-minute discounts for weekly or short breaks. Optional breakfasts available in the Meadow Barn dining room.*

Unit ▥ 📺 ▣ � ▣ ▣ ⊟ ⬚ ⬚ ⬚ ✿
General ⬚ ▥ ⚲ ◉ Ⓢ   Leisure ⬚ ∪ ⬚   Shop 2 miles   Pub 3 miles

---

HILLFARRANCE, Somerset Map ref 1D1   SELF CATERING

★ ★ ★ ★ ★
SELF CATERING

The Long Barn, Hillfarrance, Taunton

Units **1**
Sleeps **2–14**

contact Mrs Lucy Fielding-Johnson, Pontispool Farm, Allerford, Hillfarrance, Taunton TA4 1BG
t (01823) 461508 & 07776 188646 **f** (01823) 462945 **e** info@somersetlongbarn.co.uk
w somersetlongbarn.co.uk

Low season per wk
£1,700.00–£2,100.00
High season per wk
£2,400.00–£3,500.00

open All year
payment Credit/debit cards, cash/cheques

Large, five-bedroomed house, en suite throughout (six bedrooms from spring 2008). Large garden, summer house, hot tub, indoor pool. Great for large groups and families.

✤ *M5 jct 26. A38 Taunton. Left past Sheppeys Cider, Oake, Bradford-on-Tone. First right, 2 miles, left over bridge. Allerford Inn, left past 3 cottages, turn right into drive.*

Unit ▥ 📺 ▣ ▣ ⊟ ⬚ ⬚ ⬚ ⬚ ✿
General ⬚ ▥ ⚲ P ✂ ◉ Ⓢ   Leisure ⬚ ◉ ∪ ⬚ ▸ 🚲   Shop 1.5 miles   Pub 1 mile

---

MARTOCK, Somerset Map ref 2A3   GUEST ACCOMMODATION

★ ★ ★ ★
INN

The White Hart Hotel

B&B per room per night
s Min £45.00
d Min £62.00
Evening meal per person
Min £10.25

East Street, Martock TA12 6JQ **t** (01935) 822005 **f** (01935) 822056
e enquiries@whiteharthotelmartock.co.uk **w** whiteharthotelmartock.co.uk

Pleasant Hamstone, Grade II Listed coaching inn. Centre of Martock, seven miles from Yeovil and two miles off the A303. Top-class, fresh food served. Real ales, fine wines.

open All year except Christmas and New Year
bedrooms 5 double, 5 family
bathrooms All en suite
payment Credit/debit cards, cash/cheques, euros

Room ☎ 📺 ⬚ ⬚   General ⬚ ▥ ⚲ P ⚡ ✕ ⬚ 🐾

---

enjoy**England**.com

Big city buzz or peaceful panoramas? Take a fresh look at England and you may be surprised at what's right on your doorstep. Explore the diversity online at enjoyengland.com

---

MINEHEAD, Somerset Map ref 1D1   **HOTEL**

★★
HOTEL

B&B per room per night
s £38.50–£42.50
d £65.00–£68.00
HB per person per night
£48.50–£50.00

Gascony Hotel

The Avenue, Minehead TA24 5BB **t** (01643) 705939 **f** (01643) 709926 **e** info@gasconyhotel.co.uk
w gasconyhotel.co.uk

Comfortable and well-appointed Victorian house hotel. Ideally positioned on the level, close to seafront. Home cooking. Large secure car park. Short breaks available.

open All year except Christmas and New Year
bedrooms 8 double, 6 twin, 3 single, 3 family
bathrooms All en suite
payment Credit/debit cards, cash/cheques

Room 🛏 📺 👓 🍵   General 👜 🛏 🏧 P ✂ 🍷 🎱 🍴   Leisure ⚑

MINEHEAD, Somerset Map ref 1D1   **SELF CATERING**

★★★
SELF CATERING

Units   1
Sleeps   5

Low season per wk
Min £200.00
High season per wk
Min £380.00

Fishermans Cottage, Minehead

contact Mr Martin, 57 Quay Street, Minehead TA24 5UL
t (01643) 704263

open All year
payment Cash/cheques
Situated overlooking the harbour and Minehead Bay. With two bedrooms, one double, the other with double and single beds. All linen, towels and cloths provided. Electricity included.

Unit 📶 📺 📼 🔲 💻 ✿   General 👜5 P ⊙   Leisure ⚓⚑   Shop 1 mile   Pub < 0.5 miles

---

MONTACUTE, Somerset Map ref 2A3   **SELF CATERING**

★★★★
SELF CATERING

Units   1
Sleeps   4

Low season per wk
£275.00–£340.00
High season per wk
£340.00–£475.00

Far End Cottage, Montacute

contact Mrs Adrienne Wright, 39 The Avenue, Crowthorne RG45 6PB
t (01344) 772461 **f** (01344) 778389 **e** aawright@btopenworld.com **w** somersetcottageholidays.co.uk

Golden hamstone cottage in beautiful village. Country walks. Many NT properties and gardens nearby. Two bedrooms. Well-equipped kitchen with dishwasher. Open log fire. Lovely garden. Private parking. Linen provided. Brochure.

open All year
payment Credit/debit cards, cash/cheques

Unit 📶 📺 📟 📼 🔲 💻 🔐 🍵 ✿   General 👜 🛏 🏧 P ✂ 🔲 🐾   Leisure 🏊   Shop < 0.5 miles   Pub < 0.5 miles

---

OTTERFORD, Somerset Map ref 1D2   **SELF CATERING**

★★★★
SELF CATERING

Units   1
Sleeps   1–11

Low season per wk
£395.00–£445.00
High season per wk
£650.00–£750.00

Tamarack Lodge, Chard

contact Matthew Sparks, Tamarack Lodge, Fyfett Farm, Chard TA20 3QP
t (01823) 601270 **e** matthew.sparks@tamaracklodge.co.uk **w** tamaracklodge.co.uk

open All year
payment Cash/cheques
Luxurious log cabin-style ranch house on beautiful Blackdown Hills of Somerset. As seen on TV and in Daily Telegraph article. Suitable for disabled. Stabling available. Situated on family livestock farm. Two wildlife sites. Coast 35 minutes away.

⊕ B3170 to Corfe. Pass through Corfe, travel up hill for 3 miles. At top of hill, pass over crossroads and take 2nd left to Fyfett Farm.

Unit 📶 📺 📟 📼 🔲 💻 🔐 🍵 ✿   General 👜 🛏 🏧 P ✂ 🔲 🐾   Leisure ∪ ⚓ ⚑ 🏄   Shop 1 mile   Pub 0.5 miles

---

Somerset **Places to stay**

SHEPTON MALLET, Somerset Map ref 2A2 — **GUEST ACCOMMODATION**

Bowlish House

★★★★
RESTAURANT WITH ROOMS

B&B per room per night
s £65.00–£80.00
d £80.00–£110.00
Evening meal per person
£15.00–£27.50

Wells Road, Bowlish, Shepton Mallet BA4 5JD t (01749) 342022 f (01749) 345311
e info@bowlishhouse.com w bowlishhouse.com

open All year
bedrooms 4 double, 2 twin
bathrooms All en suite
payment Credit/debit cards, cash/cheques

Grade II* Listed Georgian Palladian house with character and period charm close to the cathedral city of Wells and other major attractions. Continental breakfast included in price of room.

Room ☎ 📺 ♿ General 🏠♨P✳️♉️🛏️🎱🐾❄️ Leisure ▶️

STOGUMBER, Somerset Map ref 1D1 — **GUEST ACCOMMODATION**

The White Horse Inn

★★★
INN

B&B per room per night
s £35.00–£40.00
d £64.00–£70.00
Evening meal per person
£5.95–£15.95

High Street, Stogumber, Taunton TA4 3TA t (01984) 656277 f (01984) 656873
w whitehorsestogumber.co.uk

open All year except Christmas
bedrooms 2 double, 1 twin
bathrooms All en suite
payment Credit/debit cards, cash/cheques

The White Horse is a Grade II Listed, traditional freehouse in the picturesque village of Stogumber, hidden away from the rat race on the slopes of the Quantock Hills. The extensive menu uses fresh, local produce, and award-winning, locally brewed real ales are a speciality.

⊕ A358 Taunton to Minehead; approx 14 miles from Taunton, village signposted on left. In centre of village turn right at T-junction, and right again (White Horse signposted).

Room 📺 ♿🍽 General 🔥♨P♉️✕🛏️❄️🐾 Leisure 🔍∪▶️🏛️

STOKE SUB HAMDON, Somerset Map ref 1D2 — **SELF CATERING**

Fairhaven, Stoke sub Hamdon

★★★★
SELF CATERING

Units 1
Sleeps 2
Low season per wk
£160.00–£180.00
High season per wk
£180.00–£280.00

contact Mrs Margaret Wilson, Fairhaven, Montacute Road, East Stoke, Stoke sub Hamdon TA14 6UQ
t (01935) 823534 e fairhaven@onetel.com w fairhavensomerset.co.uk

open All year
payment Cash/cheques, euros

A warm welcome awaits you in this comfortable, self-contained wing of owners' home. Beautiful, forever-changing view of wooded hills to rear. Close to Montacute House and Ham Hill Country Park. Private garden for guests, off-road parking. Excellent touring base for Somerset, Dorset and East Devon. Frequently revisited.

⊕ From A303 take A3088 towards Yeovil. Turn right after 1 mile then right again at top of hill. House on left.

♥ Reduction for 2-week bookings. Reduction for over 65s. £99.00 for 4 nights off-season.

Unit 🏠📺📶📺📟🍽🍳🎱❄️ General P✳️⑤ Leisure ⌇∪▶️🏛️ Shop < 0.5 miles Pub 0.5 miles

---

Key to symbols
Open the back flap for a key to symbols.

For key to symbols open the back-cover flap.

WELLS, Somerset Map ref 2A2 — SELF CATERING

★★★★
SELF CATERING

Units **1**
Sleeps **1–5**
Low season per wk
£300.00–£450.00
High season per wk
£475.00–£575.00

Honeysuckle Cottage, Wells

contact Mrs Luana Law, Honeysuckle Cottage, Worth, Wookey, Wells BA5 1LW
t (01749) 678971 e honeycroft2@aol.com

open All year
payment Cash/cheques

Barn conversion on working farm in beautiful countryside. One double en suite and one double with adjoining single bedrooms. Large bathroom upstairs, shower room downstairs. Spacious kitchen/diner/lounge leading to large patio and garden overlooking stunning Mendip Hills. All modern equipment from dishwasher to DVD.

⊕ M5 jct 22. A38 towards Bristol for 500m. Right at Fox and Goose to Mark. Two miles, left towards Wells/Wedmore. Ten miles, Worth village. Cottage on left.

♥ Short stays available.

Unit ▥ 📺 ▯ ▨ ▣ 🖫 🖫 ▯ ▯ ▯ ▯ ▯
General 🕭 ♟ P ✂ Ⓢ Leisure ∪ ♪ ▶ 🏛 Shop 0.5 miles Pub < 0.5 miles

WEST PORLOCK, Somerset Map ref 1D1 — GUEST ACCOMMODATION

★★★★
GUEST ACCOMMODATION

B&B per room per night
s Min £35.00
d £64.00–£69.00

West Porlock House

West Porlock, Minehead TA24 8NX t (01643) 862880 e westporlockhouse@amserve.com

A small country house overlooking the sea and countryside on the road from Porlock to Porlock Weir. Lovely woodland garden set in five acres with exceptional sea views. Open March to November.

bedrooms 2 double, 2 twin, 1 family
bathrooms 2 en suite, 3 private
payment Credit/debit cards, cash/cheques

Room 📺 🕯 General 🕭6 P ✂ 🗎 ✿

WESTON-SUPER-MARE, Somerset Map ref 1D1 — HOTEL

★★★
HOTEL

B&B per room per night
s £50.00–£65.00
d £110.00–£130.00
HB per person per night
£64.50–£80.00

Beachlands Hotel

Uphill Road North, Weston-super-Mare BS23 4NG t (01934) 621401 f (01934) 621966
e info@beachlandshotel.com w beachlandshotel.com

open All year except Christmas and New Year
bedrooms 8 double, 5 twin, 2 single, 6 family
bathrooms All en suite
payment Credit/debit cards, cash/cheques

On the level, overlooking Weston Golf Course and 300yds from beach. This delightful hotel is small enough to be able to recognise that you, as an individual, have individual requirements, yet large enough to provide the facilities that you need. Highly reputed restaurant and well-appointed, individually designed, en suite bedrooms.

⊕ M5 jct 21, follow signs for hospital. At hospital roundabout follow signs for beach. Hotel 6.5 miles from motorway, overlooking golf course, 300yds before beach.

♥ Bargain breaks from £62.75pppn DB&B, including use of indoor pool and sauna.

Room 🛏 ☎ 📺 🕯 🗎 🕳 General 🕭 🛏 ♟ P ✂ 🍽 🗎 ⓘ ☎ ✿ 🚌 Leisure 🎣 🏊 ∪ ▶

Take a break

Look out for special promotions and themed breaks. This could be your chance to indulge an interest, find a new one, or just relax and enjoy exceptional value. Offers (highlighted in colour) are subject to availability.

WESTON-SUPER-MARE, Somerset Map ref 1D1 — HOTEL

★★★
HOTEL

B&B per room per night
s £54.00–£66.00
d £69.00–£110.00

Royal Hotel

South Parade, Weston-super-Mare BS23 1JP t (01934) 423100 f (01934) 415135
e reservations@royalhotelweston.com w royalhotelweston.com

open All year
bedrooms 20 double, 3 twin, 6 single, 5 family,
3 suites
bathrooms All en suite
payment Credit/debit cards, cash/cheques

One of Weston's oldest hotels, 50yds from shopping centre and high street. Views over large lawns and seafront, well appointed with air of elegance. Excellent conference and wedding facilities, civil licence and ample car parking. Our Ala Restaurant includes dishes to excite all tastes. Live entertainment in our licensed bar.

⊕ M5 jct 21 follow signs to seafront, pass the pier next door to Winter Gardens Pavilion.

♥ Stay 2 nights get 3rd night free – £99.00 DB&B per person.

Room 🛏 📞 📺 👆 🔧 🔩 General ⚊ 🛏 🅿 🍽 🎱 🔕 ● 🎱 ● 🍴 ✱ 🚐 Leisure ♫ ⤢ ↟ 🚣

WINCANTON, Somerset Map ref 2B3 — HOTEL

COUNTRY HOUSE HOTEL

B&B per room per night
d £140.00–£250.00

Holbrook House Hotel and Spa

Wincanton BA9 8BS t (01963) 824466 f (01963) 32681 e enquiries@holbrookhouse.co.uk
w holbrookhouse.co.uk

open All year
bedrooms 16 double, 1 family, 4 suites
bathrooms All en suite
payment Credit/debit cards, cash/cheques

Holbrook House . . . a luxury home from home. A traditional country-house hotel, set in 17 acres of beautiful parkland and gardens. Boasting an award-winning restaurant, luxury accommodation and a fully equipped spa, Holbrook is the perfect place for a relaxing break. All located within easy reach of the A303 and just outside the racing town of Wincanton.

⊕ Holbrook is located just 2 minutes from Wincanton junction on the A303. By rail the nearest stations are Castle Cary and Templecombe.

♥ See website for special breaks and seasonal breaks, as well as last-minute deals.

Room 🧹 🛏 📞 📺 👆 🔧 🔩 General ⚊ 🛏 🅿 🍽 🎱 🔕 ● 🍴 ✱ 🚐 🐴 Leisure ⌖ ♨ ✷ ⚲ ∪ ⤢ ↟ 🚣

WINFORD, Somerset Map ref 2A2 — SELF CATERING

★★★
SELF CATERING

Units   2
Sleeps 2–4

Low season per wk
£185.00–£255.00
High season per wk
£315.00–£445.00

Regilbury Farm, Bristol

contact Mrs Keedwell, Regilbury Farm, The Street, Regil, Winford, Bristol BS40 8BB
t (01275) 472369 e janekeedwell@yahoo.co.uk w regilburyfarm.co.uk

A working farm with cattle, sheep and chickens, all set in a beautiful, quiet hamlet. Wonderful rambling and lots to see. Guided walks available. Cowshed – double, Parlour – double and twin.

open All year
payment Cash/cheques

Unit 🏠 📺 📹 🖥 🔧 🔥 🍴 🔌✱
General ⚊ 🛏 🅿 ✂ Leisure ⤢ Shop 2 miles Pub 1 mile

Using map references

Map references refer to the colour maps at the front of this guide.

For key to symbols open the back-cover flap.

YEOVIL, Somerset Map ref 2A3   **CAMPING & CARAVANNING**

★★★★
HOLIDAY, TOURING
& CAMPING PARK

🚐 (30)	£16.00
🚏 (30)	£16.00
⛺ (30)	£16.00
🏠 (3)	£350.00–£800.00

60 touring pitches

Long Hazel Park

High Street, Sparkford, Yeovil BA22 7JH **t** (01963) 440002 **f** (01963) 440002
e longhazelpark@hotmail.com **w** sparkford.f9.co.uk/lhi.htm

Adult-only park set in 3.5 acres of level, landscaped grounds. Recreation area, picnic tables and full disabled facilities. Two fully heated lodges. Close to restaurant, bar, shop, post office, garage and bus stop.

open All year
payment Credit/debit cards, cash/cheques, euros

General 🛏 🚲 P 🅿 🌡 ☕ 🍽 🛆 ⊙ 📼 🔭 ☼ Leisure ∪ 🎣 🚲

Walkers and cyclists welcome

Look out for quality-assessed accommodation displaying the Walkers Welcome and Cyclists Welcome signs.

Participants in these schemes actively encourage and support walking and cycling. In addition to special meal arrangements and helpful information, they'll provide a water supply to wash off the mud, an area for drying wet clothing and footwear, maps and books to look up cycling and walking routes and even an emergency puncture-repair kit! Bikes can also be locked up securely undercover.

The standards for these schemes have been developed in partnership with the tourist boards in Northern Ireland, Scotland and Wales, so wherever you're travelling in the UK you'll receive the same welcome.

Stonehenge   Stourhead

Iford Manor Gardens

Explore Wiltshire

Visit two World Heritage Sites, shrouded in mystery, and feel dizzy looking up at England's tallest cathedral spire. Find fascinating historic houses and glorious gardens or discover huge white horses carved on the hillsides.

Salisbury and Stonehenge

You'll spot the cathedral spire long before you reach the historic heart of Salisbury – at 123 metres (404 feet) it's England's tallest. Take tea in 18th-century Mompesson House and watch a fascinating film on the city's heritage in the nearby Medieval Hall. Stroll along ancient streets browsing antique shops, investigating historic inns and wander through the multi-coloured stalls on market days.

Beyond the city, clamber up to Old Sarum Iron Age hill-fort for splendid views and brush up on Old Wardour Castle's bloodthirsty past. Then prepare yourself for one of the world's greatest ancient sites – Stonehenge. It's 5,000 years since the striking stone structure was erected, but we still don't really know why. A similar sense of awe and mystery surrounds the great stone circle at Avebury, Wiltshire's other World Heritage Site, where around a hundred stones form a huge ring, a quarter of a mile across.

Houses and gardens

Wiltshire has more than its fair share of historic houses and glorious gardens. See mirror-perfect reflections of statues, pergolas and a thousand shrubs and trees in Stourhead's still lakes, or unwrap over 460 years of history at Wilton House, home of the Earl of Pembroke. At Bowood House & Gardens, landscaper 'Capability' Brown created a flowing mix of woodlands and lawn sloping down to a lake. You can also see his work at Longleat House and at Elizabethan Corsham Court. Make sure you take in Lacock Abbey and find out about photography pioneer William Fox Talbot who once lived here, or smell the heady scent of roses and mixed aromas of herbs at Malmesbury's Abbey House Gardens.

Bradford-on-Avon

Lacock Abbey

Longleat Safari Park

Salisbury Cathedral

The great outdoors

Put on the walking shoes and see the very best of the countryside on foot – there are over 7,500 paths throughout the county so it's easy to find the perfect route. White horses have been a feature of Wiltshire's downlands for centuries – massive, dazzling figures carved into the chalk hillsides. Find all eight of them by walking the White Horse Trail. Or bring your bike for leisurely exploration on traffic-free country lanes. A whole series of routes have been especially created, ranging from family-friendly off-road routes to the 160-mile long distance Wiltshire Cycleway. But for the most peaceful exploration of all, hire a boat and cruise the Kennet & Avon Canal, an idyllic waterway that glides through the heart of the county.

Family fun

For families there's everything from wildlife, farm and water parks to Steam – Museum of the Great Western Railway in Swindon. Step into the museum here and enter the world of the railway worker on Isambard Kingdom Brunel's Great Western Railway, once considered one of the most advanced in the world. Befriend a Royal Ball Python at Longleat Safari Park and explore the stunning house and grounds. Or spend a day combining shopping with fun at The Wilton Shopping Village and Swindon's McArthurGlen Designer Outlet.

Food & drink

Fancy a bite to eat, a relaxing drink or some fresh local produce? Here's a selection of food and drink venues to get you started. For lots more ideas go online at enjoyengland.com/taste.

Restaurants

Beechfield House Hotel
English
Beanacre, Melksham SN12 7PU
t (01225) 703700
w beechfieldhouse.co.uk

The Bybrook Restaurant at Manor House
British
Castle Combe,
Chippenham SN14 7HR
t (01249) 782206
w exclusivehotels.com

The Harrow at Little Bedwyn
British
Little Bedwyn,
Marlborough SN8 3JP
t (01672) 870871
w theharrowatlittlebedwyn.co.uk

Lucknam Park Hotel
Fine dining
Colerne, Chippenham SN14 8AZ
t (01225) 742777
w lucknampark.co.uk

LXIX New Street Restaurant
English
69 New Street, Salisbury
SP1 2PH
t (01722) 340000

The Mulberry Restaurant at Bishopstrow House
British
The Wylye Valley, Warminster
BA12 9HH
t (01985) 212312
w bishopstrow.co.uk

The Pear Tree at Purton
English
Church End, Swindon SN5 4ED
t (01793) 772100
w peartreepurton.co.uk

Red or White
English
Evolution House, 46 Castle Street,
Trowbridge BA14 7AY
t (01225) 781666
w redorwhite.biz

The Refectory Restaurant
English
Salisbury Cathedral, The Close,
Salisbury SP1 2EN
t (01722) 555172
w salisburycathedral.org.uk

The Sign of the Angel
English
Church Street, Lacock SN15 2LB
t (01249) 730230
w lacock.co.uk

Whatley Manor
French
Easton Grey, Malmesbury
SN16 0RB
t (01666) 822888
w whatleymanor.com

Widbrook Grange Hotel
English
Trowbridge Road,
Bradford-on-Avon BA15 1UH
t (01225) 864750
w widbrookgrange.com

Woolley Grange
British
Woolley Green,
Bradford-on-Avon BA15 1TX
t (01225) 864705
w woolleygrangehotel.co.uk

Tearooms, coffee shops and cafes

The Bridge Tea Rooms
24a Bridge Street,
Bradford-on-Avon BA15 1BY
t (01225) 865537

Pubs

The Flemish Weaver
63 High Street, Corsham
SN13 0EZ
t (01249) 701929

The George & Dragon
High Street, Rowde SN10 2PN
t (01380) 723053

The Old Bear Inn
Staverton, Trowbridge BA14 6PB
t (01225) 782487
w theoldbear.co.uk

The Red Lion
Axford, near Marlborough
SN8 2HA
t (01672) 520271
w redlionaxford.com

The Tollgate Inn
Ham Green, Holt,
Bradford-on-Avon BA14 6PX
t (01225) 782326
w tollgateholt.co.uk

Farm shops and local produce

Britford Farm Shop
Lower Road, Britford,
Salisbury SP5 4DY
t (01722) 413400
w britfordfarmshop.co.uk

The Cheese Board
30a Silver Street,
Bradford-on-Avon BA15 1JX
t (01225) 868043
w cheeseboardboa.co.uk

Old Forge Butcher & Delicatessen
Unit 4, Stonehenge Walk,
Amesbury SP4 7DB
t (01980) 624921
w oldforgefarmshop.co.uk

Whitehall Farm Shop
Whitehall Garden Centre,
Corsham Road, Lacock,
SN15 2LZ
t (01249) 730204
w whitehallgardencentre.co.uk

where to stay in
Wiltshire – Salisbury & Stonehenge

Maps
All place names in the blue bands are shown on the maps at the front of this guide.

Accommodation symbols
Symbols give useful information about services and facilities. Inside the back-cover flap you can find a key to these symbols. Keep it open for easy reference.

BRADFORD-ON-AVON, Wiltshire Map ref 2B2   **GUEST ACCOMMODATION**

★★★★
BED & BREAKFAST
SILVER AWARD

B&B per room per night
d £50.00–£60.00

Honeysuckle Cottage

95 The Common, Broughton Gifford, Melksham SN12 8ND   **t** (01225) 782463
e info@honeysuckle-cottage.org.uk   **w** honeysuckle-cottage.org.uk

open All year except Christmas
bedrooms 1 double, 1 twin
bathrooms 1 en suite, 1 private
payment Cash/cheques

Comfortable country cottage dating back to the 18th century. Tranquil situation facing village common. Ideal base for Bath, Bradford-on-Avon, Lacock and numerous historic locations. Accommodation in double en suite and twin/family with private facilities. Breakfast is freshly prepared using local produce when possible.

⊕ *Information on location will be sent when the booking is confirmed.*

Room 📺 🕭 ♍   General 🛏 ▦ ♿ P ⊬ 𝄞 ✿   Leisure ♻ 🎣

BROAD CHALKE, Wiltshire Map ref 2B3   **GUEST ACCOMMODATION**

★★★★
BED & BREAKFAST

B&B per room per night
s £25.00–£30.00
d £50.00–£60.00

Lodge Farmhouse Bed & Breakfast

Lodge Farmhouse, Broad Chalke, Salisbury SP5 5LU   **t** (01752) 519242   **f** (01725) 519597
e mj.roe@virgin.net   **w** lodge-farmhouse.co.uk

open All year except Christmas and New Year
bedrooms 1 double, 2 twin
bathrooms All en suite
payment Credit/debit cards, cash/cheques

Peaceful brick and flint farmhouse with Wiltshire's finest views overlooking 1,000 square miles of Southern England. Comfortable and welcoming, the perfect tour base for Wessex. Lying on the Ox Drove 'green lane', a paradise for walkers and byway cyclists. For neighbouring nature reserves and archaeological sites see website.

⊕ *A354 from Salisbury (8 miles) or Blandford (14 miles). Turn to Broad Chalke at crossroads on only stretch of dual carriageway on the A354. One mile signposted.*

Room 📺 🕭 ♍   General 🛏12 P ⊬ ✿ 🐾   Leisure ∪ ↻ 🎣

COLLINGBOURNE KINGSTON, Wiltshire Map ref 2B2 　　　　　**GUEST ACCOMMODATION**

★★★★
FARMHOUSE

B&B per room per night
s £40.00–£45.00
d £60.00–£65.00

Manor Farm B&B

Collingbourne Kingston, Marlborough SN8 3SD　t (01264) 850859　f (01264) 850859
e stay@manorfm.com　w manorfm.com

open All year
bedrooms 1 double, 1 twin, 1 family
bathrooms 2 en suite, 1 private
payment Credit/debit cards, cash/cheques, euros

An attractive, Grade II Listed, period village farmhouse with comfortable and spacious rooms (all en suite/private) on a working family farm. Sumptuous traditional, vegetarian, gluten-free and other special-diet breakfasts. Beautiful countryside with superb walking and cycling from the farm. Horses and pets welcome.

⊕ Opposite the church in the centre of the small village of Collingbourne Kingston, nine miles south of Marlborough.

♥ Pleasure flights from our private airstrip over Wiltshire's ancient places, white horses and crop circles by balloon, aeroplane and helicopter.

Room 📺 ⚘　General 🐾 ♿ P ✗ 🍴 ✿ 🐕　Leisure ∪ ♪ 🏹 🚴 🏛

CORSHAM, Wiltshire Map ref 2B2　　　　　**GUEST ACCOMMODATION**

★★★★
BED & BREAKFAST
GOLD AWARD

B&B per room per night
s £42.00–£49.00
d £62.00–£69.00

Heatherly Cottage

Ladbrook Lane, Gastard, Corsham SN13 9PE　t (01249) 701402　f (01249) 701412
e pandj@heatherly.plus.com　w heatherlycottage.co.uk

open All year except Christmas and New Year
bedrooms 2 double, 1 twin
bathrooms All en suite
payment Cash/cheques

Delightful 17thC cottage in a quiet lane with two acres and beautiful views across open countryside. Guests have a separate wing of the house with their own entrance. All rooms en suite, one with king-size bed. Colour TV, clock radio, hospitality tray, hairdryer. Many pubs serving good food nearby. Off-road parking.

⊕ Take the B3353 out of Corsham towards Gastard and Melksham. Ladbrook Lane is 0.8 miles from Corsham.

Room ♿ 📺 ⚘ 🍵　General 🐾10 P ✗ 🍴 ✿　Leisure ∪ 🚴

DEVIZES, Wiltshire Map ref 2B2　　　　　**GUEST ACCOMMODATION**

★★★★
GUEST ACCOMMODATION

B&B per room per night
s Min £35.00
d Min £60.00

Rosemundy Cottage

London Road, Devizes SN10 2DS　t (01380) 727122　f (01380) 720495
e info@rosemundycottage.co.uk　w rosemundycottage.co.uk

open All year
bedrooms 2 double, 1 twin, 1 family
bathrooms All en suite
payment Credit/debit cards, cash/cheques

Canal-side cottage, short walk to Market Place. Fully equipped rooms, include a four-poster and a ground floor room. Sitting room with guides provided. Guest office, Wi-Fi Internet. Garden with barbecue and heated pool in summer. Wiltshire Breakfast Award. Off-road parking. Perfect for business or leisure.

⊕ A361 just north of Devizes centre, towards Avebury. Right just past County Police HQ. On Wessex Ridgeway and bridge 137 on canal routes.

♥ Double en suite at single occupancy rate. Discount for 3 or more consecutive nights.

Room ♿ 📺 ⚘ 🍵　General ♿ P ✗ 🍴 ✿ 🐾 ✿　Leisure ⚓ ∪ ♪ 🚴 🏛

DEVIZES, Wiltshire Map ref 2B2 — SELF CATERING

Fourbee, Devizes

★★★★
SELF CATERING

Units **1**
Sleeps **6**

Low season per wk
£425.00–£525.00
High season per wk
£550.00–£625.00

contact Mr & Mrs Bernard & Susan Foreman, Rushley Mount, 50 High Street, Littleton Panell, Devizes SN10 4ES
t (01380) 816919 **f** (01380) 818093 **e** fourbeecontact@aol.com **w** fourbee.biz

High-quality converted self-catering accommodation in charming market town of Devizes. Ideally situated for all West Country attractions. Sleeps six en suite. Cot and highchair available. Highly recommended.

open All year
payment Cash/cheques, euros

Unit ⬛ 📺 🛢🖥 ⬛ 🔲🔲 🖲 🔲 🔲 ❄
General 🍳 🛏 🍴 P ✂ S Leisure ∪ ⏛ ↑ 🚲 🚣 Shop < 0.5 miles Pub < 0.5 miles

LACOCK, Wiltshire Map ref 2B2 — CAMPING & CARAVANNING

Piccadilly Caravan Park Ltd

★★★★★
TOURING &
CAMPING PARK

🚐 (39) £12.50–£14.50
🚏 (39) £12.50–£14.50
Å (4)   £12.50–£14.50
43 touring pitches

Folly Lane (West), Lacock, Chippenham SN15 2LP **t** (01249) 730260 **e** piccadillylacock@aol.com

This well-maintained and peaceful site stands in open countryside 0.5 miles from the historic National Trust village of Lacock. Open April to October.

payment Cash/cheques

General P 🔲 ⏻ 🍴 🌣 ⊙ 🖼🔲 ↑ ☼ Leisure △ ⏛

MARKET LAVINGTON, Wiltshire Map ref 2B2 — GUEST ACCOMMODATION

The Green Dragon

★★★
INN

B&B per room per night
s £25.00–£40.00
d £50.00–£60.00
Evening meal per person
£6.00–£20.00

26-28 High Street, Market Lavington, Devizes SN10 4AG **t** (01380) 813235
e greendragonlavington@tiscali.co.uk **w** greendragonlavington.co.uk

Family-run public house, situated in the heart of the village; comfortable, non-smoking rooms; good home-cooked food. Ideal for walkers and cyclists.

open All year
bedrooms 1 double, 1 single, 1 family
bathrooms 1 en suite
payment Credit/debit cards, cash/cheques

Room 📺 🍴 🍵 General 🍳 🛏 P ✂ ⏛ ✕ 🍽 🌣 ↑ Leisure ⏛ ↑ 🚲 🚣

MARLBOROUGH, Wiltshire Map ref 2B2 — GUEST ACCOMMODATION

Crofton Lodge

★★★★
BED & BREAKFAST
SILVER AWARD

B&B per room per night
s £32.50–£37.50
d £65.00–£75.00
Evening meal per person
£15.00–£20.00

Crofton, Marlborough SN8 3DW **t** (01672) 870328 **e** ali@croftonlodge.co.uk **w** croftonlodge.co.uk

open All year except Christmas and New Year
bedrooms 1 double, 1 twin, 1 single
bathrooms 1 en suite, 2 private
payment Cash/cheques, euros

Comfortable, welcoming home with large gardens in hamlet next to Kennet and Avon Canal, Crofton Beam Engines and Savernake Forest. Close to Great Bedwyn and good pubs. Easy reach Marlborough and Hungerford. Excellent base for walkers and cyclists. Home grown or local produce.

⊕ *From Great Bedwyn (2 miles south of A4 between Marlborough and Hungerford) follow Crofton Beam Engine signs. Crofton Lodge is 1.5 miles on right.*

♥ *Stay for 3 nights and enjoy a free dinner.*

Room 📺 🍴 🍵 General 🍳 12 ✕ 🍽 🌣 ✂ ↑ Leisure ⏛ 🚲 🚣

Place index

If you know where you want to stay, the index at the back of the guide will give you the page number listing accommodation in your chosen town, city or village. Check out the other useful indexes too.

For key to symbols open the back-cover flap.

ROWDE, Wiltshire Map ref 2B2 — **SELF CATERING**

★★★★
SELF CATERING

Units **2**
Sleeps **2–6**

Low season per wk
Min £275.00
High season per wk
Max £650.00

The Canal Barn, Nr Devizes

contact Mr & Mrs Patrick & Louise Dawe-Lane, Upper Foxhangers Farm, Marsh Lane, Rowde, Devizes SN10 1RE
t (01380) 728883 e mail@canalbarn.co.uk w canalbarn.co.uk

The Canal Barn consists of two holiday units, providing luxury en suite accommodation with a contemporary feel. In the heart of Wiltshire at foot of Caen Hill flight of locks.

open All year
payment Cash/cheques

Unit
General Shop 1 mile Pub 1 mile

SALISBURY, Wiltshire Map ref 2B3 — **GUEST ACCOMMODATION**

★★★
GUEST HOUSE

B&B per room per night
s £38.00–£60.00
d £50.00–£75.00

Byways House

31 Fowlers Road, Salisbury SP1 2QP t (01722) 328364 f (01722) 322146
e info@bywayshouse.co.uk w bywayshouse.co.uk

open All year except Christmas and New Year
bedrooms 8 double, 7 twin, 4 single, 4 family
bathrooms 19 en suite
payment Credit/debit cards, cash/cheques

Attractive, large, Victorian guesthouse in quiet location alongside the city centre/restaurants. Free car parking on site. Licensed drinks lounge. Clean and comfortable en suite rooms. Special rates for long stays. Wi-Fi Internet access.

⊕ Arriving in Salisbury follow A36, then follow Youth Hostel signs until outside hostel. Fowlers Road is opposite. Byways is a large Victorian house on the left.

Room General Leisure

SALISBURY, Wiltshire Map ref 2B3 — **GUEST ACCOMMODATION**

★★★★
GUEST HOUSE
SILVER AWARD

B&B per room per night
s £45.00–£55.00
d £45.00–£80.00

The Rokeby Guest House

3 Wain-A-Long Road, Salisbury SP1 1LJ t (01722) 329800 f (01722) 329800
e karenrogers@rokebyguesthouse.co.uk w rokebyguesthouse.co.uk

open All year
bedrooms 3 double, 2 twin, 3 family
bathrooms 7 en suite, 1 private
payment Cash/cheques

2007 Salisbury Tourism Award and Recognition Scheme winner in the B&B category. Beautiful, nostalgic, Victorian guesthouse, quietly situated, ten minutes' stroll city centre/cathedral. Large landscaped gardens, summer house, elegant two-storey conservatory, gymnasium. Free internet access available. Brochure available. Come and see for yourself.

⊕ Take Laverstock exit off St Mark's Church roundabout on A30 London road into Wain-a-Long Road. The Rokeby is 2nd house on left.

Room General

It's all quality-assessed accommodation

Our commitment to quality involves wide-ranging accommodation assessment. Rating and awards were correct at the time of going to press but may change following a new assessment. Please check at time of booking.

SALISBURY, Wiltshire Map ref 2B3 — SELF CATERING

★★★★
SELF CATERING

Units **1**
Sleeps **5**

Low season per wk
£310.00–£370.00
High season per wk
£380.00–£560.00

Rustic Cottage, Salisbury

contact Mrs Cheryl Beeney, 75 Church Rd, Laverstock SP1 1QS
t (01722) 337870 **e** cheribeen@aol.com **w** rustic-cottage-salisbury.co.uk

open All year
payment Credit/debit cards, cash/cheques, euros

Cosy, newly renovated character cottage (1810) close to historic centre of the cathedral city of Salisbury and tourist attractions of Stonehenge, the New Forest and south coast. Delightful country walks start from doorstep. Furnished and equipped throughout to high standard. Terraced garden with a tranquil pond and large decking area with barbecue.

⊕ At junction A338 and A30 follow signpost Laverstock onto Church Road. Immediately beyond church (on right) turn left into driveway of 2 Church Road.

♥ Special rates for last minute bookings, short breaks and extended stays in off-peak periods. See website or telephone for details.

Unit 🏠 📺 🚿 🔌 🖥 🗑 🍽 🔥 📻 🛏 💡 ❋
General 🐕5 P ⚬ Ⓢ Leisure ∪ ⚓ ► 🚲 Shop < 0.5 miles Pub < 0.5 miles

SALISBURY PLAIN

See under Market Lavington, Salisbury, Warminster

TROWBRIDGE, Wiltshire Map ref 2B2 — GUEST ACCOMMODATION

★★★
GUEST HOUSE

B&B per room per night
s £40.00–£45.00
d £65.00–£70.00

Ring O' Bells

321 Marsh Road, Hilperton Marsh, Trowbridge BA14 7PL **t** (01225) 754404 **f** (01225) 340325
e ringobells@blueyonder.co.uk **w** ringobells.biz

open All year
bedrooms 1 double, 1 twin, 2 single, 2 family
bathrooms All en suite
payment Credit/debit cards, cash/cheques

Two miles north of Trowbridge. Formerly a pub, we now offer non-smoking, comfortable en suite rooms on the ground and first floors. Rooms have TV, tea/coffee facilities, radio/alarm, hairdryer and room safes. Private car park, disabled access, Wi-Fi internet via BT Openzone, friendly atmosphere. Child- and pet-friendly. CCTV operating.

⊕ From the A361 follow B3105 into Hilperton, Staverton & Holt. Ring O' Bells is a mile down on your left. Car park in Horse Road.

Room 🛋 📺 💧 ☕ General 🐕 🏠 ♿ P ⚬ 🖥 🔥 ❋ 🐾 Leisure ∪ ⚓ ► 🚲 🎣

WARMINSTER, Wiltshire Map ref 2B2 — CAMPING & CARAVANNING

★★★★★
TOURING PARK

🚐(165) £14.30–£27.70
🚙(165) £14.30–£27.70
165 touring pitches

Longleat Caravan Club Site

Longleat, Warminster BA12 7NL **t** (01985) 844663 **w** caravanclub.co.uk

payment Credit/debit cards, cash/cheques

Close to Longleat House, this is the only site where you can hear lions roar at night! Cafés, pubs and restaurants within walking distance. Non-members welcome. Open March to November.

⊕ Take A362, signed for Frome, 0.5 miles at roundabout turn left (2nd exit) onto Longleat Estate. Through toll booths, follow caravan and camping pennant signs for 1 mile.

♥ Special member rates mean you can save your membership subscription in less than a week. Visit our website to find out more.

THE
CARAVAN
CLUB

General 🔌 P ⚡ 🚽 🚿 🚐 📶 ⊙ 🖥 🐾 ☼ Leisure ⛺ ⚓

For key to symbols open the back-cover flap.

Places to visit

On the following pages you'll find an extensive selection of indoor and outdoor attractions in South West England. Get to grips with nature, stroll around a museum, have an action-packed day with the kids and a whole lot more...

Attractions are ordered by county, and if you're looking for a specific kind of experience each county is divided into the following sections.

 Family fun

 Entertainment and culture

 Nature and wildlife

 Food and drink

 Historic England

Relaxing and pampering

 **Outdoor activities**

Look out, too, for the Quality Assured Visitor Attraction sign. This indicates that the attraction is assessed annually and meets the standards required to receive the quality marque. So rest assured, you'll have a great time.

The index on page 243 will help you to locate specific attractions with ease. For more great ideas for places to visit contact a local Tourist Information Centre or log on to **enjoyengland.com**.

Please note, as changes often occur after press date, it is advisable to confirm opening times and admission prices before travelling.

KEY TO ATTRACTIONS

Cafe/restaurant . . . . 🍵

Picnic area . . . . 🪑

No dogs except service dogs . . . . 🐕

Partial disabled access . . . . ♿

Full disabled access . . . . ♿

Where prices aren't specified, use the following guide for an adult admission:

£   up to £5
££   between £5 and £10
£££   between £10 and £15
££££   more than £15

Spot Lemurs at
Bristol Zoo Gardens

Bristol & Bath

FAMILY FUN

Bailey Balloons
44 Ham Green, Bristol BS20 0HA
t (01275) 375300 **w** baileyballoons.co.uk
open All year, Mon-Fri 0900-1730, Sat 1000-1400.
admission ££££
Champagne balloon flights from Bristol, Bath, South Wales and nationwide. Flight approximately one hour, but whole experience three to four hours. In-flight photos, flight certificates, gift vouchers.

Bristol Blue Glass Ltd
Unit 7, Whitby Road, Brislington BS4 3QF
t (0117) 972 0818 **w** bristol-glass.co.uk
open All year, Mon-Sat 1000-1600.
admission £
Watch Bristol blue glass being made by a skilled team of glassmakers in the new visitor centre, and purchase direct from the factory shop.

Explore-At-Bristol
Anchor Road, Harbourside, Bristol BS1 5DB
t 0845 345 1235 **w** at-bristol.org.uk
open Weekdays during term time 1000-1700. Weekends and local school holidays 1000-1800.
admission ££
Explore-At-Bristol is one of the UK's most exciting hands-on science centres! Discover interactive exhibits, special exhibitions and tour the night sky in the Planetarium.

NATURE AND WILDLIFE

Ashton Court Estate
Long Ashton BS41 9JN
t (0117) 963 9174 **w** bristol.gov.uk/ashtoncourtestate
open Apr, daily 0730-2015. May-Aug, daily 0730-2115. Sep, daily 0730-2015. Oct, daily 0730-1915. Nov-Jan, daily 0730-1715. Feb, daily 0730-1815.
admission Free
Woodlands, mansion, coach house cafe, garden, Rose Garden, golf courses, orienteering course, Avon Timberland Mountain Bike Trail, miniature railway, deer parks, visitor centre, horse-riding trail, car parking and weddings.

Bristol Zoo Gardens
Clifton BS8 3HA
t (0117) 974 7399
w bristolzoo.org.uk
open Apr-Oct, daily 0900-1730. Nov-Mar, daily 0900-1700.
admission £££
Voted Zoo of the Year 2004 by the Good Britain Guide, Bristol Zoo Gardens has something for everyone, from the world's smallest and rarest tortoise to the largest ape.

HorseWorld Visitor Centre
Staunton Manor Farm, Staunton Lane, Whitchurch BS14 0QJ
t (01275) 540173
w horseworld.org.uk
open Apr-Oct, daily 1000-1700. Nov-Mar, Tue-Sun 1000-1600.
admission ££
Meet our friendly horses, ponies and donkeys and enjoy our touch-and-groom areas, pony rides, live shows, adventure playground, slides, nature trail and video theatre.

Prior Park Landscape Garden
Ralph Allen Drive, Combe Down BA2 5AH
t (01225) 833422
w nationaltrust.org.uk
open Mar-Oct, Wed-Mon 1100-1730. Nov-Jan, Sat-Sun 1100-dusk.
admission £
Beautiful and intimate 18thC landscaped garden created by Bath entrepreneur Ralph Allen (1693-1764) with advice from the poet Alexander Pope and Capability Brown.

HISTORIC ENGLAND

Assembly Rooms
Bennett Street, Bath BA1 2QH
t (01225) 477789
w fashionmuseum.co.uk
open Mar-Oct, daily 1100-1700. Nov-Feb, daily 1100-1600.
admission Free
Designed by John Wood the Younger in 1769, this is one of Bath's finest Georgian buildings. Includes the Fashion Museum (admission charge) housing a world-class collection of contemporary and historical dress.

Bath Abbey
Abbey Church Yard, Bath BA1 1LT
t (01225) 422462
w bathabbey.org
open Apr-Oct, daily 0900-1800. Nov-Mar, daily 0900-1630.
admission Free
Late 15thC abbey illustrating a magnificent example of the Perpendicular period of English Gothic architecture. Display of history of Christianity in Bath in Heritage Vaults Museum.

Bristol Cathedral
College Green, Bristol BS1 5TJ
t (0117) 926 4879
w bristol-cathedral.co.uk
open Daily 0800-1730.
admission Free
Once an Augustinian abbey and splendid 12thC Norman chapter house. Magnificent 13thC and 14thC architecture.

Bristol St John the Baptist
Broad Street, Bristol BS1 2EZ
t (020) 7213 0660
w visitchurches.org.uk
open Daily, please phone for details.
admission Free
The elegant perpendicular spire of St John's rises above the Gothic city gate, and the interior of the church is impressively tall and graceful. Also home to a fine collection of monuments.

Clifton Cathedral
Clifton Park, Clifton BS8 3BX
t (0117) 973 8411
w cliftoncathedral.org.uk
open Daily 0730-1800.
admission Free
Modern Roman Catholic cathedral. The Cathedral was consecrated on 29 June 1973, replacing a wooden-framed pro-Cathedral that had been built in the mid-19th century.

The New Room – John Wesley's Chapel
36 The Horsefair, Bristol BS1 3JE
t (0117) 926 4740
w newroombristol.org.uk
open All year, Mon-Sat 1000-1600.
admission Free
The oldest Methodist building in the world. Built as a meeting room and accommodation after Wesley began to preach in the open air in Bristol in 1739.

Pump Room
Abbey Church Yard, Bath BA1 1LZ
t (01225) 477785
w romanbaths.co.uk
open Mar-Jun, daily 0900-1800. Jul-Aug, daily 0900-2100. Sep-Oct daily 0900-1800. Nov-Feb, daily 0930-1730.
admission Free
With its elegant interior of c1795, the Pump Room is the social heart of Bath. Stop for refreshments or lunch and sample a glass of spa water from the fountain.

St Mary Redcliffe Church
12 Colston Parade, Bristol BS1 6RA
t (0117) 929 1487
w stmaryredcliffe.co.uk
open Apr-Oct, Mon-Sat 0830-1700, Sun 0800-1930. Nov-Mar, Mon-Sat 0900-1600, Sun 0800-1930.
admission Free
One of the finest examples of Gothic architecture in England. The north porch is ornate Early English and the spire was completed c1872.

Temple Church
Temple Street, off Victoria Street, Bristol BS1 6EN
t (0117) 975000
w english-heritage.org.uk
open Daily.
admission Free
Walls and tower of 15thC church bombed in World War II, which stands on the site of a 12thC Knights Templar church.

OUTDOOR ACTIVITIES

The Bristol Packet Boat Trips
Wapping Wharf, Gas Ferry Road, Bristol BS1 6UN
t (0117) 926 8157
w bristolpacket.co.uk
open City Dock Tours: all year, Sat-Sun 1100-1600. School holidays, daily 1100-1600. River cruises: please see website for details.
admission £
Trips around the historic harbour and up and down the River Avon. Suitable and available for the general public, for private charter and educational cruises.

ENTERTAINMENT AND CULTURE

Alexander Gallery
122 Whiteladies Road, Bristol BS8 2RP
t (0117) 973 4692
w alexander-gallery.co.uk
open All year, Mon-Sat 0900-1730.
admission Free
One of Bristol's leading galleries specialising in oil paintings and watercolours.

Arnolfini
16 Narrow Quay, Bristol BS1 4QA
t (0117) 917 2300
w arnolfini.org.uk
open All year, daily 1000-1800.
admission Free
Arnolfini is one of Europe's centres for the contemporary arts, presenting new and innovative work in visual arts, performance, dance and film. Also offering an arts bookshop and cafe bar.

Bath Aqua Theatre of Glass
105-107 Walcot Street, Bath BA1 5BW
t (01225) 428146
w bathaquaglass.com
open All year, Mon-Sun, Bank Hols 0930-1700.
admission £
Discover the Bath Aqua Theatre of Glass, Bath's visitor centre in the heart of the city's artisan quarter.

Bath Postal Museum

27 Northgate Street, Bath BA1 1AJ
t (01225) 460333
w bathpostalmuseum.org
open Mar-Nov, Mon-Sat 1100-1700. Dec-Feb, Mon-Sat 1100-1630.
admission £

To discover the truly fascinating story of 4,000 years of written communication, visit the Bath Postal Museum in the very city from which the first stamp in the world, the Penny Black, was posted.

Bristol City Museum & Art Gallery

Queen's Road, Bristol BS8 1RL
t (0117) 922 3571
w bristol-city.gov.uk/museums
open Daily 1000-1700.
admission Free

Collection representing applied, oriental and fine art, archaeology, geology, natural history, ethnography and Egyptology.

Bristol Hippodrome

St Augustine's Parade, Bristol BS1 4UZ
t (0117) 302 3333
w bristolhippodrome.org.uk
open All year. See website for details.
admission ££££

The West's main theatrical venue for large-scale West End musicals, opera, ballet, comedy, children's shows and much more.

British Empire & Commonwealth Museum

Clock Tower Yard, Temple Meads BS1 6QH
t (0117) 925 4980
w empiremuseum.co.uk
open Daily 1000-1700.
admission ££

A major national museum exploring the dramatic history and heritage of the British Empire and its development into the modern Commonwealth.

Brunel's ss Great Britain

Great Western Dockyard, Gas Ferry Road,
Bristol BS1 6TY
t (0117) 926 0680
w ssgreatbritain.org
open Apr-Oct, daily 0900-1730. Nov-Mar, daily 0900-1630.
admission ££

Brunel's steam ship, the ss Great Britain, is a unique survival from Victorian times and the forerunner of all modern shipping. The world's first iron-hulled, screw propeller-driven, steam-powered passenger liner.

Building of Bath Museum

The Huntingdon Chapel, The Vineyards, Bath BA1 5NA
t (01225) 333895
w bath-preservation-trust.org.uk
open All year, Tue-Sun, Bank Hols 1030-1700.
admission £

The Building of Bath Museum tells the story of how Georgian Bath was built. Exhibitions include a huge model of the entire city.

Fashion Museum

Assembly Rooms, Bennett Street,
Bath BA1 2QH
t (01225) 477173
w fashionmuseum.co.uk
open All year, daily.
admission ££

A world-class collection of contemporary and historical dress housed the Assembly Rooms, one of Bath's finest Georgian buildings. Exhibitions, displays and special events.

Herschel Museum of Astronomy

19 New King Street, Bath BA1 2BL
t (01225) 446865
w bath-preservation-trust.org.uk
open All year, Mon-Tue, Thu-Fri 1300-1700, Sat-Sun, Bank Hols 1100-1700.
admission £

18thC house of astronomer, scientist, musician and composer, William Herschel and his sister Caroline. The Star Astronomy auditorium introduces their work and its impact on modern space exploration. Georgian garden.

The Clifton Suspension Bridge spanning the River Avon

Admission is based on an adult price. Please check opening times and admission before travelling.

Holburne Museum of Art
Great Pulteney Street, Bath BA2 4DB
t (01225) 466669
w bath.ac.uk/holburne
open All year, Tue-Sat 1000-1700, Sun 1100-1700, Bank Holidays 1100-1700.
admission £

Fine collection of sliver, porcelain, miniatures and furniture. Picture gallery contains paintings by Turner, Stubbs and Gainsborough, including The Byam Family.

The Jane Austen Centre
40 Gay Street, Queen Square, Bath BA1 2NT
t (01225) 443000
w janeausten.co.uk
open Apr-Sep, daily 1000-1730. Oct-Mar, Mon-Fri, Sun 1100-1630, Sat 1000-1730.
admission ££

Celebrating Bath's most famous resident, the centre offers a snapshot of life during Regency times and explores how living in this magnificent city affected Jane Austen's life and writing.

The Museum of East Asian Art
12 Bennett Street, Bath BA1 2QJ
t (01225) 464640
w meaa.org.uk
open All year, Tue-Sat, Bank Hols 1000-1700, Sun 1200-1700.
admission £

Museum displaying over 500 art objects from the East, on three floors of a Georgian house.

Roman Baths
Abbey Church yard, Bath BA1 1LZ
t (01225) 477785
w romanbaths.co.uk
open Jan-Feb, Nov-Dec 0930-1630 (excl 25-26 Dec). Mar-Jun, Sep-Oct 0900-1700. Jul-Aug 0900-2000. Exit one hour after these times.
admission £££

The Roman Baths and Temple of Sulis Minerva are among the finest Roman remains in Britain. State-of-the-art computer reconstructions of Roman Britain bring the experience to life.

Royal West of England Academy
Queens Road, Clifton, Bristol BS8 1PX
t (0117) 973 5129
w rwa.org.uk
open All year, Mon-Sat 1000-1730, Sun 1400-1700.
admission £

One of the finest buildings in Bristol housing seven galleries which show major solo, group and open exhibitions of contemporary fine art as well as a Permanent Collection.

Victoria Art Gallery
Pulteney Bridge, Bridge Street, Bath BA2 4AT
t (01225) 477233
w victoriagal.org.uk
open All year, Tue-Sat 1000-1700, Sun 1330-1700.
admission Free

Permanent collection of British and European fine and decorative art from 15th-21stC. Also major touring exhibitions from national museums and other places.

Watershed Media Centre
1 Canons Road, Harbourside, Bristol BS1 5TX
t (0117) 927 6444
w watershed.co.uk
open Daily 0900-2300.
admission Free

Watershed offers an electric programme of independent film, digital media and events with a relaxed and welcoming cafe/bar overlooking Bristol's harbourside.

Sally Lunn's House
4 North Parade Passage, Bath BA1 1NX
t (01225) 461634
w sallylunns.co.uk
open All year, Mon-Sat, Bank Hols 1000-2200, Sun 1100-2200.
admission Free

The oldest house in Bath. A Tudor-style building on a monastic site with excavations showing early medieval and Roman building. Now a licensed restaurant.

Thermae Bath Spa
Hot Bath Street, Bath BA1 1SJ
t 0844 888 0848
w thermaebathspa.com
open All year, daily, Bank Hols 0900-2200.
admission ££££

Britain's original and most remarkable spa. The only place in the UK where you can bathe in natural hot waters, as the Romans and Celts did over 2,000 years ago.

Cornwall & the Isles of Scilly

 FAMILY FUN

Bodmin and Wenford Railway
Bodmin General Station, Lostwithiel Road,
Bodmin PL31 1AQ
t (01208) 73666 w bodminandwenfordrailway.co.uk
open See website for details.
admission ££
Cornwall's only preserved standard-gauge steam railway which combines the nostalgia of a branch line in the heyday of steam with the beauty of the Fowey and Camel River valleys.

Cornwall's Crealy Great Adventure Park
Tredinnick PL27 7RA
t (01841) 540276 w crealy.co.uk/cornwall_pages
open Apr-Oct, daily 1000-1700.
admission £££
Maximum magical fun and unforgettable adventures. Discover Cornwall's best value all-weather family attraction.

Dairyland Farm World
Tresillian Barton, Summercourt TR8 5AA
t (01872) 510246 w dairylandfarmworld.com
open Apr-Oct, daily 1000-1700.
admission ££
Adventure playground, country life museum, nature trail, farm park, pets and daily events, including 120 cows milked in Clarabelle's space-age orbiter.

Delabole Slate Quarry
Pengelly, Delabole PL33 9AZ
t (01840) 212242 w delaboleslate.co.uk
open Quarry: all year. Tours: May-Aug, Mon-Fri 1400.
admission £
Come to Delabole, England's oldest working slate quarry. Visit our showroom and viewing platform then see a presentation or take a short guided tour of the quarry's operation.

The Extreme Academy
On the Beach, Watergate Bay, Newquay TR8 4AA
t (01637) 860840 w watergatebay.co.uk
open Apr-Sep, daily, Bank Hols 0830-1830. Oct-Mar, daily, Bank Hols 0930-1630.
admission £££
Cornwall's ski resort on a beach. Take your pick from waveski, kitesurf, mountain board, kite buggy, land board or traction kite lessons, or try them all with an awesome Extreme Day.

Flambards Experience
Culdrose Manor, Helston TR13 0QA
t (01326) 573404 w flambards.co.uk
open Apr-Oct, daily 1030-1730. Winter: please call for details.
admission £££
Flambards Victorian village, Britain in The Blitz exhibition and the best thrill rides in Cornwall. There's mountains of fun both indoors and out. Family tickets available.

Goonhilly Satellite Earth Station Experience

The Visitors Centre, Goonhilly Downs TR12 6LQ
t 0800 679593 w goonhilly.bt.com
open Mar-Jun, daily 1000-1700. Jul-Aug, daily 1000-1800. Sep-Nov, daily 1000-1700.
admission ££
The world's largest satellite earth station. Guided bus tour around the complex. Visitor centre with film show, and interactive displays. Children's play area.

Holywell Bay Fun Park

Holywell Bay, Newquay TR8 5PW
t (01637) 830095 w holywellbay.co.uk
open Easter-Oct, daily. Please see website for details.
admission Free
Landscaped park with quality rides. Includes go-karts, crazy golf, battle boats, maze, indoor adventure play area and fun rides, bumper boats, Bugs Buggies, golf, panning for gold, trampolines and more.

Lappa Valley Steam Railway
St Newlyn East TR8 5HZ
t (01872) 510317 w lappavalley.co.uk
open Apr-Sep, School Hols, daily. Oct, Tue-Thu, Sun. Please see website for details.
admission ££
A two-mile steam train journey. Leisure park, paddle boats, canoes, miniature railways, crazy golf, maze. Listed mine building, video of mine disaster.

Oasis Fun Pool

Hendra Holiday Park, Lane TR8 4NY
t (01637) 870711 w oasis-hendra.co.uk
open Daily 1000-1800.
admission ££
Fun pools with three water flumes, the Hendra River Rapid Ride, water cannon, fountains, waterfall and much more. It includes a toddlers' area and slide.

For key to symbols see page 171.

Poldark Mine
Wendron TR13 0ER
t (01326) 573173
w poldark-mine.co.uk
open Apr, Jul-Aug, daily 1000-1730. May-Jun, Sep-Oct, Mon-Fri, Sun 1000-1730.
admission Free
Genuine 18thC Cornish tin mine featuring guided underground tours. Museum, entertainment, gardens, restaurant, gift shops and craft workshops.

Shire Horse Farm and Carriage Museum
Lower Gryllis Farm, Treskillard TR16 6LA
t (01209) 713606
open Apr-Oct, Mon-Fri, Sun 1000-1730.
admission ££
Over 40 commercial and pleasure horse-drawn vehicles. All three breeds of heavy English horses – Shire, Suffolk Punch and Clydesdale.

Spirit of the West American Theme Park
Retallack, Winnards Perch TR9 6DE
t (01637) 881160
w chycor.co.uk/spirit-ofthe-west
open All year, Mon-Fri, Sun 1030-1700.
admission ££
Wild West theme park, museums of cowboys, Indians and American collections. Live action shows, a complete living history museum of the 1800s set in 100 acres.

Trethorne Leisure Farm
Kennards House PL15 8QE
t (01566) 86324
w trethorneleisure.com
open Daily 1000-1800.
admission ££
All-weather attraction for all ages. Large indoor and outdoor play areas plus animal activities. Tenpin bowling, restaurant, bars, gift shop, and games room.

Waterworld
Trenance Leisure Park, Newquay TR7 2LZ
t (01637) 853828
w newquaywaterworld.co.uk
open Daily. Please see website for details.
admission ££
Two swimming pools, 25m fun pool, Wooden Waves ramp park, superb life fitness gym and aerobics classes.

World of Model Railways
Meadow Street, Mevagissey PL26 6UL
t (01726) 842457
w model-railway.co.uk
open Apr-Oct, daily 1000-1700. Nov-Feb, Sat-Sun 1000-1600.
admission £
Extensive layout with detailed scenery. Nearly 50 trains automatically programmed. A world in miniature with over 2,000 models of trains from many countries.

NATURE AND WILDLIFE

Antony Woodland Gardens and Woodland Walk
Nr Antony House, Antony Road, Torpoint PL11 2QA
t (01752) 812364   **w** nationaltrust.org.uk
open Garden: Mar-Oct, Tue-Thu, Sat-Sun 1100-1730.
admission £
Woodland garden bordering the Lynher estuary containing fine shrubs, magnolias, camellias and rhododendrons set in a Humphrey Repton landscape. Further 50 acres of woods.

Blue Reef Aquarium
Towan Promenade, Newquay TR7 1DU
t (01637) 878134   **w** bluereefaquarium.co.uk
open Mar-Oct, daily 1000-1700. Nov-Feb, daily 1000-1600.
admission ££
Blue Reef Aquarium brings the magic of the undersea world alive. Enjoy close encounters with tropical sharks, rays and seahorses.

Burncoose Gardens and Nursery
Gwennap TR16 6BJ
t (01209) 860316   **w** burncoose.co.uk
open All year, Mon-Sat 0830-1700, Sun 1100-1700.
admission £
A 30-acre woodland garden featuring rhododendrons, magnolias, azaleas and other ornamental trees and shrubs alongside a working nursery.

Caerhays Castle Gardens
Caerhays, Gorran PL26 6LY
t (01872) 501310   **w** caerhays.co.uk
open Mid Feb-May, daily 1000-1700.
admission ££
A 60-acre woodland garden renowned for its collections of camellias, magnolias, rhododendrons and oaks.

Cromwells Castle, Tresco

Carnglaze Slate Caverns
Carnglaze, St Neot PL14 6HQ
t (01579) 320251 **w** carnglaze.com
open Apr-Jul, Mon-Sat 1000-1700. Aug, Mon-Sat
1000-2000. Sep-Mar, Mon-Sat 1000-1700.
admission ££
*Centuries-old caverns, created by local slate miners.
Subterranean lake with crystal-clear blue-green water.
Also visit The Rum Store concert and event venue. Dogs
welcome in gardens and woodland walk.*

Colliford Lake Park
Bolventor, Bodmin Moor, St Neot PL14 6PZ
t (01208) 821469 **w** collifordlakepark.com
open See website for details.
admission ££
*An all-weather adventure park with over 30,000 sq ft
undercover offering loads of fun and exciting
entertainment for all the family. Set in a beautiful
country park on Bodmin Moor.*

Cornish Birds of Prey Centre
Meadowside Farm, Winnards Perch,
St Columb Major TR9 6DH
t (01637) 880544 **w** cornishbirdsofprey.co.uk
open Daily 1000-1700.
admission ££
*Birds of prey centre, animal park and fishing lakes set in
a beautiful valley. Flying displays twice daily, over 60
birds to see, plus much more!*

Eden Project
Bodelva, St Austell PL24 2SG
t (01726) 811911 **w** edenproject.com
open Apr-Oct, daily 1000-1800. Nov-Mar, daily
1000-1630.
admission £££
*An unforgettable experience in a breathtaking epic
location. A gateway into the fascinating world of plants
and people.*

Glendurgan Garden
Mawnan Smith TR11 5JZ
t (01326) 250906 **w** nationaltrust.org.uk
open Feb-Oct, Tue-Sat, Bank Hols 1030-1730. Aug,
Mon 1030-1730.
admission ££
*A valley garden of great beauty, created in the 1820s
and running down to the tiny village of Durgan and its
beach. There are many fine trees and rare and exotic
plants.*

Kit Hill Country Park
Kit Hill Office, Clitters, Callington PL17 8HW
t (01579) 370030 **w** cornwall.gov.uk
open Daily.
admission Free
*A wild, rugged, granite hilltop, famous for its fine views
and fascinating history. Kit Hill Country Park forms a
dominating feature, to be seen for miles around.*

The Lost Gardens of Heligan
Heligan, Pentewan PL26 6EN
t (01726) 845100
w heligan.com
open Mar-Oct, daily 1000-1800. Nov-Feb, daily
1000-1700.
admission ££
*The nation's favourite garden offers 200 glorious
acres of exploration, which include extensive
productive gardens and pleasure grounds,
sustainably-managed farmland, wetlands, ancient
woodlands and a pioneering wildlife conservation
project.*

The Monkey Sanctuary Trust
Looe PL13 1NZ
t (01503) 262532
w monkeysanctuary.org
open Apr-Sep, Mon-Thu, Sun 1100-1630. Oct, School
hols, Mon-Thu, Sun 1100-1630.
admission ££
*Protected colony of woolly monkeys. Talks given
throughout the day and monkeys can be seen in
extensive enclosures and trees. Also a rescue centre for
ex-pet Capuchin monkeys.*

National Seal Sanctuary
Gweek, Helston TR12 6UG
t (01326) 221361
w sealsanctuary.co.uk
open All year, daily from 1000.
admission ££
*Britain's leading marine mammal rescue centre.
Celebrating 50 years of grey seal rescue,
rehabilitation and release. The National Seal
Sanctuary is also home to resident seals, sea lions
and Asian short-clawed otters.*

Newquay Zoo
Trenance Gardens, Newquay TR7 2LZ
t (01637) 873342
w newquayzoo.org.uk
open Oct-Mar 1000-1700 (excl 25 Dec). Apr-Sep
0930-1800.
admission ££
*Discover hundreds of animals from all around the
world set amongst lakeside gardens, from the
smallest monkey, the Pygmy Marmoset, to African
lions. Enjoy talks and feeding times throughout the
day.*

Paradise Park
Glanmor House, Trelissick Road, Hayle TR27 4HB
t (01736) 751020
w paradisepark.org.uk
open Daily 1000-1800.
admission ££
*Cornwall's award-winning wildlife sanctuary. Large
aviaries set around sheltered Victorian gardens with
flamingos, tropical birds, otters, red pandas and
farmyard. Daily events and huge 'Jungle Barn' indoor
play area for children.*

Penjerrick Garden
Budock Water TR11 5ED
t (01872) 870105 **w** penjerrickgarden.co.uk
open Mar-Sep, Wed, Fri, Sun, 1330-1630.
admission £

Spring flowering, ten acre garden with camellias, rhododendrons, tree ferns, magnificent trees and ponds. Very tranquil, wild and non-commercial. Best to wear wellington boots.

Pine Lodge Gardens & Nursery
Holmbush, St Austell PL25 3RQ
t (01726) 73500 **w** pine-lodge.co.uk
open Daily 1000-1800.
admission ££

Thirty acres with over 6,000 plants. Herbaceous and shrub borders, many water features. Lake with waterfowl and black swans. Plant-hunting expeditions every year. New Winter Garden of three acres.

Porfell Animal Land
Trecangate, Nr Lanreath, Liskeard PL14 4RE
t (01503) 220211 **w** PorfellAnimalLand.co.uk
open Good Friday-Oct, daily 1000-1800.
admission ££

Porfell Animal Land with its gently sloping fields, streams, woodland walks and a variety of exotic wild and domesticated animals allows visitors to enjoy close contact with nature.

Screech Owl Sanctuary
Trewin Farm, Goss Moor, St Columb TR9 6HP
t (01726) 860182 **w** screechowlsanctuary.co.uk
open Feb-Oct, daily 1000-1800.
admission ££

Owl rescue and rehabilitation centre. Guided tours of sanctuary, approximately 160 owls and an education centre on a conservation theme. Flying displays twice daily.

Springfields Fun Park and Pony Centre
Ruthvoes TR9 6HU
t (01637) 882130 **w** springfieldsponycentre.co.uk
open See website for details.
admission ££

Lots of indoor and outdoor activities. Springfields is not just a day out, it's what childhood memories are made of.

Stithians Lake
Menherion TR16 6NW
t (01209) 860301 **w** swlakestrust.org.uk
open All year, daily.
admission Free

Stithian's reputation as one of England's windiest inland waters make it a favourite with windsurfers and sailors, and a fantastic location to learn new watersports including canoeing or rowing.

Tamar Lakes
Kilkhampton EX23 9SB
t (01288) 321712 **w** swlakestrust.org.uk
open All year, daily.
admission Free

Near Bude on the North Cornwall coast, these two lakes offer a variety of activities including watersports, angling and walking. The Bude Aqueduct Walk starts and finishes at Lower Tamar.

Tamar Otter & Wildlife Centre
North Petherwin PL15 8GW
t (01566) 785646 **w** tamarotters.co.uk
open Apr-Oct, daily, Bank Hols 1030-1800.
admission ££

Wooded valley with collection of otters in large, open, natural enclosures. Water-fowl lakes, aviaries, woodland trail with deer, peacocks and pheasants. Breeding owls. Tearoom with homemade produce.

Tamar Valley Donkey Park

St Ann's Chapel, Gunnislake PL18 9HW
t (01822) 834072 **w** donkeypark.com
open Apr-Oct, daily 1000-1730. Nov-Mar, Sat-Sun, School Hols 1030-1630.
admission ££

Donkey rides, feed the animals, rabbit warren, goat mountain, large indoor play barn, two outdoor playgrounds, cafe, shop, picnic garden and adopt a donkey.

Trebah Garden
Trebah, Mawnan Smith TR11 5JZ
t (01326) 252200 **w** trebah-garden.co.uk
open All year. Please see website for details.
admission ££

A 26-acre ravine garden leading to a private beach on Helford River. Extensive collection of rare and sub-tropical plants and trees. Play areas and trails for children of all ages.

Trelissick Garden
Feock TR3 6QL
t (01872) 862090 **w** nationaltrust.org.uk
open Feb-Oct, daily 1030-1730. Nov-Jan, daily 1100-1600.
admission ££

Large garden, lovely in all seasons. Superb views of estuary and Falmouth harbour. Woodland walks beside the River Fal.

Trengwainton Garden
Madron TR20 8RZ
t (01736) 363148 **w** nationaltrust.org.uk
open Feb-Oct, Sun-Thu, Good Friday 1030-1700.
admission ££

Garden rich in exotic plants, views to Mount's Bay, stream and walled gardens with many plants which cannot be grown anywhere else on mainland UK.

Tresco Abbey Gardens
Tresco TR24 0QQ
t (01720) 424108
w tresco.co.uk
open All year, daily.
admission ££

The Abbey Garden is a glorious exception – a perennial Kew without the glass – shrugging off salt spray and Atlantic gales to host 20,000 exotic plants.

Trevarno
Crowntown TR13 0RU
t (01326) 574274
w trevarno.co.uk
open Daily 1030-1700.
admission ££

Do not miss a visit to the historic Trevarno Estate where you can explore the magnificent gardens, grounds and woodland walks which date back to 1246.

Trewithen
Grampound Road TR2 4DD
t (01726) 883647
w trewithengardens.co.uk
open Feb-May, daily 1000-1630. Jun-Sep, Mon-Sat 1000-1630.
admission £

Gardens renowned for camellias, rhododendrons, magnolias and many rare plants. An 18thC landscaped parkland. House built in 1720. Audiovisual on history of Trewithen.

Fisherman's Bay

HISTORIC ENGLAND

The Arthurian Centre
Slaughterbridge, Camelford PL32 9TT
t (01840) 213947
w arthur-online.co.uk
open Apr-Oct, daily 1000-1700.
admission £

Site of King Arthur's last battle. 6thC King Arthur's Stone, Lady Falmouth's 18thC garden, exhibition room, video loop, brass rubbings, gift shop. A totally unique experience. Beautiful riverside walks.

Charlestown Shipwreck and Heritage Centre
Quay Road, Charlestown PL25 3NJ
t (01726) 69897
w shipwreckcharlestown.com
open Mar-Oct, daily 1000-1700.
admission ££

Visual history of Charlestown including life-size tableaux of old inhabitants, blacksmith and cooper. Outstanding display of shipwreck material. Diving and RNLI exhibitions. Ocean Liner exhibits including Titanic.

Chysauster Ancient Village
New Mill, Penzance TR20 8XA
t 07831 757934
w english-heritage.org.uk/chysauster
open Apr-Jun, daily 1000-1700. Jul-Aug, daily 1000-1800. Sep, daily 1000-1700. Oct, daily 1000-1600.
admission £

Originally occupied almost 2,000 years ago, the village contained eight stone-walled homesteads, each with a central courtyard surrounded by thatched rooms.

Cornish Mines & Engines
Pool TR15 3NP
t (01209) 315027
w nationaltrust.org.uk
open Apr-Nov, Mon, Wed-Fri, Sun 1100-1700.
admission £

Cornwall's engine houses are dramatic reminders of the time when the county was a powerhouse of tin, copper and china-clay mining.

Cotehele
St Dominick PL12 6TA
t (01579) 351346
w nationaltrust.org.uk
open House: Mar-Oct, Mon-Thu, Sat-Sun 1100-1630. Gardens: all year, daily 1000-dusk.
admission ££

Medieval house with superb collections of textiles, armour and furniture, set in extensive grounds. Home of the Edgcumbe family for centuries, its granite and slatestone walls contain intimate chambers adorned with tapestries.

 For key to symbols see page 171.

The Courtroom Experience
Shire Hall, Mount Folly, Bodmin PL31 2DQ
t (01208) 76616
w bodminmoor.co.uk/bodmintic
open Apr-Oct, Mon-Sat 1100-1600. Nov-Mar, Mon-Fri 1100-1600.
admission £
Guilty or not guilty: you must decide! What will the verdict be in this Victorian murder trial?

King Arthur's Great Halls
Fore Street, Tintagel PL34 0DA
t (01840) 770526
w kingarthursgreathalls.com
open Summer: daily 1000-1700. Winter: daily 1100-1500.
admission £
Dedicated to the Arthurian legend, this is the home of Robert Powell's narrated light show about the deeds of the Knights of the Round Table.

Land's End
Sennen TR19 7AA
t 0870 458 0099
w landsend-landmark.co.uk
open Apr-Sep, daily 1000-1700. Oct-Mar, daily 1000-1500.
admission ££
Spectacular cliffs with breathtaking vistas. Superb multi-sensory Last Labyrinth show and other exhibitions.

Lanhydrock
Bodmin PL30 5AD
t (01208) 265950
w nationaltrust.org.uk
open House: Mar-Sep, Tue-Sun 1100-1730. Oct, Tue-Sat 1100-1700. Gardens: all year, daily 1000-1800.
admission ££
A 17thC house largely rebuilt after a fire in 1881. The 116ft gallery with magnificent plaster ceiling illustrates scenes from the Old Testament. Park, gardens, walks.

Mount Edgcumbe House and Park
Cremyll PL10 1HZ
t (01752) 822236
w mountedgcumbe.gov.uk
open Apr-Sep, Mon-Thu, Sun 1100-1630.
admission £
Restored Tudor mansion, past home of Earl of Mount Edgcumbe. French, Italian and English formal gardens with temples and 800 acres of parkland.

Pencarrow House and Gardens
Washaway, Bodmin PL30 3AG
t (01208) 841369
w pencarrow.co.uk
open House: 23 Mar-19 Oct, Sun-Thu 1100-1700. Gardens: 1 Mar- 31 Oct, daily 0930-1730.
admission ££
Historic family-owned Georgian house, superb collection of paintings, furniture and china. Extensive Grade II Listed grounds, picnic area, craft centre, children's play area, pets' corner and tearooms.*

Pendennis Castle
Falmouth TR11 4LP
t (01326) 316594 w english-heritage.org.uk/pendennis
open Apr-Jun, Sep, Mon-Fri, Sun 1000-1700, Sat 1000-1600. Jul-Aug, Mon-Fri, Sun 1000-1800, Sat 1000-1600. Oct-Mar, daily 1000-1600.
admission ££
Guards the entrance to the Fal estuary, along with its sister castle, St Mawes. Well-preserved coastal fort built by Henry VIII c1540. Discover the gun deck, barrack room displays, underground tunnels and tea room.

Prideaux Place
Padstow PL28 8RP
t (01841) 532411 w prideauxplace.co.uk
open May-Oct, Mon-Thu, Sun 1230-1700.
admission ££
A 16thC Elizabethan mansion with contemporary embossed plaster ceiling in the Great Chamber. Forty acres of grounds including deer park.

Restormel Castle
Castleton, Near Lostwithiel PL22 0BD
t (01208) 872687 w english-heritage.org.uk/restormel
open Apr-Jun, Sep, daily 1000-1700. Jul-Aug, daily 1000-1800. Oct, daily 1000-1600.
admission £
Surrounded by a deep, dry moat and perched on a high mound, the huge circular keep of this Norman castle survives in good condition.

Roseland St Anthony's Church
Roseland, Portscatho TR2 5EY
t (020) 7213 0660 w visitchurches.org.uk
open Daily 1000-1630.
admission Free
Picturesquely situated looking across the creek to St Mawes, the church retains its original medieval plan and appearance. It also features notable Victorian work, and impressive monuments to members of the Spry family.

St Mawes Castle
St Mawes TR2 3AA
t (01326) 270526 w english-heritage.org.uk/stmawes
open Apr-Oct, daily from 1000. Nov-Mar, Fri-Mon from 1000. See website for closing times.
admission £
On edge of Roseland Peninsula, erected by Henry VIII for coastal defence. Clover-leaf shaped and still intact. Fine example of military architecture. Lovely gardens.

St Michael's Mount
Marazion TR17 0EF
t (01736) 710507 w stmichaelsmount.co.uk
open 16 Mar-Nov, Mon-Fri, Sun 1030-1700.
admssion ££
Rocky island crowned by medieval church and castle, home to a living community.

Tintagel Castle
Tintagel PL34 0HE
t (01840) 770328
w english-heritage.org.uk/tintagel
open Apr-Sep, daily 1000-1800. Oct, daily 1000-1700.
Nov-Mar. daily 1000-1600.
admission £
*Medieval ruined castle on wild, wind-swept coast.
Famous for associations with Arthurian legend. Built
largely in 13thC by Richard, Earl of Cornwall.*

Truro Cathedral
The Cathedral Office, 14 St Mary's Street,
Truro TR1 2AF
t (01872) 276782
w trurocathedral.org.uk
open All year, Mon-Sat 0730-1800, Sun 0900-1900.
admission Free
*Outstanding example of the work of Victorian architect,
John Pearson, who favoured the Gothic style, with
strong influences from French churches.*

Tamar Cruising
Cremyll Quay, Cremyll PL10 1HX
t (01752) 822105
w tamarcruising.com
open Daily. Please see website for details.
admission ££
*Cruises from the Mayflower Steps, Barbican and
Plymouth around the dockyard to see warships. Also
along the River Tamar and River Yealm. Ferry lands at
Mount Edgcumbe Country Park.*

Westward Airways & Land's End Flying School
Land's End Airport, St Just TR19 7RL
t (01736) 788771
w landsendairport.co.uk
open Daily.
admission ££££
*Experience flying over the Penwith Peninsula for an
unforgettable bird's eye view with Westward Airways.
Alternatively, have a go yourself with a trial flying lesson
at Land's End Flying School.*

OUTDOOR ACTIVITIES

ENTERTAINMENT AND CULTURE

Isles of Scilly Travel
Quay Street, Penzance TR18 4BZ
t 0845 710 5555
w ios-travel.co.uk
open Office: Mon-Sat. Skybus: all year. Scillonian III:
17 Mar-1 Nov, Mon-Sat.
admission ££££
*Discover the beautiful Isles of Scilly. Fly with
Skybus from Southampton, Bristol, Exeter,
Newquay or Land's End (shuttle service available).
Alternatively relax and sail with Scillonian III from
Penzance.*

Barbara Hepworth Museum and Sculpture Garden
Barnoon Hill, St Ives TR26 1AD
t (01736) 796226
w tate.org.uk/stives
open Mar-Oct, Mon-Sun 1000-1720. Nov-Feb, Tue-Sun
1000-1620.
admission £
*Home of the late Dame Barbara Hepworth from
1949-75. Sculptures in wood, stone and bronze inside
the museum and in the sub-tropical garden. Archive
section with photographs.*

The catch of the day, Porthloe

British Cycling Museum
The Old Station, Camelford PL32 9TZ
t (01840) 212811
w chycorco.uk/britishcyclingmuseum
open All year, Sun-Thu 1000-1700.
admission £   卉 ㋨ ㋡
A history of cycles and cycling memorabilia from c1818 to modern times. The nation's foremost museum of cycling history.

Falmouth Art Gallery
Municipal Buildings, The Moor, Falmouth TR11 2RT
t (01326) 313863
w falmouthartgallery.com
open All year, Mon-Sat 1000-1700.
admission Free   卉 ㋨ ㋡
Family-friendly exhibitions, internationally acclaimed artists and one of the best collections in the South West featuring Pre-Raphaelites and British Impressionists.

Geevor Tin Mine
Pendeen TR19 7EW
t (01736) 788662
w geevor.com
open Apr-Oct, Mon-Fri, Sun 0900-1600. Nov-Mar, Mon-Fri, Sun 0900-1500.
admission ££   ㋛ 卉 ㋡
Cornish mining museum, tours of surface plant and underground tours of the site.

The Minack Theatre and Visitor Centre
Porthcurno TR19 6JU
t (01736) 810181
w minack.com
open Apr-Oct, daily, Bank Hols 0930-1730. Nov-Mar, daily, Bank Hols 1000-1600.
admission £   ㋛ ㋨ ㋡
Open-air cliff-side theatre with breathtaking views, presenting a 17-week season of plays and musicals. Visitor centre telling the theatre's story.

The Museum of Witchcraft
The Harbour, Boscastle PL35 0HD
t (01840) 250111
w museumofwitchcraft.com
open Apr-Oct, Mon-Sat 1030-1800, Sun 1130-1800.
admission £   ㋡
Museum devoted to the study of witchcraft in England during the past and present day. Home to the world's largest collection dedicated to witchcraft.

National Maritime Museum Cornwall
Discovery Quay, Falmouth TR11 3QY
t (01326) 313388
w nmmc.co.uk
open Daily 1000-1700 (excl 25-26 Dec).
admission ££   ㋛ ㋨ ㋡
Located on the edge of Falmouth's stunning harbour, this museum is a hands-on, new generation of visitor attraction that will appeal to landlubbers and sailors alike.

North Cornwall Museum and Gallery
The Clease, Camelford PL32 9PL
t (01840) 212954
open Apr-Sep, Mon-Sat 1000-1700.
admission £   ㋨ ㋡
Reconstruction of the upstairs and downstairs of a Cornish cottage. Farm tools, carpentry, cobbling and quarrying tools. Wagons, domestic bygones and clothes.

Porthcurno Telegraph Museum
Eastern House, Porthcurno TR19 6JX
t (01736) 810966
w porthcurno.org.uk
open Apr-Oct, Mon-Tue, Thu-Sun 1000-1700, Wed 1000-1930.
admission £   卉 ㋨ ㋡
Award-winning museum housed in secret underground communications bunker. Superb collection tells the story of Empire communications from 1850 to World War II.

Royal Cornwall Museum
River Street, Truro TR1 2SJ
t (01872) 272205
w royalcornwallmuseum.org.uk
open All year, Mon-Sat 1000-1700 (excl Bank Hols).
admission Free   ㋛ ㋨
World-famous mineral collection, Old Master drawings, ceramics, oil paintings by the Newlyn School and others, archaeology, local history, national history, genealogy library.

St Ives Society of Artists
Norway Square, St Ives TR26 1NA
t (01736) 795582
w stisa.co.uk
open Mar-early Jan, Mon-Sat 1030-1730. Whitsun to Oct half-term, Sun 1430-1730.
admission Free
Housed in the former Mariners Church, the St Ives Society of Artists' Members and Mariners galleries show members' work in exhibitions throughout the year, as well as a variety of invited and open exhibitions.

Tate St Ives
Porthmeor Beach, St Ives TR26 1TG
t (01736) 796226
w tate.org.uk/stives
open Mar-Oct, Mon-Sun 1000-1720. Nov-Feb, Tue-Sun 1000-1620.
admission ££   ㋛ ㋨ ㋡
On a spectacular site overlooking Porthmeor Beach, enjoy the very best of a varied international, modern and contemporary art exhibition programme, in the unique cultural context of St Ives.

Tunnels Through Time
St Michael's Road, Newquay TR7 1RA
t (01637) 873379
w tunnelsthroughtime.co.uk
open Apr-Oct, Mon-Fri, Sun. Please phone for details.
admission £
Exhibition of over 70 full-sized characters portraying Cornish stories and legends.

FOOD AND DRINK

Camel Valley Vineyards
Nanstallon PL30 5LG
t (01208) 77959
w camelvalley.com
open Apr-Sep, Mon-Sat 1000-1700. Oct-Mar, Mon-Fri 1000-1700.
admission Free
Cornwall's largest vineyard. New modern winery, tours, tasting. Wine by the glass, bottle or case. International Gold Medal winner.

Cornish Cyder Farm
Penhallow TR4 9LW
t (01872) 573356
w thecornishcyderfarm.co.uk
open All year, Mon-Sun. See website for details.
admission Free
Visit a real working cider farm and take a guided tour to learn the art of cider making. Taste the international award-winning cider. Complete your visit with a home-made cream tea.

Polmassick Vineyard
Polmassick, St Ewe PL26 6HA
t (01726) 842239
open May-Sep, daily, Bank Hols 1100-1700.
admission £
Vine growing and wine making to produce wine for sale. Wine-making equipment on display. Harvest usually from end of September through October, at weekends.

RELAXING AND PAMPERING

Boscastle Pottery
The Old Bakery, Boscastle PL35 0HE
t (01840) 250291
open All year, Mon-Sun, Bank Hols 0930-1730.
admission Free
The world's only dedicated mocha-ware maker, with an on site showroom. Visitors can watch trees grow on the pots as if by magic.

Cornish Goldsmiths
Tolgus Mill, New Portreath Road,
Portreath TR16 4HN
t (01209) 218198
w cornishgoldsmiths.com
open All year, Mon-Sat 0930-1730, Sun 1030-1630.
admission Free
Showroom offering the largest collection of gold and silver jewellery in the South West, with many hand finished and carefully crafted pieces.

Cotswolds & Forest of Dean

FAMILY FUN

Avon Valley Railway
Bitton Station, Bath Road,
Bitton, Bristol BS30 6HD
t (0117) 932 7296 w avonvalleyrailway.org
open Apr-Oct, Sun 1100-1600. Easter, May, Aug, Oct School Hols, Tue-Thu 1100-1600.
admission ££
A 2.5-mile standard-gauge steam railway offering a journey back in time to the glorious days of steam, and a collection of locomotives and rolling stock.

Bourton Model Railway Exhibition
Box Bush, High Street, Bourton-on-the-Water GL54 2AN
t (01451) 820686 w bourtonmodelrailway.co.uk
open Jun-Aug, daily 1100-1700. Sep-May, Sat-Sun 1100-1700. Feb, Mar, May School Hols, daily.
admission £
Approximately 500 sq ft of some of the finest scenic model railway layouts in the country.

Butts Farm Rare Farm Animals and Farm Shop
The Butts Farm, Cricklade Road,
Near South Cerney GL7 5QE
t (01285) 869414 w buttsfarmshop.com
open See website for details.
admission £
A traditional farm where you can enjoy a unique hands-on experience amongst our friendly farm animals. A must for all animal lovers.

Clearwell Caves and Ancient Iron Mines
Clearwell, Coleford GL16 8JR
t (01594) 832535 w clearwellcaves.com
open Mar-Oct, daily 1000-1700.
admission £
A natural cave system tunnelled into by miners for over 5,000 years. There are nine large caverns and geological displays throughout. A great underground experience.

For key to symbols see page 171.

Cotswold Farm Park
Guiting Power GL54 5UG
t (01451) 850307 w cotswoldfarmpark.co.uk
open Apr-Aug, daily 1030-1700. Sep-Oct, Sat-Sun
1030-1700.
admission ££
Over 50 flocks and herds of British rare breeds of farm animals, seasonal farming demonstrations, lots of fun children's activities, cafe and gift shop.

Dean Forest Railway
Forest Road, Lydney GL15 4ET
t (01594) 845840 w deanforestrailway.co.uk
open See website for details.
admission ££
Heritage steam (and occasional diesel) railway running between Lydney Junction and Parkend. As well as the regular timetable there are also special events, a luxury dining train, museum, gift shop and cafe.

The Dick Whittington Farm Park
Little London, Longhope GL17 0PH
t (01452) 831000 w dickwhittington.info
open Mar-Sep, Dec, daily 1000-1700. Jan-Feb, Oct-Nov,
Tue-Sun 1000-1700.
admission £
Fun for all the family with an indoor play barn, aquarium and reptile/insect house, outdoor play/adventure zones, giant sandpit, pedal course, farm animals and deer, small pets corner, walks and views.

Forest Model Village and Gardens
Old Park, Lydney Park Estate, Aylburton GL15 6BU
t (01594) 845244 w forest-model-village.co.uk
open See website for details.
admission £
Discover a miniature Forest of Dean set within five spectacular landscaped gardens in a shady woodland glade. Come face to face with what makes the Forest of Dean a magical, special place.

Gloucestershire Warwickshire Railway
The Railway Station, Toddington GL54 5DT
t (01452) 539062 w gwsr.com
open See website for details.
admission ££
Fully operational narrow-gauge railway. Exhibits from Britain and abroad. Steam rides available.

Go Ape! Forest of Dean
Queen Street, Lydney GL15 5LY
t 0870 444 5562 w goape.co.uk
open 10 Feb-25 Feb, 23 Mar-2 Nov, daily 0900-1700.
Nov, Sat-Sun 0900-1700.
admission ££££
Live life adventurously and take to the trees, experiencing an exhilarating course of rope bridges, Tarzan Swings and zip slides up to 40 feet above the forest floor.

St Augustine's Farm
High Street, Arlingham GL2 7JN
t (01452) 740720 w staugustinesfarm.co.uk
open Mar-Oct, Tue-Sun 1100-1700.
admission £
Organic dairy farm lying in the middle of a horseshoe bend in the River Severn. Visitor centre, cafe and museum.

NATURE AND WILDLIFE

Batsford Arboretum
Batsford Park, Batsford GL56 9QB
t (01386) 701441 w batsarb.co.uk
open Feb-Nov, daily 1000-2000. Dec-Jan, Mon-Tue,
Thu-Sun 1000-2000.
admission ££
Fifty-acre arboretum containing one of the largest private collections of rare trees in the country, most spectacular in spring and autumn. Falconry, nursery and tearooms.

Birdland Park
Rissington Road, Bourton-on-the-Water GL54 2BN
t (01451) 820480 w birdland.co.uk
open Apr-Oct, daily 1000-1800. Nov-Mar, daily
1000-1600.
admission ££
A natural setting of woodland, river and gardens, Birdland is home to over 500 birds of 130 different species.

Bonsai World of Cheltenham
Two Hedges Road, Woodmancote,
Cheltenham GL52 9PT
t (01242) 674389 w bonsai-world.co.uk
open All year, Mon-Wed, Fri-Sat 0900-1700, Sun
1000-1600.
admission Free
One of the largest Bonsai collections in Gloucestershire.

Cotswold Falconry
Batsford Park, Moreton-in-Marsh GL56 9QB
t (01386) 701043 w cotswold-falconry.co.uk
open 9 Feb-16 Nov, daily 1030-1700.
admission ££
Collection of over 120 birds of prey. Flying demonstrations of eagles, owls, hawks, vultures and falcons. Breeding aviaries, owl wood, hawk walk and gift shop.

Hidcote Manor Garden (National Trust)
Hidcote Bartrim, Chipping Campden GL55 6LR
t (01386) 438333 w nationaltrust.org.uk
open 15 Mar-Jun, Sep, Mon-Wed, Sat-Sun 1000-1700.
Jul-Aug, Mon-Wed, Fri-Sun 1000-1700. Oct, Mon-Wed,
Sat-Sun 1000-1600.
admission ££
One of England's great gardens, famous for its rare trees and shrubs, outstanding herbaceous borders and unusual plants from all over the world.

Keynes Country Park/Cotswold Water Park
Cotswold Water Park, Spratsgate Lane,
Shorncote GL7 6DF
t (01285) 861459 **w** waterpark.org
open See website for details.
admission £

Includes nature reserve. Facilities for angling, bathing, windsurfing and sailing. Tourism centre, Coots cafe and retail area.

Lydney Park Gardens
Lydney GL15 6BU
t (01594) 842844
open 23 Mar-1 May, Wed, Sun, Bank Hols 1000-1700.
2 May-8 Jun, Sun-Thu 1000-1700.
admission £

Extensive rhododendron, azalea and flowering shrub gardens in Lakeland Valley with unique Roman temple site and museum.

Mill Dene Garden
Mill Dene, School Lane, Blockley GL56 9HU
t (01386) 700457 **w** milldenegarden.co.uk
open 18 Mar-Oct, Tue-Fri 1000-1700.
admission £

Cotswold garden surrounding a water mill with millpond, stream and grotto. Steep valley hides surprises of colour, views, planting ideas and fun.

Painswick Rococo Garden Trust
Painswick GL6 6TH
t (01452) 813204 **w** rococogarden.org.uk
open Jan-Oct, daily, Bank Hols 1100-1700.
admission ££

Eighteenth-century Rococo garden, set in a hidden combe, with garden buildings, vistas and woodland paths.

Prinknash Bird Park
Prinknash Park, Cranham GL4 8EU
t (01452) 812727 **w** prinknash-bird-and-deerpark.com
open Apr-Oct, daily 1000-1700. Nov-Mar, daily
1000-1600.
admission £

A deer park with fallow deer, pygmy goats and peacocks, both Indian blue and white and crown cranes. New aviary. Numerous species of waterfowl and exotic pheasants.

Robinswood Hill Country Park
Reservoir Road, Gloucester GL4 6SX
t (01452) 303206
open Daily, Bank Hols 0800-dusk.
admission Free

Open countryside park of 250 acres with viewpoint, pleasant walks, way-marked nature trails and Gloucestershire visitor centre.

The Sculpture Trail & Beechenhurst Lodge
Speech House Road, Forest of Dean GL16 7EG
t (01594) 833057 **w** forestofdean-sculpture.org.uk
open All year, Mon-Sun, Bank Hols 0800-1800.
admission Free

Since 1984 The Forest of Dean Sculpture Trust has raised funds to commission artists to celebrate the life of the forest.

Westbury Court Garden (National Trust)
Westbury-on-Severn GL14 1PD
t (01452) 760461 **w** nationaltrust.org.uk
open 12 Mar-Jun, Wed-Sun 1000-1700. Jul-Aug, daily
1000-1700. Sep-26 Oct, Wed-Sun 1000-1700.
admission £

Formal water garden with canals and yew hedges laid out between 1696 and 1705.

Traditional stone cottages in the village of Bibury

Admission is based on an adult price. Please check opening times and admission before travelling.

Westonbirt Arboretum
Forest Enterprise, Westonbirt GL8 8QS
t (01666) 880220
w forestry.gov.uk/westonbirt
open All year, daily 0900-dusk.
admission £

Six-hundred acres with the finest collections of trees, beautiful spring flowers, stunning autumn colours and a wide range of events.

Wildfowl & Wetlands Trust Slimbridge
WWT Slimbridge Wetland Centre,
Slimbridge GL2 7BT
t (01453) 891900
w wwt.org.uk
open Apr-Oct 0930-1730. Nov-Mar 0930-1700 (excl 25 Dec).
admission ££
WWT Slimbridge Wetland Centre is a fantastic day out for everyone. Visit our wonderful reserve, relax in our restaurant, browse in our gallery and shop, or enjoy one of our many events and activities.

HISTORIC ENGLAND

Blackfriars
Ladybellegate Street, Gloucester
t 07795 223870
w english-heritage.org.uk
open See website for details.
admission £
One of the most complete surviving friaries of Dominican 'black friars' in England, later converted into a Tudor house and cloth factory. Notable features include the church and the fine scissor-braced dormitory roof.

Chedworth Roman Villa (National Trust)
Yanworth GL54 3LJ
t (01242) 890256
w nationaltrust.org.uk
open Apr-Oct, Tue-Sun 1000-1700. Nov, Tue-Sun 1000-1600.
admission ££
Remains of a well-preserved Roman villa set in wooded Cotswold combe. A chance to see Roman Britain at its grandest.

Church of Saint John Baptist
Market Place, Cirencester GL7 2BQ
t (01285) 659317
w cirenparish.co.uk
open Apr-Oct, daily 1000-1700. Nov-Mar, daily 1000-1600.
admission Free
One of the wool churches of the Cotswolds with 15thC pulpit, tower, three-storey fan-vaulted porch and Anne Boleyn cup.

Dean Heritage Centre
Camp Mill, Soudley GL14 2UB
t (01594) 822170
w deanheritagemuseum.com
open Mar-Oct, daily 1000-1700. Nov-Feb, Sat-Sun 1000-1600.
admission £
Museum displays housed in an old corn mill in a woodland setting. Explore Forest of Dean history, see a beam engine, waterwheel and ponds, woodland walks and an art gallery.

Dyrham Park
Dyrham SN14 8ER
t (0117) 937 2501
w nationaltrust.org.uk
open Park: Daily 1100-1730. House: Mar-Oct, Mon-Tue, Fri-Sun 1200-1700.
admission ££
Mansion built between 1691 and 1710 for William Blathwayt. A herd of deer has roamed the 263-acre parkland since Saxon times.

Gloucester Cathedral
Westgate Street, Gloucester GL1 2LR
t (01452) 528095
w gloucestercathedral.org.uk
open All year, Mon-Fri 0730-1815, Sat 0730-1715, Sun 0730-1600.
admission £
An architectural gem made of honey-coloured limestone with crypt, cloisters and Chapter House set in its precincts.

Hailes Abbey
Winchcombe GL54 5PB
t (01242) 602398
w english-heritage.org.uk/hailes
open Apr-Jun, daily 1000-1700. Jul-Aug, daily 1000-1800. Sep, daily 1000-1700. Oct, daily 1000-1600.
admission £
Standing in secluded Cotswold pastureland are the remains of this 13thC Cistercian abbey, built by Richard, Earl of Cornwall.

Historic Gloucester Docks
1 Albion Cottages, The Docks, Gloucester GL1 2ER
t (01452) 311190
w glosdocks.co.uk
open Daily.
admission Free
Collection of restored Victorian warehouses, with shops, museums, restaurants and cafe bars. Boat trips and guided walks in summer months.

Kingswood Abbey Gatehouse
Kingswood
t 0870 333 1181
w english-heritage.org.uk
open See website for details.
admission Free
This 16thC gatehouse, with carved mullioned window, is all that remains of the Cistercian abbey which prospered in the Middle Ages due to the wool trade.

Lodge Park & Sherborne Estate
Aldsworth GL54 3PP
t (01451) 844130 w nationaltrust.org.uk
open Grandstand/Deer Park: Mar-Oct, Mon, Fri, Sun
1100-1600. Estate: all year, daily.
admission £
Lodge Park is part of the Sherborne Estate, an ornate building dating from 1635, overlooking the deer course and surrounding countryside.

Odda's Chapel (English Heritage)
Deerhurst
t (01684) 295027 w english-heritage.org.uk
open Apr-Oct, daily 1000-1800. Nov-Mar, daily 1000-1600.
admission Free
Rare Saxon chapel dating back to 1056, attached to a half-timbered farmhouse. It lay undiscovered for many years and has been partly rebuilt and restored.

Old Baptist Chapel and Court
Church Street, Tewkesbury GL20 5RZ
t (01684) 295027 w tewkesbury.gov.uk
open All year, daily.
admission Free
Constructed in the 15th century as a three-bay house and later adapted as a chapel for worship. Modernised in 1720 and restored 1976-1979.

'Out of the Hat' – Tewkesbury Heritage & Visitor Centre
100 Church Street, Tewkesbury GL20 5AB
t (01684) 272096 w outofthehat.org.uk
open All year, daily.
admission £
A brand new unique attraction for Tewkesbury. Visitors can explore and contemplate 17thC life and learn about the town's fascinating history. Interactive exhibitions and hands-on experiences.

Parish Church of St Mary
Painswick GL6 6UT
t (01452) 814795 w beaconbenefice.co.uk
open Apr-Sep, daily 0930-1800. Oct-Mar, daily 0930-1600.
admission Free
Fourteenth-century church gradually extended in later centuries. The tower houses 14 bells, the earliest of which dates from 1731. There are 100 yew trees in the churchyard.

Pittville Pump Room
Pitville Park, Cheltenham GL52 3JE
t (01242) 523852
open All year, Mon, Wed-Sun 1000-1600.
admission Free
Pittville Pump Room is a beautiful, historic Grade I Listed property set in parkland at Pittville used for commercial and some cultural events.

St Mary The Virgin with St Mary Magdalene Church
Church Street, Tetbury GL8 8DN
t (01666) 502333
w tetburychurch.co.uk
open Daily 0900-1700.
admission Free
Built in 1781 in Georgian Gothic style. The spire is the fourth highest in England, measuring 186ft, and is part of the old medieval church. Recently restored.

St Mary's Church
Kempley
t (01531) 822468
w english-heritage.org.uk
open Apr-Oct, Mon-Sun 1000-1800.
admission Free
A delightful Norman church with superb wall paintings from the 12th-14th centuries which were only discovered beneath whitewash in 1871.

Sezincote House and Garden
Nr Moreton-in-Marsh GL56 9AW
t (01386) 700444
w sezincote.co.uk
open Garden: Jan-Nov, Thu-Fri, Bank Hols 1400-1800. House: May-Sep, Thu-Fri, Bank Hols 1430-1730.
admission ££
Sezincote is a unique Indian house, built in 1805. The garden, with its Hindu Temple, seven pools and Persian Paradise Garden, is one of the most remarkable examples of the Picturesque style in the UK.

Snowshill Manor (National Trust)
Snowshill WR12 7JU
t (01386) 852410
w nationaltrust.org.uk
open House: 19 Mar-2 Nov, Wed-Sun, Bank Hols 1200-1700. Gardens: all year, daily 1100-1730.
admission ££
A Cotswold manor packed to the rafters with a spectacular collection of craftmanship, set in an intimate Arts and Crafts garden run on organic principles.

'The Giant's Throne', Forest of Dean

For key to symbols see page 171.

Stanway Water Gardens
Stanway GL54 5PQ
t (01386) 584469
w stanwayfountain.co.uk
open House and Fountain: Jun-Aug, Tue, Thu
1400-1700.
admission ££

Golden-stoned Jacobean manorhouse with exquisite
gatehouse set amid 20 acres of landscaped grounds.
Important 14thC tythe barn. Tudor great hall with
shuffleboard.

Sudeley Castle, Gardens and Exhibition
Winchcombe GL54 5JD
t (01242) 602308
w sudeleycastle.co.uk
open 15 Mar-26 Oct, daily, Bank Hols 1030-1700.
admission ££

Nestled in the Cotswold hills, Sudeley Castle not only
celebrates its rich history but explores the new. Various
exhibitions and tours give an insight into Sudeley
throughout the ages.

Tewkesbury Abbey
Church Street, Tewkesbury GL20 5RZ
t (01684) 850959
w tewkesburyabbey.org.uk
open All year, daily 0800-1800.
admission Free

Superb Norman abbey with 14thC vaulting and
windows. Largest surviving Norman tower in the
country. Formerly a Benedictine monastery.
Services at 0800, 0915, 1100 and 1800 on
Sundays.

Westonbirt School, Gardens & House
Westonbirt School, Westonbirt GL8 8QG
t (01666) 881338
w westonbirt.gloucs.sch.uk
open Easter, Summer School Hols, Thu-Sun 1100-1630.
Oct School Hols, Daily 1100-1630.
admission £

Exquisite gardens surrounding the splendid country seat
of Robert Holford, the great Victorian collector of plants
who founded Westonbirt Arboretum.

Telstar Cruises
Riverside Walk, Tewkesbury GL20 5UR
t (01684) 294088
open Apr-Sep, daily 1100-1700.
admission £

Take a leisurely cruise along the beautiful River
Avon in peace and tranquillity to the village of
Twyning. Or hire a self-drive boat and enjoy the
river at your own pace.

Beatrix Potter Museum & Shop
The House of the Tailor of Gloucester plc,
9 College Court, Gloucester GL1 2NJ
t (01452) 422856
w tailor-of-gloucester.org.uk
open All year, daily 1000-1600.
admission Free

The location chosen by Beatrix Potter as the
home of The Tailor of Gloucester – a true
story. Shop and museum of Potter
memorabilia.

Burlington Contemporary Art
The Courtyard, Montpellier Street,
Cheltenham GL50 1SR
t (01242) 515165
w burlingtoncontemporaryart.com
open All year, Mon-Sat 1000-1730.
admission Free

Gallery selling paintings and original etchings, glass,
jewellery, sculpture and ceramics. Crafts Council
selected.

Cheltenham Art Gallery and Museum
Clarence Street, Cheltenham GL50 3JT
t (01242) 237431
w cheltenham.artgallery.museum
open All year, Mon-Sat 1000-1720.
admission Free

World-renowned Arts and Crafts Movement collection,
inspired by William Morris. Three-hundred years of
painting by Dutch and British artists. Special exhibitions
throughout the year.

Corinium Museum
Park Street, Cirencester GL7 2BX
t (01285) 655611
w cotswold.gov.uk/go/museum
open All year, Mon-Sat 1000-1700, Sun 1400-1700.
admission £

Award-winning museum, featuring one of the
finest collections of antiquities from Roman
Britain.

Cotswold Motoring Museum & Toy Collection
Bourton-on-the-Water GL54 2BY
t (01451) 821255
w cotswold-motor-museum.com
open Feb-Dec, daily 1000-1800.
admission £

A snapshot in time. Wonderful cars, motorbikes, toys
and pedal cars. A large collection of enamel signs and
fascinating motoring memorabilia. Home to Brum, the
children's TV character.

Edward Jenner Museum and Gardens
Church Lane, Berkeley GL13 9BN
t (01453) 810631 **w** jennermuseum.com
open Apr-Sep, Tue-Sat 1230-1730, Sun 1300-1730. Oct,
Sun 1300-1730. Bank Hols, 1230-1730.
admission £
Celebrating the life and work of Edward Jenner, the
discoverer of the vaccination against smallpox, housed
in Jenner's Queen Anne home.

Gloucester City Museum and Art Gallery
Brunswick Road, Gloucester GL1 1HP
t (01452) 396131
open All year, Tue-Sat 1000-1700.
admission Free
Housed in a fine Victorian building in the heart of the city,
among the spectacular collection are the archaeological
finds, fine and decorative arts, and natural history
specimens representing Gloucester's rich heritage.

Gloucester Folk Museum
99-103 Westgate Street, Gloucester GL1 2PG
t (01452) 396467 **w** livinggloucester.co.uk
open All year, Tue-Sat 1000-1700.
admission Free
A 15th-17thC timber-framed museum. Pin factory,
Victorian agricultural implements and Civil War armour.
Also includes wheelwright, carpenter and ironmonger.

Gloucester Ski & Snowboard Centre
Robinswood Hill, Gloucester GL4 6EA
t (01452) 874842 **w** gloucesterski.com
open See website for details.
admission ££
One of the UK's best and longest artificial ski slopes.

Holst Birthplace Museum
4 Clarence Road, Pittville, Cheltenham GL52 2AY
t (01242) 524846 **w** holstmuseum.org.uk
open Feb-Dec, Tue-Sat 1000-1600.
admission £
This Regency terraced house, where the composer of
'The Planets' was born, shows the upstairs/downstairs
way of life in Victorian times.

Keith Harding's World of Mechanical Music
The Oak House, High Street, Northleach GL54 3ET
t (01451) 860181 **w** mechanicalmusic.co.uk
open All year, daily 1000-1800.
admission ££
A 17thC wool merchant's house with antique musical
boxes, automata and mechanical musical instruments
presented as live entertainment.

Museum in the Park
Stroud District Museum Service,
Stratford Park, Stratford Road, Stroud GL5 4AF
t (01453) 763394 **w** stroud.gov.uk/museum
open Apr-Jul, Tue-Fri 1000-1700, Sat-Sun, Bank Hols
1100-1700. August, daily 1000-1700. Sep, Tue-Fri
1000-1700, Sat-Sun 1100-1700. Oct-Nov, Tue-Fri
1000-1600, Sat-Sun, Bank Hols 1100-1600. Jan-Mar,
Tue-Fri 1000-1600, Sat-Sun, Bank Hols 1100-1600.
admission Free
Family-friendly museum in historic parkland setting.
Colourful displays including dinosaur remains, a Roman
temple, the world's first lawnmower and much more.

National Waterways Museum
Llanthony Warehouse, Gloucester Docks,
Gloucester GL1 2EH
t (01452) 318200 **w** nwm.org.uk
open Apr-Oct, daily 1000-1700. Nov-Mar, daily
1100-1600.
admission ££
Three floors of a Victorian warehouse with interactive
displays and galleries, charting the story of Britain's
waterways. Historic craft, working forge, cafe and shop.

Nature in Art
Wallsworth Hall, Main A38, Twigworth GL2 9PA
t 0845 450 0233 **w** nature-in-art.org.uk
open All year, Tue-Sun, Bank Hols 1000-1700.
admission £
The world's first museum dedicated exclusively to fine,
decorative and applied art inspired by nature from any
period, any culture and in any media.

Broadway Tower, the Cotswolds

Admission is based on an adult price. Please check opening times and admission before travelling.

Soldiers of Gloucestershire Museum
Custom House, Gloucester Docks, Gloucester GL1 2HE
t (01452) 522682 **w** glosters.org.uk
open Apr-May, Tue-Sun 1000-1700. Jun-Sep, daily,
Bank Hols 1000-1700. Oct-Mar, Tue-Sun 1000-1700.
admission £

*Listed Victorian building in historic docks. The story of
the soldiers of Gloucestershire over the last 300 years,
highlighting their contribution to the nation's history.*

The Toy Museum
8 Park Street, Stow-on-the-Wold GL54 1AQ
t (01451) 830159 **w** thetoymuseum.co.uk
open All year, Wed-Sat 1000-1300, 1400-1630.
admission £

*The Sutton Collection of teddy bears, dolls and doll-
related items, many other Victorian and later toys,
games and books. Also on show are textiles, lace and
porcelain.*

Wellington Aviation Museum
Bourton/Broadway Road, Moreton-in-Marsh GL56 0BG
t (01608) 650323 **w** wellingtonaviation.org
open All year, Tue-Sun 1000-1230, 1400-1700.
admission £

*Aviation museum of Royal Air Force treasures, with
permanent exhibition of World War II memorabilia.*

Winchcombe Folk and Police Museum
Town Hall, High Street, Winchcombe GL54 5LJ
t (01242) 609151 **w** winchcombemuseum.org.uk
open Apr-Oct, Mon-Sat 1000-1630.
admission £

*The heritage and history of the ancient town of
Winchcombe and its people with the Police Collection of
British and International Uniforms and Equipment.*

Winchcombe Railway Museum and Garden
23 Gloucester Street, Winchcombe GL54 5LX
t (01242) 609305 **w** rag-mag.co.uk
open Please phone for details.
admission £

*A hands-on museum of railway life. Includes working
signals, signal box and booking office. Set in half an acre
of Victorian Cotswold gardens.*

FOOD AND DRINK

Three Choirs Vineyards
Baldwins Farm, Newent GL18 1LS
t (01531) 890223 **w** threechoirs.com
open All year, Tue-Sat 0900-2030, Sun-Mon 0900-1700.
admission ££

*Self-guided tours take visitors around the vineyards and
into the winery for a video, story of winemaking and
viewing gallery. Wine tasting. A la carte restaurant.
Audio trail. Vineyard walks.*

RELAXING AND PAMPERING

The New Brewery Arts
Brewery Court, Cirencester GL7 1JH
t (01285) 657181 **w** breweryarts.org.uk
open All year, Mon-Fri 1000-1700, Sat 0930-1730, Sun
1100-1600.
admission Free

*The New Brewery Arts comprises a gallery, craft shop,
cafe, 12 resident craft workshops, and education,
performance, sculpture and ceramics studios.*

Prinknash Abbey Visitors Centre
Cranham GL4 8EX
t (01452) 812066 **w** prinknashabbey.org.uk
open All year, daily 0900-1730.
admission Free

*Benedictine abbey set in the heart of the Cotswolds. Gift
shop, tearoom, bird and deer park, Roman mosaic
exhibition and children's play area.*

Devon

FAMILY FUN

Babbacombe Model Village
Hampton Avenue, Babbacombe TQ1 3LA
t (01803) 315315 **w** babbacombemodelvillage.co.uk
open See website for details.
admission ££

*A unique journey into a miniature world. Picturesque by
day, magical at night.*

Brannam Pottery
C H Brannam Limited, Roundswell Industrial Estate,
Barnstaple EX31 3NJ
t (01271) 343035
open All year, Mon-Sat 0900-1700.
admission Free

*Terracotta earthenware. Firing in kiln, hand-throwing
and decorating. Museum.*

Branscombe – The Old Bakey, Manor Mill & Forge
Branscombe EX12 3DB
t (01297) 680333
w nationaltrust.org.uk
open See website for details.
admission £
A stone-built and partially rendered building beneath thatch, which until 1987 was the last traditional working bakery in Devon.

Cascades Tropical Adventure Pool
Ruda Holiday Park, Croyde Bay EX33 1NY
t (01271) 890671
w parkdeanholidays.co.uk
open Mid Mar-mid Nov, daily from 1000.
admission £
Tropical adventure pool with giant 230ft flume and rapids ride. Safe pools and mini-waterfalls for younger children. Award-winning spectacular sandy beach.

Dartington Crystal Limited
Linden Close, Torrington EX38 7AN
t (01805) 626242
w dartington.co.uk
open Mon-Fri 0900-1700, Sat-Sun 1000-1600.
admission £
Watch skilled craftsmen creating the world-famous crystal. Enjoy the fascinating history of glass in the visitor centre, and browse the dazzling collection in the factory shops.

Devon Railway Centre
The Station, Bickleigh EX16 8RG
t (01884) 855671
w devonrailwaycentre.co.uk
open See website for details.
admission ££
Set in the Exe Valley, this railway attraction includes a preserved GWR station, a passenger-carrying 2ft gauge railway, model railways and a museum.

Devon's Crealy Great Adventure Park
Sidmouth Road, Clyst St Mary, Exeter EX5 1DR
t (01395) 233200
w crealy.co.uk
open Apr-Oct, daily 1000-1700 (Summer Hols, daily 1000-1800). Nov-Mar, Thu-Sun 1000-1700.
admission £££
An unforgettable day with magic, fun and adventure for all the family. Exciting rides, all-weather attractions and the friendliest animals! The South West's favourite family adventure.

Devonshire's Country Living Centre
Bickleigh Mill, Bickleigh EX16 8RG
t (01884) 855419
w bickleighmill.co.uk
open See website for details.
admission Free
Watermill, fishing centre and gift shop with restaurant, specialising in quality, locally produced crafts and foods.

Diggerland
Verbeer Manor, Cullompton EX15 2PE
t 0870 034 4437 **w** diggerland.com
open Feb-Nov, Sat-Sun, School Hols 1000-1700.
admission £££
An adventure park based on JCBs, where children of all ages can ride and drive diggers and small dumpers. A huge variety of equipment is available for a day of family fun.

The Gnome Reserve and Wild Flower Garden
West Putford EX22 7XE
t (01409) 241435 **w** gnomereserve.co.uk
open Mar-Oct, daily 1000-1800.
admission £
Over 1,000 gnomes and pixies in woodland garden with stream. Wild-flower garden with 250 species. Studio making kiln-fired, hand-painted pottery pixies. Prints of landscape paintings inhabited by gnomes.

Hedgehog Hospital at Prickly Ball Farm
Prickly Ball Farm, Denbury Road, East Ogwell, Newton Abbot TQ12 6BZ
t (01626) 362319 **w** pricklyballfarm.co.uk
open Easter-Oct, daily 1000-1700.
admission ££
Visit the Hedgehog Hospital and meet hedgehogs from around the world, cuddle pets in Pets Corner, meet all our farm animals, groom ponies, walk goats, ride on our pony and cart.

House of Marbles and Teign Valley Glass
The Old Pottery, Pottery Road, Bovey Tracey TQ13 9DS
t (01626) 835358 **w** houseofmarbles.com
open All year, Mon-Sat 0930-1700, Sun 1100-1700.
admission Free
Former pottery where visitors may watch glass-blowing and learn of the history of the pottery, glass and the making of glass marbles, in the museums.

The Milky Way Adventure Park
Downland Farm, Clovelly EX39 5RY
t (01237) 431255 **w** themilkyway.co.uk
open Apr-Oct, daily 1030-1800. Nov-Mar, Sat-Sun, School Hols 1030-1800.
admission ££
All-weather family attraction featuring Cosmic Typhoon, Devon's tallest and fastest rollercoaster, Time Warp indoor adventure play area, pets' corner, toddlers' area and much, much more.

Norman Lockyer Observatory and James Lockyer Planetarium
Salcombe Hill Road, Sidmouth EX10 0NY
t (01395) 579941 **w** ex.ac.uk/nlo
open See website for details.
admission £
An opportunity to observe the planets, moon and sunspots through 10 Victorian telescopes, planetarium and much more. A must for those interested in astronomy, radio and weather.

For key to symbols see page 171.

Paignton and Dartmouth Steam Railway
Queen's Park Station, Torbay Road, Paignton TQ4 6AF
t (01803) 553760
w paignton-steamrailway.co.uk
open See website for details.
admission ££
Steam train trip from Paignton to Kingswear (for ferry to Dartmouth). Coastal and country scenery. Services combine with trips on the River Dart.

Paignton Pier
Paignton Sands, Paignton TQ4 6BW
t (01803) 522139
w paigntonpier.co.uk
open Summer: daily 1000-2200. Winter: daily 1000-1700.
admission Free
Amusements, children's rides and prize bingo. Trampolines, crazy golf.

Pennywell – Devon's Farm and Wildlife Centre
Buckfastleigh TQ11 0LT
t (01364) 642023
w pennywellfarm.co.uk
open Feb-Oct, daily 0900-1700.
admission ££
Hands-on activities, shows and displays. The biggest farm activity park in the South West. Fun for all the family!

Quaywest Waterpark
Quaywest, Goodrington Sands, Paignton TQ4 6LN
t (01803) 555550
w quaywest.co.uk
open May-Jun, Mon-Sun, Bank Hols 1100-1700. Jul-Aug, Mon-Sun, Bank Hols 1000-1800. Sep, Mon-Sun, Bank Hols 1100-1700.
admission ££
Enjoy the wettest and wildest fun at the English Riviera's outdoor water park. Choose from eight different flumes. Also go-karts, amusement rides, bumper boats and crazy golf.

The Riviera International Centre
Chestnut Avenue, Torquay TQ2 5LZ
t (01803) 299992
w rivieracentre.co.uk
open See website for details.
admission £
Waves leisure pool, flume and wave machine. Children's water spray area, health and fitness suite and restaurant.

Seaton Tramway
Harbour Road, Seaton EX12 2NQ
t (01297) 20375
w tram.co.uk
open See website for details.
admission ££
Journey through East Devon's beautiful Axe valley by open-top or enclosed tramcar. A great way to enjoy panoramic views of the estuary and wildlife.

South Devon Railway
The Station, Buckfastleigh TQ11 0DZ
t (01364) 642338
w southdevonrailway.org
open See website for details.
admission ££
A seven-mile Great Western Railway country branch line through the superb scenery of the River Dart. Picnic grounds at Buckfastleigh. Now accessible from Totnes over footbridge.

Tuckers Maltings
Teign Road, Newton Abbot TQ12 4AA
t (01626) 334734
w tuckersmaltings.com
open Apr-Oct, Mon-Sat 1000-1600.
admission ££
A guided tour of England's only working malthouse open to the public. Speciality bottled beer shop. View Teignworthy Brewery and sample 'real' ale.

Woodlands Leisure Park
Blackawton TQ9 7DQ
t (01803) 712598
w woodlandspark.com
open Mar-Nov, daily. See website for details.
admission ££
All-weather fun guaranteed. Unique combination of indoor and outdoor attractions, three water coasters, toboggan run, indoor venture centre with rides. Falconry and animals.

NATURE AND WILDLIFE

Becky Falls Woodland Park
Manaton TQ13 9UG
t (01647) 221259
w beckyfalls.com
open Mar-Oct, 1000-1700.
admission ££
Over 60 acres of natural oak woodland with a 70ft waterfall and river walks. Site of Special Scientific Interest. One of Devon's most beautiful places.

Beer Quarry Caves
Quarry Lane, Beer, Nr Seaton EX12 3AS
t (01297) 680282 & (01297) 625830
w beerquarrycaves.fsnet.co.uk
open Daily from Monday before Easter to 31 Oct. Other times by appointment.
admission ££
Guided tours of vast man-made Roman caverns give the visitor an amazing insight into the lives of those who quarried Beer stone for many historic buildings. Secret catholic chapel and hiding place for contraband.

Bicton Park Botanical Gardens
East Budleigh, Budleigh Salterton EX9 7BJ
t (01395) 568465 **w** bictongardens.co.uk
open Apr-Sep, daily 1000-1800. Oct-Mar daily
1000-1700.
admission ££
Grade I Listed historical gardens featuring palm house, Italian and American gardens, indoor and outdoor play areas, shell house, museum, glass houses, garden centre, train ride.

Buckfast Butterfly Farm and Dartmoor Otter Sanctuary
Buckfastleigh Steam and Leisure Park,
Buckfastleigh TQ11 0DZ
t (01364) 642916 **w** ottersandbutterflies.co.uk
open See website for details.
admission ££
Tropical landscaped garden with waterfalls and large undercover pond where exotic butterflies and moths from all over the world fly free. Also otters, birds, terrapins and fish.

Canonteign Falls
Canonteign, Christow EX6 7NT
t (01647) 252434 **w** canonteignfalls.com
open Mar-Oct, daily 1030-1730. Nov-Dec, Sat-Sun
1030-1700.
admission £
Highest waterfall in England, situated in private parkland and ancient woodland in the Teign Valley. Lakes, grounds, natural gardens and lots of wildlife. Cafe and shop.

Cockington Country Park
Cockington Court, Cockington TQ2 6XA
t (01803) 606035 **w** countryside-trust.org.uk
open Daily, dawn-dusk.
admission Free
A country park of 450 acres with a Craft Centre at its heart, featuring demonstrations of a wide range of craft skills.

Combe Martin Wildlife and Dinosaur Park
Combe Martin EX34 0NG
t (01271) 882486 **w** dinosaur-park.com
open Mar-Oct, Mon-Sun 1000-1500.
admission £££
The land that time forgot. A subtropical paradise with hundreds of birds and animals, and animatronic dinosaurs, so real they're alive!

Dartington Hall Gardens
Dartington, Totnes TQ9 6EL
t (01803) 862367 **w** dartington.org
open See website for details.
admission £
Medieval courtyard and Great Hall, landscaped gardens. The hall and gardens are part of a working environment and visitors are asked to respect the residents' privacy.

Docton Mill and Gardens
Docton Mill, Spekes Valley, Hartland EX39 6EA
t (01237) 441369 **w** doctonmill.co.uk
open Mar-Oct, daily 1000-1800.
admission £
Working watermill of Saxon origin. Eight acres of woodland, lawns and streams. Coastal waterfalls and beach within one mile of gardens.

The Donkey Sanctuary

Slade House Farm, Sidmouth EX10 0NU
t (01395) 578222 **w** thedonkeysanctuary.org.uk
open Daily 0900 to dusk.
admission Free
The Donkey Sanctuary is open 365 days a year from 0900 until dusk. Admission and parking are free. Visitors return time and again to meander among the donkeys and absorb the serene and relaxed surroundings.

Escot Fantasy Gardens, Maze and Woodland
Escot Park, Ottery St Mary EX11 1LU
t (01404) 822188 **w** escot-devon.co.uk
open All year, Mon-Sun 1000-1700.
admission ££
Enjoy the natural historical gardens and fantasy woodland which surround the ancestral home of the Kennaway family. Here, in 220 acres of parkland, you'll find an arkful of animals with paths, trails and vistas.

Exmoor Zoological Park
South Stowford, Bratton Fleming EX31 4SG
t (01598) 763352 **w** exmoorzoo.co.uk
open See website for details.
admission ££
A unique zoo in natural surroundings! Ideal for all generations. Relax or be entertained with activities every half hour. A family-run, family attraction supporting worldwide conservation on Exmoor.

The Garden House
Buckland Monachorum PL20 7LQ
t (01822) 854769 **w** thegardenhouse.org.uk
open Mar-Oct, daily 1030-1700.
admission £
Stunning, innovative planting centred on a lovely walled garden surrounding the romantic ruins of a medieval vicarage. Various themed gardens and glorious year-round colour. Plants for sale.

Grand Western Canal Country Park
The Moorings, Canal Hill, Tiverton EX16 4HX
t (01884) 254072
w devon.gov.uk/grand_western_canal
open All year, daily.
admission Free
Opened in 1814, this peaceful, 11 mile canal is great for walking, boating, angling, cycling, picnics and nature watching.

Greenway
Greenway Road, Galmpton TQ5 0ES
t (01803) 842382 **w** nationaltrust.org.uk
open Mar-Oct, Wed-Sun 1030-1700.
admission ££

A glorious woodland garden in a tranquil setting on the banks of the River Dart. Renowned for rare half-hardy plants underplanted with native wild flowers.

High Moorland Visitor Centre
Tavistock Road, Princetown PL20 6QF
t (01822) 890414 **w** dartmoor-npa.gov.uk
open Daily 1000-1600.
admission Free

Dartmoor's major visitor and interpretation centre in the heart of the moor. Exciting displays for all the family about Dartmoor's natural and cultural heritage.

Ilfracombe Aquarium
The Old Lifeboat House, The Pier,
Ilfracombe EX34 9EQ
t (01271) 864533
open Feb-Mar, daily 1000-1500. Apr-Jun, daily
1000-1630. Jul-Aug, daily 1000-1730. Sep-Oct, daily
1000-1630.
admission £

Award-winning, all-weather family attraction providing a fascinating journey of discovery into the aquatic life of North Devon.

Jungleland
St John's Garden Centre, St John's Lane,
Barnstaple EX32 9DD
t (01271) 343884 **w** stjohnsgardencentre.co.uk
open All year, Mon-Sat 0900-1800, Sun 1030-1630.
admission Free

Chipmunks, terrapins, birds and fish in an exotic setting of giant cacti, tropical jungle plants and waterfalls. All under cover.

Kents Cavern Prehistoric Caves
Ilsham Road, Wellswood, Torquay TQ1 2JF
t (01803) 215136 **w** kents-cavern.co.uk
open Mar-Jun, daily 1000-1600, Jul-Aug, daily
1000-1630, Sep-Oct daily 1000-1600, Nov-Feb
1000-1530.
admission ££

The most important Stone Age cave in Britain reveals more about Palaeolithic Britain than anywhere else.

Lee Ford Gardens
Lee Ford, Budleigh Salterton EX9 7AJ
t (01395) 445894 **w** leeford.co.uk
open All year, Mon-Thu 1000-1600 by prior
appointment only.
admission £

Forty acres of parkland, formal and woodland gardens with extensive display of spring bulbs, camellias, rhododendrons, azaleas and magnolias. Adam pavilion.

Living Coasts
Torquay Harbourside, Beacon Quay,
Torquay TQ1 2BG
t (01803) 202470
w livingcoasts.org.uk
open Daily 1000-dusk.
admission ££

Living Coasts features a range of fascinating coastal creatures from loud and loveable penguins to playful fur seals, colourful puffins to waders and sea ducks.

Lydford Gorge
The Stables, Lydford EX20 4BH
t (01822) 820320
w nationaltrust.org.uk
open Mar-Sep, daily 1000-1700. Oct, daily 1000-1600.
Nov-Dec, Sat-Sun 1100-1530.
admission ££

On the western edge of Dartmoor, a beautiful woodland walk along the top of the gorge leads down to the spectacular 90ft White Lady waterfall.

Marwood Hill Gardens
Marwood Hill, Marwood EX31 4EB
t (01271) 342528
w marwoodhillgarden.co.uk
open Daily 0930-1730.
admission ££

An 18-acre garden with three small lakes, unusual trees and shrubs, bog garden, national collection of astilbes, iris ensata and tulbaghias.

The Miniature Pony Centre
Wormhill Farm, North Bovey TQ13 8RG
t (01647) 432400
w miniatureponycentre.com
open See website for details.
admission ££

Miniature ponies, donkeys and many other animals. Indoor and outdoor play area for the children. A wealth of wildlife in and around the ponds and Willow Garden.

The Mythic Garden Sculpture Exhibition
Stone Lane Gardens, Stone Farm, Chagford TQ13 8JU
t (01647) 231311
w mythicgarden.com
open Daily 1400-1800.
admission £

Unusual and attractive five-acre landscaped arboretum and water garden with national collections of wild-origin birch and alder. Imaginative summer sculpture exhibition. Specialist tree nursery.

National Marine Aquarium
Rope Walk, Coxside, Plymouth PL4 0LF
t (01752) 600301
w national-aquarium.co.uk
open Jan-Mar, daily 1000-1700, Apr-Oct, daily
1000-1800, Nov-Dec, daily 1000-1700.
admission ££

Britain's biggest aquarium has just got even bigger thanks to their brand new three-floor, multi-million-pound interactive centre at the National Marine Aquarium, Plymouth.

Northam Burrows Country Park
Northam EX39 1LY
t (01237) 479708 w torridge.gov.uk
open Daily.
admission Free
Coastal country park with visitor centre, beach access and golf course. Walks and activities programme available from ranger staff in the summer.

Orchid Paradise
Forches Cross, Newton Abbot TQ12 6PZ
t (01626) 352233 w orchids.uk.com
open Daily 1000-1600.
admission £
Wander amongst the beautiful, exotic orchid blooms around our rainforest pool. Cool in summer and warm in winter. All under cover and open all year. Plant and sundries for sale.

Paignton Zoo Environmental Park
Totnes Road, Paignton TQ4 7EU
t (01803) 697500 w paigntonzoo.org.uk
open Daily 1000-dusk.
admission £££
One of England's largest zoos with over 1,200 animals in the beautiful setting of 75 acres of botanical gardens. One of Devon's most popular family days out.

Pecorama Pleasure Gardens and Exhibition
Underleys, Beer EX12 3NA
t (01297) 21542 w peco-uk.com
open Apr-May, Mon-Fri 1000-1730, Sat 1000-1300.
Jun-Sep, Sun-Fri 1000-1730, Sat 1000-1300. Sep-Oct,
Mon-Fri 1000-1730, Sat 1000-1300.
admission ££
Spectacular Millennium Celebration Gardens, passenger-carrying miniature railway with steam and diesel locomotives, Peco Model Railway exhibition, shop and play areas.

RHS Garden Rosemoor
Great Torrington EX38 8PH
t (01805) 624067
w rhs.org.uk/rosemoor
open Apr-Sep, daily 1000-1800, Oct-Mar, daily
1000-1700.
admission ££
Rosemoor, an enchanting 65-acre garden, offers year-round interest. Visit us for inspiration, tranquillity or simply a marvellous day out.

River Dart Adventures
Holne Park, Ashburton TQ13 7NP
t (01364) 652511
w riverdart.co.uk
open See website for details.
admission ££
A 90-acre Victorian country estate offering parkland, picnic meadow, nature/tree trails and woodland adventure playgrounds.

Roadford Lake
Broadwoodwidger, Lifton PL16 0JL
t (01566) 784859
w swlakestrust.org.uk
open All year, daily.
admission Free
Located on the edge of Dartmoor between Okehampton and Launceston, Roadford is the largest inland water in the South West. A visit won't leave you short of something to do.

Totnes Rare Breeds Farm
Totnes TQ9 5JR
t (01803) 840387
w totnesrarebreeds.co.uk
open Mar-Oct, daily 0930-1700.
admission Free
An ideal place for all the family to visit. Good food, beautiful views, lovely animals and spectacular owls.

Torquay Harbour

For key to symbols see page 171.

HISTORIC ENGLAND

Arlington Court
Arlington EX31 4LP
t (01271) 850296
w nationaltrust.org.uk
open Mar-Oct, Mon-Fri, Sun 1030-1700.
admission ££
Historic house with interesting collection. Gardens with rhododendrons, azaleas and hydrangeas. Carriage collection and rides. Extensive estate walks.

Berry Pomeroy Castle
Berry Pomeroy TQ9 6LJ
t (01803) 866618
w english-heritage.org.uk/berrypomeroy
open Apr-Jun, daily 1000-1700. Jul-Aug, daily 1000-1800. Sep, daily 1000-1700. Oct, daily 1000-1600.
admission £
A romantic ruined castle set in a picturesque Devon valley. The gatehouse dates from the late 15thC with Elizabethan remains behind, steeped in folklore.

Buckfast Abbey
Buckfastleigh TQ11 0EE
t (01364) 645500
w buckfast.org.uk
open All year, Mon-Thur 0900-1700, Fri 1000-1700, Sun 1200-1700.
admission Free
Large Benedictine monastery rebuilt on medieval foundations. Many art treasures in the Abbey church. Also unusual shops, exhibition and excellent restaurant.

Buckland Abbey
Yelverton PL20 6EY
t (01822) 853607
w nationaltrust.org.uk
open See website for details.
admission ££
Originally a Cistercian monastery, then home of Sir Francis Drake. Ancient buildings, exhibitions, herb garden, craft workshops and estate walks. Elizabethan garden.

Bygones
Fore Street, St Marychurch, Torquay TQ1 4PR
t (01803) 326108
w bygones.co.uk
open See website for details.
admission ££
Life-size Victorian street and period rooms. Large, scenic model railway and a 28 ton steam engine. 1940s/50s shopping arcade, medals and militaria. Walk through a WW1 trench. Interactive illuminated Fantasy Land and much more.

Cadhay
Ottery St Mary EX11 1QT
t (01404) 813511 **w** cadhay.org.uk
open May-Sep, Fri 1400-1730.
admission ££
Historic Elizabethan manorhouse built c1550 around a courtyard. Fine timber roof of Great Hall and Elizabethan Long Gallery. Magnificent gardens.

Castle Drogo
Drewsteignton EX6 6PB
t (01647) 433306 **w** nationaltrust.org.uk
open Mar-Oct, Wed-Sun 1100-1700. Dec, Sat-Sun 1200-1600.
admission ££
Granite castle, built between 1910 and 1930 by Sir Edwin Lutyens, standing at over 900ft overlooking the wooded gorge of the River Teign. Views of Dartmoor.

Clovelly
The Estate Office, Clovelly, Nr Bideford EX39 5SY
t (01237) 431781 **w** clovelly.co.uk
open Summer: 0930-1730. Winter: 1000-1600.
admission £
Picturesque fishing village with cobbled streets leading to a 14thC harbour. Audio-visual show in the visitor centre, the Kingsley Museum and the 1930s Fisherman's Cottage are all included in the admission price.

The Collegiate Church of the Holy Cross
Church Street, Crediton EX17 2AH
t (01363) 773226 **w** creditonparishchurch.org.uk
open All year, 0800-dusk.
admission Free
On the site of this magnificent 15thC collegiate church, Devon's first cathedral stood for 200 years. Here Boniface, patron saint of Germany and the Netherlands, was born in AD680.

Crownhill Fort
Crownhill Fort Road, Plymouth PL6 5BX
t (01752) 793754 **w** crownhillfort.co.uk
open See website for details.
admission Free
Tunnels of fun for everyone! Underground tunnels to explore. Step back to 1890 to experience history and adventure. Daily gun firings at 1330.

Dartmouth Castle
Castle Road, Dartmouth TQ6 0JN
t (01803) 833588
w english-heritage.org.uk/dartmouth
open Apr-Jun, Sep, daily 1000-1700, Jul-Aug, daily 1000-1800, Oct daily 1000-1600. Nov-Mar, Sat-Sun 1000-1600.
admission £
This brilliantly positioned defensive castle juts out into the narrow entrance to the Dart Estuary. One of the first castles constructed with artillery in mind.

Exeter Cathedral – Church of Saint Peter
The Cloisters, Exeter EX1 1HS
t (01392) 255573
w exeter-cathedral.org.uk
open Daily 0930-1700.
admission £
Medieval cathedral. Fine example of Gothic Decorated style. Longest unbroken stretch of Gothic vaulting in the world.

Exeter Quay House Visitor Centre
46 The Quay, Exeter EX2 4AN
t (01392) 271611
w exeter.gov.uk/visiting
open Apr-Oct 1000-1700. Nov-Mar, Sat-Sun 1100-1600.
admission Free
The history of Exeter's Quayside is brought to life with displays, illustrations and artefacts. An exciting audio-visual presentation depicts 2,000 years from Roman times to the present day.

Exeter's Underground Passages
2 Paris Street, Exeter EX1 1GA
t (01392) 665887
w exeter.gov.uk/passages
open Please phone for details.
admission £
Visit the new heritage centre with interactive exhibits, exciting interpretation and a full-size passage replica. Then take a guided tour through vaulted medieval passages under the streets of Exeter.

Hartland Abbey and Gardens
Hartland EX39 6DT
t (01237) 441234
w hartlandabbey.com
open Good Friday-23 May, Wed-Thu, Sun, Bank Hols 1200-1700. 26 May-5 Oct, Mon-Thu, Sun 1200-1700.
admission ££
Family home since the dissolution in 1539. Woodland gardens leading to bog garden and 18thC walled gardens. Beautiful walk to beach. Location for filming of BBCs 'Sense and Sensibility' 2007.

Hemyock Castle
Hemyock EX15 3RJ
t (01823) 680745
w hemyockcastle.co.uk
open Mar-Sep, Bank Hols 1400-1700.
admission Free
Medieval moated castle and gatehouse remains. Interpretation centre illustrating the history of the site. Life-size historical tableaux including extended Civil War display.

Killerton House and Garden
Broadclyst, Exeter EX5 3LE
t (01392) 881345
w nationaltrust.org.uk
open See website for details.
admission ££
An 18thC house built for the Acland family. Hillside garden of 18 acres with rare trees and shrubs.

Knightshayes Court
Bolham, Tiverton EX16 7RQ
t (01884) 254665
w nationaltrust.org.uk
open House: Mar-Nov, Mon-Thu, Sat-Sun 1100-1700. Shop, garden, restaurant: all year, daily 1100-1700.
admission ££
House built c1870 by William Burges. Celebrated garden features a water lily pool, topiary, fine specimen trees, formal terraces, spring bulbs and rare shrubs.

Loughwood Meeting House
Dalwood EX13 7DU
t (01392) 881691
w nationaltrust.org.uk
open Daily 1000-1700.
admission Free
Built c1653 by the Baptist congregation of Kilmington. The interior, fitted in the early 18th century, remains unaltered.

Okehampton Castle
Castle Lodge, Okehampton EX20 1JB
t (01837) 52844
w english-heritage.org.uk/okehampton
open Apr-Jun, daily 1000-1700, Jul-Aug, daily 1000-1800, Sep, daily 1000-1700.
admission £
The ruins of the largest castle in Devon, including the jagged remains of the keep. Picnic area and enchanted woodland walks.

Parracombe, St Petrock
Parracombe EX31 4RA
t (020) 7213 0660
w visitchurches.org.uk
open See website for details.
admission Free
The modest medieval exterior of St Petrock's conceals a remarkable Georgian interior almost unchanged in 200 years, with wonderful 18thC fittings.

Powderham Castle
Kenton EX6 8JQ
t (01626) 890243
w powderham.co.uk
open Apr-Oct, daily 1000-1730.
admission ££
Built c1390 and restored in the 18thC. Georgian interiors, china, furnishings and paintings. Family home of the Courtenays for over 600 years. Fine views across deer park and River Exe.

The Royal Citadel
The Hoe, Plymouth PL1 2PD
t (01752) 266030
w english-heritage.org.uk/visits
open May-Sep, Tue, Thu 1430 by guided tour only.
admission £
A dramatic 17thC fortress built to defend the coastline from the Dutch. It is still in use today.

St Lawrence Chapel (Old Grammar School)
St Lawrence Lane, Ashburton TQ13 7DD
t (01364) 653414
w stlawrencechapel.ik.com
open May-Sep, Tue, Thu-Sat 1400-1630.
admission Free
A former chantry chapel and a grammar school, the chapel has long been the traditional meeting place of the Ancient Courts Leet and Baron.

St Mary's Church
The College, Ottery St Mary EX11 1DQ
t (01404) 812062
w otterystmary.org.uk
open See website for details.
admission Free
Dating from the 13thC, the church was enlarged and modelled on Exeter Cathedral c1342. Given five star rating in 'England's Thousand Best Churches.'

St Mary's Church
High Street, Totnes TQ9 5NN
t (01803) 866045
w stmarystotnes.org.uk
open See website for details.
admission Free
This 15thC church contains many items of architectural interest including a 15thC stone screen, pulpit and font, 19thC Kempe window and Willis organ.

Saltram
Plympton PL7 1UH
t (01752) 333500
w nationaltrust.org.uk
open See website for details.
admission ££
George II mansion with magnificent interiors designed by Robert Adam. Fine period furniture, china and paintings. Garden with orangery. Art gallery and play area.

Tapeley Park
Instow EX39 4NT
t (01271) 342558
w tapeleypark.com
open Mar-Oct 1000-1700.
admission £
Devon home of the Christie family of Glyndebourne, overlooking the estuary to the sea. Beautiful Italian garden with many rare plants and woodland walk.

Tiverton Castle
Park Hill, Tiverton EX16 6RP
t (01884) 253200
w tivertoncastle.com
open Apr-Oct, Thu, Sun, Bank Hols 1430-1730.
admission £
All ages of architecture from medieval to modern. Important Civil War armoury – try some on. Beautiful gardens with romantic ruins.

Torbryan Holy Trinity
Torbryan TQ12 5UR
t (020) 7213 0660
w visitchurches.org.uk
open Daily 1000-1600.
admission Free
Church of considerable size and grandeur, with dramatic octagonal stair turret on the fine perpendicular tower. Also features a magnificent rood screen with delicate woodcarving spanning the full width of the interior.

Torrington 1646
Castle Hill, South Street, Great Torrington EX38 8AA
t (01805) 626146
w torrington-1646.co.uk
open Mar-Sep, Mon-Sat 1030-1700, Oct-Feb, Mon-Fri 1100-1630.
admission ££
At Torrington 1646 meet colourful 17thC characters and learn what it was like to live, work and play during the Civil War.

Totnes Castle
Castle Street, Totnes TQ9 5NU
t (01803) 864406
w english-heritage.org.uk/totnes
open Apr-Jun, daily 1000-1700. Jul-Aug, daily 1000-1800. Sep, daily 1000-1700. Oct, daily 1000-1600.
admission £
One of the best-preserved Norman shell keeps, this motte and bailey castle offers splendid views over the River Dart.

Ugbrooke House and Park
Chudleigh TQ13 0AD
t (01626) 852179
w ugbrooke.co.uk
open 13 Jul-11 Sep, Tue, Wed, Thur, Sun, Aug Bank Hol 1300-1730.
admission ££
Robert Adam-designed house and chapel, Capability Brown-designed park and grounds. Fine furniture, paintings, needlework, costume and uniforms.

OUTDOOR ACTIVITIES

Dart Pleasure Craft Limited (River Link Operators)
5 Lower Street, Dartmouth TQ6 9AJ
t (01803) 834488
w riverlink.co.uk
open See website for details.
admission ££
Operating between Dartmouth and Totnes, dependent on tide. Circular trips in Dartmouth for one hour. Large boats with covered accommodation and commentary given.

Sound Cruising Ltd
Hexton Quay, Hooe, Plymouth PL9 9RE
t (01752) 408590 w soundcruising.com
open Please phone for details.
admission £

Daily cruises around the naval harbour, also regular cruises to Calstock on the River Tamar and sea trips to the River Yealm, east of Plymouth. Ferries from Saltash to Plymouth.

Stuart Line Cruises
Exmouth Marina, Exmouth Docks, Exmouth EX8 1DU
t (01395) 222144 w stuartlinecruises.co.uk
open See website for details.
admission £

Sailing from Exmouth, enjoy relaxing River Exe cruises and trips along the Devon coastline. Sailing throughout the year.

Tiverton Canal Company
The Wharf, Canal Hill, Tiverton EX16 4HX
t (01884) 253345 w tivertoncanal.co.uk
open Apr-Oct, see website for details.
admission ££

Indulge your senses and relax on this rare horse-drawn barge, now one of only five in Britain today. Daytime and evening trips.

ENTERTAINMENT AND CULTURE

Allhallows Museum
High Street, Honiton EX14 1PG
t (01404) 44966 w honitonmuseum.co.uk
open See website for details.
admission £

Comprehensive display of lace and lace-making demonstrations June-August. Local historical documents and artefacts.

Barometer World
Quicksilver Barn, Merton EX20 3DS
t (01805) 603443 w barometerworld.co.uk
open All year, Tue-Fri, 1st and 3rd Sat of each month 0900-1700.
admission £

New exhibition housing an incredible variety of weather predictors from the normal to the very bizarre.

Cobbaton Combat Collection
Chittlehampton EX37 9RZ
t (01769) 540740 w cobbatoncombat.co.uk
open Apr-Jun and Sep-Oct, Mon-Fri, Sun 1000-1700. Jul-Aug, daily 1000-1700. Winter: by appointment only.
admission ££

Private collection of World War II British, Canadian and Warsaw Pact tanks, trucks, armoured cars and allied equipment. Items from the Home Front.

Coldharbour Mill Museum
Coldharbour Mill, Uffculme, Cullompton EX15 3EE
t (01884) 840960 w coldharbourmill.org.uk
open Daily 1100-1600.
admission £

Museum of the Devon textiles industry in an 18thC woollen mill. Working demonstrations of traditional textile machinery. Waterwheel and steam engines. Riverside walks. Factory tours at Steam Ups – see website.

The Devon Guild of Craftsmen
Riverside Mill, Bovey Tracey TQ13 9AF
t (01626) 832223 w crafts.org.uk
open Daily 1000-1730.
admission Free

The largest contemporary craft centre in the South West. A Grade II Listed building with shop, exhibition gallery and cafe. Recent £1 million refurbishment.

Dingles Fairground Heritage Centre
Milford, Lifton PL16 0AT
t (01566) 783425 w fairground-heritage.org.uk
open Apr-Oct, Mon, Thu-Sun 1030-1700.
admission ££

Indoor live steam and working displays for all the family. The National Fairground Collection. Shop and cafeteria in a rural setting.

Dunkeswell Memorial Museum
Flightway Business Park, Sea Bees Place, Unit C4, Dunkeswell EX1 4PG
t (01404) 891943
w dunkeswellmemorialmuseum.org.uk
open Mar-Sep, Mon, Wed-Sun 1000-1800. Oct-Feb, Sat-Sun 1000-1700.
admission £

Original artefacts and photographic archives of the history of the World War II United States Navy airbase at Dunkeswell.

Exeter Red Coat Guided Tours
Tourist Information Centre, Civic Centre, Dix's Field, Exeter EX1 1RQ
t (01392) 265203 w exeter.gov.uk/visiting
open Daily (excl 25-26 Dec).
admission Free

Free guided 90 minute walking tours of historic Exeter. Explore a catacomb by torchlight, visit a house that moved and learn why Exeter is reputed to be one of England's most haunted cities!

Finch Foundry
Sticklepath EX20 2NW
t (01837) 840046 w nationaltrust.org.uk
open Mar-Oct, Mon, Wed-Sun 1100-1700.
admission £

A 19thC water-powered forge with three working waterwheels, driving trip hammers, grindstone and other machinery producing agricultural and mining hand tools.

For key to symbols see page 171.

Marine House at Beer

Fore Street, Beer EX12 3EF
t (01297) 625257
w marinehouseatbeer.co.uk
open Apr-Oct, daily 1000-1730. Nov-Mar, daily
1000-1700, Marine House closed Mon, Steam Gallery
closed Tue.
admission Free
*Two galleries in the historic fishing village of Beer. A
constantly changing range of paintings, sculpture,
ceramics, glassware and jewellery.*

Monks Withecombe Gallery

Monks Withecombe, Chagford TQ13 8JY
t (01647) 432854
w strategic-art.com
open All year, Tue-Sun 1100-1800.
admission Free
*The Monks Withecombe Gallery exhibits the work of
outstanding contemporary artists in the beautiful
surroundings of the Dartmoor National Park.*

Morwellham Quay The Morwellham & Tamar Valley Trust

Morwellham Quay, Tavistock PL19 8JL
t (01822) 832766
w morwellham-quay.co.uk
open Jan-Mar, daily 1000-1630. Mar-Oct, daily
1000-1730. Nov-Dec, daily 1000-1630.
admission ££
*An award-winning, evocative museum and visitor centre
based around the historic port and mine workings on the
River Tamar.*

Museum of Barnstaple and North Devon

The Square, Barnstaple EX32 8LN
t (01271) 346747
w devonmuseums.net/barnstaple
open All year, Mon-Sat 0930-1700.
admission Free
*Major regional museum displaying and interpreting the
natural and human history of North Devon. Housed in a
fine Victorian brick building.*

North Devon Maritime Museum

Odun House, Odun Road, Appledore EX39 1PT
t (01237) 422064
w devon.gov.uk
open Apr, daily 1400-1730. May-Sep Mon-Fri
1100-1300, daily 1400-1730. Oct, daily 1400-1730.
admission Free
*All aspects of North Devon's maritime history illustrated
by models, photographs, paintings and film show.
Interpretation centre for the area and museum.*

Plymouth Pavilions

Millbay Road, Plymouth PL1 3LF
t 0845 146 1460
w plymouthpavilions.com
open See website for details.
admission £
*A fun pool and ice rink complement this leading rock,
pop and entertainment venue.*

Plymouth Ski Centre – John Nike Leisuresport Complex

Alpine Park, Marsh Mills, Plymouth PL6 8LQ
t (01752) 600220
w jnll.co.uk
open See website for details.
admission ££££
*Largest ski slope in the South West. Main slope 150m
long and 20m wide and two nursery slopes. Largest
toboggan run of its type in the South West.*

Spacex Gallery

45 Preston Street, Exeter EX1 1DF
t (01392) 431786
w spacex.co.uk
open All year, Tue-Sat 1000-1700.
admission Free
*Public contemporary art gallery presenting the latest
developments in visual art. Engage with art, artists and
ideas through the acclaimed programme of exhibitions
and events.*

Teignmouth and Shaldon Museum

29 French Street, Teignmouth TQ14 8ST
t (01626) 777041
w teignmuseum.org.uk
open May-Oct, Mon-Sat 1000-1630.
admission £
*Exhibits include 16thC and c1877 cannons, artefacts
from the Armada wreck, c1920s pier machines and local-
history exhibits.*

Tiverton Museum of Mid Devon Life

Beck's Square, Tiverton EX16 6PJ
t (01884) 256295
w tivertonmuseum.org.uk
open Feb-Dec, Mon-Fri 1030-1630, Sat 1000-1300.
admission £
*Comprehensive regional museum. Railway gallery
contains a Great Western Railway locomotive. Heathcoat
lace machine gallery. Collection of agricultural and
domestic implements.*

Totnes Elizabethan House Museum

70 Fore Street, Totnes TQ9 5RU
t (01803) 863821
w devonmuseums.net/totnes
open Mon-Fri 1030-1700.
admission £
*A 16thC Tudor merchant's house. Period furniture,
costumes, dolls' houses, toys and archaeology. Victorian
grocer's shop. Charles Babbage (father of the computer)
room.*

Watermouth Castle

Ilfracombe EX34 9SL
t (01271) 863879
w watermouthcastle.com
open Apr-Oct, see website for details.
admission £££
*Castle with Victorian museum, model railway and
dungeons. Underground water fountain show. Gardens
with children's animations, mini golf, tube slide, river
ride, spinning cooking pots and much more.*

Yelverton Paperweight Centre
Leg O'Mutton, Yelverton PL20 6AD
t (01822) 854250
w paperweightcentre.co.uk
open Apr-Oct, daily 1030-1700.
admission Free   ♿

Exhibition of the Broughton Collection of hundreds of antique and modern glass paperweights, plus a large selection of gifts and collectable paperweights, including limited edition pieces from leading glass studios.

FOOD AND DRINK

Countryman Cider
Felldownhead, Milton Abbot PL19 0QR
t (01822) 870226
w crying-fox.com
open All year, Mon-Sat 0900-1830.
admission Free

Stable buildings dating from the 15thC, converted for cider pressing and the manufacture of traditional, still farm cider. Demonstration orchard. Tastings, off-licence shop with gifts including pottery.

Plymouth Gin Distillery
Black Friars Distillery, 60 Southside Street, Barbican PL1 2LQ
t (01752) 665292
w plymouthgin.com
open Daily 0900-1730.
admission Free   ♿

Tour the Black Friars Distillery, England's oldest working gin distillery, where Plymouth Gin has been distilled for over 200 years.

Sharpham Vineyard
Sharpham Estate, Ashprington TQ9 7UT
t (01803) 732203
w sharpham.com
open Mar-Jun, Mon-Sat 1000-1700, Jun-Aug, daily 1000-1700, Sep-Dec, Mon-Sat 1000-1700.
admission £   ♿

A beautifully situated working vineyard and winery on the edge of the River Dart, renowned for the quality of its wine. Self-guided vineyard trail.

RELAXING AND PAMPERING

Abbot Pottery
Hopkins Lane, Newton Abbot TQ12 2EL
t (01626) 334933
w abbotpottery.com
open See website for details.
admission Free   ♿

A working craft pottery producing traditional Devon slipware by throwing, turning, decorating and glazing.

Atlantic Village
Clovelly Road, Bideford EX39 3QU
t (01237) 473901
w atlanticvillage.co.uk
open All year, Mon-Wed, Fri-Sat 1000-1800, Thu 1000-2000, Sun 1030-1630.
admission Free   ♿

North Devon's largest discount shopping outlet with themed leisure attractions. A family day out.

Barbican Glassworks
The Old Fish Market, Barbican, Plymouth PL1 2LT
t (01752) 224777
w dartington.co.uk
open All year, Mon-Sat 0900-1800, Sun, Bank Hols 1100-1700.
admission Free   ♿

Large retail shop offering exquisite gifts from world-famous glass maker, Dartington Crystal.

Cardew Teapottery
Newton Road, Bovey Tracey TQ13 9DX
t (01626) 832172
w cardewdesign.com
open Daily 1000-1700.
admission Free   ♿

Tour of working pottery with painting area and pottery studio. Award-winning gifts at factory prices in our shops. Licensed restaurant with sundeck. Free large car park.

The Famous Lee Mill
Lee Mill, Plymouth Road, Ivybridge PL21 9EE
t (01752) 691100
open All year, Mon-Sat 0930-1700, Sun 1000-1600.
admission Free   ♿

Factory outlet offering a wide selection of branded goods at significantly reduced prices including fashion, golf, homeware, gifts and souvenirs.

Otterton Mill
Fore Street, Otterton EX9 7HG
t (01395) 568521
w ottertonmill.com
open Daily 1000-1700.
admission Free   ♿

Centuries-old working watermill, award-winning Devon food shop, artisan bakery, restaurant serving a superb menu of fresh local food, plus art gallery, three artists' studios and a live music venue.

Trago Mills
Shopping and Leisure Centre, Stover TQ12 6JD
t (01626) 821111
w trago.co.uk
open Mon-Sat 0900-1730, Sun 1000-1600.
admission Free   ♿

Large shopping complex with superb leisure attractions, including super karts, trawler boats, steam and model railways plus an interactive animal enclosure.

Dorset

FAMILY FUN

Adventure Wonderland
Merritown Lane, Hurn BH23 6BA
t (01202) 483444
w adventurewonderland.co.uk
open 15 Mar-7 Sep, 25 Oct-2 Nov, daily 1000-1800.
8 Sep-19 Oct, Sat-Sun 1000-1800. Wild Thing: all year,
daily 1000-1830.
admission ££
Exciting Adventure Wonderland with rides and attractions galore including Wild Thing indoor play centre, scary ghostly galleon plus lots more besides.

The Bournemouth Eye
The Lower Gardens, Bournemouth BH1 2AQ
t (01202) 317697
w bournemouthballoon.com
open Apr-Sep, see website for details.
admission ££
Tethered balloon flight to 500ft, giving spectacular views of the coastline, town and countryside for over 20 miles.

Corfe Castle Model Village and Gardens
The Square, Corfe Castle BH20 5EZ
t (01929) 481234
w corfecastlemodelvillage.co.uk
open Apr-Oct, Mon-Thu, Sat-Sun 1000-1700. Nov-Mar,
Sat-Sun 1000-1700. School Hols, daily 1000-1700.
admission £
Detailed scale model of Corfe Castle and village before its destruction by Cromwell. Old English country garden. Working stocks and pillories, giant games and enchanted fairy garden.

Dorset Quadbiking
Manor Farm, East Bloxworth, Wareham BH20 7EB
t (01929) 459083
w dorsetquadbiking.co.uk
open All year, phone for details.
admission ££££
Quadbike trekking perfect for all times of the year. With challenging terrain and capable quads, a unique outdoor adventure.

The Dorset Teddy Bear Museum
East Gate, Corner of High East Street/Salisbury Street,
Dorchester DT1 1JU
t (01305) 266040 **w** teddybearmuseum.co.uk
open Apr-Oct, daily 1000-1700. Nov-Mar, daily
1000-1630.
admission ££
A museum devoted to the wonderful world of the teddy bear. It contains a wealth of bears for you to delight in, including Edward Bear and a family of people-sized bears.

Farmer Palmer's Farm Park
Organford, Poole BH16 6EU
t (01202) 622022 **w** farmerpalmers.co.uk
open 9 Feb-15 Mar, daily 1000-1600. 16 Mar-25 Oct,
daily 1000-1730. 26 Oct-28 Dec, Fri-Sun 1000-1600.
admission ££
National Farm Attraction of the Year 2006. Family-run and designed for children eight years and under. There are hands-on animal events, many play facilities and fresh farmhouse fayre in the large, child-friendly restaurant.

Go Ape!
Moors Valley Country Park, Horton Road,
Ashley Heath BH24 2ET
t 0870 444 5562 **w** goape.co.uk
open Apr-Nov, daily 0800-1730.
admission ££££
Tackle a high-wire forest adventure course of rope bridges, Tarzan swings and zip slides up to 35ft above the forest floor.

Swanage Railway
Station House, Swanage BH19 1HB
t (01929) 425800 **w** swanagerailway.co.uk
open All year, see website for details.
admission ££
Travel to the seaside by steam train and make the most of the Jurassic Coast. Start your journey from Norden Park & Ride, the most convenient way to visit Corfe Castle.

The Tutankhamun Exhibition
High West Street, Dorchester DT1 1UW
t (01305) 269571 **w** tutankhamun-exhibition.co.uk
open Apr-Oct, daily 0930-1730. Nov-Mar, Mon-Fri
0930-1700, Sat-Sun 1000-1630.
admission ££
Tutankhamun's tomb, treasures and mummy are perfectly reconstructed. Facsimiles of magnificent treasures including his golden burial mask and the golden throne.

Wimborne Model Town and Gardens
16 King Street, Wimborne Minster BH21 1DY
t (01202) 881924 **w** wimborne-modeltown.com
open Apr-Oct, daily 1000-1700.
admission £
Charming 1/10th scale recreation of 1950s Wimborne, a delightful historic market town, set in beautiful award-winning gardens. Wendy Street play area, putting and working model railway. Tearooms and gift shop.

NATURE AND WILDLIFE

Abbotsbury Sub Tropical Gardens
Bullers Way, Abbotsbury DT3 4LA
t (01305) 871387 **w** abbotsbury-tourism.co.uk
open Apr-Aug, daily 1000-1800. Sep-Oct, Feb-Mar, daily 1000-1700. Nov-Jan, daily 1000-1600.
admission ££
Twenty acres of woodland valley. Exotic plants from all over the world, teahouse and gift shop. Voted 'Our Favourite Garden' by The Daily Telegraph.

Abbotsbury Swannery
New Barn Road, Abbotsbury DT3 4JG
t (01305) 871858 **w** abbotsbury-tourism.co.uk
open Apr-Aug, daily 1000-1800. Sep-Oct, daily 1000-1700.
admission ££
The only place in the world where up to 1,000 swans can be viewed during their nesting and hatching time. Feeding at 1200 and 1600 daily. Ugly Duckling Trail. No dogs allowed.

Bennett's Water Gardens
Putton Lane, Chickerell DT3 4AF
t (01305) 785150 **w** waterlily.co.uk
open Apr-Sep, Tue-Fri, Sun, Bank Hols 1000-1700.
admission ££
Eight acres of gardens. Outstanding displays of water lilies in summer. Monet-style bridge and gazebo. Nursery, gift shop and tearooms.

The Blue Pool
Furzebrook, Wareham BH20 5AR
t (01929) 551408 **w** bluepooluk.com
open Mar-Nov, daily 0930-1700.
admission £
A unique 25 acres of pine trees, gorse and heather. A traditional teahouse, gift shops, museum and plant centre.

Brownsea Island
Poole Harbour, Poole BH13 7EE
t (01202) 707744
w nationaltrust.org.uk/brownsea
open Mar-Jul, daily 1000-1700. Aug, daily 1000-1800. Sep, daily 1000-1700. Oct, daily 1000-1600.
admission £
Beautiful island with wonderful views, wildlife and history including rare red squirrels and birds. The birthplace of Scouting and Guiding.

Compton Acres
164 Canford Cliffs Road, Canford Cliffs, Poole BH13 7ES
t (01202) 700778
w comptonacres.co.uk
open Mar-Oct, daily 0900-1800. Nov-Feb, daily 1000-1600.
admission ££
Wander through beautiful and distinct gardens of the world including Italian, Japanese and Roman gardens plus much more. One of the finest privately owned gardens in the UK.

The Dorset Heavy Horse Centre & Farm Park
Grains Hill, Edmondsham, Verwood BH21 5RJ
t (01202) 824040
w dorset-heavy-horse-centre.co.uk
open Easter-Oct, daily 1000-1700.
admission ££
Heavy horses, wagon rides, tractor and trailer rides (free), interesting daily shows, 'hands-on with the friendly farm animals', llamas and snow dogs. Vintage tractor driving. Play areas. Cafe and gift shop. Great value!

Durlston Country Park
Durlston, Lighthouse Road, Swanage BH19 2JL
t (01929) 424443
w durlston.co.uk
open Daily.
admission Free
Countryside, sea cliffs and wildlife. Visitor centre with exhibits, information, live cliff camera and underwater sounds. Themed trails, guided walks and children's events.

Corfe Castle, Isle of Purbeck

For key to symbols see page 171.

Hardy's Cottage
Higher Bockhampton DT2 8QJ
t (01305) 262366
w nationaltrust.org.uk
open 23 Mar-30 Oct, Mon-Thu, Sun 1100-1700.
admission £
Thomas Hardy was born here in 1840. It is where he wrote 'Under the Greenwood Tree' and 'Far from the Madding Crowd'.

Kingston Maurward Gardens and Animal Park
Kingston Maurward College,
Kingston Maurward DT2 8PY
t (01305) 215003
w kmc.ac.uk/gardens
open Jan-Dec, daily 1000-1730.
admission £
Set deep in Hardy's Dorset and listed by English Heritage, these gardens include a croquet lawn, rainbow beds and borders.

Lyme Regis Marine Aquarium and Cobb History
Oakfield, Launchycroft Estate, Lyme Regis DT7 3NF
t (01297) 444230
open Mar-Oct, daily 1000-1700.
admission £
Small marine aquarium with exhibits caught in local waters. History displays of the cobb and ale.

Mapperton Gardens
Estate Office, Mapperton, Beaminster DT8 3NR
t (01308) 862645
w mapperton.com
open Gardens: Mar-Oct, Mon-Fri, Sun 1100-1700.
House: Jul, Mon-Fri 1400-1630.
admission £
Romantic valley gardens in unspoilt countryside, featuring Italianate garden, topiary, 17thC fish ponds and orangery. Marvellous Elizabethan manor house.

MGFT Animal Sanctuary
Church Knowle, Nr Wareham BH20 5NQ
t (01929) 480474
w animalsanctuaryuk.com
open Daily 1000-1600 (excl 25 Dec).
admission Free
Wander around 35 acres of beautiful Purbeck countryside, home to more than 200 rescued animals awaiting new homes: cats, furries, farm animals and horses. A lovely day out for all the family.

Minterne Gardens
Minterne Magna DT2 7AU
t (01300) 341370
w minterne.co.uk
open Mar-Oct, daily 1000-1800.
admission £
Important rhododendron garden with many fine and rare trees, landscaped in the 18th century, with lakes, cascades and streams. The setting of Great Hintock House in Hardy's 'The Woodlanders'.

Moors Valley Country Park
Horton Road, Ashley Heath BH24 2ET
t (01425) 470721 w moors-valley.co.uk
open Daily 0800-dusk.
admission Free
A 1,000-acre country park and forest. Lake and riverside walks, steam railway, cycle hire centre, golf course, fishing and an adventure play area. Visitor centre housing tearoom and country shop.

Moreton Gardens & Plant Centre
Moreton DT2 8RF
t (01929) 405084 w moretondorset.co.uk
open Mar-Oct, daily 1000-1700. Nov-Dec, daily 1000-1600. Jan-Feb, Sat-Sun 1000-1600.
admission £
Moreton Gardens is a 3.5-acre landscaped garden in a beautiful south Dorset village associated with TE Lawrence (Lawrence of Arabia) who is buried in the adjacent churchyard. Plant centre. Ample parking.

Oceanarium
Pier Approach, West Beach,
Bournemouth BH2 5AA
t (01202) 311993 w oceanarium.co.uk
open Daily from 1000 (excl 25 Dec).
admission ££
Enjoy close encounters with creatures from piranhas to clownfish, and take a walk through the amazing underwater tunnel to get even closer to sharks, sea turtles, stingrays and eels.

Studland Beach and Nature Reserve
Purbeck Estate Office, Middle Beach,
Studland BH19 3AX
t (01929) 450259 w nationaltrust.org.uk
open Daily.
admission Free
Glorious sandy beaches stretching for three miles from South Haven Point to Old Harry Rocks. A haven for rare birds and other wildlife, embracing two national nature reserves.

Upton Country Park
Upton Road, Upton BH17 7BJ
t (01202) 672625 w boroughofpoole.com
open Daily 0930-dusk.
admission Free
Formal gardens, meadows, woodlands, and marshland. Heritage centre with nature trails. Upton House, historic Grade II Listed building.

Weymouth Sea Life Park and Marine Sanctuary
Lodmoor Country Park, Weymouth DT4 7SX
t (01305) 788255 w sealifeeurope.com
open Daily 1000-1600.
admission £££
An amazing array of the world's most fascinating marine life, offering a day of fun and amazement whatever the weather.

HISTORIC ENGLAND

Athelhampton House and Gardens
Athelhampton DT2 7LG
t (01305) 848363 w athelhampton.co.uk
open Apr-Oct, Mar, Mon-Thu, Sun 1030-1700.
Nov-Feb, Sun 1030-1700.
admission ££ 💷 🎜 🍴 🚻
Legendary site of King Athelstan's palace. One of the finest 15thC manorhouses, surrounded by glorious Grade I Listed garden with fountains, pools and waterfalls.

Brewers Quay and Timewalk Journey
Hope Square, Weymouth DT4 8TR
t (01305) 777622 w brewers-quay.co.uk
open Daily 1000-1730.
admission £ 💷 🍴 🚻
Converted Victorian brewery with indoor speciality shopping village, courtyard restaurant and award-winning Timewalk attraction recreating the sights, sounds and smells of Weymouth's history.

Cerne Abbas Giant
Cerne Abbas
t (01297) 561900 w nationaltrust.org.uk
open Daily.
admission Free
The 180ft-tall club-wielding man has long been regarded as a sign of fertility. He was probably created during the Roman occupation of Britain in the second century AD.

Christchurch Castle
Castle Street, Christchurch
t (01202) 495127 w visitchristchurch.info
open Daily.
admission Free
Late 11th century castle built to protect the town.

Christchurch Priory Church
Quay Road, Christchurch BH23 1BU
t (01202) 485804 w christchurchpriory.org
open Apr-Oct, daily 0930-1700. Oct-Mar, daily 0930-1600.
admission Free 🚻 🍴 🚻
Longest parish church in England, dating from 1094. The west tower can be climbed. Legendary Miraculous Beam. Memorial to the poet Shelley.

Corfe Castle
The Square, Corfe Castle BH20 5EZ
t (01929) 477063 w nationaltrust.org.uk
open Apr-Sep, daily 1000-1730. Nov-Feb, daily 1000-1530. March, Oct, daily 1000-1630.
admission ££ 💷 🚻
Ruins of former royal castle sieged and slighted in 1646 by parliamentary forces.

Edmondsham House and Garden
Edmondsham House, Edmondsham,
Cranborne BH21 5RE
t (01725) 517207
open House: Apr, Wed 1400-1700. Oct, Wed 1400-1700. Bank Hols, 1400-1700. Gardens: Apr-Oct, Wed, Sun 1400-1700.
admission £ 🚻 🍴 🚻
Fine Tudor/Georgian manorhouse, with Victorian stables and dairy. Six-acre garden and one-acre walled garden.

Forde Abbey and Gardens
Chard TA20 4LU
t (01460) 221290 w fordeabbey.co.uk
open Abbey: 18 Mar-Oct, Tue-Fri, Sun 1200-1600. Gardens: daily 1000-1630.
admission ££ 💷 🚻 🚻
More than 900 years of history and romance are encapsulated in this elegant former Cistercian monastery and its 30 acres of exquisite award-winning gardens.

Highcliffe Castle
Rothesay Drive, off Lymington Road,
Highcliffe BH23 4LE
t (01425) 278807 w highcliffecastle.co.uk
open Feb-Dec, daily 1100-1700.
admission £ 💷 🚻 🍴 ♿
Grade I Listed c1830 picturesque and romantic seaside mansion. Now fully repaired to exterior only. Six staterooms open as visitor and exhibition centre.

Kingston Lacy House and Gardens
Wimborne Minster BH21 4EA
t (01202) 883402 w nationaltrust.org.uk
open House: Apr-Oct, Wed-Sun 1100-1600. Gardens: Apr-Oct, daily 1030-1800. Nov-Dec, Fri-Sun 1030-1600. Feb-Mar, Sat-Sun 1030-1600.
admission ££ 💷 🚻 🍴 🚻
A 17thC house designed for Sir Ralph Bankes by Sir Roger Pratt, altered by Sir Charles Barry in the 19thC. Collection of paintings, 250-acre wooded park, herd of Devon cattle.

The geological wonder of Durdle Door on the Jurassic coast

Admission is based on an adult price. Please check opening times and admission before travelling.

Lulworth Castle & Park
East Lulworth, Wareham BH20 5QS
t 0845 450 1054
w lulworth.com
open Summer: Sun-Fri 1030-1800. Winter: Sun-Fri 1030-1600 (excl 24-25 Dec, 6-19 Jan).
admission ££
Idyllic castle set in extensive park with 18thC chapel, animal farm, adventure play area, woodland walks, picnic area, cafe and courtyard shop. Special events throughout the year including spectacular summer jousting shows.

Maumbury Rings
Weymouth Avenue, Dorchester
t (01305) 266861
w dorchester-tc.gov.uk
open Daily.
admission Free
Originally a sacred circle of the Stone Age, the Romans later turned the rings into a coliseum where 13,000 spectators could watch gladiatorial combats.

Max Gate
Alington Avenue, Dorchester DT1 2AA
t (01305) 262538
open 26 Mar-29 Sep, Mon, Weds, Sun 1400-1700.
admission £
Victorian house designed by Thomas Hardy, and his home from 1885 until his death in 1928. Contains several pieces of Hardy's furniture.

Milton Abbey
Milton Abbas DT11 0BP
t (01258) 880215
w ruraldorset.com
open Daily 1000-1730.
admission £
A 14thC abbey, church and abbots' hall. Gothic-style house.

Nothe Fort
The Nothe, Barrack Road, Weymouth DT4 8UF
t (01305) 766626
w fortressweymouth.co.uk
open May-Sep, daily 1030-1730.
admission £
Mid-Victorian coastal defence fort with ramparts, gun deck and magazines. Models, displays and exhibitions. Views over town, harbour and Jurassic Coast.

Portland Castle
Portland DT5 1AZ
t (01305) 820539
w english-heritage.org.uk/portlandcastle
open Apr-Jun, daily 1000-1700. Jul-Aug, daily 1000-1800. Sep, daily 1000-1700. Oct, daily 1000-1600.
admission £
A well-preserved coastal fort built by Henry VIII to defend Weymouth Harbour against possible French and Spanish attack. Exhibition detailing 400 years of the castle's history.

St Catherine's Chapel
Abbotsbury
t (01305) 820868
w english-heritage.org.uk
open All year, daily.
admission Free
A small stone chapel, set on a hilltop, with an unusual roof and small turret previously used as a lighthouse.

St Mary the Virgin
Tarrant Crawford DT11 9HU
t (020) 7213 0660
w visitchurches.org.uk
open Daily, dawn-dusk.
admission Free
This simple, unspoilt church stands on a slope above the River Tarrant. There is a series of 14thC paintings on the south wall.

Sherborne Abbey
The Close, Sherborne DT9 3LQ
t (01935) 812452
w sherborneabbey.com
open Apr-Oct, daily 0900-1800. Nov-Mar, daily 0900-1600.
admission Free
Historic abbey church dating from Saxon times. Wealth of 15thC fan-vaulting built of hamstone. Fine monuments.

Sherborne Castle
Sherborne Castle Estates, New Road, Sherborne DT9 5NR
t (01935) 813182
w sherbornecastle.com
open 22 Mar-Oct, Tue-Thur, Sat-Sun, Bank Hols 1100-1630.
admission ££
Built by Sir Walter Raleigh in 1594. Home to the Digby family since 1617. Splendid collections of decorative arts. Capability Brown lake, gardens and grounds.

Stinsford Church
Church Lane, Stinsford DT2 8PS
t (01305) 267992
open Daily 0900-1800.
admission Free
Norman church with churchyard containing the graves of Thomas Hardy and the poet Cecil Day Lewis.

Wimborne Minster
Church House, High Street, Wimborne Minster BH21 1HT
t (01202) 884753
w wimborneminster.org.uk
open Mar-Dec, daily 0930-1730. Jan-Feb, daily 0930-1600.
admission Free
Medieval church, Ethelred brass, astronomical clock, quarterjack, chained library and gift shop.

OUTDOOR ACTIVITIES

The Dorset Belles Ltd
Boat Booking Office, Bournemouth Pier,
Bournemouth BH2 5AA
t (01202) 558550 w dorsetcruises.co.uk
open Apr-Oct, daily 0700-2200. Nov-Mar, daily
0800-1700.
admission £ 💻🏠🔋
Glorious coastal and harbour cruises from Bournemouth,
Poole and Swanage. Visit islands or view the Purbeck
heritage coast and Poole Harbour. Dorset's finest
scenery.

ENTERTAINMENT AND CULTURE

Bridport Museum
South Street, Bridport DT6 3NR
t (01308) 422116 w bridportmuseum.co.uk
open Apr-Oct, Mon-Sat 1000-1700.
admission £ ✂️🔋
Learn the unique history of the town, from Romans to
rope-making. New exhibitions and galleries. A gateway
to the Jurassic Coast World Heritage Site.

Childrens Farm and Smugglers Barn
New Barn Road, Abbotsbury DT3 4JG
t (01305) 871817 w abbotsbury-tourism.co.uk
open Apr-Aug, daily 1000-1800. Sep-Oct, see website
for full details.
admission ££ 🏠✂️🔋
Children's farm and soft play with a smuggling theme for
children under 11 years. Activities include rabbit and
guinea pig handling and pony rides (extra charge).

The Dinosaur Museum
Icen Way, Dorchester DT1 1EW
t (01305) 269880 w thedinosaurmuseum.com
open Apr-Oct, daily 0930-1730. Nov-Mar, daily
1000-1630.
admission ££ ✂️🔋
Award-winning museum devoted to dinosaurs. Features
fossils, actual-size dinosaur reconstructions, video
gallery and audiovisual/hands-on displays.

Dinosaurland
Coombe Street, Lyme Regis DT7 3PY
t (01297) 443541 w dinosaurland.co.uk
open All year, Mon-Sun, Bank Hols 1000-1700.
admission £ 🏠
Jurassic fossil museum. Guided fossil-hunting walks,
fossil shop.

Gold Hill Museum and Garden
Gold Hill, Shaftesbury SP7 8JW
t (01747) 852157
open Apr-Oct, daily 1030-1630.
admission £ ✂️🔋
Take a step back in time and discover the story of
Shaftesbury, the highest market town in Wessex.

The Keep Military Museum
The Keep, Bridport Road, Dorchester DT1 1RN
t (01305) 264066
w keepmilitarymuseum.org
open Apr-Sep, Mon-Sat 0930-1700. Oct-Mar, Tue-Sat
0930-1700.
admission £ ✂️♿
Touch-screen computers and interactive and creative
displays tell the stories of the courage, tradition and
sacrifice of those who served in the regiments of Devon
and Dorset.

Lyme Regis Philpot Museum
Bridge Street, Lyme Regis DT7 3QA
t (01297) 443370
w lymeregismuseum.co.uk
open Apr-Oct, Mon-Sat 1000-1700, Sun, 1100-1700.
Nov-Mar, Sat-Sun. Please phone for details.
admission £ ✂️🔋
Fossils, geology, local history, literary connections. The
story of Lyme in its landscape.

Museum of Electricity
The Old Power Station, Bargates,
Christchurch BH23 1QE
t (01202) 480467
w scottish-southern.co.uk/museum
open Apr-Sep, Mon-Thu 1200-1600, School Hols,
Mon-Fri 1200-1600.
admission £ 🏠✂️🔋
One of the most extensive collections of historic
electrical equipment in Great Britain, the restored 1903
building houses more than 700 exhibits. Plenty to see
and do.

The Priest's House Museum and Garden
23-27 High Street, Wimborne Minster BH21 1HR
t (01202) 882533
open Apr-Oct, Mon-Sat 1000-1630.
admission £ 💻🏠✂️🔋
Award-winning museum. Period rooms, Victorian
kitchen, walled garden, East Dorset villages gallery,
childhood and archaeology galleries and hands-on
activities for all ages.

The Red House Museum and Gardens
Quay Road, Christchurch BH23 1BU
t (01202) 482860
w hants.gov.uk/museum/redhouse
open All year, Tue-Sat 1000-1700, Sun 1400-1700.
admission Free 💻🏠✂️🔋
Museum showing the archaeology, social and domestic
history of Christchurch. Changing temporary exhibitions,
costume gallery, rose and herb gardens.

For key to symbols see page 171.

RNLI Headquarters and Display
West Quay Road, Poole BH15 1HZ
t 0845 122 6999   **w** rnli.org.uk
open All year, Mon-Fri 0900-1700.
admission Free
Small display of the history and development of RNLI including pictures, models and paintings.

Royal Signals Museum
Blandford Camp, Blandford Forum DT11 8RH
t (01258) 482248   **w** royalsignalsmuseum.com
open All year, Mon-Fri 1000-1700, Sat-Sun, Bank Hols 1000-1600.
admission ££
History of army communication from Crimean War to Gulf War. Vehicles, uniforms, medals and badges on display.

Russell-Cotes Art Gallery & Museum
East Cliff, Bournemouth BH1 3AA
t (01202) 451800   **w** russell-cotes.bournemouth.gov.uk
open All year, Tue-Sun, summer Bank Hols 1000-1700.
admission Free
Part house, part museum, this late Victorian villa is both eccentric and ostentatious in character. Home to fascinating and eclectic collections from around the world and some of the finest Victorian art.

Shaftesbury Abbey Museum and Garden
Park Walk, Shaftesbury SP7 8JR
t (01747) 852910   **w** shaftesburyabbey.co.uk
open Apr-Oct, daily 1000-1700.
admission £
Explore one of the sites of Saxon England's foremost Benedictine nunnery, founded by King Alfred.

Snowtrax
Matchams Lane, Hurn BH23 6AW
t (01202) 499155
w snowtrax.eu
open Daily 1000-2200.
admission Free
A dry-ski slope with fully licensed bar and restaurant and Alpine adventure play park. Fully equipped ski and snowboard shop with hire facilities. Free admission, activities individually priced.

The Tank Museum
Bovington, Wareham BH20 6JG
t (01929) 405096
w tankmuseum.org
open Daily 1000-1700.
admission ££
The world's best collection of tanks displayed in five large halls. From the very first to the very latest, see over 250 tanks from across the globe.

Tolpuddle Martyrs Museum
Tolpuddle DT2 7EH
t (01305) 848237
w tolpuddlemartyrs.org.uk
open Apr-Oct, Tue-Sat 1000-1700, Sun, Bank Hols 1000-1700. Nov-Mar, Thu-Sat 1000-1600, Sun, Bank Hols 1000-1600. (Closed 17 Dec-2 Jan).
admission Free
Colourful banners and touch-screen computers tell the story of the six Martyrs of Tolpuddle who were transported to Australia in 1834.

Walk up the ancient cobbled street of Gold Hill, Shaftesbury

RELAXING AND PAMPERING

Poole Pottery Factory Shop Outlet
The Quay, Poole BH15 1RF
t (01202) 668681 **w** poolepottery.co.uk
open All year, Mon-Sat 0930-1630, Sun 1030-1630.
admission Free
Factory shop, teashop and Poole Pottery Experience with design-your-own area.

Stapehill Abbey, Crafts and Gardens
Wimborne Road West, Stapehill,
Wimborne Minster BH21 2EB
t (01202) 861686
open Jan-Mar, daily 1000-1600. Apr-Sep, daily 1000-1700. Oct-Dec 1000-1600.
admission £
Stapehill has magnificent award-winning gardens, 19thC buildings, nuns' chapel, cloister garden, working craftspeople and a 12,000 sq ft museum depicting life in bygone days.

Walford Mill Craft Centre
Stone Lane, Wimborne BH21 1NL
t (01202) 841400 **w** walfordmillcrafts.co.uk
open Apr-Dec, Mon-Sat 1000-1700, Sun 1100-1600.
Jan-Mar, Tue-Sat 1000-1700, Sun 1100-1600.
admission Free
A converted mill building by the river with a gallery and shop showing the best in contemporary British design. Also has workshops, a craft school and a bistro.

Somerset

FAMILY FUN

Animal Farm Adventure Park
Red Road, Berrow TA8 2RW
t (01278) 751628 **w** animal-farm.co.uk
open All year, daily 1000-1730.
admission ££
Set in 25 acres of Somerset countryside with views across to the Mendip Hills. Feed and hold many friendly animals. Indoor play area now open.

Brean Leisure Park
Coast Road, Brean Sands, Burnham-on-Sea TA8 2QY
t (01278) 751595 **w** brean.com
open See website for details.
admission Free
Fun park with over 30 rides and attractions from roundabouts to rollercoasters. Pool complex with five waterslides, golf course, garden centre, bars and restaurants.

Butlins Minehead
Warren Road, Minehead TA24 5SH
t 0870 145 0045 **w** butlins.com
open May-Dec, daily 0930-1800.
admission £££
Amusement park, outdoor splash pool and traditional funfair. Skyline pavilion, splash swimming pool, outdoor adventure play area, Hotshots ten-pin bowling alley. Fantastic live entertainment.

The Cheddar Gorge Cheese Company, Shop & Working Dairy
The Cliffs, Cheddar Gorge BS27 3QA
t (01934) 742810 **w** cheddargorgecheeseco.co.uk
open Shop: Apr-Oct, daily 1000-1730. Nov-Mar, daily 1000-1630. Visitor Centre: Apr-Oct, daily 1000-1600.
Nov-Mar, daily 1000-1600.
admission £
Working Cheddar cheese factory with dairy, visitor centre and shop. Entrance fee is for dairy only.

The East Somerset Railway
Cranmore Station, Cranmore BA4 4QP
t (01749) 880417 **w** eastsomersetrailway.com
open Mar-May, Sep-Dec, Sat-Sun. Jun-Aug, Sat-Sun, Wed-Thu, Bank Hols. Please phone for details.
admission ££
Steam through the rolling Mendip countryside on a day out at the East Somerset Railway. Train rides, engine shed and workshops, museum, cafe and shop.

Exmoor Falconry & Animal Farm
West Lynch Farm, Allerford TA24 8HJ
t (01643) 862816 **w** exmoorfalconry.co.uk
open Mar-Oct, daily 1000-1700.
admission ££
Falconry centre with owls, hawks, eagles, falcons and other animals set in medieval farmyard. Flying displays and animal handling twice daily. Falconry activities, alpaca walks, horse riding, tea gardens and herb garden.

Grand Pier
Marine Parade, Weston-super-Mare BS23 1AL
t (01934) 620238 **w** grandpierwsm.co.uk
open Mar-Dec, daily 1000-1800.
admission Free
Covered amusement park over the sea. Deck trains, dodgems, spaceflight simulator, ghost train, children's adventure play area, big wheel, slot machines and videos.

Admission is based on an adult price. Please check opening times and admission before travelling.

Middlemoor Waterpark

The Causeway, Woolavington, Bridgwater TA7 8DN
t (01278) 685578 **w** middlemoor.co.uk
open All year, Tue-Sat 1000-1800, Sun 1300-1700.
admission ££££

Middlemoor Waterpark, Somerset's premier venue for jet-skiing, wake-boarding, water-skiing and pro-karting.

Noah's Ark Zoo Farm

Moat House Farm, Failand Road, Wraxall BS48 1PG
t (01275) 852606 **w** noahsarkzoofarm.co.uk
open Feb-Oct, Mon-Sat 1030-1700.
admission ££

The most varied zoo and farm in North Somerset with hands-on animal experiences for everyone. Only five miles from Bristol, it's a beautiful, peaceful and fun place for adults and children.

West Somerset Railway

The Railway Station, Minehead TA24 5BG
t (01643) 704996 **w** west-somerset-railway.co.uk
open May-Sep, daily. Mar-Apr, Oct, Tue-Thu, Sat-Sun.
admission £££

The longest Heritage railway in the country, the West Somerset Railway runs from Bishops Lydeard, through the Quantock Hills before turning along the Somerset coastline and arriving in Minehead after a 20-mile journey.

Weston Miniature Railway

Marine Parade, Weston-super-Mare BS23 1AL
t (01934) 643510 **w** westonprom.com
open Apr-May, Sat-Sun 1030-1700. Jun-Sep, daily 1030-1700. Oct, Sat-Sun 1030-1700.
admission £

Passenger-carrying miniature railway over half a mile on the seafront. Eighteen-hole putting course.

Wookey Hole Caves and Papermill

Wookey Hole, Wells BA5 1BB
t (01749) 672243 **w** wookey.co.uk
open Apr-Oct, daily. Bank Hols 1000-1700. Nov-Mar, daily, Bank Hols 1000-1600.
admission £££

Spectacular caves and legendary home of the Witch of Wookey. Working Victorian paper mill including Old Penny Arcade, Magical Mirror Maze and Cave Diving Museum.

NATURE AND WILDLIFE

Avon Valley Country Park

Pixash Lane, Bath Road, Keynsham BS31 1TS
t (0117) 986 4929 **w** avonvalleycountrypark.co.uk
open See website for details.
admission ££

A great day out for all the family. A river-based park with animals and birds, children's play area and assault course, boating and fishing. Undercover soft play area and falconry.

Barrington Court

Barrington TA19 0NQ
t (01460) 241938
w nationaltrust.org.uk
open Mar-Oct, Mon-Tue, Thu-Sun 1100-1700.
admission ££

Series of beautiful gardens influenced by Gertrude Jekyll including a large kitchen garden designed to support the house. Barrington Court House is also open to visitors.

Cheddar Caves & Gorge

Cheddar BS27 3QF
t (01934) 742343
w cheddarcaves.co.uk
open Jul-Aug, daily 1000-1700. Sep-Jun, daily 1030-1630.
admission £££

Nature, culture and adventure. Britain's finest caves and deepest gorge. Victorian Gothic splendour and how our Stone Age ancestors survived.

Chew Valley Lake and Blagdon Lake

Wally Court Road, Chew Stoke BS40 8XN
t (0117) 966 5881
w bristolwater.co.uk
open Daily, dawn-dusk.
admission Free

Situated on the northern edge of the beautiful Mendip Hills, the picturesque surroundings make this a popular destination. Chew Valley Lake is the biggest inland waterway in South West England.

Combe Sydenham Country Park

Monksilver TA4 4JG
t 0800 783 8572
open Apr-Aug, daily 0900-1630.
admission Free

Restored west wing, gardens, deer park, woodland walks, fish ponds, Domesday corn mill.

East Lambrook Manor Gardens

East Lambrook, South Petherton TA13 5HH
t (01460) 240328
w eastlambrook.co.uk
open Daily, Bank Hols 1000-1700.
admission £

The garden at East Lambrook Manor is recognised throughout the world as the home of English cottage gardening, having been created in the 1940s, 50s and 60s by the late gardening icon, Margery Fish.

Ebbor Gorge National Nature Reserve

Wookey Hole BA5 3AH
t (01749) 679546
w naturalengland.org.uk
open Daily 0800-dusk.
admission Free

Woodland walk with excellent spring flowers, summer butterflies and autumn colour. Limestone outcrops and towering cliffs surround the gorge itself with great views across the Somerset Levels to Glastonbury Tor.

Ferne Animal Sanctuary
Chard TA20 3DH
t (01460) 65214 w ferneanimalsanctuary.org
open Daily 1000-1700.
admission Free
Fifty-one-acre sanctuary for some 300 animals. Nature trails, picnic tables and light refreshments. Tearoom and well-stocked gift shop.

Hestercombe Gardens
Cheddon Fitzpaine TA2 8LG
t (01823) 413923 w hestercombegardens.com
open All year, daily 1000-1800.
admission ££
A unique combination of Georgian landscape, Victorian terrace and Edwardian garden. Walks, streams, temples, vivid colours, formal terraces, woodlands, lakes and cascades. Cafe, shop, free parking, dogs welcome.

Kelways Plant Centre and Orchid House
Barrymore Farm, Picts Hill, Langport TA10 9EZ
t (01458) 250521 w kelways.co.uk
open All year, Mon-Sat 0900-1700, Sun, Bank Hols 1000-1600.
admission Free
Plant centre and orchid display house. National collection of peonies open during flowering season in June.

Lower Severalls Garden and Nursery
Crewkerne TA18 7NX
t (01460) 73234 w lowerseveralls.co.uk
open Mar-Jul, Tue-Wed, Fri-Sat, Bank Hols 1000-1700.
Sep, Tue-Wed, Fri-Sat, 1000-1700.
admission £
Enchanting, original garden set in front of 18thC hamstone farmhouse. The informal garden has herbaceous borders and many innovative features with a nursery.

Seaquarium
Marine Parade, Weston-super-Mare BS23 1BE
t (01934) 613361 w seaquarium.co.uk
open All year, daily, Bank Hols 1000-1700.
admission ££
It's a whole new world. See some of the weirdest and deadliest animals on the planet, from sharks to seahorses. Ticket is valid all day – come and go as you please with a hand stamp.

Tintinhull Garden
Farm Street, Tintinhull BA22 8PZ
t (01935) 823289 w nationaltrust.org.uk
open 15 Mar-2 Nov, Wed-Sun 1100-1700.
admission £
A 20thC formal garden surrounding a 17thC house. The layout is divided into areas by walls and hedges, has border colour and plant themes, shrub roses, clematis and kitchen garden.

Tropiquaria
Washford Cross, Watchet TA23 0QB
t (01984) 640688
w tropiquaria.co.uk
open 1 Apr-2 Sep 1000-1800, last entry 1630.
3 Sep-4 Nov 1100-1700, last entry 1600.
5 Nov-31 March, weekends and school holidays.
admission ££
Visit the indoor jungle, aquarium, puppet theatre and radio museum. Play on the full-size pirate ships or in the indoor play castle. Visit the animal collection in our grounds.

The Wildlife Park at Cricket St Thomas

Cricket St Thomas TA20 4DB
t (01460) 30111
w wild.org.uk
open Apr-mid Sep, daily, Bank Hols 1000-1800 (last admission 1600). Oct-Mar, daily, Bank Hols 1000-1600 (last admission 1500).
admission ££
Set in a scenic valley, over 600 species of exotic animals and birds are kept in a natural setting as part of world conservation programmes.

Wimbleball Lake
Brompton Regis, Dulverton TA22 9NU
t (01398) 371460
w swlakestrust.org.uk
open Daily.
admission Free
This scenic lake lies within Exmoor National Park and is surrounded by woodland and meadows. It offers a variety of activities including water sports, angling and walking.

Yeovil Country Park
Yeovil
t (01935) 462462
w southsomerset.gov.uk
open Daily.
admission Free
Managed by South Somerset District Council, an area of 127 acres of woodland, grassland, lake and river, open to all.

HISTORIC ENGLAND

The Bishop's Palace & Gardens
Wells BA5 2PD
t (01749) 678691
w bishopspalacewells.co.uk
open Apr-Oct, Mon-Fri 1030-1800, Sat 1030-1400, Sun 1030-1800. Nov-Dec, Wed-Sun 1030-1600.
admission £
Enjoy the tranquillity of the beautiful gardens in this unique and historic site. Discover the wells from which the city takes its name and the splendid 13thC palace buildings.

For key to symbols see page 171.

Cameley St James, Somerset
St James Church, Cameley, Temple Cloud BS39 5AH
t (020) 7213 0660
w visitchurches.org.uk
open Daily, please phone for details.
admission Free

A delightfully unspoilt church, with a tower of Mendip stone featuring a handsome parapet. The interior has fixtures and fittings from many periods and a wall painting of the Ten Commandments.

Castle Neroche
Blackdown Hills, Taunton TA20 3AB
t (01392) 832262
w forestry.gov.uk
open Daily.
admission Free

A visit to the Forest of Neroche will offer you spectacular views over the Vale of Taunton towards the Quantock Hills and Exmoor and a place to enjoy a stroll with the family.

Cleeve Abbey
Washford TA23 0PS
t (01984) 640377
w english-heritage.org.uk/cleeve
open See website for details.
admission £

One of the few 13thC monastic sites left with such a complete set of cloister buildings.

Clevedon Pier and Heritage Trust
Waterloo House, 4 The Beach, Clevedon BS21 7QU
t (01275) 341196
w clevedonpier.com
open Apr-Oct, Mon-Fri 1000-1700, Sat-Sun 1000-1800.
Nov-Mar, Mon-Fri 1000-1600, Sat-Sun 1000-1700.
admission £

Heritage display in words and pictures of how Clevedon was created. Paddle Steamer Preservation Society history.

Cothay Manor
Greenham, Wellington TA21 0JR
t (01823) 672283
w cothaymanor.co.uk
open Apr-Sep, Wed-Thu, Sun, Bank Hols 1400-1800.
admission £

Hidden for centuries, and virtually untouched since it was built in 1480. 12 acres of highly romantic gardens. Said to be the finest example of a small classic medieval manor remaining today.

Culbone Church – St Beuno
Culbone, Porlock
t (01598) 741270
open Daily.
admission Free

This Exmoor parish church is the smallest in England where regular worship is still offered. Its dimensions are 35ft by 12ft.

Dunster Castle
Dunster TA24 6SL
t (01643) 821314 **w** nationaltrust.org.uk
open Mar-Jul, Mon-Wed, Fri-Sun 1100-1600. Aug, Mon-Wed, Fri-Sun 1100-1700. Sep-Nov, Mon-Wed, Fri-Sun 1100-1600.
admission ££

Fortified home of the Luttrells for 600 years, remodelled 100 years ago. Fine 17thC staircase, plaster ceilings and garden of rare shrubs. Last entry 30 minutes before closing.

Glastonbury Abbey

Abbey Gatehouse, Magdalen Street,
Glastonbury BA6 9EL
t (01458) 832267 **w** glastonburyabbey.com
open Mar-May, Sep-Nov 0930-1800 (or dusk if earlier).
Jun-Aug 0900-1800. Dec-Feb 1000-1630.
admission £

Magnificent abbey ruins and grounds. Legendary burial place of King Arthur. Modern museum, living history presentations and outdoor summer cafe. Grounds contain an orchard, ornamental lakes and an ever-changing array of flora.

Glastonbury Tor
Glastonbury
t (01985) 843600 **w** nationaltrust.org.uk
open Daily.
admission Free

Remains of 15thC tower. Hill overlooks Glastonbury town and beyond.

Ham Hill Country Park
The Rangers Office, Stoke sub Hamdon TA14 6RW
t (01935) 823617 **w** southsomerset.gov.uk
open All year, daily.
admission Free

Open access country park of 400 acres. Superb countryside walks with Iron Age and Roman earthworks. Panoramic views of Somerset. Green Flag award winning park.

Montacute House
Montacute TA15 6XP
t (01935) 823289 **w** nationaltrust.org.uk
open 15 Mar-2 Nov, Mon, Wed-Sun 1100-1700.
admission ££

Late 16thC house built of local golden hamstone, by Sir Edward Phelips. The Long Gallery houses a collection of Tudor and Jacobean portraits. Formal gardens. Park.

Muchelney Abbey
Muchelney TA10 0DQ
t (01458) 250664 **w** english-heritage.org.uk/muchelney
open See website for details.
admission £

The abbey was first established by Ine, a 7thC King of Wessex. The Abbot's lodging is the best preserved feature of the abbey.

Oare Church – St Mary's Church
Oare EX35 6NX
t (01598) 741270
open Please phone for details.
admission **Free**

Set in the beautiful wooded valley of Oare Water, the church was the scene of Lorna Doone's wedding in the novel by R D Blackmore.

Peat Moors Centre
Shapwick Road, Westhay BA6 9TT
t (01458) 860697
open Apr-Oct, Mon-Tue, Thu-Sun 1000-1630.
admission **£**

Replica Iron Age settlement and wooden trackways. Traditional peat-cutting display, archaeology, peat and wildlife exhibition.

Priest's House
Muchelney TA10 0DQ
t (01458) 253771 w nationaltrust.org.uk
open Apr-Sep, Mon, Sun, 1400-1730.
admission **£**

Late medieval house with large Gothic hall windows, originally a residence of priests serving the parish church opposite.

Wells Cathedral
Chain Gate, Cathedral Green, Wells BA5 2UE
t (01749) 674483 w wellscathedral.org.uk
open Apr-Sep, daily 0700-1900. Oct-Mar, daily 0700-1800.
admission **Free**

Dating from the 12th century and built in the Early English Gothic style. Magnificent west front with 296 medieval groups of sculpture. Chapter House and Lady Chapel.

Willows & Wetlands Visitor Centre
Meare Green Court, Stoke St Gregory, Taunton TA3 6HY
t (01823) 490249 w englishwillowbaskets.co.uk
open Mon-Sat 0900-1700.
admission **Free**

Discover the history and art of willow growing and basketmaking. Handmade basketware and gifts for sale. Charge for optional workshop tours. See also how water has shaped the Somerset Levels.

OUTDOOR ACTIVITIES

Yeovil Alpine Village
Addlewell Lane, Yeovil BA20 1QW
t (01935) 421702
w yeovilalpinevillage.co.uk
open Please phone for details.
admission **££**

The leading skiing and snowboarding venue in the South West, offering something for everyone whatever their ability. Innovatively designed slopes are set on a natural hillside.

ENTERTAINMENT AND CULTURE

Avon Ski and Action Centre
High Action Limited, Lyncombe Lodge, Churchill BS25 5PQ
t (01934) 852335
w highaction.co.uk
open All year, daily 0900-2200.
admission **£££**

Main slope served by two lifts. Two separate nursery areas for beginners away from the main slope, plus toboggan slope, all on 130 acres of land.

The Bakelite Museum
Orchard Mill, Bridge Street, Williton TA4 4NS
t (01984) 632133
w bakelitemuseum.co.uk
open Apr-Sep, Thu-Sun 1030-1800.
admission **£**

Britain's only vintage plastics museum, from the Victorian age to World War II. A colourful feast of nostalgia, fascinating for all ages. A massive and unique collection.

Porlock Bay, Exmoor National Park

Admission is based on an adult price. Please check opening times and admission before travelling.

Bridgwater Arts Centre
11-13 Castle Street, Bridgwater TA6 3DD
t (01278) 422700
w bridgwaterartscentre.co.uk
open All year, Tue-Fri 1030-1700, Sat 1000-1300.
admission Free
Bridgwater's Community Arts Centre, combining gallery, professional performances of theatre, dance, music and film, and classes in many artforms for adults and children.

Church House Designs
Broad Street, Congresbury BS49 5DG
t (01934) 833660
w churchhousedesigns.co.uk
open All year, Mon-Tue, Thu-Sat 1000-1300, 1415-1700.
admission Free
A long established independent gallery promoting quality British contemporary crafts with particular emphasis on ceramics and glassware selected by the Crafts Council for quality.

Clevedon Craft Centre
Moor Lane, Clevedon BS21 6TD
t (01275) 872149
w clevedoncraftcentre.co.uk
open All year, Tue-Sat 1000-1700, Sun 1400-1700.
admission Free
Housing studios and workshops in the outbuildings of a 17thC Somerset 'Long Farm'. Purchase high quality craftwork directly from the designers and enjoy the quiet rural atmosphere at this free, all-year-round attraction.

Dunster Dolls Museum
Memorial Hall, High Street,
Dunster TA24 6SF
t (01643) 821220
open Easter-Sep, Mon-Fri, Bank Hols 1030-1630, Sat-Sun 1400-1700.
admission Free
This varied collection of over 900 dolls from many places and periods, baby gowns and a doll's house will revive nostalgic memories. New themed displays each year.

Fleet Air Arm Museum
RNAS Yeovilton, Ilchester BA22 8HT
t (01935) 840565
w fleetairarm.com
open Apr-Oct 1000-1730. Nov-Mar, Wed-Sun 1000-1630.
admission £££
See Europe's largest collection of naval aircraft, plus Concorde, Harriers, helicopters and the award-winning Aircraft Carrier Experience. There's even a nuclear bomb! Adventure playground, shop, restaurant, excellent parking and disabled facilities.

Haynes International Motor Museum
Sparkford BA22 7LH
t (01963) 440804 w haynesmotormuseum.co.uk
open Apr-Oct, daily 0930-1730. Nov-Mar, daily 1000-1630.
admission ££
Working museum with over 350 amazing cars and bikes ranging from bygone classics to modern-day supercars. Collection of British motorcycles, commercial and military vehicles, play area, cinema, restaurant. New exhibition halls now open.

The Helicopter Museum
The Heliport, Locking Moor Road,
Weston-super-Mare BS24 8PP
t (01934) 635227 w helicoptermuseum.co.uk
open Apr-Jul, Wed-Sun 1000-1730. Aug, daily 1000-1730. Sep, Wed-Sun 1000-1730. Nov-Mar, Wed-Sun 1000-1630.
admission ££
Unique collection of helicopters and autogyros with displays on history, developments, how they work and their uses. The only helicopter museum in the UK and the largest in the world.

King John's Hunting Lodge
The Square, Axbridge BS26 2AP
t (01934) 732012 w nationaltrust.org.uk
open 21 Mar-30 Sep, daily 1300-1600.
admission Free
Early Tudor merchant's house extensively restored in 1971, now houses museum of local history and archaeology.

Montacute TV, Radio and Toy Museum
1 South Street, Montacute TA15 6XD
t (01935) 823024 w montacutemuseum.co.uk
open Apr-Oct, Wed-Sat, Bank Hols 1230-1700, Sun 1400-1700. Nov-Mar, please phone for details.
admission £
Memories of your favourite TV programmes brought to life through a vast collection of toys, books and games. Includes full-size Dr Who Dalek and Tardis.

Museum of South Somerset
Hendford, Yeovil BA20 1UN
t (01935) 462855 w southsomerset.gov.uk
open Apr-Oct, Mon-Sat 0900-1700. Nov-Mar, Mon-Fri 0900-1700.
admission Free
Collections of glassware, costumes, agricultural and domestic bygones, reconstructed period room and temporary exhibitions.

North Somerset Museum
Burlington Street, Weston-super-Mare BS23 1PR
t (01934) 621028 w n-somerset.gov.uk/museum
open All year, Mon-Sat, Bank Hols 1000-1630.
admission £
A family-friendly museum full of displays telling the story of the district, from pre-history to the present. Cafe and gift shop.

Perry's Cider Farm
Dowlish Wake TA19 0NY
t (01460) 55195 w perryscider.co.uk
open All year, Mon-Fri 0900-1730, Sat 0930-1630, Sun
1000-1300, Bank Hols 0930-1630.
admission Free
*Traditional working cider farm. Museum of presses,
wagons, farm tools, photographic displays and video on
cider-making in 16thC thatched barn. Shop selling cider,
apple juice, West Country foods and wines.*

Radstock, Midsomer Norton and District Museum
The Market Hall, Waterloo Road, Radstock BA3 3EP
t (01761) 437722 w radstockmuseum.co.uk
open Feb-Nov, Tue-Fri, Bank Hols 1400-1700, Sat
1100-1700.
admission £
*Features reconstructed coal face, miner's cottage,
Victorian schoolroom, 1930s Co-op, joiner's shop and
blacksmith.*

Shakspeare Glass
Foundry Road, Riverside Place, Taunton TA1 1JJ
t (01823) 333422 w shakspeareglass.co.uk
open All year, Mon, please phone for details, Tue-Sat
0900-1700.
admission Free
*Studio-glass workshop and gallery. One of the country's
leading studio-glass workshops showing a wide range of
Shakspeare's own work.*

Somerset & Dorset Railway Museum
Washford Station, Washford TA23 0PP
t (01984) 640869 w sdrt.org.uk
open See website for details.
admission £
*Museum of Somerset and Dorset Railway relics, working
replica signal box, collection of rolling stock including
three six-wheel S&D coaches, 'permanent way' display
and peat works railway display.*

Somerset Cricket Museum
7 Priory Avenue, Taunton TA1 1XX
t (01823) 275893
open Apr-Sep, Tue-Fri, match days 1030-1600.
admission £
*Display of Somerset County Cricket Club and other
cricket memorabilia housed in a renovated 16thC priory
barn.*

Somerset Rural Life Museum
Abbey Farm, Chilkwell Street, Glastonbury BA6 8DB
t (01458) 831197 w somerset.gov.uk/museums
open Apr-Oct, Tue-Fri 1000-1700, Sat-Sun 1400-1800.
Nov-Feb, Tue-Sat 1000-1700.
admission Free
*Magnificent 14thC abbey barn, also Victorian farmhouse
and yard. Permanent exhibitions. Events programme
throughout the summer.*

Wells Museum
8 Cathedral Green, Wells BA5 2UE
t (01749) 673477 w wellsmuseum.org.uk
open Apr-Oct, Mon-Sat, 1000-1730, Sun 1100-1600.
Nov-Mar, daily 1100-1600.
admission £
*Local archaeology and finds from the Mendip caves,
fossils from the South West, local and international
minerals, plus embroidery samplers and some Wells
Cathedral statues.*

West Somerset Rural Life Museum
The Old School, Allerford TA24 8HN
t (01643) 862529 w victorianschool.org.uk
open May-Oct, Wed-Fri 1030-1600, Sun, Bank Hols
1330-1600.
admission £
*Museum housed in the old school building with a large
hall, smaller Victorian schoolroom, thatched roof and
garden by the river. Exhibition of past local rural life.*

Weston Scooter Parts
77 Alfred St, Weston-super-Mare BS23 1PP
t (01934) 614614 w westonscooterparts.co.uk
open All year, Wed-Sat 1000-1730.
admission Free
*The world's only collection of Lambretta scooters, 61
models in all dating from 1947 to 1971.*

FOOD AND DRINK

Avalon Vineyard
The Little House, East Pennard BA4 6UA
t (01749) 860393 w pennardorganicwines.co.uk
open Daily, please phone for details.
admission Free
*Working organic vineyard and fruit farm. Purpose-built
winery and underground cellar. Self-guided vineyard
walk, free wine and cider tasting.*

Sheppy's Cider Farm Centre
Three Bridges Farm, Bradford-on-Tone,
Taunton TA4 1ER
t (01823) 461233 w sheppyscider.com
open Jan-Easter, Mon-Sat 0830-1800. Easter-Dec,
Mon-Sat 0830-1800, Sun 1100-1300.
admission £
*Visitors may wander through orchards, taste cider in the
farm shop and visit the farm/cider museum. Children's
play area. Licensed tearoom open June to September.*

The Somerset Distillery
Burrow Hill, Kingsbury Episcopi, Martock TA12 6BU
t (01460) 240782 w ciderbrandy.co.uk
open All year, Mon-Sat, Bank Hols 0900-1730.
admission Free
*Barrels of cider and Somerset Cider Brandy, all pressed
and distilled from vintage apples grown in Somerset.*

For key to symbols see page 171.

RELAXING AND PAMPERING

Clarks Village
Farm Road, Street BA16 0BB
t (01458) 840064 **w** clarksvillage.co.uk
open Apr-Oct, Mon-Wed, Fri, Sat 0900-1800, Thu
0900-2000. Nov-Mar, Mon-Wed, Fri, Sat 0900-1730,
Thu 0900-2000.
admission Free   💻 🎄 ⚹ 🕭
*Factory shopping village including over 80 high street
name outlets plus a variety of attractions including a
shoe museum, landscaped walkways, children's play
area and art studio.*

London Cigarette Card Company Showroom and Shop
West Street, Somerton TA11 7PR
t (01458) 273452 **w** londoncigcard.co.uk
open All year, Mon-Tue,Thu-Fri 0930-1300, 1400-1700,
Wed, Sat 0930-1300.
admission Free   ⚹ 🕭
*Largest display of collectable cards in Britain. See 4,500
different sets covering all kinds of subjects from 1880s
to the present day, plus valuation catalogues, storage
albums and frames.*

Wiltshire – Salisbury & Stonehenge

FAMILY FUN

Bush Farm Bison Centre
Bush Farm, West Knoyle BA12 6AE
t (01747) 830263 **w** bisonfarm.co.uk
open Apr-Sep, Wed-Sun 1000-1700.
admission ££   💻 🎄 ⚹ 🕭
*Bison, wapiti and red deer in 100 acres of grass fields
and 30 acres of old oak woods and gardens. Gallery of
North American wildlife and Native American artefacts.
Children's farmyard and play area.*

Cholderton Rare Breeds Farm Park
Amesbury Road, Cholderton, Salisbury SP4 0EW
t (01980) 629438 **w** choldertoncharliesfarm.com
open Apr-Sep, daily 1000-1800. Oct-Mar, daily
1000-1600.
admission ££   💻 🎄 🕭
*Rare breed farm animals, baby unit, rabbit world, indoor
play barn, nature trail, adventure playground, new cafe
and shop.*

Farmer Giles Farmstead
Teffont SP3 5QY
t (01722) 716338 **w** farmergiles.co.uk
open Apr-Oct, daily 1000-1800. Nov-Mar, Sat-Sun
1000-dusk.
admission £   💻 🎄 ⚹ 🕭
*Family leisure farm with large selection of animals, set in
acres of glorious rolling Wiltshire downland. Working
dairy farm. Watch cows being milked or bottle-feed lambs.*

Oasis Leisure Centre
North Star Avenue, Swindon SN2 1EP
t (01793) 445401 **w** swindon.gov.uk/oasis
open All year, Mon, Fri 0630-2300, Tue-Thu 0900-2300,
Sat 0800-1900, Sun 0800-2130, Bank Hols 0630-1800.
admission £   💻 ⚹ 🕭
*Lagoon pool with wave machine, water cannon, three
giant water slides, four outdoor multiplayer pitches and
soft play area.*

NATURE AND WILDLIFE

Abbey House Gardens
Market Cross, Malmesbury SN16 9AS
t (01666) 822212 **w** abbeyhousegardens.co.uk
open 21 Mar-21 Oct, daily 1100-1645.
admission ££   💻 🎄 ⚹ 🖼
*With over 10,000 different plants this is a 'must see'
garden with a special atmosphere. Alan Titchmarsh
claims that the WOW factor is here in abundance.*

The Courts
Holt BA14 6RR
t (01225) 782340
open Apr-Oct, Mon-Tue, Thu-Sun 1100-1730.
admission £   💻 ⚹ 🖼
*This delightful and tranquil seven-acre English country
garden is full of charm, variety and colour with herbaceous
borders, water gardens, topiary and arboretum.*

Heale Garden & Plant Centre
Middle Woodford SP4 6NT
t (01722) 782504 **w** greatbritishgardens.co.uk
open Feb-Oct, Wed-Sun 1000-1700.
admission £   💻 🎄 ⚹ 🖼
*Mature traditional garden with herbaceous borders,
exemplary kitchen garden and woodland garden with
authentic Japanese Teahouse, specimen trees, shrubs,
roses and famous February display of snowdrops and
aconites.*

Lackham Country Park
Wiltshire College Lackham, Lacock SN15 2NY
t (01249) 466800
w lackhamcountrypark.co.uk
open Aug, Mon-Fri, Sun 1000-1700.
admission £

Idyllically situated in the Wiltshire countryside. Discover formal and historic walled gardens, a rural-life museum housed in thatched buildings and woodland walks.

Larmer Tree Gardens
Tollard Royal SP5 5PT
t (01725) 516971
w larmertreegardens.co.uk
open Apr-Jun, Aug-Sep, Mon-Thu, Sun 1100-1630.
Oct-Nov, Feb-Mar, Mon-Thu 1100-1630.
admission £

These historical gardens of General Pitt Rivers are the secret gardens of Wiltshire. Rare and unusual planting and exhibits of General Pitt Rivers' work. Regular concerts and festivals.

The Peto Garden
Iford Manor, Bradford-on-Avon BA15 2BA
t (01225) 863146
w ifordmanor.co.uk
open May-Sep, Tue-Thu, Sat-Sun 1400-1700.
admission £

Italianate garden created by Harold Peto. This romantic hillside garden is characterised by pools, terraces, sculptures, evergreen planting and rural views.

Stourhead House and Garden
The National trust
The Estate Office,
Stourton BA12 6QD
t (01747) 841152
w nationaltrust.org.uk
open Garden: all year, daily 0900-1900. House:
Apr-Oct, Mon-Tue, Fri-Sun 1130-1630.
admission £££

Often referred to as 'Paradise', Stourhead is one of the finest 18thC landscape gardens in the world and Stourhead House is home to Chippendale furniture and a Regency library.

HISTORIC ENGLAND

Avebury Manor and Garden
Avebury SN8 1RF
t (01672) 539250
w nationaltrust.org.uk
open House: Apr-Oct, Mon-Tue, Sun 1400-1640.
Garden: Apr-Oct, Mon-Tue, Fri-Sun 1100-1700.
admission £

Manorhouse of monastic origins. Present buildings date from early 16thC with Queen Anne alterations and Edwardian renovations. Charming Edwardian garden laid out in a series of delightful outdoor 'rooms'.

Admission is based on an adult price. Please check opening times and admission before travelling.

Avebury Stone Circles

Avebury SN8 1RF
t (01672) 539250 w nationaltrust.org.uk
open Daily.
admission **Free**

Originally from 4,500 years ago, many of the stones were located and re-erected in the 1930s by Alexander Keiller. The circles and henge encircle part of the village.

Bowood House and Gardens

The Estate Office, Bowood, Calne SN11 0LZ
t (01249) 812102 w bowood.org
open Apr-Oct, daily 1100-1800.
admission **££**

An 18th century house by Robert Adam. Collections of paintings, watercolours, Victoriana and porcelain. Landscaped park with lake, terraces, waterfall and grotto.

Bratton Camp and White Horse

Westbury
t (01305) 820868 w english-heritage.org.uk
open See website for details.
admission **Free**

A large Iron Age hill fort and white horse carved into the hillside.

Broad Town White Horse

Broad Town, Wootton Bassett SN4 8JN
t (01380) 734669 w wiltshirewhitehorses.org.uk
open Daily.
admission **Free**

A white horse measuring 86ft by 61ft situated on the hill to the east of the village of Broad Town was completed in 1863 by a local farmer William Simmonds.

Chisbury Chapel

Chisbury
t (01305) 820868 w english-heritage.org.uk
open See website for details.
admission **Free**

Thatched 13thC chapel. Rescued in recent years having been used as a farm building.

Fisherton Delamere, St Nicholas

Fisherton de la Mere BA12 0PZ
t (020) 7213 0660
w visitchurches.org.uk
open Daily 0900-1700.
admission **Free**

The exterior of this 14thC church is constructed in a chequerboard pattern of flint and stone. Substantially reconstructed in the 19thC, it has an elegant Edwardian screen separating nave and chancel, and interesting monuments.

Inglesham St John the Baptist

Inglesham SN6 7RD
t (020) 7213 0660
w visitchurches.org.uk
open Daily 0900-1700.
admission **Free**

A church of Saxon origin with a powerful Saxon carving and seven centuries of wall paintings. The interior is much as it would have been in the 17th century.

Lacock Abbey

Lacock SN15 2LG
t (01249) 730459
w nationaltrust.org.uk
open 15 Mar-2 Nov, Mon, Wed-Sun 1300-1730.
admission **££**

Founded in the 13thC and converted into a country house c1540 when it became the home of the Talbot family. Medieval cloisters, 18thC Gothic hall and 16thC stable court.

Malmesbury Abbey

Parish Office, The Old Squash Court,
Malmesbury SN16 0AA
t (01666) 826666
w malmesburyabbey.com
open Daily 1000-1600.
admission **Free**

Norman/Romanesque abbey, now the parish church. Founded by St Aldhelm in Saxon times c676.

River Bybrook, Castle Combe

Mompesson House
The Close,
Salisbury SP1 2EL
t (01722) 335659
w nationaltrust.org.uk
open 15 Mar-2 Nov, Mon-Wed,
Sat-Sun 1100-1700.
admission £   💻 🍴 👜

Built c1701 for Charles Mompesson, the house has a graceful staircase and magnificent plasterwork. Collection of English 18thC drinking glasses. Delightful walled garden.

Old Sarum
Castle Road, Salisbury SP1 3SD
t (01722) 335398
w english-heritage.org.uk/oldsarum
open Apr-Jun, daily 1000-1700. Jul-Aug, daily 0900-1800. Sep, daily 1000-1700. Oct, daily 1000-1600. Nov-Feb, daily 1100-1500. Mar, daily 1000-1600.
admission £   👜

Huge ramparts and earthworks covering 56 acres. First an Iron Age hill fort, later inhabited by Romans, Saxons and Normans.

St Peter's Church, Marlborough
High Street,
Marlborough SN8 1HQ
t (01672) 511453
open All year, Mon-Sat 1000-1700,
Bank Hols 1100-1600.
admission Free   💻 ♿

Permanent art and crafts display, coffee and snacks in an historic redundant church.

Salisbury Cathedral
Visitor Services,
33 The Close,
Salisbury SP1 2EJ
t (01722) 555120
w salisburycathedral.org.uk
open Daily 0715-1815. 11 Jun-24 Aug, Mon-Sat, late opening until 1915.
admission Free   💻 🎪 ♿

In 2008 the Cathedral celebrates the 750th anniversary of its dedication in 1258. Events include: Cathedral open day (26 April), medieval fair (5 May), flower festival (17-21 June) and more.

Ancient stone circle, Stonehenge

For key to symbols see page 171.

Sheldon Manor Gardens
Sheldon Manor, Chippenham SN14 0RG
t (01249) 653120
w sheldonmanor.co.uk
open Apr-Oct, Thu, Sun, Bank Hols 1400-1800.
admission £

Sheldon Manor is Wiltshire's oldest inhabited manorhouse with a 13thC porch and a 15thC chapel. Gardens with ancient yews, a mulberry tree and a profusion of old-fashioned roses blooming in May and June.

Stonehenge
Amesbury SP4 7DE
t 0870 333 1181
w english-heritage.org.uk/stonehenge
open See website for details.
admission ££

World-famous prehistoric monument built as a ceremonial centre. Started 5,000 years ago and remodelled several times over the next 1,500 years.

Wilton House
The Estate Office, Wilton SP2 0BJ
t (01722) 746720
w wiltonhouse.com
open House: Easter, Apr-Aug, Sun-Thu, Bank Hols 1200-1730. Sep, Tue, Wed, Thu 1200-1730. Garden: Easter, Apr-Sep, daily 1100-1730.
admission £££

Magnificent state rooms, world famous art collection, introductory film, recreated Victorian laundry and Tudor kitchen, landscaped parks, gardens and adventure playground.

River Kennet, Marlborough

OUTDOOR ACTIVITIES

Kennet and Avon Canal Boat Trips
K & A Cottage by Lock, 15 Frome Road,
Bradford-on-Avon BA15 1LE
t (01225) 868683 **w** katrust.org
open Please phone for details.
admission £

Boat trips along the Kennet and Avon canal. Travel along the scenic Avon Valley and Avoncliff aqueduct.

ENTERTAINMENT AND CULTURE

Alexander Keiller Museum
High Street, Avebury SN8 1RF
t (01672) 529203 **w** nationaltrust.org.uk
open See website for details.
admission £

One of the most important prehistoric archaeological collections in Britain. Includes the National Trust's Barn Gallery, which uses interactive exhibits to tell the story of the landscape and its people over the past 6,000 years.

Athelstan Museum
Cross Hayes, Malmesbury SN16 9BZ
t (01666) 829258 **w** northwilts.gov.uk
open Apr-Oct, daily 1030-1630. Nov-Mar, daily 1130-1530.
admission Free

Exhibits of local history including coins minted in Malmesbury, lace-making displays, early fire engines and tricycles and a drawing of Malmesbury by Thomas Girtin.

Atwell-Wilson Motor Museum Trust
Downside, Stockley Lane, Calne SN11 0NF
t (01249) 813119 **w** atwellwilson.org.uk
open Apr-Oct, Mon-Thu, Sun 1100-1700. Nov-Mar, Mon-Thu, Sun 1100-1600.
admission £

Motor museum with vintage, post-vintage and classic cars, including American models and classic motorbikes. Water meadow walk. Car clubs welcome for rallies. Play area.

Fox Talbot Museum of Photography
Lacock SN15 2LG
t (01249) 730459 **w** nationaltrust.org.uk/lacock
open Apr-Oct, Mar, daily 1100-1730. Nov-Feb, Sat-Sun 1100-1600.
admission ££

Displays of apparatus and photographs related to Fox Talbot. Gallery with changing exhibitions each season.

The Kennet and Avon Canal Museum
The Canal Centre, Couch Lane, Devizes SN10 1EB
t (01380) 721279 **w** katrust.org
open Apr-Sep, daily 1000-1700. Winter: Please phone for details.
admission £
Exhibition telling of the creation of the waterways link connecting London and Bristol, which emerged as a direct result of the Industrial Revolution.

The Royal Gloucestershire, Berkshire and Wiltshire Regiment (Salisbury) Museum
The Wardrobe, 58 The Close, Salisbury SP1 2EX
t (01722) 414536 **w** thewardrobe.org.uk
open Feb-Mar, Tue-Sun 1000-1700. Apr-Oct, daily, Bank Hols 1000-1700. Nov, Tue-Sun 1000-1700.
admission £
Collections include Victoria Crosses, uniforms, weapons and militaria. Buildings of historic interest and landscaped garden.

Salisbury and South Wiltshire Museum
The King's House, 65 The Close, Salisbury SP1 2EN
t (01722) 332151 **w** salisburymuseum.org.uk
open Apr-Jun, Mon-Sat 1000-1700. Jul-Aug, Mon-Sat 1000-1700, Sun 1400-1700. Sep-Mar, Mon-Sat 1000-1700.
admission £
Grade I Listed building. Home of the award-winning Stonehenge Gallery. Fascinating displays of history of Salisbury, costume, ceramics, pictures and changing temporary exhibitions. All in the glorious setting of Salisbury Cathedral Close.

STEAM – Museum of the Great Western Railway

Kemble Drive, Swindon SN2 2TA
t (01793) 466646 **w** swindon.gov.uk/steam
open All year, daily 1000-1700.
admission ££
Displays celebrating the Great Western Railway include footplate access on locomotives and detailed reconstructions of life on the railways.

Swindon Museum and Art Gallery
Bath Road, Swindon SN1 4BA
t (01793) 466556 **w** swindon.gov.uk
open All year, Mon-Sat 1000-1700.
admission Free
Changing exhibitions of 20thC and 21stC British art and studio ceramics. Collections include works by LS Lowry, Richard Hamilton, Lisa Milroy and Lucie Rie. Museum displays history, archaeology and geology of Swindon area.

Trowbridge Museum
The Shires, Court Street, Trowbridge BA14 8AT
t (01225) 751339 **w** trowbridgemuseum.co.uk
open All year, Tue-Fri 1000-1600, Sat 1000-1630.
admission £
The history of Trowbridge and its people. Includes working looms and displays on the West of England woollen industry and local history. Housed in a former woollen mill.

RELAXING AND PAMPERING

Swindon Designer Outlet
Kemble Drive, Swindon SN2 2DY
t (01793) 507622 **w** swindondesigneroutlet.com
open All year, Mon-Wed, Fri 1000-1800, Thu 1000-2000, Sat 1000-1900, Sun 1000-1700.
admission Free
McArthurGlen Great Western is the largest undercover outlet, offering top brand names at up to 50% off high street prices.

Wilton Shopping Village
Wilton, Salisbury SP2 0RS
t (01722) 741211 **w** wiltonshoppingvillage.co.uk
open All year, Mon-Sat 0930-1730, Sun 1030-1630.
admission Free
The whole family will enjoy a visit to the unique riverside setting of Wilton Shopping Village and its beautifully restored 18thC courtyard. Take a tour of the world-famous Wilton Carpet Factory.

Salisbury Cathedral

Further information

Stonehenge, Wiltshire

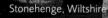

Enjoy England
Quality Rose scheme

When you're looking for a place to stay, you need a rating system you can trust. Enjoy England ratings are your clear guide to what to expect, in an easy-to-understand form.

Enjoy England professional assessors pay unannounced visits to establishments that are new to the rating scheme and stay overnight where appropriate. Once in the scheme establishments receive an annual pre-arranged day visit, with an overnight stay generally every other year for hotel and B&B guest accommodation. On these occasions the assessors book in anonymously, and test all the facilities and services.

Based on internationally recognised star ratings, the system puts great emphasis on quality, and reflects exactly what consumers are looking for. Ratings are awarded from one to five stars – the more stars, the higher the quality and the greater the range of facilities and services provided – and are the sign of quality assurance, giving you the confidence to book the accommodation that meets your expectations.

Look out, too, for Enjoy England Gold and Silver Awards, which are awarded to hotels and guest accommodation achieving the highest levels of quality within their star rating. While the overall rating is based on a combination of facilities and quality, the Gold and Silver Awards are based solely on quality.

Hotels

All hotels that are awarded a star rating will meet the minimum standards – so you can be confident that you will find the basic services that you would expect, such as:

- All bedrooms with an en suite or private bathroom
- A designated reception facility and staff members who will be available during the day and evening (24hrs in case of an emergency)
- A licence to serve alcohol (unless a temperance hotel)
- Access to the hotel at all times for registered guests

- Dinner available at least five days a week (with the exception of a Town House Hotel or Metro Hotel)
- All statutory obligations will be met.

Hotels have to provide certain additional facilities and services at the higher star levels, some of which may be important to you:

TWO-STAR hotels must provide:
- Dinner seven nights a week.

THREE-STAR hotels must provide:
- All en suite bedrooms (ie no private bathrooms)
- Direct dial phones in all rooms
- Room service during core hours
- A permanently staffed reception.

FOUR-STAR hotels must provide:
- 24-hour room service
- 50% of all en suites with bath **and** shower.

FIVE-STAR hotels must provide:
- Some permanent suites
- Enhanced services, such as concierge.

Sometimes a hotel with a lower star rating has exceptional bedrooms and bathrooms and offers its guests a very special welcome, but cannot achieve a higher rating because, for example, it does not offer dinner every evening (two star), room service (three star) or does not have the minimum 50% of bathrooms with bath and shower (four star).

Quality
The availability of additional services alone is not enough for an establishment to achieve a higher star rating. Hotels have to meet exacting standards for quality in critical areas. Consumer research has shown the critical areas to be: cleanliness, bedrooms, bathrooms, hospitality and service, and food.

Awaiting confirmation of rating
At the time of going to press some establishments/parks featured in this guide had not yet been assessed and so their new rating could not be included. Rating Applied For indicates this.

Guest accommodation

All guest accommodation that is awarded a star rating will meet the minimum standards – so you can be confident that you will find the basic services that you would expect, such as:

- A clear explanation of booking charges, services offered and cancellation terms
- A full cooked breakfast or substantial continental breakfast
- At least one bathroom or shower room for every six guests
- For a stay of more than one night, rooms cleaned and beds made daily
- Printed advice on how to summon emergency assistance at night
- All statutory obligations will be met.

Proprietors of guest accommodation have to provide certain additional facilities and services at the higher star levels, some of which may be important to you:

THREE-STAR accommodation must provide:
- Private bathroom/shower room (cannot be shared with the owners)
- Bedrooms must have a washbasin if not en suite.

FOUR-STAR accommodation must provide:
- 50% of bedrooms en suite or with private bathroom.

FIVE-STAR accommodation must provide:
- All bedrooms with en suite or private bathroom.

Sometimes guest accommodation has exceptional bedrooms and bathrooms and offers visitors a very special welcome, but cannot achieve a higher star rating because, for example, there are no en suite bedrooms, or it is difficult to put washbasins in the bedrooms (three star). This is sometimes the case with period properties.

Quality
The availability of additional facilities alone is not enough for an establishment to achieve a higher star rating. Guest accommodation has to meet exacting standards for quality in critical areas. Consumer research has shown the critical areas to be: cleanliness, bedrooms, bathrooms, hospitality and food.

Self-catering accommodation

All self-catering accommodation that is awarded a star rating will meet the minimum standards – so you can be confident that you will find the basic services that you would expect, such as:

- Clear information prior to booking on all aspects of the accommodation including location, facilities, prices, deposit, policies on smoking, children etc
- No shared facilities, with the exception of a laundry room in multi-unit sites
- All appliances and furnishings will meet product safety standards for self-catering accommodation, particularly regarding fire safety
- At least one smoke alarm in the unit and a fire blanket in the kitchen
- Clear information on emergency procedures
- Contact details for the local doctor, dentist etc
- All statutory obligations will be met including an annual gas check and public liability insurance.

Certain additional facilities and services are required at the higher star levels:

TWO-STAR accommodation must provide:
- Single beds which are a minimum of 3ft wide and double beds a minimum of 4ft 6in.

THREE-STAR accommodation must provide:
- Bed linen (with or without additional charge).

FOUR-STAR accommodation must provide:
- All sleeping space in bedrooms, unless a studio (bed settees can not be advertised)
- Bed linen included in the hire charge and beds are made up for arrival.

FIVE-STAR accommodation must provide:
- At least two of the following items: tumble-dryer, telephone, Hi-Fi, video, DVD.

Some self-catering establishments offer a choice of units that may have different star ratings. In this case, the entry shows the range.

Quality
The availability of additional facilities, such as a dishwasher or DVD, is not enough to achieve a higher star rating – the quality of the furnishings, equipment and decoration must be of a high standard. Self-catering accommodation with a lower star rating may offer some or all of the above, but to achieve the higher star ratings, the overall quality score has to be reached and exacting standards have to be met in critical areas. Consumer research has shown these to be: cleanliness, bedrooms, bathrooms, kitchens and public areas.

The British Graded Holiday Park Scheme

When you're looking for a place to stay, you need a rating system you can trust. The British Graded Holiday Parks Scheme, operated jointly by the national tourist boards for England, Scotland, Wales and Northern Ireland, was devised in association with the British Holiday and Home Parks Association and the National Caravan Council. It gives you a clear guide of what to expect in an easy-to-understand form.

The process to arrive at a star rating is very thorough to ensure that when you make a booking you can be confident it will meet your expectations. Professional assessors visit parks annually and take into account over 50 separate aspects, from landscaping and layout to maintenance, customer care and, most importantly, cleanliness.

Strict guidelines are in place to ensure that every park is assessed to the same criteria. A random check is made of a sample of accommodation provided for hire (caravans, chalets etc) but the quality of the accommodation itself is not included in the grading assessment.

In addition to The British Graded Holiday Parks Scheme, VisitBritain operates a rating scheme for Holiday Villages. The assessor stays on the site overnight and grades the overall quality of the visitor experience, including accommodation, facilities, cleanliness, service and food.

So you can rest assured that when you choose a star-rated park or holiday village you won't be disappointed.

Star ratings

Parks are required to meet progressively higher standards of quality as they move up the scale from one to five stars:

ONE STAR Acceptable
To achieve this grade, the park must be clean with good standards of maintenance and customer care.

TWO STARS Good
All the above points plus an improved level of landscaping, lighting, refuse disposal and maintenance. May be less expensive than more highly rated parks.

THREE STARS Very good
Most parks fall within this category; three stars represent the industry standard. The range of facilities provided may vary from park to park, but they will be of a very good standard and will be well maintained.

FOUR STARS Excellent
You can expect careful attention to detail in the provision of all services and facilities. Four-star parks rank among the industry's best.

FIVE STARS Exceptional
Highest levels of customer care will be provided. All facilities will be maintained in pristine condition in attractive surroundings.

Advice and information

Making a booking

When enquiring about accommodation, make sure you check prices, the quality rating and other important details. You will also need to state your requirements clearly and precisely, for example:

- Arrival and departure dates, with acceptable alternatives if appropriate
- The type of accommodation you need – for example, room with twin beds, en suite bathroom
- The terms you want – for example, room only, bed and breakfast
- The age of any children with you, whether you want them to share your room or be next door, and any other requirements, such as a cot
- Any particular requirements you may have, such as a special diet, ground-floor room.

Confirmation

Misunderstandings can easily happen over the telephone, so do request a written confirmation, together with details of any terms and conditions.

Deposits

If you make a hotel or guest accommodation reservation weeks or months in advance, you will probably be asked for a deposit, which will then be deducted from the final bill when you leave. The amount will vary from establishment to establishment and could be payment in full at peak times.

Proprietors of self-catering accommodation will normally ask you to pay a deposit immediately, and then to pay the full balance before your holiday date. This safeguards the proprietor in case you decide to cancel at a late stage or simply do not turn up. He or she may have turned down other bookings on the strength of yours and may find it hard to re-let if you cancel.

In the case of camping and caravan parks the full charge often has to be paid in advance. This may be in two instalments – a deposit at the time of booking and the balance by, say, two weeks before the start of the booked period.

Payment on arrival

Some establishments, especially large hotels in big towns, ask you to pay for your room on arrival if you have not booked it in advance. This is especially likely to happen if you arrive late and have little or no luggage.

If you are asked to pay on arrival, it is a good idea to see your room first, to make sure it meets your requirements.

Cancellations

Legal contract

When you accept accommodation that is offered to you, by telephone or in writing, you enter a legally binding contract with the proprietor. This means that if you cancel your booking, fail to take up the accommodation or leave early, the proprietor may be entitled to compensation if he or she cannot re-let for all or a good part of the booked period. You will probably forfeit any deposit you have paid, and may well be asked for an additional payment.

At the time of booking you should be advised of what charges would be made in the event of cancelling the accommodation or leaving early. If this is not mentioned you should ask so that future disputes can be avoided. The proprietor cannot make a claim until after the booked period, and during that time he or she should make every effort to re-let the accommodation. If there is a dispute it is sensible for both sides to seek legal advice on the matter. If you do have to change your travel plans, it is in your own interests to let the proprietor know in writing as soon as possible, to give them a chance to re-let your accommodation.

And remember, if you book by telephone and are asked for your credit card number, you should check whether the proprietor intends charging your credit card account should you later cancel your reservation. A proprietor should not be able to charge your credit card account with a cancellation fee unless he or she has made this clear at the time of your booking and you have agreed. However, to avoid later disputes, we suggest you check whether this is the intention.

Insurance

A travel or holiday insurance policy will safeguard you if you have to cancel or change your holiday plans. You can arrange a policy quite cheaply through your insurance company or travel agent. Some hotels also offer their own insurance schemes and many self-catering agencies insist their customers take out a policy when they book their holidays.

Arrival time

If you know you will be arriving late in the evening, it is a good idea to say so when you book. If you are delayed on your way, a telephone call to say that you will be late would be appreciated.

It is particularly important to liaise with the owner of self-catering accommodation about key collection as he or she will not necessarily be on site.

Service charges and tipping

These days many places levy service charges automatically. If they do, they must clearly say so in their offer of accommodation, at the time of booking. The service charge then becomes part of the legal contract when you accept the offer of accommodation.

If a service charge is levied automatically, there is no need to tip the staff, unless they provide some exceptional service. The usual tip for meals is 10% of the total bill.

Telephone charges

Establishments can set their own charges for telephone calls made through their switchboard or from direct-dial telephones in bedrooms. These charges are often much higher than telephone companies' standard charges (to defray the cost of providing the service).

Comparing costs

It is a condition of the Enjoy England Quality Rose assessment scheme that an establishment's unit charges are on display by the telephones or with the room information. It is not always easy to compare these charges with standard rates, so before using a telephone for long-distance calls, you may decide to ask how the charges compare.

Security of valuables

You can deposit your valuables with the proprietor or manager during your stay, and we recommend you do this as a sensible precaution. Make sure you obtain a receipt for them. Some places do not accept articles for safe custody, and in that case it is wisest to keep your valuables with you.

Disclaimer

Some proprietors put up a notice that disclaims liability for property brought on to their premises by a guest. In fact, they can only restrict their liability to a minimum laid down by law (The Hotel Proprietors Act 1956). Under that Act, a proprietor is liable for the value of the loss or damage to any property (except a car or its contents) of a guest who has engaged overnight accommodation, but if the proprietor has the notice on display as prescribed under that Act, liability is limited to £50 for one article and a total of £100 for any one guest. The notice must be prominently displayed in the reception area or main entrance. These limits do not apply to valuables you have deposited with the proprietor for safekeeping, or to property lost through the default, neglect or wilful act of the proprietor or his staff.

Bringing pets to England

Dogs, cats, ferrets and some other pet mammals can be brought into the UK from certain countries without having to undertake six months' quarantine on arrival provided they meet all the rules of the Pet Travel Scheme (PETS).

For full details, visit the PETS website at
w defra.gov.uk/animalh/quarantine/index.htm or contact the PETS Helpline
t +44 (0)870 241 1710
e quarantine@animalhealth.gsi.gov.uk
Ask for fact sheets which cover dogs and cats, ferrets or domestic rabbits and rodents.

What to expect

Hotels, guest and self-catering accommodation, holiday villages
The proprietor/management is required to undertake the following:

- To maintain standards of guest care, cleanliness and service appropriate to the type of establishment;

- To describe accurately in any advertisement, brochure or other printed or electronic media, the facilities and services provided;

- To make clear to visitors exactly what is included in all prices quoted for accommodation, including taxes, and any other surcharges. Details of charges for additional services/facilities should also be made clear;

- To give a clear statement of the policy on cancellations to guests at the time of booking ie by telephone, fax, email, as well as information given in a printed format;

- To adhere to and not to exceed prices quoted at the time of booking for accommodation and other services;

- To advise visitors at the time of booking, and subsequently if any change, if the accommodation offered is in an unconnected annexe or similar and to indicate the location of such accommodation and any difference in comfort and/or amenities from accommodation in the establishment;

- To register all guests on arrival (except self-catering accommodation);

- To give each visitor on request details of payments due and a receipt, if required;

- To deal promptly and courteously with all enquiries, requests, bookings and correspondence from visitors;

- To ensure complaint handling procedures are in place and that complaints received are investigated promptly and courteously and that the outcome is communicated to the visitor;

- To give due consideration to the requirements of visitors with disabilities and visitors with special needs, and to make suitable provision where applicable;

- To provide public liability insurance or comparable arrangements and to comply with all applicable planning, safety and other statutory requirements;

- To allow an Enjoy England assessor reasonable access to the establishment on request, to confirm the VisitBritain Code of Conduct is being observed.

What to expect

Caravan and camping parks

In addition to fulfilling its statutory obligations, including having applied for a certificate under the Fire Precautions Act 1971 (if applicable) and holding public liability insurance, and ensuring that all caravan holiday homes/chalets for hire and the park and all buildings and facilities thereon, the fixtures, furnishings, fittings and decor are maintained in sound and clean condition and are fit for the purposes intended, the management is required to undertake the following:

- To ensure high standards of courtesy, cleanliness, catering and service appropriate to the type of park;

- To describe to all visitors and prospective visitors the amenities, facilities and services provided by the park and/or caravan holiday homes/chalets whether by advertisement, brochure, word of mouth or other means;

- To allow visitors to see the park or caravan holiday homes/chalets for hire, if requested, before booking;

- To present grading awards and/or any other national tourist board awards unambiguously;

- To make clear to visitors exactly what is included in prices quoted for the park or caravan holiday homes/chalets, meals and refreshments, including service charge, taxes and other surcharges. Details of charges, if any, for heating or for additional services or facilities available should also be made clear;

- To adhere to, and not to exceed, prices current at time of occupation for caravan holiday homes/chalets or other services;

- To advise visitors at the time of booking, and subsequently if any change, if the caravan holiday home/chalet or pitch offered is in a different location or on another park, and to indicate the location of this and any difference in comfort and amenities;

- To give each visitor, on request, details of payments due and a receipt if required;

- To advise visitors at the time of booking of the charges that might be incurred if the booking is subsequently cancelled;

- To register all guests on arrival;

- To deal promptly and courteously with all visitors and prospective visitors, including enquiries, requests, reservations, correspondence and complaints;

- To allow a national tourist board representative reasonable access to the park and/or caravan holiday homes/chalet whether by prior appointment or on an unannounced assessment, to confirm that the VisitBritain Code of Conduct is being observed and that the appropriate quality standard is being maintained;

- The operator must comply with the provision of the caravan industry Codes of Practice.

Comments and complaints

The law

Places that offer accommodation have legal and statutory responsibilities to their customers, such as providing information about prices, providing adequate fire precautions and safeguarding valuables. Like other businesses, they must also abide by the Trades Description Acts 1968 and 1972 when they describe their accommodation and facilities. All the places featured in this guide have declared that they do fulfil all applicable statutory obligations.

Information

The proprietors themselves supply the descriptions of their establishments and other information for the entries, (except Enjoy England ratings and awards). VisitBritain cannot guarantee the accuracy of information in this guide, and accepts no responsibility for any error or misrepresentation. All liability for loss, disappointment, negligence or other damage caused by reliance on the information contained in this guide, or in the event of bankruptcy or liquidation or cessation of trade of any company, individual or firm mentioned, is hereby excluded. We strongly recommend that you carefully check prices and other details when you book your accommodation.

Quality Rose signage

All establishments/parks displaying a Quality Rose sign have to hold current membership of an Enjoy England Quality Rose assessment scheme or The British Graded Holiday Parks Scheme. When an establishment is sold the new owner has to reapply and be reassessed.

Problems

Of course, we hope you will not have cause for complaint, but problems do occur from time to time. If you are dissatisfied with anything, make your complaint to the management immediately. Then the management can take action at once to investigate the matter and put things right. The longer you leave a complaint, the harder it is to deal with it effectively.

In certain circumstances, VisitBritain may look into complaints. However, VisitBritain has no statutory control over establishments or their methods of operating. VisitBritain cannot become involved in legal or contractual matters, nor can they get involved in seeking financial recompense.

If you do have problems that have not been resolved by the proprietor and which you would like to bring to our attention, please write to: Quality in Tourism, Farncombe House, Broadway, Worcestershire WR12 7LJ.

Gold and Silver Awards

VisitBritain's unique Gold and Silver Awards recognise exceptional quality in serviced accommodation.

Enjoy England assessors make recommendations for Gold and Silver Awards during assessments in recognition of levels of quality over and above that expected of a particular rating.

Look for the Gold and Silver Awards in the regional sections.

About the guide entries

Entries

All the establishments/parks featured in this guide have been assessed or have applied for assessment under an Enjoy England Quality Rose assessment scheme or The British Graded Holiday Parks Scheme.

Proprietors have paid to have their establishment/park featured in either a standard entry (includes description, facilities and prices) or enhanced entry (photograph and extended details).

Locations

Places to stay are generally listed under the town, city or village where they are located. If a place is in a small village, you may find it listed under a nearby town (providing it is within a seven-mile radius).

Place names are listed alphabetically within each regional section of the guide, along with the ceremonial county they are in and their map reference.

Complete addresses for self-catering properties are not given and the town(s) listed may be a distance from the actual establishment. Please check the precise location at the time of booking.

Map references

These refer to the colour location maps at the front of the guide. The first figure shown is the map number, the following letter and figure indicate the grid reference on the map. Some entries were included just before the guide went to press, so they do not appear on the maps.

Addresses

County names, which appear in the place headings, are not repeated in the entries. When you are writing, you should of course make sure you use the full address and postcode.

Telephone numbers

Telephone numbers are listed below the accommodation address for each entry. Area codes are shown in brackets.

Prices

The prices shown are only a general guide; they were supplied to us by proprietors in summer 2007. Remember, changes may occur after the guide goes to press, so we strongly advise you to check prices when you book your accommodation.

Prices are shown in pounds sterling and include VAT where applicable. Some places also include a service charge in their standard tariff, so check this when you book.

Bed and breakfast: the prices shown are per room for overnight accommodation with breakfast. The double room price is for two people. (If a double room is occupied by one person there is sometimes a reduction in price.)

Half board: the prices shown are per person per night for room, evening meal and breakfast. These prices are usually based on two people sharing a room.

Evening meal: the prices shown are per person per night.

Some places only provide a continental breakfast in the set price, and you may have to pay extra if you want a full English breakfast.

According to the law, establishments with at least four bedrooms or eight beds must display their overnight accommodation charges in the reception area or entrance. In your own interests, do make sure you check prices and what they include.

Self catering: prices shown are per unit per week and include VAT.

Camping: Touring pitches are based on the minimum and maximum charges for one night for two persons, car and either caravan or tent. (Some parks may charge separately for car, caravan or tent, and for each person and there may be an extra charge for caravan awnings.) Minimum and maximum prices for caravan holiday homes are given per week.

Children's rates

You will find that many places charge a reduced rate for children, especially if they share a room with their parents. Some places charge the full rate, however, when a child occupies a room which might otherwise have been let to an adult. The upper age limit for reductions for children varies from one hotel to another, so check this when you book.

Seasonal packages and special promotions

Prices often vary through the year and may be significantly lower outside peak holiday weeks. Many places offer special package rates – fully inclusive weekend breaks, for example – in the autumn, winter and spring. A number of establishments taking an enhanced entry have included any special offers, themed breaks etc that are available.

You can get details of other bargain packages that may be available from the establishments themselves, regional tourism organisations or your local Tourist Information Centre (TIC). Your local travel agent may also have information and can help you make reservations.

Bathrooms (hotels and guest accommodation)

Each accommodation entry shows you the number of en suite and private bathrooms available. En suite bathroom means the bath or shower and wc are contained behind the main door of the bedroom. Private bathroom means a bath or shower and wc solely for the occupants of one bedroom, on the same floor, reasonably close and with a key provided. If the availability of a bath, rather than a shower, is important to you, remember to check when you book.

Meals (hotels and guest accommodation)

It is advisable to check availability of meals and set times when making your reservation. Some smaller places may ask you at breakfast whether you want an evening meal. The prices shown in each entry are for bed and breakfast or half board, but many places also offer lunch.

Chalets/villas for hire (camping and caravan parks)

Where a site has chalets or villas for hire this is indicated by this symbol ⛺. Please note that this type of accommodation is not necessarily included within the official quality rating for the park and it is advisable that you contact the proprietor directly if you require further information.

Opening period

If an entry does not indicate an opening period, please check directly with the establishment.

Symbols

The at-a-glance symbols included at the end of each entry show many of the services and facilities available at each establishment. You will find the key to these symbols on the back-cover flap – open it out and check the meanings as you go.

Smoking

In the UK, it is illegal to smoke in enclosed public spaces and places of work. This means that smoking is banned in the public and communal areas of hotels, guesthouses and B&Bs, and in restaurants, bars and pubs.

Some hotels, guesthouses and B&Bs may choose to provide designated smoking bedrooms, and B&Bs and guest houses may allow smoking in private areas not used by any staff. Smoking may also be permitted in self-catering accommodation if the owner chooses to allow it. If you wish to smoke, it is advisable to check whether it is allowed when you book.

Alcoholic drinks

All hotels (except temperance hotels) hold an alcohol licence. Some guest accommodation may also be licensed, however, the licence may be restricted – to diners only, for example. If a bar is available this is shown by the ♥ symbol.

Pets

Many places accept guests with dogs, but we do advise that you check this when you book, and ask if there are any extra charges or rules about exactly where your pet is allowed. The acceptance of dogs is not always extended to cats and it is strongly advised that pet owners contact the establishment well in advance. Some establishments do not accept pets at all. Pets are welcome by arrangement where you see this symbol 🐕.

The quarantine laws have changed in England, and dogs, cats and ferrets are able to come into Britain from over 50 countries. For details of the Pet Travel Scheme (PETS) please turn to page 228.

Payment accepted

The types of payment accepted by an establishment are listed in the payment accepted section. If you plan to pay by card, check that the establishment will take your particular card before you book. Some proprietors will charge you a higher rate if you pay by credit card rather than cash or cheque. The difference is to cover the percentage paid by the proprietor to the credit card company. When you book by telephone, you may be asked for your credit card number as confirmation. But remember, the proprietor may then charge your credit card account if you cancel your booking. See under Cancellations on page 227.

Getting to the South West

England is a country of perfect proportions – big enough to find a new place to discover, yet small enough to guarantee it's within easy reach. Getting from A to B can be easier than you think...

Planning your journey

Make transportdirect.info your first portal of call! It's the ultimate journey-planning tool to help you find the best way from your home to your destination by car or public transport. Decide on the quickest way to travel by comparing end-to-end journey times and routes. You can even buy train and coach tickets and find out about flights from a selection of airports.

With so many low-cost domestic flights, flying really is an option. Just imagine, you could finish work in Bristol and be in Newcastle just over an hour later for a fun-packed weekend!

If you're travelling by car and want an idea of distances check out the mileage chart overleaf. Or let the train take the strain – the National Rail network is also shown overleaf.

Think green

If you'd rather leave your car behind and travel by 'green transport' when visiting some of the attractions highlighted in this guide you'll be helping to reduce congestion and pollution as well as supporting conservation charities in their commitment to green travel.

The National Trust encourages visits made by non-car travellers. It offers admission discounts or a voucher for the tea room at a selection of its properties if you arrive on foot, cycle or public transport. (You'll need to produce a valid bus or train ticket if travelling by public transport.)

More information about The National Trust's work to encourage car-free days out can be found at nationaltrust.org.uk. Refer to the section entitled Information for Visitors.

To help you on your way you'll find a list of useful contacts at the end of this section.

By car and by train

Distance chart

The distances between towns on the chart below are given to the nearest mile, and are measured along routes based on the quickest travelling time, making maximum use of motorways or dual-carriageway roads. The chart is based upon information supplied by the Automobile Association.

To calculate the distance in kilometres multiply the mileage by 1.6

For example: Brighton to Dover
82 miles x 1.6 =131.2 kilometres

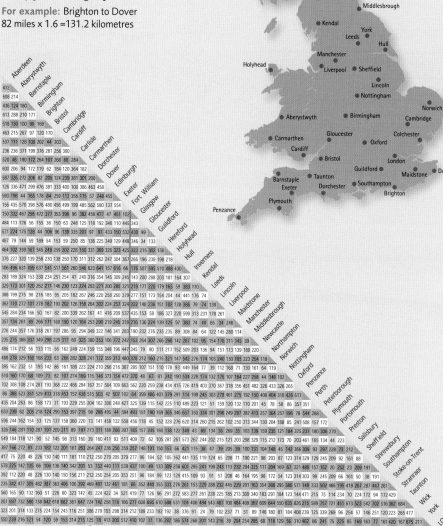

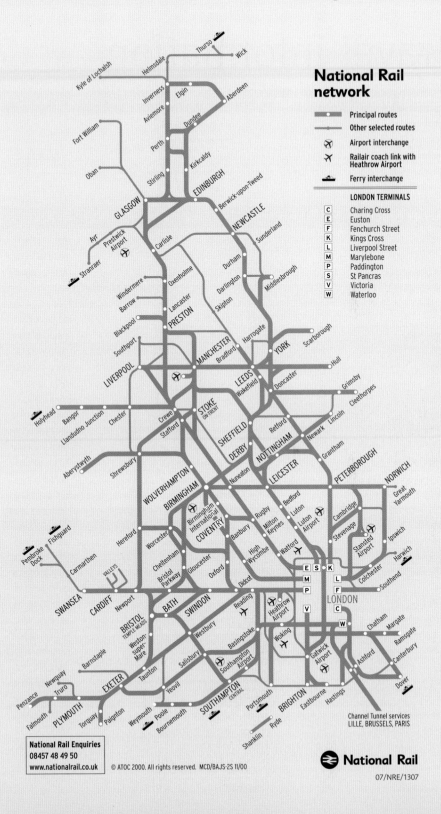

National Rail network

- ▭ Principal routes
- ── Other selected routes
- ✈ Airport interchange
- ✈ Railair coach link with Heathrow Airport
- ⛴ Ferry interchange

LONDON TERMINALS

C	Charing Cross
E	Euston
F	Fenchurch Street
K	Kings Cross
L	Liverpool Street
M	Marylebone
P	Paddington
S	St Pancras
V	Victoria
W	Waterloo

Channel Tunnel services
LILLE, BRUSSELS, PARIS

National Rail Enquiries
08457 48 49 50
www.nationalrail.co.uk   © ATOC 2000. All rights reserved. MCD/BAJS-2S 11/00

🚅 **National Rail**

07/NRE/1307

Travel information

General travel information

Streetmap	streetmap.co.uk	
Transport Direct	transportdirect.info	
Transport for London	tfl.gov.uk	(020) 7222 1234
Travel Services	departures-arrivals.com	
Traveline	traveline.org.uk	0870 200 2233

Bus & coach

Megabus	megabus.com	0901 331 0031
National Express	nationalexpress.com	0870 580 8080
WA Shearings	washearings.com	(01942) 824824

Car & car hire

AA	theaa.com	0870 600 0371
Green Flag	greenflag.co.uk	0845 246 1557
RAC	rac.co.uk	0870 572 2722
Alamo	alamo.co.uk	0870 400 4562*
Avis	avis.co.uk	0844 581 0147*
Budget	budget.co.uk	0844 581 2231
Easycar	easycar.com	0906 333 3333
Enterprise	enterprise.co.uk	0870 350 3000*
Hertz	hertz.co.uk	0870 844 8844*
Holiday Autos	holidayautos.co.uk	0870 400 4461
National	nationalcar.co.uk	0870 400 4581
Thrifty	thrifty.co.uk	(01494) 751500

Air

Airport information	a2btravel.com/airports	0870 888 1710
Air Southwest	airsouthwest.com	0870 043 4553
Blue Islands (Channel Islands)	blueislands.com	0845 620 2122
BMI	flybmi.com	0870 607 0555
BMI Baby	bmibaby.com	0871 224 0224
British Airways	ba.com	0870 850 9850
British International (Isles of Scilly to Penzance)	islesofscillyhelicopter.com	(01736) 363871*
Eastern Airways	easternairways.com	0870 366 9989
Easyjet	easyjet.com	0871 244 2366
Flybe	flybe.com	0871 522 6100
Jet2.com	jet2.com	0871 226 1737*
Ryanair	ryanair.com	0871 246 0000
Skybus (Isles of Scilly)	islesofscilly-travel.com	0845 710 5555
VLM	flyvlm.com	0871 666 5050

Train

National Rail Enquiries	nationalrail.co.uk	0845 748 4950
The Trainline	trainline.co.uk	
UK train operating companies	rail.co.uk	
Arriva Trains	arriva.co.uk	0845 748 4950
c2c	c2c-online.co.uk	0845 601 4873
Chiltern Railways	chilternrailways.co.uk	0845 600 5165
CrossCountry	crosscountrytrains.co.uk	0845 748 4950
East Midlands Trains	eastmidlandstrains.co.uk	0845 748 4950
First Capital Connect	firstcapitalconnect.co.uk	0845 748 4950
First Great Western	firstgreatwestern.co.uk	0845 700 0125
Gatwick Express	gatwickexpress.co.uk	0845 850 1530
Heathrow Express	heathrowexpress.com	0845 600 1515
Hull Trains	hulltrains.co.uk	0845 071 0222
Island Line	island-line.co.uk	0845 748 4950
London Midland	londonmidland.com	0845 748 4950
Merseyrail	merseyrail.org	0845 748 4950
Northern Rail	northernrail.org	0845 748 4950
One Railway	onerailway.com	0845 600 7245
South Eastern Trains	southeasternrailway.co.uk	0845 000 2222
South West Trains	southwesttrains.co.uk	0845 600 0650
Southern	southernrailway.com	0845 127 2920
Stansted Express	stanstedexpress.com	0845 600 7245
Transpennine Express	tpexpress.co.uk	0845 600 1671
Virgin Trains	virgintrains.co.uk	0845 722 2333*

Ferry

Ferry information	sailanddrive.com	
Condor Ferries (Channel Islands)	condorferries.co.uk	0870 243 5140*
Steam Packet Company (Isle of Man)	steam-packet.com	0871 222 1333
Isles of Scilly Travel	islesofscilly-travel.co.uk	0845 710 5555
Red Funnel (Isle of Wight)	redfunnel.co.uk	0844 844 9988
Wight Link (Isle of Wight)	wightlink.co.uk	0871 376 4342*

Phone numbers listed are for general enquiries unless otherwise stated.

* Booking line only

A selection of events for 2008

This is a selection of the many cultural, sporting and other events that will be taking place throughout Northern England during 2008. For a more comprehensive list, visit **enjoyengland.com/events**.

Please note, as changes often occur after press date, it is advisable to confirm the date and location before travelling.

March

30 Mar – 6 Apr
St Endellion Music Festival
Near Port Isaac, Cornwall
endellion.org.uk

April

4 – 6 Apr
Exeter Festival of South West Food and Drink
Northernhay Gardens, Exeter, Devon
(01392) 440745
visitsouthwest.co.uk/foodfestival

29 Apr – 5 May
Cheltenham Jazz Festival
Various venues, Cheltenham, Gloucestershire
cheltenhamfestivals.co.uk

May

1 – 4 May
Badminton Horse Trials
Badminton, Gloucestershire
0870 242 3436
badminton-horse.co.uk

8 May
Helston Flora Day
Streets of Helston, Cornwall
(01326) 572082
helston-online.co.uk

8 – 17 May
Daphne du Maurier Festival
Various venues, Fowey, Cornwall
0845 094 0428
dumaurierfestival.co.uk

15 – 17 May
Devon County Show
Westpoint Exhibition Centre, Devon County Showground, Clyst St Mary, Devon
(01392) 446000
devoncountyshow.co.uk

23 May – 8 Jun
Bath Fringe Festival
Various venues, Bath, Somerset
(01225) 480079
bathfringe.co.uk

23 – 26 May
Chippenham Folk Festival
Various venues, Chippenham, Wiltshire
(01249) 657190
chippfolk.co.uk

23 – 26 May
Run to the Sun
Trevelgue Holiday Park, Newquay, Cornwall
(01637) 851851
runtothesun.co.uk

23 May – 8 Jun
Salisbury International Arts Festival
various venues, Salisbury
0845 241 9651
salisburyfestival.co.uk

28 May – 31 May
The Royal Bath & West Show
Bath & West Showground, Shepton Mallet, Somerset
(01749) 822200
bathandwest.co.uk

June

5 – 7 Jun
Royal Cornwall Show
Royal Cornwall Showground, Wadebridge,
Cornwall
(01208) 812183
royalcornwall.co.uk

13 – 15 Jun
Wimborne Folk Festival
Town centre, Wimborne Minster, Dorset
(01202) 623740
wimbornefolkfestival.co.uk

20 – 22 Jun
Goldcoast Oceanfest
Croyde, Devon
(01271) 817000
goldcoastoceanfest.co.uk

22 – 29 Jun
Golowan Festival incorporating Mazey Day
Various venues, Penzance, Cornwall
(01736) 363405
golowan.org

July

12 – 13 Jul
Royal International Air Tattoo
RAF Fairford, Gloucestershire
airtattoo.com

19 Jul – 2 Aug
Gloucester Festival
Various venues, Gloucester, Gloucestershire
(01452) 396370
gloucester.gov.uk

19 – 26 Jul
Westival Arts Fest
Taunton, Somerset
(01823) 336344
westival.co.uk

25 – 27 Jul
Weymouth National Beach Volleyball
The Beach, Pavilion End, Weymouth, Dorset
(01305) 785747
weymouth.gov.uk

25 – 27 Jul
WOMAD
Charlton Park, Malmesbury, Wiltshire
0870 720 2128
womad.org

August

1 – 3 Aug
Bristol Harbour Festival
Bristol harbour, Bristol
bristol.gov.uk

1 – 8 Aug
Sidmouth Folk Week
Various venues, Sidmouth, Devon
(01395) 578627
sidmouthfolkweek.co.uk

7 – 10 Aug
Bristol International Balloon Fiesta
Ashton Court, Bristol
(0117) 953 5884
bristolfiesta.co.uk

7 Aug
Honiton Agricultural Show
The Showground, A30 Honiton Bypass,
Honiton, Devon
(01823) 601022
Bookings: (01404) 43716
honitonshow.co.uk

9 – 16 Aug
Henri-Lloyd Falmouth Week
Falmouth Bay, Cornwall
(01326) 211555
pofsa.co.uk

11 – 17 Aug
Ripcurl Boardmasters
Newquay, Cornwall
(020) 8789 6655
ripcurlboardmasters.com

27 Aug – 31 Aug
Great Dorset Steam Fair
South Down Farm, Tarrant Hinton, Dorset
(01258) 860361
Bookings: (01258) 488928
steam-fair.co.uk

27 Aug – 30 Aug
Port of Dartmouth Royal Regatta
Various venues, Dartmouth, Devon
(01803) 834912
dartmouthregatta.co.uk

September

12 – 14 Sep
Poole Animal Windfest
Sandbanks, Poole, Dorset
(01202) 708555
animalwindfest.co.uk

15 – 20 Sep
Agatha Christie Festival
Various venues, Torquay, Devon
(01803) 211211
englishriviera.co.uk

October

16 – 19 Oct*
Falmouth Oyster Festival
Falmouth, Cornwall
(01326) 312300
falmouthoysterfestival.co.uk

November

5 Nov
Tar Barrels
Town centre, Ottery St Mary, Devon
(01404) 813964
tarbarrels.co.uk

7 Nov
Bridgwater Guy Fawkes Carnival
Town centre, Bridgwater, Somerset
(01278) 421795
bridgwatercarnival.org.uk

* provisional date at time of going to press

Farmers' markets

Every Sat, 0900-1400
Bath Farmers' Market
Green Park Station, Bath Somerset

Every Wed, 0930-1430
Bristol Farmers' Market
Corn Street, Bristol

Every Tue, 0900-1400
Falmouth Farmers' Market
The Moor, Falmouth, Cornwall

Every Fri, 0900-1500
Gloucester Gate Streets Farmers' Market
The Cross & Southgate Street, Gloucester,
Gloucestershire

1st Thu monthly (Apr-Sep), 1000-1400
Isles of Scilly Local Produce Market
Holgates Green (weather permitting) or the Town
Hall, St Mary's, Isles of Scilly

2nd & 4th Sat monthly, 0900-1300
Malmesbury Farmers' Market
Top of High Street Market Cross, Malmesbury,
Wiltshire

Every Tue, 0900-1600
Newton Abbot Farmers' Market
Courtenay Street, Newton Abbot, Devon

2nd & 4th Sat monthly, 0800-1600
Plymouth Farmers' Market
Sundial, Armada Way, City Centre, Plymouth,
Devon

1st & 3rd Wed monthly, 1000-1400
Salisbury Farmers' Market
Main Market Square, Salisbury, Wiltshire

Every Sat, 0900-1400
Stroud Farmers' Market
Cornhill Market Place & surrounding streets,
Stroud, Gloucestershire

Every Thu, 0900-1500
Taunton Farmers' Market
High Street, Taunton, Somerset

2nd Sun monthly, 1000-1500
Weymouth Farmers' Market
Westham Bridge, Weymouth, Dorset

Tourist Information Centres

When you arrive at your destination, visit an Official Partner Tourist Information Centre for quality assured help with accommodation and information about local attractions and events, or email your request before you go. To search for attractions and Tourist Information Centres on the move just text INFO to 62233, and a web link will be sent to your mobile phone.

Bristol & Bath

Bath	Abbey Church Yard	0906 711 2000**	tourism@bathtourism.co.uk
Bristol: Harbourside	Harbourside	0906 711 2191**	ticharbourside@destinationbristol.co.uk

Cornwall & the Isles of Scilly

Bodmin	Mount Folly Square	(01208) 76616	bodmintic@visit.org.uk
Bude	The Crescent	(01288) 354240	budetic@visitbude.info
Camelford*	The Clease	(01840) 212954	manager@camelfordtic.eclipse.co.uk
Falmouth	11 Market Strand	(01326) 312300	info@falmouthtic.co.uk
Looe*	Fore Street	(01503) 262072	looetic@btconnect.com
Padstow	North Quay	(01841) 533449	padstowtic@btconnect.com
Truro	Boscawen Street	(01872) 274555	tic@truro.gov.uk
Wadebridge	Eddystone Road	0870 122 3337	wadebridgetic@btconnect.com

Cotswolds & the Forest of Dean

Bourton-on-the-Water	Victoria Street	(01451) 820211	bourtonvic@btconnect.com
Cheltenham	77 Promenade	(01242) 522878	info@cheltenham.gov.uk
Chipping Camden	High Street	(01386) 841206	information@visitchippingcamden.com
Cirencester	Market Place	(01285) 654180	cirencestervic@cotswold.gov.uk
Coleford	High Street	(01594) 812388	tourism@fdean.gov.uk
Gloucester	28 Southgate Street	(01452) 396572	tourism@gloucester.gov.uk
Moreton-in-Marsh	High Street	(01608) 650881	moreton@cotswolds.gov.uk
Stow-on-the-Wold	The Square	(01451) 831082	stowvic@cotswold.gov.uk
Stroud	George Street	(01453) 760960	tic@stroud.gov.uk
Tewkesbury	64 Barton Street	(01684) 295027	tewkesburytic@tewkesburybc.gov.uk
Winchcombe	High Street	(01242) 602925	winchcombetic@tewkesbury.gov.uk

Devon

Brixham	The Quay	(01803) 211211	holiday@torbay.gov.uk
Paignton	The Esplanade	(01803) 211211	holiday@torbay.gov.uk
Plymouth Mayflower	3-5 The Barbican	(01752) 306330	barbicantic@plymouth.gov.uk
Torquay	Vaughan Parade	(01803) 211211	holiday@torbay.gov.uk

Dorset

Bridport	47 South Street	(01308) 424901	bridport.tic@westdorset-dc.gov.uk
Christchurch	49 High Street	(01202) 471780	enquiries@christchurchtourism.info
Dorchester	11 Antelope Walk	(01305) 267992	dorchester.tic@westdorset-dc.gov.uk
Lyme Regis	Church Street	(01297) 442138	lymeregis.tic@westdorset-dc.gov.uk

Sherbourne	Digby Road	(01935) 815341	sherborne.tic@westdorset-dc.gov.uk
Swanage	Shore Road	(01929) 422885	mail@swanage.gov.uk
Wareham	South Street	(01929) 552740	tic@purbeck-dc.gov.uk
Weymouth	The Esplanade	(01305) 785747	tic@weymouth.gov.uk

Somerset

Burnham-on-Sea	South Esplanade	(01278) 787852	burnham.tic@sedgemoor.gov.uk
Cartgate	A303/A3088 Cartgate Picnic Site	(01935) 829333	cartgate.tic@southsomerset.gov.uk
Cheddar	The Gorge	(01934) 744071	cheddar.tic@sedgemoor.gov.uk
Somerset	Sedgemoor Services	(01934) 750833	somersetvisitorcentre@somerset.gov.uk
Taunton	Paul Street	(01823) 336344	tauntontic@tauntondeane.gov.uk
Wells	Market Place	(01749) 672552	touristinfo@wells.gov.uk
Weston-Super-Mare	Beach Lawns	(01934) 888800	westontouristinfo@n-somerset.gov.uk
Yeovil	Hendford	(01935) 845946	yeoviltic@southsomerset.gov.uk

Wiltshire - Salisbury & Stonehenge

Avebury	Green Street	(01672) 539425	all.atic@kennet.gov.uk
Chippenham	Market Place	(01249) 665970	tourism@chippenham.gov.uk
Corsham	31 High Street	(01249) 714660	enquiries@corshamheritage.org.uk
Devizes	Market Place	(01380) 729408	all.dtic@kennet.gov.uk
Malmesbury	Market Lane	(01666) 823748	malmesburyip@northwilts.gov.uk
Salisbury	Fish Row	(01722) 334956	visitorinfo@salisbury.gov.uk
Swindon	37 Regent Street	(01793) 530328	infocentre@swindon.gov.uk
Warminster	off Station Rd	(01985) 218548	visitwarminster@westwiltshire.gov.uk

* seasonal opening
** calls are charged at premium rate

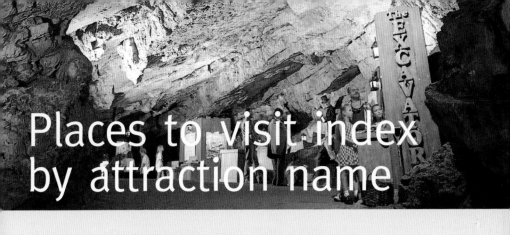

Places to visit index by attraction name

All places to visit featured in this guide are listed below.

2008 Calendar

JANUARY

M	T	W	T	F	S	S
	1	2	3	4	5	6
7	8	9	10	11	12	13
14	15	16	17	18	19	20
21	22	23	24	25	26	27
28	29	30	31			

FEBRUARY

M	T	W	T	F	S	S
				1	2	3
4	5	6	7	8	9	10
11	12	13	14	15	16	17
18	19	20	21	22	23	24
25	26	27	28	29		

MARCH

M	T	W	T	F	S	S
31					1	2
3	4	5	6	7	8	9
10	11	12	13	14	15	16
17	18	19	20	21	22	23
24	25	26	27	28	29	30

APRIL

M	T	W	T	F	S	S
	1	2	3	4	5	6
7	8	9	10	11	12	13
14	15	16	17	18	19	20
21	22	23	24	25	26	27
28	29	30				

MAY

M	T	W	T	F	S	S
			1	2	3	4
5	6	7	8	9	10	11
12	13	14	15	16	17	18
19	20	21	22	23	24	25
26	27	28	29	30	31	

JUNE

M	T	W	T	F	S	S
30						1
2	3	4	5	6	7	8
9	10	11	12	13	14	15
16	17	18	19	20	21	22
23	24	25	26	27	28	29

JULY

M	T	W	T	F	S	S
	1	2	3	4	5	6
7	8	9	10	11	12	13
14	15	16	17	18	19	20
21	22	23	24	25	26	27
28	29	30	31			

AUGUST

M	T	W	T	F	S	S
				1	2	3
4	5	6	7	8	9	10
11	12	13	14	15	16	17
18	19	20	21	22	23	24
25	26	27	28	29	30	31

SEPTEMBER

M	T	W	T	F	S	S
1	2	3	4	5	6	7
8	9	10	11	12	13	14
15	16	17	18	19	20	21
22	23	24	25	26	27	28
29	30					

OCTOBER

M	T	W	T	F	S	S
		1	2	3	4	5
6	7	8	9	10	11	12
13	14	15	16	17	18	19
20	21	22	23	24	25	26
27	28	29	30	31		

NOVEMBER

M	T	W	T	F	S	S
					1	2
3	4	5	6	7	8	9
10	11	12	13	14	15	16
17	18	19	20	21	22	23
24	25	26	27	28	29	30

DECEMBER

M	T	W	T	F	S	S
1	2	3	4	5	6	7
8	9	10	11	12	13	14
15	16	17	18	19	20	21
22	23	24	25	26	27	28
29	30	31				

Accommodation index by property name

Accommodation with a detailed entry in this guide is listed below.

Establishments listed here have a detailed entry in this guide.

Index by property name

Establishments listed here have a detailed entry in this guide.

Accommodation index by place name

The following places all have accommodation in this guide. If the place where you wish to stay is not shown, the location maps (starting on page 26) will help you to find somewhere to stay in the area.

Index by place name

Turn to the pages indicated for detailed accommodation entries in these places.

enjoyEngland ™

official tourist board guides

Hotels, including country house and town house hotels, metro and budget hotels in England 2008

£10.99

Guest accommodation, B&Bs, guest houses, farmhouses, inns, restaurants with rooms, campus and hostel accommodation in England 2008

£11.99

Self-catering holiday homes, including serviced apartments and approved caravan holiday homes, boat accommodation and holiday cottage agencies in England 2008

£11.99

Touring parks, camping holidays and holiday parks and villages in Britain 2008

£8.99

informative, easy to use and great value for money

Pet-friendly hotels, B&Bs and self-catering accommodation in England 2008

£9.99

Great ideas for places to visit, eat and stay in England

£10.99

Places to stay and visit in South West England

£9.99

Places to stay and visit in Northern England

£9.99

Accessible places to stay in Britain

£9.99

Now available in good bookshops.
For special offers on VisitBritain publications,
please visit **enjoyenglanddirect.com**

Published by: VisitBritain, Thames Tower, Blacks Road, London W6 9EL
in partnership with England's tourism industry
enjoyEngland.com
Publishing Manager: Tess Lugos
Production Manager: Iris Buckley
Compilation, design, copywriting, production and advertisement sales:
Jackson Lowe Marketing, 3 St Andrews Place, Southover Road, Lewes,
East Sussex BN7 1UP
t (01273) 487487 jacksonlowe.com
Typesetting: Marlinzo Services, Somerset and Jackson Lowe Marketing
Accommodation maps: Based on digital map data © ESR Cartography, 2007
Printing and binding: Emirates Printing Press, Dubai, United Arab Emirates

Front cover: Portloe, Cornwall (britainonview.com/Philip Fenton)

Back cover (from top)**:** Calcot Manor, Nr Tetbury; britainonview.com/
Martin Brent; The Salty Monk Restaurant with Rooms, Sidford;
Tone Dale House, Wellington

Photography credits: Bath Tourism; Bristol Balloon Fiestas Limited;
britainonview.com/David Angel /Daniel Bosworth/Martin Brent/
East Midlands Tourism/Eden Project/Rod Edwards/Klaus Hagmeier/
Adrian Houston/Pawel Libera/McCormick-McAdam/David Noton/Tony
Pleavin; The Caravan Club; Dorset County Council; English Riviera Tourist
Board; Forest of Dean District Council; Paul Frost; Gloucester City Council;
Michael Jackson; Longleat Safari Park; Oceanarium; Restormel Borough
Council; Somerset Tourism; South West Tourism; Thermae Bath Spa/
Matt Cardy; Visit Bristol

Important note: The information contained in this guide has been
published in good faith on the basis of information submitted to
VisitBritain by the proprietors of the premises listed, who have paid for
their entries to appear. VisitBritain cannot guarantee the accuracy of the
information in this guide and accepts no responsibility for any error or
misrepresentation. All liability for loss, disappointment, negligence or
other damage caused by reliance on the information contained in this
guide, or in the event of bankruptcy, or liquidation, or cessation of trade
of any company, individual or firm mentioned, is hereby excluded to the
fullest extent permitted by law. Please check carefully all prices, ratings
and other details before confirming a reservation.

© British Tourist Authority (trading as VisitBritain) 2008
ISBN 978-0-7095-8438-4

A VisitBritain Publishing guide

visit**Britain**™